HARDEN'S

Top UK Restaurants 2001

including Eire

Visit www.hardens.com

- **Register for free updates and newsletters, and to take part in next year's survey**
- **Restaurant searches**
- **News of latest openings**
- **Corporate gift service**
- **Order Harden's guides**

Customised editions – the ideal corporate gift
Harden's Top UK Restaurants and *Harden's London Restaurants* are both available in specially customised corporate gift formats. For information, please call (020) 7839 4763 or visit www.hardens.com.

© Harden's Limited 2000

ISBN 1-873721-36-6 (paperback)
ISBN 1-873721-40-4 (bonded leather)

British Library Cataloguing-in-Publication data:
a catalogue record for this book is available from
the British Library.

Printed and bound in Finland by
WS Bookwell Ltd

Research Manager: Antonia Russell

Harden's Limited
14 Buckingham Street
London WC2N 6DF

Cube8.com plc is an investor in Harden's Limited

Distributed in the United States of America by
Seven Hills Book Distributors,
1531 Tremont Street, Cincinnati, OH45214

CONTENTS

HOW THIS BOOK IS ORGANISED

As response to the format of our London guide has generally been very favourable, we have tried, to the extent possible, to observe the same principles here.

London is covered first, and, in recognition of the scale and diversity of its restaurant scene, has an extensive introduction and indexes, as well as its own maps. After the London section, the guide is organised strictly by place name – we could see no logic in separating England from Scotland, Wales, Northern Ireland or the Republic of Ireland, so Chester, Clachan and Cork alike appear under 'C'.

For *cities and larger towns*, you can therefore turn straight to the relevant section. In the major restaurant centres you will find a brief introduction before the reviews.

In *less densely populated areas*, you will generally find it easiest to start with the map of the relevant area at the back of the book, which will guide you to the appropriate place names.

HOW THIS BOOK IS RESEARCHED

This book is the result of a research effort involving some 15,000 people – our 'reporters'. This year, over 5,000 contributed to our tenth annual survey of London restaurant-goers. Our second survey of restaurant-goers outside the capital attracted over 11,500 participants. Some people participated in both surveys.

The density of the feedback on London (where many of the top places attract several hundred reviews each) is such that the ratings for the metropolitan restaurants included in this edition are almost exclusively statistical in derivation. We have, as it happens, visited all the restaurants in the London section, anonymously, and at our own expense, but we use our personal experiences only to inform the standpoint from which to interpret the consensus opinion.

In the case of the more commented-upon provincial restaurants, we have adopted an approach very similar to London. In the case of less-visited provincial establishments, however, the interpretation of survey results owes as much to art as it does to science. In our experience, smaller establishments are – for better or worse – generally quite consistent, and we have therefore felt able to place a relatively high level of confidence in a lower level of commentary. Conservatism on our part, however, will undoubtedly have led to some smaller places being under-rated compared to their more visited peers.

RATINGS & PRICES

We see little point in traditional rating systems, which generally tell you nothing more than that expensive restaurants are 'better' than cheap ones because they use costlier ingredients and attempt more ambitious dishes. You probably knew that already – our system assumes that, as prices rise, so do diners' expectations.

Prices and ratings are shown as follows:

£ Price
The cost of a three-course *dinner* for one person. We include half a bottle of house wine, coffee and service (or a 10% tip if there is no service charge).

Food
The following symbols indicate that, ***in comparison with other restaurants in the same price-bracket***, the cooking at the establishment is:

★★ **Exceptional**

★ **Very good**

Ambience
Restaurants which provide a setting which is very charming, stylish or 'buzzy' are indicated as follows:

𝔸 **Particularly atmospheric**

Small print

Telephone number – *All numbers in the London section are (020) numbers. Eire numbers are shown for dialling within the republic (the international code for which is + 353).*

Sample dishes – *these dishes exemplify the style of cooking at a particular establishment. They are merely samples – it is unlikely that these specific dishes will be available at the time of your visit.*

Value tip – *if we know of a particularly good-value set menu or some similar handy tip, we note this. Details change, so always check ahead.*

Details – *the following information is given where relevant.*

Directions – *to help you find the establishment.*

Website – *if applicable.*

Last orders time – *at dinner (Sunday may be up to 90 minutes earlier).*

Opening hours – *unless otherwise stated, restaurants are open for lunch and dinner seven days a week.*

Credit and debit cards – *unless otherwise stated, Mastercard, Visa, Amex and Switch are accepted.*

Dress – *where appropriate, the management's preferences concerning patrons' dress are given.*

Smoking – *cigarette smoking restrictions are noted. Pipe or cigar smokers should always check ahead.*

Children – *if we know of a specified minimum age for children, we note this.*

Accommodation – *if an establishment has rooms, we list how many and the minimum price for a double.*

FROM THE EDITORS

Although we have been in the business of publishing restaurant guides (to London) for the past ten years, this is only the third edition of our guide to the UK as a whole. (For the last two years it has also included some coverage of Eire.)

London restaurants have undergone a complete transformation during the period over which we have been writing guides about them. The period since we began publishing the UK guide has – no doubt coincidentally – seen the stirring of a similar revolution across the British Isles as a whole. It is exciting to play a part in recording what on any analysis is an important period of evolution and improvement of the British and Irish restaurant scenes.

It would be a very arrogant – and, indeed, stupid – publisher who claimed any guide book as perfect, and we certainly make no such claim for this one. However, thanks largely to the much increased level of survey feedback, we have been able to make this third edition of the guide much bigger and, we believe, better balanced and more accurate than the previous editions. We hope that readers will think so too.

In this edition, we have considerably expanded the number of entries. Our coverage in some areas is more patchy than we would like – especially in Ireland, and particularly in the Republic. Even in the heartland of England, however, there are surely deserving places which have been passed over. If you perceive omissions, please remember that the solution lies partially in your own hands.

Assembling a large number of people interested to contribute their views on restaurants is no easy task, and we are once again most grateful to readers of the *Observer* who completed survey forms distributed with the newspaper. We are no less grateful to the growing band of our "own" reporters who also took part.

All restaurant guides are the subject of continual revision. This is especially true when the restaurant scene is undergoing a period of rapid change, as at present. **Please help us to make the next edition even more comprehensive and accurate.** If you register for your free update (by returning the reply-paid card at the back of the book, by e-mail, or on the web at www.hardens.com) you will be invited, in the spring of 2001, to participate in our next survey. **If you take part you will, on publication, receive a complimentary copy of *Harden's Top UK Restaurants 2002*.**

Richard Harden   **Peter Harden**

LONDON INTRODUCTION

LONDON INTRODUCTION

There is no doubt that the 1990s saw a great revolution in dining out in the capital. Some of its effects have been extremely benign: there is now a range of places to eat – especially in the inner suburbs – which would have been unthinkable a decade ago. However not all developments can be classed as progress – the number of places, especially in the West End, where you can pay a great deal for very little is now larger than ever.

To help to guide you through the minefield, see the results from our London survey, which start on page 16. Please do *use* these tables: they tell you which restaurants regular London diners-out think are the pick of the crop. (Do note that the Most Mentioned list simply tells you which are the restaurants which are attracting popular attention. It means just what it says – inclusion on the list may just indicate that a restaurant has achieved a high public profile, which may, or may not, be an indication of inherent quality.)

Owing to the sheer breadth of the London scene, this initial review is very selective. The 'Area overviews' (starting on page 62) will help you identify many excellent places not mentioned below.

Fine dining

There are surprisingly few truly world-class restaurants in London. Arguably, there are only two – *Gordon Ramsay* and *Le Gavroche* (the most traditional, 'grand restaurant'). Other restaurants offering cooking of a very high level include *Pied à Terre*, *Aubergine* and the Japanese *Tatsuso*. None of these, however, offers the trappings generally associated with restaurants of the highest level.

Grandeur and tradition

Though perhaps not generally in quite the same league for cooking as the Fine Dining restaurants, some of the top hotel dining rooms are worth seeking out for their stylish and comfortable settings and very good service. The *Connaught* is often held up as the capital's benchmark of culinary consistency. Its less culinarily ambitious Mayfair competitor, the *Dorchester Grill*, is now also back on top form. At a more modest price-point, London's oldest restaurant, *Rules,* still has a lot to recommend it, and, if money is no particular object, *Wilton's* typifies a certain traditional style.

'In' places

The most perennially 'in' restaurants in London are the (very difficult to book) duo, *The Ivy* and *Le Caprice*.

Two years old (in its new guise), the *Mirabelle* is consolidating its claim to be considered a modern classic. For the media and fashion world the choice of trendy place to eat becomes more and more difficult: should it stick with the undoubted virtues of *Nobu,* or prefer one of the gimmicky dining rooms of American design-hotelier Ian Schrager – *Asia de Cuba* or the more recent *Spoon+?* For what used to be called the jet-set, the decision is much simpler – as always, Knightsbridge's upmarket Italian restaurants are the destinations of choice.

Tourist traps

One of the undesirable products of the '90s was the creation of very large restaurants, with major marketing budgets which have enabled them to achieve a very high profile regardless of their inherent quality, or lack of it. Many of the restaurants in the Conran group – most notably *Bluebird, Mezzo* and *Quaglino's* – are in this category. So is the *Oxo Tower* (run by Harvey Nichols), which offers a great view but little else. By all means check out these restaurants if you feel you must to complete your tourism of London, but don't be surprised if you emerge feeling you have paid an unreasonably high price for the experience.

Key cuisines

Here are some foreign cuisines in which London excels.

Modern Italian
London's Italian cooking has in recent years emerged with a vengeance from the Anglicised torpor which has dominated since the '50s. Modern Italian establishments now offer the most exciting continental cuisine available in London. Notable followers of the new school include *Assaggi, The River Café, Tentazioni* and *Zafferano.*

Indian
London has the finest selection of Indian restaurants in the world, with outstanding places at all price-levels. At the grander end of the market, the best names include *Tamarind, Vama* and *Zaika,* as well as the more established *Salloos* and *Star of India.* Some of the best subcontinental food in London is incredibly cheap – see the list on page 19 for the best inexpensive places.

Thai
London's most consistently successful grand ethnic restaurant is the *Blue Elephant,* which offers a lot of theatre, as well as some very good, if not inexpensive, cooking. There are concentrations of good, less expensive Thai restaurants in Soho, south west London and west London. The most central Thai all-rounder is the *Chiang Mai.* A London speciality is the adoption of

Thai cooking by pubs or places which, by day, are 'greasy spoons' – Notting Hill's *Walmer Castle* is one example.

East-meets-West

Three fashionable US-originated restaurants which 'fuse' disparate cuisines – *Nobu* (Japanese/South American), *Vong* (French/Thai) and *Asia de Cuba* (self-explanatory) – have opened in the last few years. The first two mentioned, at least, have made a considerable success of offering cooking combining the culinary traditions of different continents. The same can be said of the home-grown *Sugar Club*.

Gastropubs

Gastropubs are an area of undoubted improvement over the past few years. The original 'super-pub', *The Eagle*, in ever-trendier Clerkenwell, is still one of the best, but there is now a host of worthy imitators. *The Havelock Tavern* in Olympia is one of the better examples.

Budget ethnics

Ethnic restaurants are almost invariably the top choice for budget dining. The best of them tend to cluster in particular parts of town. Chinatown is in the heart of the West End, and there are also quite a lot of Chinese establishments – some of them better than their more central cousins – in Bayswater. There are several concentrations of Indian restaurants, of which the most accessible are in the Little India by Euston Station and the East End's Brick Lane – the southern Indians of Tooting are a little further away. There are many good, inexpensive Thai restaurants around Hammersmith and Chiswick. For Lebanese restaurants, look around the Edgware Road.

Vegetarians

Most London restaurants (but not some of the classic French establishments) can provide some vegetarian option, perhaps explaining the existence of relatively few specialist vegetarian restaurants of any interest – *Blah!Blah!Blah!* and *The Gate* are notable exceptions. Some of the best vegetarian food is ethnic. Southern Indian restaurants offer some delicious and extremely inexpensive cooking. Fine examples of the type include *Kastoori* and *Rasa*. Veggies should also be very happy with the meze dishes available at Middle Eastern restaurants – the *Maroush* group being notable in this respect.

LONDON
SURVEY RESULTS
DIRECTORY

LONDON – MOST MENTIONED

These are the restaurants which were most frequently mentioned by reporters. (Last year's position is given in brackets. An asterisk* indicates a first appearance in the list of a recently opened or re-launched restaurant.)

1	The Ivy (1)
2	Oxo Tower (2)
3	Mirabelle (3)
4	Nobu (13)
5	Bluebird (6)
6	Le Caprice (5)
7	Blue Elephant (11)
8	Le Pont de la Tour (9)
9	The Square (10)
10	The River Café (12)

11	Gordon Ramsay (21)
12	Bank (4)
13	Chez Bruce (24)
14	Zafferano (18)
15	Quaglino's (8)
16	J Sheekey (-)
17=	The Criterion (17)
17=	La Poule au Pot (29)
19	Le Gavroche (25)
20	Bibendum (15)

21	Club Gascon (-)
22	City Rhodes (26)
23	Pétrus (-)
24	The Sugar Club (21)
25	Coq d'Argent (23)
26	Vong (16)
27	Andrew Edmunds (31)
28	Mezzo (19)
29	Chutney Mary (27)
30	Le Palais du Jardin (20)

31	Zaika (-)
32	The Eagle (-)
33	1 Lombard Street (39)
34	Axis (27)
35	Clarke's (-)
36	Kensington Place (40)
37	La Tante Claire (30)
38	Moro (-)
39	Rules (35)
40	Joe Allen (-)

LONDON – NOMINATIONS

Ranked by the number of reporters' votes for:

Top gastronomic experience

1 Gordon Ramsay (1)
2 The Ivy (2)
3 Mirabelle (3)
4 Nobu (7)
5 Chez Bruce (6)
6 The Square (4)
7 Le Gavroche (5)
8 Pétrus (-)
9 Club Gascon (10)
10 The River Café (8)

Favourite

1 The Ivy (1)
2 Chez Bruce (3)
3 Le Caprice (2)
4 Mirabelle (6)
5 Nobu (5)
6 Gordon Ramsay (-)
7 The River Café (4)
8 Zafferano (7)
9 Oxo Tower (-)
10 Le Palais du Jardin (8)

Best for business

1 City Rhodes (1)
2 1 Lombard Street (5)
3 The Square (8)
4 Bank (2)
5 The Ivy (7)
6 Le Pont de la Tour (6)
7 Coq d'Argent (9)
8 Savoy Grill (3)
9 Oxo Tower (4)
10 Prism (-)

Best for romance

1 La Poule au Pot (1)
2 Andrew Edmunds (2)
3 The Ivy (3)
4 Oxo Tower (5)
5 Odette's (8)
6 Julie's (4)
7 Blue Elephant (7)
8 Le Caprice (9)
9 Launceston Place (6)
10 Le Pont de la Tour (-)

constantly updated at www.hardens.com

LONDON – HIGHEST RATINGS

These are the restaurants which received the best average food ratings.

We have divided the most represented restaurant cuisines (opposite) into two price-brackets – under and over £35.

Where the less represented cuisines (below) are concerned just the best three performers in the survey are shown.

British, Traditional
1 Dorchester Grill
2 Connaught
3 Wiltons

Vegetarian
1 The Gate
2 Blah! Blah! Blah!
3 Mildreds

Burgers, etc
1 Hard Rock Café
2 Wolfe's
3 Sticky Fingers

Pizza
1 Pizza Metro
2 Pizzeria Castello
3 La Spiga

East/West
1 Nobu
2 Vong
3 Sugar Club

Thai
1 Thailand
2 Esarn Kheaw
3 Talad Thai

Fish & Chips
1 Faulkners
2 Two Brothers
3 Seashell

Fish & Seafood
1 Chez Liline
2 Bibendum Oyster Bar
3 Poissonnerie de l'Ave

Greek
1 Vrisaki
2 The Real Greek
3 Lemonia

Spanish
1 Lomo
2 Cambio de Tercio
3 Gaudi

Turkish
1 Tas
2 Ozer
3 Iznik

Lebanese
1 Ranoush
2 Phoenicia
3 Al Hamra

constantly updated at www.hardens.com

Modern British

£35 and over
1. Chez Bruce
2. Clarke's
3. The Glasshouse
4. City Rhodes
5. The Ivy

Under £35
1. Kennington Lane
2. Parade
3. Mesclun
4. The Havelock Tavern
5. The Apprentice

French

£35 and over
1. Gordon Ramsay
2. Monsieur Max
3. Pétrus
4. Le Gavroche
5. Chinon

Under £35
1. Soulard
2. Brass. du Marché
3. Le P'tit Normand
4. 6 Clarendon Road
5. Boudin Blanc

Italian/Mediterranean

£35 and over
1. Assaggi
2. Zafferano
3. Toto's
4. Tentazioni
5. The River Café

Under £35
1. Metrogusto
2. Enoteca Turi
3. La Spighetta
4. Al Duca
5. Osteria Basilico

Indian

£35 and over
1. Zaika
2. Vama
3. Salloos
4. Tamarind
5. Rasa Samudra

Under £35
1. Vijay
2. Geeta
3. Kastoori
4. Lahore Kebab House
5. Babur Brasserie

Chinese

£35 and over
1. Dorchester, Oriental
2. The Orient
3. Ken Lo's Memories
4. ZeNW3
5. Zen Central

Under £35
1. Hunan
2. Mandarin Kitchen
3. Royal China
4. Fung Shing
5. Joy King Lau

Japanese

£35 and over
1. Shogun
2. Tatsuso
3. Defune
4. Matsuri
5. Suntory

Under £35
1. Inaho
2. K10
3. Café Japan
4. Kulu Kulu
5. Itsu

LONDON DIRECTORY

Abeno WC1   £ 28   𝔸★
47 Museum St   7405 3211   1–1C
This "civilised" Japanese newcomer, specialising in 'okonomi-yaki'
(a bit like an omelette, cooked at your table) is a worthy
replacement for the "much-missed" Museum Street Café (RIP),
whose former Bloomsbury site it occupies. / *Sample dishes:* no
starters; pork, squid and prawn egg pancake; no puddings. *Details:* 10 pm;
closed Sun D; no Amex; no smoking area.

The Admiralty WC2   £ 43
Strand   7845 4646   1–2D
Somerset House's external grandeur is only partially reflected
in the cosy rooms occupied by Oliver Peyton's new bar/restaurant;
some early reports rate the 'cuisine du terroir' as "superb",
but it seemed to us to lack inspiration – the café on the large
river terrace may offer a more interesting prospect. / *Sample
dishes:* salmon tartare with watercress soup; roast squab with thyme; Brittany
shortbread with raspberries. *Details:* 10.45 pm; closed Sun D; no smoking.

Afghan Kitchen N1   £ 14   ★
35 Islington Gn   7359 8019
"Cheap", "yummy" cooking – albeit from a "limited" selection –
ensure that this "tiny" Islington Green "gem" is always
"crowded". / *Sample dishes:* no starters; chicken in yoghurt; baklava.
Details: 11 pm; closed Mon & Sun; no credit cards.

Al Duca SW1   £ 32   ★
4-5 Duke Of York St   7839 3090   2–3D
Choice is "quite limited", but "very good" modern Italian food
at "reasonable" prices wins strong praise for restaurateur
Claudio Pulze's "noisy" and "business-like" St James's yearling.
/ *Sample dishes:* sturgeon & salmon carpaccio; char-grilled lamb with pepper
ratatouille; white chocolate mousse. *Details:* 10.15 pm, Fri-Sat 10.45 pm;
closed Sun.

Al Hamra W1   £ 39
31-33 Shepherd Mkt   7493 1954   2–4B
Infamously "slow" and "grudging" service can take the edge off
a visit to this "good but pricey" Shepherd Market Lebanese;
its outside tables, though, undoubtedly have a "great location".
/ *Sample dishes:* tabbouleh salad & houmous; Lebanese mixed grill; honey &
cream cheese halva. *Details:* 11.30 pm.

Al Sultan W1   £ 36   ★
51-52 Hertford St   7408 1155   2–4B
This Shepherd Market Lebanese is a gentler experience than the
more celebrated Al Hamra, nearby; it's a touch "dull", but "good
for the price". / *Sample dishes:* tabbouleh; lamb with lentils; baklava.
Details: www.alsultan.co.uk; 11.30 pm.

Alastair Little W1   £ 47   ★
49 Frith St   7734 5183   3–2A
"Fresh" and "straightforward" modern British cooking is founding
quite a renaissance for this once-celebrated Soho fixture; there
are still doubters, though, who say it's "incredible that this was
once a place to be really reckoned with". / *Sample dishes:* grilled
squid with chermoula; roast sea bass with potato cakes; panna cotta with
apricot sauce. *Details:* 11 pm; closed Sat L & Sun.

Alastair Little, Lancaster Rd W11   £ 36   ★

136a Lancaster Rd   7243 2220
"First-rate food, imaginatively prepared and disarmingly priced"
makes this *"cramped"* Notting Hill spot *"the perfect local
restaurant"* for many reporters; joy is mitigated, however,
by the occasional *"very dull"* experience. / **Sample dishes:** mixed
seafood platter; roast lamb with bean brandade; panna cotta with raspberries.
Details: 11 pm; closed Sun.

Alba EC1   £ 35   ★

107 Whitecross St   7588 1798
"Consistently interesting" regional cooking and a *"great selection
of quality wines"* make this Barbican-side spot *"the best Italian
in the City"* for some; the décor, though, is on the *"bland"* side.
/ **Sample dishes:** mushroom risotto; grilled swordfish; tiramisu.
Details: 11 pm; closed Sat & Sun.

Andrew Edmunds W1   £ 31   🄰

46 Lexington St   7437 5708   2–2D
"Nowhere is more romantic", say the many fans of this *"real
gem"* – a phenomenally *"popular"* and *"cramped"*, candlelit Soho
townhouse, where *"consistently good"*, if simple, modern British
cooking is washed down with a *"fabulous"*, top-value wine list;
book ahead. / **Sample dishes:** duck & red onion tart; swordfish steak with
roast fennel; tarte Tatin. **Details:** 10.45 pm.

L'Anis W8   £ 35   ★★

1 Kensington High St   7795 6533   4–1A
Stepping into the shoes of the Good Cook (RIP), this
modestly-priced Kensington newcomer has an excellent pedigree
(Claudio Pulze's ex-Frith Street team); a very early visit found
notably deft, light Mediterranean cooking and charming efficient
service; the listed interior is impressive but echoey. / **Sample
dishes:** roast scallops with braised oxtail; braised beef with snail & garlic mash;
chocolate fondant with pistachio ice cream. **Details:** 10.45 pm; closed Sat L &
Sun.

The Apprentice SE1   £ 28   ★

31 Shad Thames   7234 0254
It's *"haphazard"* and has a bit of a *"non-atmosphere"*, but results
at this South Bank catering school *"can be stunning for the
price"*, and these *"kids learning the ropes"* do *"try so hard"*.
/ **Sample dishes:** duck terrine; grilled fish with aubergine gateau; lemon tart.
Details: www.chef-school.co.uk; 8.30 pm; closed Sat & Sun; no smoking area.

Arancia SE16   £ 24   ★

52 Southwark Park Rd   7394 1751
"It's impossible to get to easily" – unless you live in Bermondsey,
that is – but this small, cosy local prepares its simple short Italian
menu to good effect, and at *"very reasonable"* prices. / **Sample
dishes:** prawns with fennel fritters; braised lamb shank with pappardelle;
chocolate semi-freddo. **Details:** 11 pm; D only; no Amex.

Arkansas Café E1   £ 19   ★

Unit 12, Old Spitalfield Mkt   7377 6999
"You can't beat Bubba's authentic BBQ" – and some think his
"simple" City-fringe market café does *"the best burgers in town"*.
/ **Sample dishes:** potato salad; BBQ rib steak; pecan pie. **Details:** L only;
closed Sat; no Amex; no smoking.

Asia de Cuba WC2 £ 58 A

45 St Martin's Ln 7300 5500 3–4C

This wackily-designed Theatreland yearling has become "a great place to see and be seen", but without managing to create the excitement surrounding its NYC sibling; the "fun-to-share" fusion fare may be "far too expensive", but, perhaps surprisingly, is generally thought (almost) worth it. / Sample dishes: calamari salad 'Asia de Cuba'; coriander-crusted sirloin steak; Havana banana & chocolate mousse. Details: midnight, Sat 1 am; closed Sat L.

Assaggi W2 £ 44 A★★

39 Chepstow Pl 7792 5501

"The best Italian cuisine in London" – with "the best maître d'" too – ensures that it is "impossible to get a table" at this "wonderful" (if "noisy") dining room above a Bayswater pub. / Sample dishes: pan-fried scallops with Parma ham ; veal chop with rosemary; chocolate tart with white chocolate ice-cream. Details: 11.30 pm; closed Sun.

The Atlas SW6 £ 24 A★

16 Seagrave Rd 7385 9129 4–3A

"Interesting Mediterranean-influenced pub food" has helped this "buzzing" backstreet boozer, near Earl's Court 2, "to come seriously up in the world" (and it's often "crowded"); there's a "great garden at the rear". / Sample dishes: antipasti; grilled lamb chops; chocolate cake. Details: 10.30 pm; no Amex; no booking.

Aubergine SW10 £ 65 ★

11 Park Wk 7352 3449 4–3B

William Drabble's "superior" modern French cooking wins much support for this famed Chelsea site; many find it "exceedingly expensive", though, and an atmosphere which is "romantic" to some, just seems "slightly sterile" to others. / Sample dishes: warm roast vegetable salad; roast pork with summer vegetables; apricot bavarois. Value tip: set weekday L £33(FP). Details: 10.30 pm; closed Sat L & Sun; jacket required.

L'Aventure NW8 £ 40 A★★

3 Blenheim Ter 7624 6232

"Intimate" St John's Wood gem that's "perfect for romance" (especially when the "lovely terrace" is in use); "steep" wine prices and "overcrowding" prompt the odd quibble, but few dispute the "attention to detail" shown by the Gallic cooking. / Sample dishes: scallops; roast rack of lamb with garlic; grilled peaches. Details: 11 pm; closed Sat L (& Sun in winter); no Switch.

Axis WC2 £ 45 ★

1 Aldwych 7300 0300 1–2D

"Discreet" and "efficient" service and a "sophisticated" (if "stark") setting are helping this Theatreland-fringe basement carve out quite a name – especially "for business" – thanks to its "imaginative" modern British cooking. / Sample dishes: Thai beef, coconut & shallot salad; king prawn linguine with Parmesan; chocolate mousse cake. Details: 11.15 pm; closed Sat L & Sun.

Babur Brasserie SE23 £ 28 A★★

119 Brockley Rise, Forest Hl 8291 2400

"What's a place this good doing in Brockley?"; the "refined" cuisine of this "welcoming" Indian is shown off to special advantage by its "interesting seasonal menus". / Sample dishes: deep-fried avari leaves with spiced chick peas; chicken piri-piri ; white chocolate truffles. Details: 11.15 pm; closed Fri L; no smoking area.

Back to Basics W1   £ 34   ★★

21a Foley St   7436 2181   1–1B

"Great" seafood and "imaginative" fish cooking ensure that this unpretentious but "relentlessly good" Fitzrovia bistro is often "crowded"; "get there early" for maximum menu choice. / **Sample dishes:** marinated herrings with sour cream; poached salmon salad; apple tart. **Details:** www.backtobasics.co.uk; 10 pm; closed Sat & Sun.

Bali Sugar W11   £ 43   ★

33a All Saints Rd   7221 4477

The "innovative", "stylish" fusion cooking is "surprisingly good" at the Notting Hill premises that once housed The Sugar Club; the slightly "clinical" setting appears to best advantage "in summer". / **Sample dishes:** scallops with sweet chilli sauce; roasted lamb & cherry tomatoes with couscous; strawberry & cherry soup. **Details:** 11 pm; closed Mon L; no smoking area.

Bangkok SW7   £ 30   ★

9 Bute St   7584 8529   4–2B

It's a touch "uncomfortable", but this "reliable" and "relaxed" Thai veteran, near South Kensington tube, is a "safe" choice; its sheer staying power makes it a "special place" for some people. / **Sample dishes:** chicken satay; beef in chilli sauce; ice cream. **Details:** 11 pm; closed Sun; no Amex.

Bank WC2   £ 44

1 Kingsway   7234 3344   1–2D

This "noisy" Theatreland venue is "one of the better big brasseries" – "as long as you don't forget your gold card" – and its "consistently good" cooking and "professional" air make it a major business favourite; "great breakfasts" are a speciality. / **Sample dishes:** spicy gazpacho; braised duck with cherry gravy; trio of sorbets. **Value tip:** pre-th. £28(FP). **Details:** 11 pm; no Switch.

Belvedere W8   £ 55   Ⓐ

Holland Park, off Abbotsbury Rd   7602 1238

'Plus ça change...' at this glamorously revamped landmark, "perfectly situated" in "beautiful" Holland Park; hopes that the new régime's grand-Gallic-brasserie-style cooking would outshine its predecessor's are fading – "given the MPW aura, we expected better". / **Sample dishes:** scallops with chives & ginger; roast Bresse chicken with pea risotto; caramelised apple tart. **Value tip:** pre-th. £31(FP). **Details:** www.whitestarline.org.uk; 11 pm.

Bengal Clipper SE1   £ 30   ★

Shad Thames   7357 9001

This "classy" South Bank Indian produces "interesting", "fresh" and "zesty" cooking; it's a shame that its slightly "cavernous" premises – to which "a pianist adds a bizarre colonial note" – can seem rather "empty". / **Sample dishes:** vegetable samosas; Karahi chicken; kulfi. **Value tip:** set Sun L £16(FP). **Details:** www.bengalrestaurants.com; 11 pm.

Bentley's W1   £ 44   ★

11-15 Swallow St   7734 4756   2–3D

"Suitable for business or romance", this traditional, "subdued" – but quite charming – Mayfair seafood institution is currently "on better form than it's been for some time". / **Sample dishes:** dressed crab; grilled Dover sole; bread & butter pudding. **Details:** 11.30 pm.

Bibendum SW3 £ 60
81 Fulham Rd 7581 5817 4–2C
London's original "beautiful" and "sophisticated" modern restaurant "rests on its laurels" nowadays, and its Gallic fare is "not as good as it used to be"; service is "condescending" too, leaving "terrific" wines as the only undoubted plus. / **Sample dishes:** fish soup with rouille & croutons; sea bass with oysters & watercress sauce; raspberry macaroon. **Details:** www.bibendum.co.uk; 10.30 pm.

Bibendum Oyster Bar SW3 £ 34 𝔸★★
81 Fulham Rd 7589 1480 4–2C
"Great seafood" (all cold) that's "surprisingly" inexpensive (considering), plus "good people-watching" ensure the Conran Shop's foyer bar is ever-popular as a "fun lunch-stop"; "too bad they don't take reservations". / **Sample dishes:** rock oysters; smoked salmon; mini chocolate pot. **Details:** www.bibendum.co.uk; 10.30 pm; no booking.

Bistro I W1 £ 18
75 Beak St 7287 1840 2–2D
This new Soho bistro, offers an all-too-rare 'plain vanilla' formula – simple fare, pleasantly served in a congenial, if basic, setting. / **Sample dishes:** pâté; pork chop; lemon tart. **Details:** 11 pm.

The Black Truffle NW1 £ 34 ★
40 Chalcot Rd 7483 0077
Enthusiasm for this "great addition to Primrose Hill" is moderated by "haphazard" service and Italian food whose simplicity verges on "basic"; the "stark" setting is "beautiful" to some, but "packed" and "dungeon-like" to others. / **Sample dishes:** grilled cuttlefish in black ink sauce; roast cod with chick pea salad; amaretto parfait. **Details:** 10.45 pm; D only Mon-Fri, closed Sun; no Amex.

Blah! Blah! Blah! W12 £ 23 𝔸★
78 Goldhawk Rd 8746 1337
"Inspirational" and "flavoursome" cooking can make this Shepherd's Bush vegetarian "a fantastic discovery"; some think the atmospheric, but "seedy" décor "could use a face-lift", though, and find the smoke "a pain"; BYO. / **Sample dishes:** saffron risotto; goat's cheese with roast vegetable tart; sticky toffee apple pudding. **Details:** 11 pm; closed Sun; no credit cards.

Bleeding Heart EC1 £ 40 𝔸★
Bleeding Heart Yd, Greville St 7242 8238
"A great hidden-away gem", this rambling brasserie/restaurant near Holborn offers "consistent" Gallic fare and an "adventurous" wine list, all at "good-value" prices; lunchtime is for business, but evenings can be "romantic". / **Sample dishes:** grilled vegetable terrine; salmon fishcakes with spinach; apple tart. **Details:** 10.30 pm; closed Sat & Sun.

Blue Elephant SW6 £ 42 𝔸★
4-6 Fulham Broadway 7385 6595 4–4A
"Belying the touristy, if charming, atmosphere", London's most popular and romantic ethnic (complete with "gardens-and-pond décor") is a great all-rounder, where "considerate" staff dish up "delicious" Thai food. / **Sample dishes:** prawns & chicken in rice paper; green seafood curry; mint sake. **Value tip:** set Sun L £26(FP). **Details:** www.blueelephant.com; 11 pm; closed Sat L.

Blue Jade SW1 £ 26 ★
44 Hugh St 7828 0321 1–4B
"Spicy" Thai cooking in "generous portions" ensures local popularity for this "oriental gem", hidden "in the murky backstreets of Pimlico". / **Sample dishes:** baby sweetcorn cakes; red Thai chicken curry; coconut ice-cream. **Details:** 11 pm; closed Sat L & Sun.

Bluebird SW3 £ 45
350 Kings Rd 7559 1000 4–3C
"Conran at its worst"; this huge, "spacious" Chelsea "landmark" restaurant gets multiple drubbings for "very standard" and "overpriced" cooking and "absolutely terrible" service. / **Sample dishes:** Thai fishcakes; Irish lamb stew with polenta; espresso parfait. **Value tip:** set Sun L £29(FP). **Details:** www.conran.com; 11 pm.

Bombay Bicycle Club SW12 £ 32 Ⓐ★
95 Nightingale Ln 8673 6217
"Delicate, subtly flavoured" Indian cooking served in a "very pleasant", "Western-style" environment makes this "consistently good" Wandsworth subcontinental a top south London destination; the "take-aways are excellent" too – in Battersea (7720 0500), Putney (8785 1188) and Wimbledon (8540 9997). / **Sample dishes:** pakoras; lamb tikka; kulfi. **Details:** 11 pm; D only, closed Sun.

Bombay Brasserie SW7 £ 38 Ⓐ★
Courtfield Clo, Gloucester Rd 7370 4040 4–2B
The "wonderful conservatory" and "colonial-style" décor of this "steady" South Kensington fixture win it much support, as does the "lovely" cooking (especially the Sunday buffet); for no particularly objective reasons, some just "can't bring" themselves to like the place. / **Sample dishes:** scallops piri-piri; quail in spiced yoghurt sauce; halva. **Details:** www.bombaybrasserielondon.com; midnight.

Bombay Palace W2 £ 32 Ⓐ★★
50 Connaught St 7723 8855
"Interesting" cooking of "great variety and flavour" makes it worth seeking out this "quiet" and rather under-appreciated Bayswater Indian. / **Sample dishes:** Bombay tiffin; lamb chop masala; kulfi. **Details:** 11.30 pm; no smoking area.

Boudin Blanc W1 £ 34 Ⓐ
5 Trebeck St 7499 3292 2–4B
Even post-expansion, conditions remain "cramped" at this Shepherd Market bistro; the "cheerful" buzz and "honest" Gallic cooking have more or less survived (and pre-7pm menus still offer good value), but it's not quite the place it used to be. / **Sample dishes:** fish soup; coq au vin; tarte Tatin. **Value tip:** set always available £20(FP). **Details:** 11 pm.

Bradley's NW3 £ 42 ★
25 Winchester Rd 7722 3457
"Real care and flair" makes this "tasteful", "no-fuss" modern British restaurant (majoring in fish) much more than just a "useful" spot in "dud" Swiss Cottage. / **Sample dishes:** artichoke, basil & tomato salad; roast duck with apples; chocolate pudding & marmalade ice-cream. **Value tip:** set Sun L £26(FP). **Details:** 11 pm; closed Sat L.

Brady's SW18 £ 20 ★
513 Old York Rd 8877 9599
"Very tasty" fish and chips (with "proper mushy peas") underpin the enduring appeal of Mr Brady's Wandsworth bistro. / **Sample dishes:** potted shrimps; battered haddock & chips; apple crumble. **Details:** 10.30 pm; closed Sun; no credit cards; no booking.

Brass. du Marché aux Puces W10   £ 34   A★
349 Portobello Rd   8968 5828
*"You could be in France itself" at this "relaxed" and "intimate"
Notting Hill corner brasserie; "very reliable" food (and a "lovely
wine list" too) helps make it a "great place for a late breakfast,
lunch or dinner".* / **Sample dishes:** *Burgundy snails in garlic butter; duck
magret with celeriac dauphinoise; tarte Tatin.* **Value tip:** *set Sun L £22(FP).*
Details: *11 pm; closed Sun D.*

Brick Lane Beigel Bake E1   £ 4   ★★
159 Brick Ln   7729 0616
*"Best at 3am after a night on the town", this "unique", 24/7
East End take-away offers "generously filled bagels at generously
low prices"; the "queue looks worse than it is".* / **Sample
dishes:** *salmon & cream cheese beigel; salt beef sandwich; no puddings.*
Details: *open 24 hours; no credit cards; no smoking.*

Busaba Eathai W1   £ 23   A★
106-110 Wardour St   7255 8686   2–2D
*"Cheap and cheerful", but "slick and stylish" too – this "funky"
new Soho oriental (one of whose backers invented the
Wagamama concept) serves tasty Thai noodle and curry dishes
at large, shared tables; service with "attitude" can be a problem,
but "go and queue" – "it's worth it".* / **Sample dishes:** *Thai calamari;
crispy pork & Chinese chive stir-fry; jasmine smoothie.* **Details:** *11 pm, Fri
& Sat 11.30pm; no smoking; no booking.*

Café Bagatelle W1   £ 31
Manchester Sq   7563 9505   2–1A
*Take your shades for maximum enjoyment of a sunny-day lunch
at the Wallace's impressively-glazed and spaciously laid out new
atrium; the modern British fare is well above 'institutional'
standards.* / **Sample dishes:** *rillettes of duck; peppered tuna with garlic &
olive oil mash; lemon tart.* **Details:** *www.wallace-collection.com; L only;
no smoking.*

Café du Marché EC1   £ 38   A★
22 Charterhouse Sq   7608 1609
*"A lovely City find"; this "intimate", "friendly" and "reliable"
farmhouse-style restaurant is "good value" and exudes
a "genuinely French" appeal – both to business lunchers and
to evening romantics and jazz-lovers.* / **Sample dishes:** *fish soup with
garlic croutons; steak with béarnaise sauce; chocolate tart.* **Details:** *10 pm;
closed Sat L & Sun; no Amex.*

Café Japan NW11   £ 27   ★
626 Finchley Rd   8455 6854
*"Excellent sushi at reasonable price" wins widespread praise for
this unpretentious Nipponese, near Golders Green BR; "it's still
good, in spite of its reputation and popularity".* / **Sample
dishes:** *yakitori; chicken teriyaki; Japanese ice cream.* **Value tip:** *set
weekday L £10(FP).* **Details:** *10.30 pm; closed Mon & Tue L; no Amex;
no smoking area.*

Café Spice Namaste   £ 31   A★
247 Lavender Hl, SW11   7738 1717
16 Prescot St, E1   7488 9242
*"Cyrus Todiwala redefines Indian food", say the many admirers
of the "eclectic" dishes served at his "colourful" east London HQ
(the Battersea offshoot "is not a patch on the original"); critics
say the food's "over-rated" or just "too unusual".* / **Sample
dishes:** *pan-fried chicken with chutney; tiger prawns, crab & squid curry;
coconut & pineapple ice cream.* **Value tip:** *set Sun L £17(FP).*
Details: *10.30 pm, Sat 10 pm; E1 closed Sat L & Sun – SW11 closed Mon,
Tue-Sat D only, Sun open for L & D.*

Cambio de Tercio SW5   £ 35   A★

163 Old Brompton Rd   7244 8970   4–2B
"Good things are happening" at this colourful and *"busy"* South
Kensington Spaniard, where *"professional"* staff serve up
"innovative" dishes in a *"very pleasant"* atmosphere. / **Sample
dishes:** sweetcorn & prawn ravioli; grilled tuna with caramelised vinegar; citrus
sorbets. **Details:** 11 pm.

Cantinetta Venegazzú SW11   £ 33   ★

31–32 Battersea Sq   7978 5395   4–4C
The *"only restaurant in London serving authentic Venetian food"*
is proclaimed by advocates of this *"charming"* and *"homely"*,
if rather *"cramped"*, Battersea spot, which has pleasant outside
tables. / **Sample dishes:** deep-fried scallops; fritto misto; tiramisu. **Value
tip:** set weekday L £18(FP). **Details:** 11 pm.

Capital Hotel SW3   £ 68   ★

22-24 Basil St   7589 5171   4–1D
Eric Chavot's *"assured"* modern French cooking maintains this
small, *"calm"* Knightsbridge dining room in London's gastronomic
Premier League; some find that its *"strange"* décor creates
a rather *"impersonal"* atmosphere. / **Sample dishes:** roast pepper &
goat's cheese salad; stuffed pigeon with truffle consommé; strawberry & white
chocolate trifle. **Value tip:** set weekday L £35(FP).
Details: www.capitalhotel.co.uk; 11 pm; jacket & tie required at D.

Le Caprice SW1   £ 45   A★

Arlington Hs, Arlington St   7629 2239   2–4C
"Sophisticated" and *"consistently reliable"*, this St James's
brasserie is *"sheer bliss"* for its huge fan club, who award
"10/10 for honest food, honest prices, and great waiters";
whether the deadpan glamour can survive Messrs Corbin and
King's departure remains to be seen. / **Sample dishes:** plum tomato
tart with basil oil; salmon fishcakes with lemon sauce; iced red berries.
Details: midnight.

Carnevale EC1   £ 25   ★

135 Whitecross St   7250 3452
"Inventive" food makes this *"intimate"* but *"cramped"* spot
a *"treasure"* for City vegetarians, and *"useful pre-Barbican"*
for those of any persuasion. / **Sample dishes:** pan-fried halloumi; roast
cassava with white beans; peach & cherry compote.
Details: www.carnevalerestaurant.co.uk; 10.30 pm; closed Sat L & Sun;
no Visa, Mastercard or Amex.

Cassia Oriental W1   £ 35

12 Berkeley Sq   7629 8886   2–3B
"Amazing value, considering the location" wins many plaudits
for this new Mayfair oriental (whose menu covers a ragbag
of cuisines); it took over from short-lived China Jazz (RIP)
and has inherited its *"luxurious"* Bond-movie-esque décor.
/ **Sample dishes:** banana heart & lime salad; Thai herb-crusted rack of lamb;
sweet Chinese buns. **Details:** www.cassiaoriental.com; 11.30 pm.

Chez Bruce SW17   £ 41   A★★

2 Bellevue Rd   8672 0114
Bruce Poole's short menu of *"extremely consistent"* and
"genuinely delicious" modern British fare – together with
"superb" service and *"sensible"* prices – has made this
"intimate", *"unpretentious"* Wandsworth Common-sider
one of the most popular places in town. / **Sample dishes:** gnocchi
gratin with roast plum tomatoes; pink bream with tomato & courgette tart;
pear tarte Tatin. **Details:** 10.30 pm; closed Sun D; booking: max 6.

Chez Liline N4 £ 34 ★★
101 Stroud Green Rd 7263 6550
"Finsbury Park's finest" may "look like it's falling apart", but the
"interesting" Mauritian fish menu delivers some "amazing"
flavours. / **Sample dishes:** spicy fishcakes; red snapper with pickled lime
sauce; fresh mango. **Value tip:** set weekday L £19(FP). **Details:** 10.30 pm;
closed Sun.

Chezmax SW10 £ 43 A★★
168 Ifield Rd 7835 0874 4–3A
"Gorgeous" French cooking and a "fantastically OTT" maître d' –
"it's worth a visit just to hear the menu run down" – have made
this "cosy" and "tucked away" Chelsea-fringe basement
a well-known destination, especially for those with romance in
mind. / **Sample dishes:** goat's cheese tart; lobster with caramelised root
vegetables; fresh figs in Amaretto. **Details:** 11 pm; closed Sun.

cheznico W1 £ 67 ★
90 Park Ln 7409 1290 2–3A
It's both good and bad that Nico's much-hyped 'new' approach –
"more choice and (some) cheaper options" – has impacted
barely at all on estimations of this grand Mayfair dining room;
there's been "no slipping" in culinary standards, but the ambience
is as "underwhelming" as ever. / **Sample dishes:** griddled foie gras; veal
cutlets with roast garlic; lemon tart. **Details:** 11 pm; closed Sat L & Sun;
no Switch; jacket & tie required.

Chiang Mai W1 £ 32 ★★
48 Frith St 7437 7444 3–2A
"Fabulous" Thai cooking – the best in the West End – leads
many to brave the iffy service, "cramped" conditions and
"deadly" ambience of this Soho veteran. / **Sample dishes:** fishcakes
with sweet chilli sauce; green chicken curry with coconut rice; exotic fruit salad.
Value tip: set weekday L £17(FP). **Details:** 11 pm; closed Sun L.

China House W1 £ 26 A
160 Piccadilly 7499 6996 2–3C
"Spectacular interior design" of an "impressive" Edwardian
building (originally a car showroom) provides a very "stylish"
setting for this new noodle bar, which is notably "reasonably
priced" for the area; "great dim sum" also wins praise. / **Sample
dishes:** deep-fried squid rolls; seafood soup noodles; ice cream.
Details: www.chinahouse.co.uk; midnight; no smoking area.

Chinon W14 £ 35 ★★
23 Richmond Way 7602 4082
"Flawless but rich" modern French cooking (and "great
presentation" too) makes it well worth truffling out this famously
"idiosyncratic" and "tucked away" Shepherd's Bush backstreet
spot. / **Sample dishes:** smoked fish platter; fillet steak with morels; chocolate
sorbet. **Details:** 10.45 pm; D only, closed Sun.

Chives SW10 £ 36 ★★
204 Fulham Rd 7351 4747 4–3B
The name of the Red Pepper Group's latest offshoot is without
colour, but the same can't be said of the splendid Mediterranean
cooking – already among the group's best; these Chelsea
premises, though, are awkwardly proportioned. / **Sample
dishes:** tortellini of rabbit; pan-fried sea bass; lemon bread & butter pudding.
Details: 10.30 pm; D only, Sat & Sun open L only.

Chutney Mary SW10 £ 38 A★
535 King's Rd   7351 3113   4–4B
"Imaginative" cooking that's "very different from your usual
Indian" wins a wide-ranging fan club for this "roomy"
distant-Chelsea fixture; it benefits from a "pretty conservatory".
/ *Sample dishes:* Punjabi vegetable samosas; sea bass in spicy Goan masala
sauce; kulfi. *Details:* www.realindianfood.com; 11.30 pm; no smoking area.

Cibo W14 £ 40 ★
3 Russell Gdns   7371 6271
"Imaginative" (though sometimes "inconsistent") cooking has
established quite a name for this "tucked away" Olympia
"neighbourhood" Italian; it can be an "intimate" place, too,
"but only if you get a decent table". / *Sample dishes:* gnocchi with
courgette flowers; liver with sage & prosciutto; ice cream.
Details: www.ciborestaurant.com; 11 pm; closed Sat L & Sun D.

Cinnamon Cay SW11 £ 28 ★
87 Lavender HI   7801 0932
"Different" (western Pacific) and "varied" cooking has already
earned quite a following for this "understated" Battersea
newcomer. / *Sample dishes:* warm beetroot & orange salad; char-grilled
beef with baby vegetables; grilled figs. *Value tip:* set weekday L £13(FP).
Details: www.cinnamoncay.co.uk; 11 pm; closed Mon L & Sun D.

City Rhodes EC4 £ 52 ★
New Street Sq   7583 1313
Gary Rhodes's "fabulous" and "wonderfully presented" English
cooking together with "slick and attentive" service make this
dining room near Fleet Street the City's top choice "for a posh
business lunch". / *Sample dishes:* tomato cake with peppered goat's
cheese; sea bream with herb & oyster tartare; strawberry custard tart.
Details: 9 pm; closed Sat & Sun.

Clarke's W8 £ 55 A★★
124 Kensington Ch St   7221 9225
"You get what you are given" at Sally Clarke's "intimate"
and "civilised" Kensington fixture – zero-menu choice (except
at lunch) is part of a Californian-influenced approach which
makes "superb" use of "outstanding, fresh, seasonal ingredients".
/ *Sample dishes:* broad bean & ricotta ravioli; Welsh lamb with mushrooms &
leaf spinach; baked white nectarine with raspberries.
Details: www.sallyclarke.com; 10 pm; closed Sat & Sun; no smoking area at L,
no smoking at D.

Club Gascon EC1 £ 35 A★★
57 West Smithfield   7796 0600
"Foie gras is a must" at this "sparkling", "vibrant" and
"romantic" Smithfield yearling; its "sensational" and "unique"
approach – featuring tapas-style dishes from Gascony – has
propelled it to instant stardom. / *Sample dishes:* foie gras with sweet
onion marmalade; baby squid with fried herbs; crème Catalan.
Details: 11 pm; closed Sat L & Sun; no Amex.

Connaught W1 £ 76 A
Carlos Pl   7499 7070   2–3B
This "old world" Mayfair bastion offers a "memorable" and
"very English" experience, with "unimpeachable" service
that "pampers without pomposity"; the time warp Anglo-French
cooking is as pricey as you might fear, but it's "reliable". / *Sample
dishes:* fresh asparagus; pan-fried entrecôte with roasted tomatoes; crème
brûlée. *Value tip:* set weekday L £48(FP). *Details:* www.the-connaught.co.uk;
10.45 pm; Grill closed Sat L; jacket & tie for dinner, jacket for lunch;
appreciated if guests try to refrain from smoking.

constantly updated at www.hardens.com

Il Convivio SW1 £ 39 A★
143 Ebury St   7730 4099   1–4A
"A welcome arrival" in benighted Belgravia (on the site that was
Mijanou, RIP), this glitzy new Italian has "great décor", "really
good" service and cooking that, if "slightly up and down",
generally delivers "good value". / *Sample dishes: scorpion fish pâte;
semolina risotto with crab & fennel; roast peaches. Details: 10.45 pm; closed
Sun.*

Coq d'Argent EC3 £ 49
1 Poultry   7395 5000
"On those rare sunny lunchtimes", it's a "delight" to have a drink
outside Conran's "stunningly located" 6th-floor venture near
Bank; the restaurant itself is "disappointing", though, with "dull"
cooking that's "grossly overpriced". / *Sample dishes: moules marinière;
rib-eye steak with garlic & snail butter; strawberry millefeuille. Value tip: set
Sun L £32(FP). Details: www.conran.com; 10 pm; closed Sat L & Sun D.*

The Cow W11 £ 28 A★
89 Westbourne Park Rd   7221 0021
The "simple, fresh seafood" served in the "packed" ground-floor
Irish bar of this trendy Notting Hill boozer inspires more
commentary than the quite ambitious, but equally crowded dining
room upstairs; standards, though, are "reliable" throughout.
/ *Sample dishes: leek & lobster salad; sea bass with parsley; passion fruit
sorbet. Details: 11 pm; D only, closed Sun – bar open all week.*

The Criterion W1 £ 44 A
224 Piccadilly Circus   7930 0488   2–3D
"Appalling" service – "inversely proportional" to the "splendour"
of the neo-Byzantine setting – has always been the bugbear
of this MPW 'diffusion' outlet; sadly, the grand brasserie food's
now "gone down" too, and even former supporters find it
"mediocre". / *Sample dishes: crab & clam risotto with parsley; halibut with
wild mushrooms ; lemon tart. Details: 11.30 pm; closed Sun L.*

Crivelli's Garden WC2 £ 27
Trafalgar Sq   7747 2869   3–4B
The feel is a touch institutional (unless you book ahead for
a fountain-view table), but the food is "surprisingly reasonable"
at this new gallery concession, run by the Red Pepper Group;
there's a grander 'French' bit and a cheaper pizza section.
/ *Sample dishes: red pepper mousse; couscous tartare; lemon tart.
Details: 8 pm; L only, Wed open L & D; no smoking.*

Defune W1 £ 44 ★★
61 Blandford St   7935 8311   1–1A
"Has it been painted in years?" – Japanese aficionados, though,
are blind to the "run down" décor of this "tiny" Marylebone café,
noting only its "excellent" fare, including the "best sushi ever".
/ *Sample dishes: crispy noodle salad; sushi & sashimi selection; sweet bean
curd. Value tip: set always available £26(FP). Details: 10.30 pm; closed Sun.*

Del Buongustaio SW15 £ 34 ★
283 Putney Br Rd   8780 9361
It "looks awful from the outside", but this Putney Italian has a big
reputation for its "great", "simple" food, "friendly" service and
"warm" atmosphere; declining ratings, though, reflect rising
disappointments of late. / *Sample dishes: mixed seafood salad; ricotta &
spinach ravioli; custard tart. Value tip: set weekday L £22(FP).
Details: www.theitalianrestaurant.net; 10.30 pm; closed Sat L.*

Diverso W1 £ 42 ★

85 Piccadilly 7491 2222 2–4C
*Though it offers "good value, given the location", this luxuriously
rustic Italian near the Ritz remains curiously "undiscovered" –
"you can always get a table". / **Sample dishes:** beef carpaccio; wild
mushroom & pancetta risotto; tiramisu. **Details:** 11.30 pm; closed Sun L.*

Dorchester Grill W1 £ 60 Ⓐ

53 Park Ln 7629 8888 2–3A
*"Real British traditional food" is an undoubted plus of this "lovely"
Mayfair dining room, decked out in Spanish Baronial splendour;
it's the service, though – "unobtrusive", but "always there when
needed" – that wins highest praise. / **Sample dishes:** mackerel &
pumpkin with couscous; chicken with provençale vegetables; bread & butter
pudding with clotted cream. **Value tip:** set Sun L £39(FP).
Details: www.dorchesterhotel.com; 11 pm.*

Dorchester, Oriental W1 £ 77

53 Park Ln 7629 8888 2–3A
*London's grandest Chinese may offer "delicious" food, but it's
"very overpriced", and the "lavish" décor strikes reporters as
somewhere between "boring" and "creepy". / **Sample dishes:** prawn
& water chestnut dumplings; pan-fried beef & aubergines in chilli sauce; chilled
mango pudding. **Value tip:** set weekday L £25(FP).
Details: www.dorchesterhotel.com; 11 pm; closed Sat L & Sun.*

The Eagle EC1 £ 22 Ⓐ★

159 Farringdon Rd 7837 1353
*"Hectic", "smoky" and "difficult to get a seat in", it may be but,
when it comes to gastropubs, this legendary Farringdon fixture –
with its "innovative" Mediterranean cooking – is still "the original
and the best" for many reporters. / **Sample dishes:** grilled sardine
bruschetta; wild sea bass with chicory salad; Portuguese custard tarts.
Details: 10.30 pm; closed Sun D; no credit cards; no booking.*

Elistano SW3 £ 29 Ⓐ★

25-27 Elystan St 7584 5248 4–2C
*"Fun", "busy" and "noisy" Chelsea "stand-by" serving "simple"
Italian grub at "reasonable prices"; it's best to book. / **Sample
dishes:** beef carpaccio salad; grilled tuna salad; lemon mousse.
Details: 11 pm.*

Emile's £ 26 ★

144 Wandsworth Br Rd, SW6 7736 2418
96-98 Felsham Rd, SW15 8789 3323
*The prix-fixe formula of "very good-value" and "reliable if
unexciting" Anglo-French fare is eliciting ever more praise for
these "informal" Putney and Fulham locals; they are "always
enjoyable" or "dull", to taste. / **Sample dishes:** tiger prawn wonton
baskets; calves liver with sweetcorn pancakes & proscuitto; treacle tart.
Details: 11 pm; D only; closed Sun; no Amex.*

Enoteca Turi SW15 £ 34 Ⓐ★

28 Putney High St 8785 4449
*"Particularly warm and likeable" service, a "stunning selection"
of Italian wines and "very good regional cooking" makes this
a notable Putney fixture; perhaps its revamp – underway as we
go to press – will earn it more of the recognition it deserves.
/ **Sample dishes:** buffalo Mozzarella salad; tagliatelle with pork belly &
Parmesan; tiramisu. **Details:** 11 pm; closed Sun.*

Esarn Kheaw W12 £ 26 ★★

314 Uxbridge Rd 8743 8930
*"Delicious" Thai food – perhaps "the most authentic in London"
– makes it worth braving this slow and drearily decorated
Shepherd's Bush spot. / Sample dishes: spring rolls; green chicken curry;
ice cream. Details: 11 pm; closed Sat L & Sun L.*

L'Escargot W1 £ 40 A★

48 Greek St 7437 2679 3–2A
*"Swift" and "unobtrusive" service and "creative" modern French
cooking ensure it's "always a pleasure" to visit this "opulent" but
"understated" Soho veteran – either downstairs or in the "lovely"
Picasso Room above (formula price £75). / Sample dishes: Scottish
langoustines with caviar; lamb chump with butter beans; champagne fruit jelly.
Details: www.whitestarline.org; 11.30 pm; closed Sat L & Sun.*

Exhibition SW7 £ 38 ★

19 Exhibition Rd 7584 8359 4–2C
*South Kensington's Tui was long London's "top Thai" for many
reporters, and it was something of a surprise to see it relaunched
in summer 2000; it's still run by the same team, but it's pricier
now and both menu and décor have been given a more European
gloss. / Sample dishes: crispy oriental pancakes; grilled sea bream with
minted lime juice; sweet sticky rice. Details: 11 pm; closed Mon; bookings:
max 10.*

Faulkner's E8 £ 20 ★★

424-426 Kingsland Rd 7254 6152
*It has an "impossible" Dalston location, but "the best fish and
chips in town" justify the pilgrimage to this eminent East End
chippy; it's licensed, but you can BYO. / Sample dishes: smoked
salmon; roast salmon in lemon sauce; sticky toffee pudding. Details: 10 pm;
no Amex; no smoking area.*

Feng Shang NW1 £ 31 A★

Opp 15 Prince Albert Rd 7485 8137
*This large, oriental barge, moored by Regent's Park, delivers
a "lovely", festive experience for most reporters – the cooking
is surprisingly good, and the staff "do everything but eat the food
for you". / Sample dishes: baked lobster with spring onions; deep-fried
pomegranate chicken; red bean cake. Details: 11 pm.*

Florians N8 £ 30 A★

4 Topsfield Parade 8348 8348
*The "good bar menu" is tops at this "noisy" Hornsey Italian,
but some also rate the romantic potential of the "good local
restaurant" at the rear. / Sample dishes: polenta, cheese & tomato
terrine; char-grilled steak with oregano & lemon; strawberry ice vacherin.
Details: 10.45 pm; no Amex.*

Foliage SW1 £ 50 ★

66 Knightsbridge 7235 2000 1–3A
*The press have raved about David Nicholls's modern French
cuisine in the rather preciously remodelled dining room of this
grand Knightsbridge Edwardian hotel; our early-days meal was
too much of a 'curate's egg' to put the cooking in the very front
rank, but, at £32.50 (prix-fixe), it was undoubtedly good value.
/ Sample dishes: crab & trout millefeuille with grapefruit; roasted cod with
beetroot Tatin; fruit cappuccino with lime syrup. Details: 10.30 pm; closed Sat
L & Sun.*

Il Forno W1 — £ 28 ★
63-64 Frith St   7734 4545   3–2A
Replacing "the excellent Frith Street restaurant", this low key Soho newcomer is most popular as a "good, unfussy lunch spot" serving "reasonably-priced" and "wholesome" Italian dishes; fans of the former régime, see L'Anis. / **Sample dishes:** *Mozzarella & aubergine salad; smoked swordfish pizza; tiramisu.* **Details:** *10.30 pm, Fri & Sat 11 pm; closed Sun.*

Fox & Anchor EC1 — £ 22   A★
115 Charterhouse St   7253 4838
For an "absolutely historic breakfast" — washed down with "a side-order of Guinness" (thanks to the local Smithfield licensing laws) — this "characterful" pub dining room is just "unbeatable". / **Sample dishes:** *prawn cocktail; fillet steak with mushrooms; apple pie.* **Details:** *10 pm, Fri & Sat 10.30 pm; closed Sun.*

Frederick's N1 — £ 36   A★
106 Camden Pas   7359 2888
"A fine tradition maintained", proclaim fans of this Islington institution, which "suits any occasion", thanks to its dependable modern British cooking and "really pretty" conservatory setting. / **Sample dishes:** *goat's cheese with roast red peppers; baked halibut with croutons; vodka & lime parfait.* **Value tip:** *set weekday L £24(FP).* **Details:** *11.30 pm; closed Sun; no smoking area.*

French House W1 — £ 36   A★
49 Dean St   7437 2477   3–3A
"Intimate, unpretentious and romantic", this "cramped" dining room above the famous ("echos of de Gaulle") pub makes a "wonderful", "casual" destination for Soho Bohemians; the "not very French" cooking is "solidly good" ("especially for meat-lovers"). / **Sample dishes:** *ox tongue with sauce vierge; rabbit & chicory in mustard sauce; Cambridge Cream.* **Details:** *11.15 pm; closed Sun.*

Fryer's Delight WC1 — £ 9 ★
19 Theobald's Rd   7405 4114   1–1D
It can't be the "Formica"-chic design, so it must be the "bargain" fish and chips that ensure this BYO chippy, behind Gray's Inn, is always "full of cabbies". / **Sample dishes:** *bread & butter; cod & chips; no puddings.* **Details:** *10 pm; closed Sun; no credit cards.*

Fung Shing WC2 — £ 32   ★★
15 Lisle St   7437 1539   3–3A
"Great food, but rather a grey atmosphere" — the low-down on "the best Chinese in Chinatown" is the same as ever; the range of "dishes not seen in other places" (especially seafood) is a major plus. / **Sample dishes:** *scallops; crispy duck pancakes; fruit & ice cream.* **Details:** *11.30 pm.*

Gaby's WC2 — £ 20 ★
30 Charing Cross Rd   7836 4233   3–3B
"The best salt beef sandwich in the West End" and an "interesting mix of Mediterranean and Middle Eastern grub" win fans for this "central", "quick" and "cheap" café. / **Sample dishes:** *falafel salad; chicken kebabs; cheesecake.* **Details:** *www.gabys.net; 11.15 pm; no credit cards.*

constantly updated at www.hardens.com

The Gate W6 £ 27 A★★

51 Queen Caroline St   8748 6932

Even "carnivores don't notice the lack of meat" at this "hidden-away" Hammersmith "veggie heaven"; "you can visit often, thanks to the regularly-changing menu" (though "you must book"); an offshoot opens at 72 Belsize Lane NW3 in late-2000. / **Sample dishes:** plantain fritters & coconut chutney; Gruyère & butternut filo with pesto; bread & butter pudding. **Details:** www.gateveg.co.uk; 10.45 pm; closed Sat L & Sun.

Gaucho Grill £ 30 A★

19-25 Swallow St, W1   7734 4040
64 Heath St, NW3   7431 8222
12 Gracechurch St, EC3   7626 5180

For some of "the best steaks in town", make tracks for these "bustling", funkily-decorated South American grills, where "great Argentinian beef and robust wines" create a winning formula. / **Sample dishes:** aubergine & Mozzarella salad; fillet steak with garlic mushrooms; lemon Mascarpone tart. **Details:** 11.45 pm – EC3 11 pm; EC3 closed Sat & Sun (open for breakfast).

Gaudi EC1 £ 40

63 Clerkenwell Rd   7608 3220

The annual dispute about this Clerkenwell Spaniard rages on; on balance, the reporters claiming it as an "excellent find" with "lovely" cooking slightly outnumber those who say it's an "odd" and "overpriced" place. / **Sample dishes:** goat's cheese lasagne with ceps; Iberian pork with paprika & roasted peppers; Spanish rice pudding crepes. **Value tip:** set weekday L £23(FP). **Details:** www.turnmills.com; 10.30 pm; closed Sat L & Sun.

Le Gavroche W1 £ 99 ★★

43 Upper Brook St   7408 0881   2–2A

Michel Roux Jr's "brilliant" Gallic gastronomy leads many reporters to award "top prize" to this grand, old Mayfair basement; an "amazing" wine list and "impeccable" service are further attractions, but some do find prices "stupid", and the perennial pleas for "redecoration" are getting louder. / **Sample dishes:** crab salad with glass noodles; herb-crusted veal; bitter chocolate & praline indulgence. **Value tip:** set weekday L £43(FP). **Details:** www.le-gavroche.co.uk; 11 pm; closed Sat & Sun; jacket required.

Geeta NW6 £ 17 ★★

59 Willesden Ln   7624 1713

You would need "transcendent" cooking "to cope with the dreary surroundings" of this Kilburn south Indian – fortunately, that's just what you get, and it's "tremendous value". / **Sample dishes:** lentil pancakes with tomato chutney; lamb tandoori; strawberry pie. **Details:** 10.30 pm, Fri & Sat 11.30 pm; no Switch.

The Glasshouse TW1 £ 38 A★★

14 Station Pde   8940 6777

Chez Bruce's year-old sibling, "right by Kew Gardens station", is "way ahead of anything else in the area"; conditions may be "cramped", but the "faultless" modern British cooking and "good-natured", "knowledgeable" service already make it a notable destination. / **Sample dishes:** tomato & Mozzarella risotto ; veal with white asparagus; lemongrass & vanilla yoghurt. **Details:** 10.30 pm; closed Sun D.

Good Earth SW3   £ 36   ★

233 Brompton Rd   7584 3658   4–2C

*You get "good menu advice" at this grand, if comfortably worn-in Knightsbridge Chinese, which is consistently praised for its "reliably fresh" cooking. / **Sample dishes:** spare ribs with seaweed; char sui pork with crispy noodles; red bean pudding. **Details:** 10.45 pm.*

Goolies W8   £ 37   𝔸★

21 Abingdon Rd   7938 1122   4–1A

*We've never quite seen it, but Kensington folk insist that this "lively local", just off the High Street, offers "imaginative" modern British cooking and "great" service. / **Sample dishes:** crab cakes with caramelised pineapple; fillet of beef with sweet potatoes & foie gras; bitter chocolate brownies. **Value tip:** set weekday L £22(FP). **Details:** www.goolies-bar.com; 10.30 pm.*

Gordon Ramsay SW3   £ 81   𝔸★★

68-69 Royal Hospital Rd   7352 4441   4–3D

*"Infinite care and attention to detail" have won Gordon Ramsay's "exquisite" modern French cooking the best food ratings ever recorded in the survey; the service at his small and "formal" Chelsea dining room is perhaps a touch "over-attentive", but it's "outstandingly professional" too. / **Sample dishes:** salad of crispy pig trotters; sea bass with crab stuffing; tarte Tatin & vanilla pod ice cream. **Value tip:** set weekday L £48(FP). **Details:** 11 pm; closed Sat & Sun.*

Granita N1   £ 34   ★

127 Upper St   7226 3222

*"Really interesting", "ever-changing" modern British menus and "friendly" service ensure that this eminent Islington spot is "always packed"; its notoriously stark décor was undergoing a major refurbishment as we went to press. / **Sample dishes:** roast peppers & artichokes; char-grilled lamb chops with minted mash; passion fruit cheesecake. **Details:** 10.30 pm; closed Mon & Tue L; no Amex.*

Grano W4   £ 42   ★

162 Thames Rd   8995 0120

*It may be "off the beaten track", but this "lovely local", near Strand on the Green, is "well above average", and offers a "rich" and "inventive" (if "limited") Italian menu, and "outstanding" wines. / **Sample dishes:** Parmesan risotto; ravioli with asparagus & peas; fresh fruit. **Details:** 10.30 pm; closed Mon L, Sat L & Sun D.*

The Grapes E14   £ 37   𝔸★

76 Narrow St   7987 4396

*"Simple food served well" is a boon in Docklands, and the small first-floor fish restaurant at this "great" old riverside pub "does what it does brilliantly"; there's a superb view from the window seats. / **Sample dishes:** lobster bisque; bangers & mash with green beans; apple crumble. **Details:** 9.15 pm; closed Sat L & Sun D; no children.*

Hard Rock Café W1   £ 27   𝔸

150 Old Park Ln   7629 0382   2–4B

*A "great, fun atmosphere" ("if you're in the mood") and "the best" burgers, keep 'em queueing at this large Mayfair diner – the original of the worldwide chain; it's "too loud" – "take people you don't want to talk to". / **Sample dishes:** onion rings; char-broiled burger with fries; ice cream. **Details:** www.hardrock.com; 12.30 am, Fri & Sat 1 am; no Switch; no smoking area; no booking.*

The Havelock Tavern W14   £ 28   ★★

57 Masbro Rd   7603 5374

"Get there early" if you want to enjoy the "great, upmarket pub-food" at this "casual", "smoky" and "loud" Olympia boozer; "boy, the staff have attitude". / **Sample dishes:** spinach & ricotta fritters; home-cured salmon with beetroot cake; fruit pavlova. **Details:** 10 pm; no credit cards; no booking.

Home EC1   £ 32   𝔸

100-106 Leonard St   7684 8618

"Ultra-hip", "nicely Bohemian" Shoreditch bar restaurant; since the dining room moved from basement (tiny) to ground floor (much bigger) it's not quite as good as it was, but the eclectic grub (with lots of fish) can still be "surprisingly good" for such a groovy place. / **Sample dishes:** mushrooms with dill & garlic; tandoori monkfish with Indian salsa; poached white cherries. **Details:** www.homebar.co.uk; 10 pm; closed Sat L & Sun; no smoking area.

Hunan SW1   £ 32   ★★

51 Pimlico Rd   7730 5712   4–2D

It looks like a (rather tired) "neighbourhood" joint, but this "imaginative" Pimlico Chinese offers "spicy" cooking which really is "first class" – "leave the ordering to them", and you will "always feel well looked after". / **Sample dishes:** pigeon soup; roast beef in wine sauce; red bean & sesame cake. **Details:** 11 pm; closed Sun.

Ibla W1   £ 38   ★

89 Marylebone High St   7224 3799   1–1A

"There's a creative genius at the stove", say those who laud the "fresh" and "imaginative" Italian fare of this improving Marylebone "sleeper"; it can hit an off note, though, and some find the experience a touch "dull". / **Sample dishes:** crab & artichoke salad; sea bass with spinach & walnuts; honey mousse with red wine sauce. **Details:** 10.30 pm; closed Sun.

Imperial City EC3   £ 34   𝔸★

Royal Exchange, Cornhill   7626 3437

This cellar under the Royal Exchange may be "full of suits", but its "buzzing" atmosphere "takes you to Hong Kong", and the "glammed up" Chinese cooking and "attentive" service make for a "very good all-round" experience. / **Sample dishes:** steamed scallops with black beans; spicy Kung Po Chicken; firecracker sweet wontons. **Details:** www.imperial-city.co.uk; 9.30 pm; closed Sat & Sun.

Inaho W2   £ 30   ★★

4 Hereford Rd   7221 8495

"The finest, cheapest Japanese food on the planet" (well, almost) is found at this "small", "crowded" Bayswater café – "a sort of Swiss chalet with chopsticks"; "service can be slow, but what's the rush when food's this good?" / **Sample dishes:** yakitori chicken; salmon & tuna sushi rolls; green tea ice crem. **Value tip:** set weekday L £17(FP). **Details:** 11 pm; closed Sat L & Sun; no Amex & no Switch.

Incognico WC2   £ 39   𝔸★

117 Shaftesbury Ave   7836 8866   3–2B

Nico Ladenis's West End newcomer rises well above the Theatreland norm, offering "delicious" Gallic haute-brasserie classics in a setting whose downtown-chic style is more NYC than London. / **Sample dishes:** Parmesan risotto; duck confit with borlotti beans; citrus fruit in champagne jelly. **Details:** midnight; closed Sun.

Indian Ocean SW17   £ 21   ★
216 Trinity Rd   8672 7740
*This Wandsworth spot is "a cut above the usual curry-house",
though fans fret that it's "getting seedier". / **Sample dishes:** tandoori
chicken; prawn & cardamom curry with lemon rice; mango sorbet.
Details: 11.30 pm.*

Isola SW1   £ 52
145 Knightsbridge   7838 1044   4–1D
*The "fantastic wine list" aside, nothing has really clicked at Oliver
Peyton's long-awaited Knightsbridge Italian – not the "cold" décor
("is that a light fixture or a UFO?"), not the "incompetent"
service, and certainly not the "really overpriced" menu; a revamp
is rumoured. / **Sample dishes:** stuffed baby squid; roast rack of lamb; hot
chocolate cake. **Details:** 10.30 pm; closed Sun.*

Italian Kitchen WC1   £ 30   ★
43 New Oxford St   7836 1011   1–1C
*They "cram you in like sardines", but the "proper home cooking"
at this Italian joint near the British Museum is "excellent value"
(especially the set menus); its former sibling – "ruined" by
refurbishment – is no more. / **Sample dishes:** deep-fried Mozzarella;
veal escalopes in cream & wine sauce; apple panini pudding. **Value tip:** set
weekday L £19(FP). **Details:** 11 pm; restricted booking Fri & Sat.*

Itsu SW3   £ 25   𝔸
118 Draycott Ave   7584 5522   4–2C
*A "fun fusion" place – this fashionable Brompton Cross
conveyor-sushi parlour offers some "innovative" East/West dishes,
and "decent" sushi; a Soho branch is in the pipeline. / **Sample
dishes:** tofu & sweetcorn roll; sushi selection; fresh fruit.
Details: www.itsu.co.uk; 11 pm; smoking only allowed in bar; no booking.*

The Ivy WC2   £ 47   𝔸★
1 West St   7836 4751   3–3B
*London holds its breath! – founders Christopher Corbin and
Jeremy King have finally quit this legendary Theatrelander,
which has for the past five years been reporters' No. 1 Favourite;
can the Belgo group maintain standards (and a star-studded
following) without them? – only time will tell. / **Sample dishes:** pea
soup with creamed Gorgonzola; roast duck with sweet potato mash; baked fig
tart with honey. **Value tip:** set Sun L £29(FP). **Details:** midnight.*

Iznik N5   £ 21   𝔸
19 Highbury Pk   7354 5697
*"Lovely", "Aladdin's cave" décor still makes this "delightful"
Islington Turk a "jewel in the heart of north London"; some,
though, have found the "meze and other staples below
expectations" on recent visits. / **Sample dishes:** falafel & houmous;
chicken with aubergines; baklava. **Details:** 11 pm; no Amex.*

Jenny Lo's Tea House SW1   £ 19   ★
14 Eccleston St   7259 0399   1–4B
*"Flavourful", "healthy" Chinese cooking is served at this
"bustling", "no-fuss", "refectory-style" noodle-parlour, near
Victoria. / **Sample dishes:** prawn & coconut laksa; pork with chestnuts &
crispy seaweed; coconut cream cake. **Details:** 10 pm; closed Sun;
no credit cards; no booking.*

Jin Kichi NW3 £ 28 ★

73 Heath St   7794 6158

There's "not much space" at this tiny Hampstead Japanese, but the staff "are always eager to please" and they serve an "excellent variety" of dishes. / Sample dishes: chicken yakitori; tuna & squid sushi with pickles; Japanese green tea sorbet. Details: 11 pm; closed Mon, Tue-Fri D only, Sat & Sun open L & D.

Joe Allen WC2 £ 35 𝔸

13 Exeter St   7836 0651   3–3D

This perennially popular, NYC-style Theatreland basement may only serve up "complacent" American fare, but it's "a good place to spot B-list celebrities", and the (off-menu) burgers are "superb"; book early for a late table. / Sample dishes: fishcakes with lemon & lime aioli; steak with saffron mash & snow peas; pecan pie. Details: www.joeallen.co.uk; 12.45 am; no smoking area.

Joy King Lau W1 £ 21 ★

3 Leicester St   7437 1132   3–3A

"Unusually cheerful… for Chinatown", this large and unremarkable-looking Chinese, just off Leicester Square, offers very "consistent" cooking and "good value for money". / Sample dishes: prawn toast & crispy seaweed; sizzling beef in peppercorn sauce; lemon pie. Details: 11.30 pm; no Switch.

Julie's W11 £ 48 𝔸

135 Portland Rd   7229 8331

"The atmosphere and the décor" are the "chief assets" of this "very pretty", "Gothic" labyrinth in Holland Park, and it's recommended "for all young lovers" and "for celebrations"; the modern-ish British cooking is "extremely average". / Sample dishes: smoked salmon; goat's cheese strudel; chocolate mousse. Details: 11.15 pm; closed Sat L.

K10 EC2 £ 20 ★★

20 Copthall Ave   7562 8510

The "variety and creativity" of Japanese-inspired dishes has made an instant lunchtime hit of this futuristic, new conveyor-sushi basement, near Liverpool Street; service is "polite and efficient". / Sample dishes: salmon sashimi; chicken teriyaki with Peruvian mash; mango & sticky rice. Details: www.k10.net; 10 pm; closed Sat & Sun; no smoking; no booking.

Kastoori SW17 £ 19 ★★

188 Upper Tooting Rd   8767 7027

"Outstanding Indo-African" cuisine, with "extraordinary flavour and texture", maintains the fame of this eminent Tooting vegetarian. / Sample dishes: onion bhaji; chicken, tomato & coriander curry; curd cheese yoghurt. Details: 10.30 pm; closed Mon L & Tue L; no Amex & no Switch.

Kavanagh's N1 £ 31 ★

26 Penton St   7833 1380

"Every bit the equal of more fashionably-situated modern British places" – Islington locals proclaim an "undiscovered gem", with "good food and service" and "unpretentious" décor. / Sample dishes: grilled aubergine salad; Parmesan risotto; raspberry crème brûlée. Details: 10.30 pm; closed Sun D; no Amex.

Ken Lo's Memories SW1 £ 45 ★

67-69 Ebury St   7730 7734   1–4B

"This is still the best Chinese in town", say supporters of this "top-notch" Belgravia veteran, whose "slightly staid" setting is its only real drawback. / Sample dishes: crispy fried king prawns; steamed salmon with ginger; ice cream. Details: 10.45 pm; closed Sun L.

Kennington Lane SE11　£ 32　A★
205-209 Kennington Ln　7793 8313
This "chic" newcomer would be a welcome addition to
Kensington, never mind Kennington, and it delivers well-oiled
service and an "inventive" mix of "first-rate" modern British
dishes; there's a "pleasant" courtyard too. / **Sample dishes:** chilled
cucumber soup; roast turbot with fennel & clams; bitter chocolate torte.
Details: 10.30 pm; closed Sun D.

Kensington Place W8　£ 39
201-205 Kensington Ch St　7727 3184
Critics say it "trades on its name", but to its loyal fan club this
notoriously "uncomfortable" and "noisy" modern British
brasserie, just off Notting Hill Gate, is "still a great place".
/ **Sample dishes:** chilled cucumber soup; shrimp & tomato risotto; home-
made sorbet. **Value tip:** set always available £25(FP). **Details:** 11.45 pm, Sun
10.15 pm.

Konditor & Cook SE1　£ 21　★★
66 The Cut　7620 2700
"Those cakes" – twinned with "good home-made soups and
panini" and "attentive and cheerful staff" – help make this
modernistic South Bank café, attached to the Young Vic, an
"outstanding" performer. / **Sample dishes:** soup with herb & cheese
scones; smoked haddock & oyster mushroom risotto; summer berry compote.
Details: 10.30 pm; closed Sun; no Amex & no Switch.

Kulu Kulu W1　£ 18　★★
76 Brewer St　7734 7316　2–2D
A "great conveyor-belt" of some of "the best sushi in London
at the price" wins unanimous acclaim for this "unpretentious"
Soho café. / **Sample dishes:** nigiri sushi; sushi selection; fresh fruit.
Details: 10 pm; closed Sun; no Amex; no smoking; no booking.

Lahore Kebab House E1　£ 15　★★
2 Umberston St　7488 2551
"Great kebabs, shame about the atrocious décor and service" –
no change, then, at this celebrated East Ender, which "still can't
be beaten for value"; BYO. / **Sample dishes:** lamb kebab; Karahi style
lamb & tomato curry; rice pudding. **Details:** 11.30 pm; no credit cards.

Latymers W6　£ 21　★
157 Hammersmith Rd　8741 2507
"Very cheap, if maybe not so cheerful" – the rear dining room
of this grim-looking Hammersmith gin palace is a "well
established" local destination, thanks to budget Thai cooking
that's "full of flavour". / **Sample dishes:** spring rolls; chicken satay; fruit
selection. **Details:** 10 pm; closed Sun; bookings taken for D only.

Launceston Place W8　£ 43　A★
1a Launceston Pl　7937 6912　4–1B
"Still a consistently excellent place" (under new ownership),
this "refined" and "tranquil" townhouse in a Kensington
backwater is a particular "romantic favourite", and offers very
dependable modern British cooking. / **Sample dishes:** penne with
char-grilled vegetables; roast cod with asparagus ; fruit selection.
Details: 11.30 pm; closed Sat L & Sun D.

Laurent NW2　£ 23　★
428 Finchley Rd　7794 3603
The "best couscous in London" is served at this celebrated
Cricklewood café, whose small premises "have no atmosphere
at all". / **Sample dishes:** deep-fried tuna & egg parcels; lamb tajine with
couscous; pistachio & honey pastries. **Details:** 11 pm; closed Sun; no Switch.

constantly updated at www.hardens.com　　37

Lemonia NW1 £ 25 Ⓐ
89 Regent's Pk Rd 7586 7454
A staff of "friendly" characters and a "relaxing" taverna
ambience with "real buzz" have made this Primrose Hill
"stalwart" famous up north London way, though the "reliable"
Greek fare doesn't set the world on fire. / **Sample dishes:** houmous
with pitta bread; grilled sea bass; yoghurt with honey & nuts. **Value tip:** set
weekday L £15(FP). **Details:** 11.30 pm; closed Sat L & Sun D; no Amex.

The Light E1 £ 32 Ⓐ★
233 Shoreditch High St 7247 8989
Airy and "refreshingly different" new bar/club/restaurant, just
north of Liverpool Street; its modern British fare was above
expectations on an early visit. / **Sample dishes:** crab claws with lemon
aioli; goat's cheese & leek tart with shallots; plum tart. **Details:** •; 11 pm;
closed Sat L.

The Light House SW19 £ 39 ★
75-77 Ridgway 8944 6338
"At last, a proper restaurant in SW19" – fans positively gush
("the most brilliant food of the year") about this "bright and airy"
modern British newcomer; results "fluctuate", though and some
find the place rather "stark". / **Sample dishes:** deep-fried prawns with
oyster mushrooms; roast red snapper with baby leeks; spiced red pears.
Details: 10.45 pm; no smoking area.

Lisboa Patisserie W10 £ 6 ★★
57 Golborne Rd 8968 5242
"Boy, can it get crowded and noisy" at this "fun" Portuguese
pâtisserie in North Kensington, famed for its "wicked" coffee
and "outstanding" pastries. / **Sample dishes:** tuna salad; chicken pie;
Portugese custard tart. **Details:** 8 pm; no credit cards; no booking.

Lobster Pot SE11 £ 36 ★
3 Kennington Ln 7582 5556
This small and "really French" Kennington outfit is "tackily"
decked out like a sunken schooner; "excellent" fish dishes and
"wonderful" fruits de mer are widely lauded, though some do find
the cooking a bit "heavy" and "old-fashioned". / **Sample dishes:** fish
soup with croutons & cheese; sea bass in Pernod & cream sauce; chocolate
profiteroles. **Value tip:** set weekday L £23(FP). **Details:** 11 pm; closed Mon &
Sun.

Lomo SW10 £ 21 Ⓐ★
222-224 Fulham Rd 7349 8848 4–3B
To say it's a "super-groovy tapas experience" may be to overcook
this Chelsea 'Beach' spot somewhat, but its "really imaginative"
snacks can justifiably claim to be "the ultimate in bar food".
/ **Sample dishes:** no starters; seasoned tiger prawns; vanilla ice-cream with
sherry. **Details:** 11.30 pm; no booking after 7.30 pm.

Ma Goa SW15 £ 27 ★
244 Upper Richmond Rd 8780 1767
Goan cooking is "an interesting variant on standard Indian",
and the "dependably delicious" dishes served by this "charming"
family-run Putney bistro make it of more than local interest.
/ **Sample dishes:** Goan pork & cinnamon sausage; seafood in coconut broth
with saffron rice; yoghurt. **Details:** www.magoa.co.uk; 11 pm; D only, closed
Mon.

Malabar W8   £ 25   ★

27 Uxbridge St   7727 8800
"Amazing consistency", "year after year", has made this "good all-round" modern Indian an ever-"likeable" fixture, off Notting Hill Gate. / **Sample dishes:** grilled chicken in yoghurt; spiced lamb with garlic naan; ice cream. **Value tip:** set weekday L £12(FP). **Details:** 11.15 pm; no Amex.

Malabar Junction WC1   £ 33   ★

107 Gt Russell St   7580 5230   1–1C
"Don't be put off by the exterior" – "high standards are maintained" at this "friendly" and surprisingly smart south Indian near the British Museum, which serves some "interesting" dishes. / **Sample dishes:** brown rice patties with masala sauce; Malabar fish curry; sweet plantains. **Details:** 11.30 pm; no smoking area.

Mandalay W2   £ 19   ★

444 Edgware Rd   7258 3696
"Delightful" owners give the "warmest of welcomes" at this Burmese café, grottily located near Edgware Road tube; the "delicious" cooking – a cross between Indian and Chinese – is "ideal if you're hungry and broke". / **Sample dishes:** shrimp & beansprout fritters; chicken & lemongrass with coconut rice; coconut jelly. **Value tip:** set weekday L £11(FP). **Details:** www.bcity.com/mandalay; 10.30 pm; closed Sun; no smoking.

Mandarin Kitchen W2   £ 27   ★★

14-16 Queensway   7727 9012
"Even if you've booked", you'll probably "have to wait for your table" at this "cavernous" and "manic" Bayswater oriental; it's worth it, though – this is the "best Chinese seafood restaurant in the UK". / **Sample dishes:** steamed scallops; crispy aromatic duck pancakes; fresh fruit salad. **Details:** 11.15 pm.

Manzi's WC2   £ 39   ★

1 Leicester St   7734 0224   3–3A
Owned by the Manzi family since time immemorial, this "distinctive" and "dependable" Theatreland "old favourite" is still a top destination for traditionalists, thanks to its "good fresh fish and seafood" and its "cheerful" service. / **Sample dishes:** citrus salad with lemon sole goujons; grilled salmon with hollandaise; crème brûlée. **Value tip:** pre-th. £24(FP). **Details:** 11.30 pm, Cabin Room 10.30 pm; closed Sun L.

Mao Tai SW6   £ 31   𝔸★

58 New King's Rd   7731 2520
"Not being a typical naff Chinese" has always been the key selling point of this "slick" Parsons Green oriental; the cooking is still "a cut about the average", but the ratings are looking less robust than they were. / **Sample dishes:** crispy curried wontons; Szechuan squid in hot bean sauce; toffee apples & bananas. **Details:** www.maotai.co.uk; 11.30 pm; no smoking area.

Maroush   £ 37   ★

III) 62 Seymour St, W1   7724 5024
II) 38 Beauchamp Pl, SW3   7581 5434
I) 21 Edgware Rd, W2   7723 0773
London's pre-eminent Lebanese chain offers "quick, tasty" food at "decent prices" in its café sections (at I and II), and all its locations have "Beirut-standard" restaurants (which "can turn out expensive"); "as late-night venues, they're always top-class". / **Sample dishes:** houmous salad; garlic chicken; baklava. **Details:** W1 1 am – W2 2 am – SW3 5 am.

The Marquis W1   £ 35   ★

121a Mount St   7499 1256   2–3B

It's a pity that this Mayfair spot has a rather "dull" atmosphere, because it provides a "friendly" reception, and the reliable modern British cooking is "good value" (especially "for the area"). / **Sample dishes:** salmon with yellow pepper pesto; roast venison with juniper berries; pannetonne ice cream with mango. **Details:** 10.45 pm; closed Sat & Sun.

Matsuri SW1   £ 49   ★★

15 Bury St   7839 1101   2–3D

"It's a pity about the ambience", but this central oriental remains highly rated for its "entertaining teppan-yaki" and "hospitable" service; some gripe it's "overpriced", but "it is in St James's, and it is Japanese!" / **Sample dishes:** fresh shellfish platter; Japanese pizza; ice cream. **Details:** 10.30 pm; closed Sun; no Switch.

Mediterraneo W11   £ 36   A★

37 Kensington Park Rd   7792 3131

"Gorgeous" seafood dishes, "excellent" pasta and "service with a smile" make this "bustling" (if "crowded" and "smoky") trattoria reporters' top choice in Notting Hill's principal restaurant row. / **Sample dishes:** char-grilled tuna with rocket; flat spaghetti with clams; ice cream selection. **Details:** 11.30 pm.

Melati W1   £ 25   ★

21 Great Windmill St   7437 2745   2–2D

"The food is tastier than the rip-off location would suggest" at this "busy" but "reliable" Malaysian canteen, not far from Piccadilly Circus. / **Sample dishes:** chicken satay; Penang beef curry with coconut rice; ice cream with mango coulis. **Details:** 11.30 pm, Fri & Sat 12.30 am.

Mesclun N16   £ 25   A★

24 Stoke Newington Ch St   7249 5029

Thanks to "W1 cooking at N16 prices", this "very workmanlike" modern British bistro offers "fantastic value" – it's by no means of interest only to "trendy Stoke Newingtonians". / **Sample dishes:** avocado & Mozzarella salad; roasted bream with thick tomato sauce; sticky toffee pudding. **Details:** 11 pm; D only; no Amex.

Metrogusto   £ 28   A★

13 Theberton St, N1   7226 9400
153 Battersea Park Rd, SW8   7720 0204

"Deserving more success than its insalubrious location suggests" – it's a bone's throw from Battersea Dogs' Home – this "entertaining" pub-conversion offers "excellent" Italian cooking and "very friendly" service; an offshoot opens on the site of Islington's Maremma (RIP) as we go to press. / **Sample dishes:** goat's cheese salad; gnocchi with char-grilled chicken & green pesto; pear tart with Pecorino. **Details:** 10.45 pm; closed Sun D; no Amex; no smoking area.

Mezzo W1   £ 44

100 Wardour St   7314 4000   2–2D

In five short years, Conran's "overblown" Soho Leviathan has tumbled from being the survey's most often mentioned establishment to No. 28; that's impressively low for one of Europe's biggest restaurants, but – given "bad" service, "airport-lounge" ambience and "rip-off" pricing – why would anyone go back? / **Sample dishes:** seared tuna with wasabi; Thai red pork curry with fragrant rice; pain perdu. **Details:** www.conran.com; midnight, Thu-Sat 1 am (crustacea till 3am); closed Sat L.

Mildreds W1 £ 21 A★
58 Greek St 7494 1634 3–2A
"Always solidly packed and deservedly so", this "small" and "buzzy" Soho veggie café offers "interesting" tucker from a menu which "changes a lot". / **Sample dishes:** spinach & goat's cheese wontons; white bean falafel tortilla with sweet chilli sauce; Greek yoghurt with honey & nuts. **Details:** 11 pm; closed Sun D; no credit cards; no smoking; no booking.

Mirabelle W1 £ 50 A★
56 Curzon St 7499 4636 2–4B
With its "glamorous setting in the heart of Mayfair", this modern classic is London's No. 1 all-rounder, so far as many reporters are concerned; "top drawer" modern French cuisine and a "glorious" wine list are leading attractions. / **Sample dishes:** salmon tartare with cucumber spaghetti; baked red mullet with wilted greens; lemon & cinnamon tart. **Value tip:** set Sun L £32(FP). **Details:** www.whitestarline.org.uk; 11.30 pm; no smoking area; booking: max 12.

Mon Plaisir WC2 £ 38 A★
21 Monmouth St 7836 7243 3–2B
"Standards are still maintained after all these years" at this "charmingly disarming" Gallic 'super bistro', whose rambling premises are a top "romantic" destination in Theatreland; lunch and pre-show set menus offer particularly good value. / **Sample dishes:** chicken liver parfait; pan-fried plaice with red pepper sauce; fresh fruit salad. **Value tip:** pre-th. £15(FP). **Details:** www.mon-plaisir.co.uk; 11.15 pm; closed Sat L & Sun.

Monkeys SW3 £ 50 A★
1 Cale St 7352 4711 4–2C
"Lots of old-school charm" and a "terrific" wine list distinguish this "quaint" and "intimate" Anglo-French Chelsea Green fixture at any time of year; "during the game season", however, "nowhere compares". / **Sample dishes:** smoked fish platter; venison steak with juniper & lentils; rich chocolate torte. **Details:** 10.30 pm; closed Sat & Sun; no Amex.

Monte's SW1 £ 40
164 Sloane St 7245 0896 4–1D
Housewives' choice Jamie Oliver now offers the public the opportunity (at lunch only) to sample his Italian cooking at this pukka Knightsbridge club; given that the Naked Chef has never actually presided over a restaurant kitchen before, the results are broadly as you would expect – run-of-the-mill. / **Sample dishes:** beef carpaccio with roast baby beetroots; roasted salmon with prosciutto & lentils; apricot tarte Tatin. **Details:** www.montes.co.uk; 11.15 pm; L only (open for D to members only), closed Sun.

Monza SW3 £ 37 A★
6 Yeoman's Rw 7591 0210 4–2C
"Attentive", "friendly" service is helping to make this "cramped" and "buzzy" backstreet Italian a "neighbourhood favourite"; some find prices "high", but that's Knightsbridge for you. / **Sample dishes:** calamari; risotto with Parmesan & baby spinach; tiramisu. **Details:** 11.30 pm; closed Mon L.

Moro EC1 £ 32 A★
34-36 Exmouth Mkt 7833 8336
"Flavours always stand out" at this "vibrant" ("noisy") and trendy Clerkenwell venture, which offers a distinctive brand of "Spanish/North African cooking" – "exceptional" bread and "interesting" fish win particular praise. / **Sample dishes:** grilled squid with harissa; roast sea bass with pomegranate molasses; chocolate & apricot tart. **Details:** 10.30 pm; closed Sat L & Sun.

Moxon's SW4 £ 31 ★★
14 Clapham Park Rd   7627 2468
Fans of this "superb" Clapham local (opposite the entrance to Sainsbury's car park) say it's "better and cheaper than anything in the West End"; the "excellent" seafood is certainly "very fresh and interesting", and the only real gripe is the slightly "nondescript modern setting". / *Sample dishes:* sweetcorn & smoked haddock velouté; mackerel with fried tomato tart; lemon & lime tart. *Details:* 11.15 pm; D only, closed Sun; no Amex.

Mr Kong WC2 £ 20 ★
21 Lisle St   7437 7341   3–3A
"Reliable food one notch above the rest of Chinatown" is doled out at this Cantonese "stand-by"; conditions are "dingy", though, especially in the basement. / *Sample dishes:* spring rolls; sweet & sour chicken; fruit selection. *Details:* 2.45 am.

The New End NW3 £ 39 ★
102 Heath St   7431 4423
Opinions divide on this ambitious newcomer; most agree it's a "decent" place – so "it can't last, in Hampstead!" – whose modern British dishes offer "rarely-found complexities of flavour"; critics, though, feel "it all takes far too long", and decry a "return of nouvelle cuisine". / *Sample dishes:* smoked haddock tortellini with pancetta; pigeon, wild mushroon & black pudding lasagne; cherry & almond tart. *Details:* www.thenewend.co.uk; 10.30 pm; closed Mon & Tue L.

Nobu W1 £ 55 Ⓐ★★
Old Park Ln   7447 4747   2–4A
"Outstanding" dishes "justify the dizzying prices" at this "chic" and "minimal" Manhattan-to-Mayfair import, whose "inspirational" Japanese/South American fusion cooking has made it one of the top dining rooms in town... and one of the most difficult to book. / *Sample dishes:* Matsuhisa shrimp with caviar; pasta with squid & garlic sauce; chocolate fondant bento box. *Details:* 10.15 pm, Sat 11.15 pm; closed Sat L & Sun; no smoking area.

Noor Jahan SW5 £ 29 ★
2a Bina Gdns   7373 6522   4–2B
A "classic Indian", whose "solid", "traditional" curries, "comfortable" décor and "ever-reliable" standards make it South Kensington's "local favourite". / *Sample dishes:* onion bhaji; Karahi lamb; kulfi. *Details:* 11.30 pm; no Switch.

North Sea Fish WC1 £ 23 ★
7-8 Leigh St   7387 5892
"What it does, it does very well" – this Bloomsbury fixture serves "really fresh, good basic fish and chips" in a setting reminiscent of a seaside tearoom. / *Sample dishes:* fishcakes; cod & chips; apple charlotte. *Details:* 10.30 pm; closed Sun.

Odette's NW1 £ 38 Ⓐ★
130 Regent's Pk Rd   7586 5486
"You can't beat it for romance", but this mirror-bedecked Primrose Hill fixture doesn't just provide "soft and flattering lighting" – it "makes you feel welcome and special", and the modern British menu can deliver some "exquisite" results. / *Sample dishes:* red mullet with vine tomatoes; Gressingham duck with caramelised onions; warm chocolate truffle cake. *Value tip:* set Dinner £23(FP). *Details:* 11 pm; closed Sat L & Sun.

constantly updated at www.hardens.com

The Old School Thai SW11   £ 26   ★
147 Lavender HI   7228 2345
It's "a gem", say fans of this family-run Battersea local – the "owner is a star", and "his wife provides delicious Thai food". / **Sample dishes:** mussels in lemongrass & sweet basil broth; green chicken curry with jasmine rice; sticky rice with mango & coconut cream. **Details:** 11 pm; D only, closed Sun; no smoking area; bookings taken for D only.

1 Lombard Street EC3   £ 46
1 Lombard St   7929 6611
With the help of Herbert Berger's "solid" modern French cooking, this "pricey" two-year-old by Bank is the City's No. 2 choice for a "slick business lunch"; it "can be a bit noisy" in the bar/brasserie, though – the slightly more expensive restaurant area is quieter. / **Sample dishes:** foie gras with caramelised mango; scallops with tomato coulis & red rice; caramel & almond parfait with roast apricots. **Details:** www.1lombardstreet.com; 10 pm; closed Sat & Sun; bookings: max 6.

L'Oranger SW1   £ 55   𝔸★
5 St James's St   7839 3774   2–4D
"They've done well since Marcus Wareing's departure" from this "cosy" and "discreet" St James's parlour; it's now almost "back to its original form", with "fabulous" service and some "very polished" and "imaginatively executed" modern French cooking. / **Sample dishes:** salmon mousse with scallops; roast John Dory with asparagus; peach soufflé. **Details:** 11.15 pm; closed Sat L & Sun.

The Orient W1   £ 40   ★
160 Piccadilly   7499 6888   2–3C
"Sophisticated" décor and "discreet" service win a "beautiful people" following for this hidden newcomer, above the China House; the cooking – an "unusual mix of oriental cuisines" (with western influences) – is "expensive", but it's also "light" and "clean-tasting", and can be "extremely good". / **Sample dishes:** salt & pepper baby squid; honey & soy pork with crispy vegetables; green tea ice cream. **Details:** www.chinahouse.co.uk; 11.30 pm; closed Sat L & Sun; no smoking area.

Oslo Court NW8   £ 42   ★
Prince Albert Rd   7722 8795
"A throwback to the '60s" it may be, but "everyone wants to return" to this dining room at the foot of a Regent's Park apartment block; it's "always busy" thanks to its "cosseting" service (especially for "elderly relatives") and its "good old-fashioned cooking". / **Sample dishes:** crab à la Rochelle; rack of lamb with vegetables; strawberry tart. **Details:** 11 pm; closed Sun.

Osteria Basilico W11   £ 33   𝔸★
29 Kensington Pk Rd   7727 9957
"Take your ear plugs" when you go to this "squashed but great" Notting Hill "local" – its atmosphere is "tops", and it serves "authentic and good-value" pizza and pasta dishes. / **Sample dishes:** calamari; rigatoni with crispy pork belly; tiramisu. **Details:** 11 pm; no booking, Sat L.

Osteria d'Isola SW1   £ 39
145 Knightsbridge   7838 1055   4–1D
The glamorously retro basement osteria of Oliver Peyton's swanky new Italian works "much better than the upstairs restaurant" (Isola); the "really authentic peasant food" is quite pricey, but then this is Knightsbridge. / **Sample dishes:** pasta with ricotta, sage & beetroot; breaded veal escalopes with capers; tiramisu. **Details:** 10.45 pm; no smoking area.

Oxo Tower SE1   £ 53   𝔸

Barge House St   7803 3888
"Fantastic view… pity about the lousy food and the snotty
service"; Harvey Nics's "shameless" standards seem set to turn
their South Bank landmark brasserie/restaurant into a venue fit
only for "wannabes" and out-of-towners; "stick to the bar".
/ **Sample dishes:** gnocchi with creamy basil pesto; pan-fried veal escalope
with garlic mash; chocolate marquise with caramelised apples.
Details: 11.15 pm.

Ozer W1   £ 40   ★

5 Langham Pl   7323 0505   2–1C
"Wonderfully refreshing and un-concept-like", this Turkish-inspired
restaurant (from the creator of Sofra) offers "interesting" and
"reasonably priced" cooking, "charmingly" served, in "chic" new
premises north of Oxford Circus. / **Sample dishes:** seared tuna with
ginger & figs; roast lamb with kumquat marmalade; panna cotta.
Details: 11 pm; no jeans.

Le Palais du Jardin WC2   £ 39   𝔸

136 Long Acre   7379 5353   3–3C
It's "a good all-round experience" to visit this always "buzzy"
Covent Garden brasserie, where "very good fish" and "excellent
lobster" are top tips from a "consistent" French menu; though
mega-restaurants are hardly in vogue at the moment, it remains
a top-ten favourite. / **Sample dishes:** crabcakes with lemon butter; pan-
fried chicken with avocado salsa; roasted peaches. **Details:** 11.45 pm.

La Pampa SW11   £ 34   𝔸★

60 Battersea Rise   7924 4774
"Great steaks and excellent party atmosphere" make this
Battersea Argentinian "huge fun for a lively night out". / **Sample
dishes:** deep-fried meat pasties; Argentinean steak & chips; Latin American
crepes. **Details:** 11 pm; D only; no Amex.

The Papaya Tree W8   £ 29   ★

209 Kensington High St   7937 2260
"Not what you'd expect on the High Street", this "charmingly
hidden" Thai basement is a "welcoming" place with "decent",
if fairly "standard", cooking. / **Sample dishes:** glass noodle salad; green
chicken curry; sticky rice & lychees. **Details:** 11 pm; no smoking area.

Parade W5   £ 34   𝔸★

18-19 The Mall   8810 0202
"At last, a good non-ethnic restaurant in Ealing!"; praise resounds
for this "large but calm" new arrival – "a good spin-off from
Sonny's" – where "knowledgeable" staff serve "interesting" and
"well-executed" modern British cooking. / **Sample dishes:** deep-fried
sardines with aioli; lamb with spiced aubergine couscous; figs in red wine with
cinnamon biscuits. **Details:** 11 pm; closed Sat L & Sun D.

The Pepper Tree SW4   £ 17   ★

19 Clapham Common S'side   7622 1758
"Fresh and cheap Thai food" at "very reasonable prices"
makes this "canteen-style" spot an ever-popular Clapham choice;
"the quality of the food is incredible, considering how quickly it's
served". / **Sample dishes:** mushroom tom yam soup; chicken stir-fry
noodles; steamed Thai custard. **Details:** 11 pm, Mon & Sun 10.30 pm;
no Amex; no smoking area; bookings taken for L only.

Le P'tit Normand SW18 £ 24
185 Merton Rd   8871 0233
"Those feeling nostalgic about holidays in France" should take
a trip to this Southfields stalwart; *"welcoming staff"* offer
"well-cooked, old-fashioned French food" in an *"authentic,
if twee"* setting. / **Sample dishes:** moules marinière; pan-fried pork with
red pepper sauce; tarte Tatin. **Details:** 10 pm, Fri & Sat 11 pm; closed Sat L.

Pétrus SW1 £ 58   A★★
33 St James's St   7930 4272   2–4C
Marcus Wareing's *"very grown up"* St James's dining room offers
"careful but powerfully flavoured" modern French cuisine,
a *"fabulous"* wine list and *"old-fashioned"* service – but it's still
"surprisingly good value for money"! / **Sample dishes:** roast quail
stuffed with oysters; roast sea bass with potato dumplings; crème brûlée.
Details: 10.45 pm; closed Sat L & Sun; booking: max 6.

Phoenicia W8 £ 35
11-13 Abingdon Rd   7937 0120   4–1A
"Courteous and helpful" service adds lustre to this long-time
"favourite", family-run Kensington Lebanese; it's famed for its
"fantastic lunchtime buffet". / **Sample dishes:** spiced aubergine salad;
chicken kebabs with couscous; Lebanese pastries. **Details:** 11.45 pm;
no smoking area.

Phoenix Bar & Grill SW15 £ 34   ★
Pentlow St   8780 3131
Not everyone goes a bundle on the *"airy"* setting, but this
well-run Putney sibling to Barnes's Sonny's delivers *"imaginative"*
and *"well-prepared"* modern British fare. / **Sample dishes:** clam &
bacon chowder; duck with roast turnips & girolles; banana fritters with
raspberries. **Value tip:** set Sat L £22(FP). **Details:** 11.30 pm, Sun 10 pm.

Pie2 Mash NW1 £ 26   ★
9-11 Jamestown Rd   7482 2770
An early visit to this tastefully-understated new Camden Town
brasserie found a short and well-realised English menu; the
simplicity of the cooking, however, made it hard to sympathise
with the slowness of the service. / **Sample dishes:** chicken mousse
with tarragon; steak & kidney pie with garlic mash; sticky toffee pudding.
Details: 11 pm, Fri & Sat 11.30 pm; no Amex; no smoking area.

Pied à Terre W1 £ 70   ★
34 Charlotte St   7636 1178   1–1C
After chef Tom Aikens's departure, ratings at this eminent
Fitzrovian have 'blipped' somewhat; that said, enthusiasm for the
place's *"adventurous and rich"* Gallic cooking remains strong,
though reporters remain ambivalent about the somewhat *"bland"*
modern setting. / **Sample dishes:** guinea fowl with French salad; beef with
potato purée; quartet of chocolate desserts. **Value tip:** set weekday L £40(FP).
Details: www.pied.a.terre.co.uk; 10.45 pm; closed Sat L & Sun.

Pizza Metro SW11 £ 28   A★★
64 Battersea Rise   7228 3812
"Straight out of Naples"; *"the best pizza in London"* (priced
by the metre) served *"with real Italian spirit"* has made quite
a name for this *"chaotic"* and *"very noisy"* Battersea spot;
"starters and pasta dishes are also a big draw". / **Sample
dishes:** Parmesan & tomato antipasti; spaghetti with crayfish; Italian ice cream.
Details: 11 pm; closed Mon, Tue-Fri D only, Sat & Sun open L & D.

Pizzeria Castello SE1　　　　£ 19　　★★

20 Walworth Rd　7703 2556

The "Elephant and Castle's finest"; this "convivial" joint delivers "great value", if chewy pizza with "flair" – it gets "awfully busy". / **Sample dishes:** garlic mushrooms; goat's cheese pizza; chocolate gateau. **Details:** www.pizzeria-castello.co.uk; 11 pm, Fri & Sat 11.30 pm; closed Sat L & Sun.

The Place Below EC2　　　　£ 20　　★

St Mary-le-Bow, Cheapside　7329 0789

"Sturdy vegetarian dishes" – with "vibrant flavours" and "wholesome" ingredients – are served "canteen-style" at this "deservedly popular" fixture, in an impressive City church crypt; BYO. / **Sample dishes:** leek & butter bean soup; spring onion, potato & cheddar quiche; apple & gooseberry crumble. **Details:** www.theplacebelow.co.uk; L only, closed Sat & Sun; no Amex; no smoking; no booking.

Poissonnerie de l'Avenue SW3　　£ 49　　★★

82 Sloane Ave　7589 2457　4–2C

"It's a bit of a stuffy, old-school-tie type of place" and the "seating is cramped", but this Brompton Cross stalwart is fêted for its "simple and delicious" fish dishes and its "perfect" seafood. / **Sample dishes:** Parmesan risotto; salmon & cod fishcakes with lemon sauce; crème brûlée. **Details:** 11.30 pm; closed Sun.

Le Pont de la Tour SE1　　　　£ 66

36d Shad Thames　7403 8403

Conran's Tower Bridge-side flagship readied itself for its 10th anniversary with a further dramatic fall in standards – its "inherently romantic" location (which is also convenient for City lunching) and an "exquisite" wine list are now its only undoubted attractions. / **Sample dishes:** salmon fillet with green pesto; baked lobster with lemon coucous; dark chocolate tart. **Value tip:** pre-th. £32(FP). **Details:** www.conran.com; 11.30 pm; closed Sat L.

Popeseye　　　　　　　　　　£ 31　　★

108 Blythe Rd, W14　7610 4578
277 Upper Richmond Rd, SW15　8788 7733

"Steak, chips and claret are the only options at these places, and they are all superb"; the humble décor is "not great", though, in either Olympia or Putney. / **Sample dishes:** no starters; fillet steak; rhubarb crumble. **Details:** 10.30 pm; D only; closed Sun; no credit cards.

The Portrait WC2　　　　　　£ 36　　Ⓐ

St Martin's Place　7312 2490　3–4B

A "glorious" panoramic view of Westminster is not the only strength of the NPG's "noisy", new top-floor restaurant; it delivers impressively consistent modern British fare on quite a scale, albeit rather slowly. / **Sample dishes:** chorizo & artichoke salad; Lancashire cheese tartlet with poached egg; brown sugar meringue with bananas. **Details:** 8.30 pm; closed D, Mon-Wed, Sat & Sun; smoking only allowed in bar; booking: max 8.

La Poule au Pot SW1　　　　£ 40　　Ⓐ★

231 Ebury St　7730 7763　4–2D

"Heaven if you're trying to seduce someone" – and yet again the Survey's No. 1 for romance – this "dark", "cramped" and "moody" Pimlico Green survivor is "always a winner for that special evening"; the cooking, inevitably, is "good, old-fashioned French". / **Sample dishes:** snails in garlic butter; roast sea bass with spinach; chocolate mousse. **Value tip:** set weekday L £26(FP). **Details:** 11.15 pm.

Prism EC3 £ 49

147 Leadenhall St   7256 3875

Housed in an impressive converted banking hall, Harvey Nics's City yearling still serves some "very good" modern British cooking; it's more "variable" than it was, though, and the evening ambience, in particular, can seem "impersonal". / Sample dishes: Asian pear & Roquefort salad; rare seared tuna steak; banana crumble. Details: www.prismrestaurant.co.uk; 10 pm; closed Sat & Sun.

Quaglino's SW1 £ 44

16 Bury St   7930 6767   2–3D

This year reporters voted the '93 début of Conran's quintessential mega-brasserie in St James's as 'most exciting opening of the past decade'; all the sadder then that — with its "deeply average" grills-and-seafood cooking and "inept" service — it's "such a let-down" nowadays. / Sample dishes: potted prawns with melba toast; braised oxtail with garlic mash; melon with elderflower sorbet. Value tip: preth. £26(FP). Details: www.conran.com; midnight, Fri & Sat 1 am.

Ranoush W2 £ 20 ★★

43 Edgware Rd   7723 5929

"Excellent juices and delicious kebab sandwiches" make this brilliant take-away a top late-night pit stop; NB cash only. / Sample dishes: tricolore salad; chicken with Parmesan; tiramisu. Details: www.maroush.com; 3 am; no credit cards.

Ransome's Dock SW11 £ 38 🄰★

35 Parkgate Rd   7223 1611   4–4C

A "wonderful" and "idiosyncratic" wine list twinned with "interesting" modern British cooking makes Martin Lam's "relaxed" but "crowded" brasserie (just over Albert Bridge) a very popular destination. / Sample dishes: char-grilled quail with spinach; Guernsey veal with vegetables; warm chocolate tart. Details: www.ransomesdock.co.uk; 11 pm, Sat midnight; closed Sun D.

Rapscallion SW4 £ 28 🄰★

75 Venn St   7787 6555

It may be "noisy" and "cramped", but this "trendy and imaginative" spot by Clapham's Picture House is "fun" too, and locals think it's "brilliant" all round. / Sample dishes: beef with cashews & lime leaf salad; grilled lamb with butternut squash; deep-fried plantain with mango. Details: 11 pm.

Rasa £ 28 ★★

6 Dering St, W1   7629 1346
55 Stoke Newington Ch St, N16   7249 0344

"Amazing food with incredibly subtle, exotic flavours" makes these vegetarian Indians (specialising in Kerala cuisine) a choice that "even confirmed carnivores should enjoy"; "charming" service attracts special praise. / Sample dishes: Indian bread & pickles; aubergine & tamarind curry with basmati rice; ice cream. Details: www.rasarestaurants.com; 11 pm; N16 closed Mon L-Thu L; W1 closed Sun L; no smoking.

Rasa Samudra W1 £ 37 ★

5 Charlotte St   7637 0222   1–1C

In spite of what some see as "outlandish" prices, many reporters find this "different" fish-and-vegetarian Indian "an adventure to be recommended"; its Fitzrovia premises, however, "lack atmosphere" to a signal extent. / Sample dishes: spiced crab with pickles; fish curry in thick coconut cream; mango & cashew nut cake. Details: midnight; closed Sun L; no smoking area.

The Real Greek N1 £ 33 A★★

15 Hoxton Market 7739 8212
*"A new look at Greek cooking – a must"; this "transcendental" yearling has earned widespread attention with its "really imaginative" menu and "lovely" service; its once-sparse premises in über-trendy Hoxton have already been considerably cosied up. / **Sample dishes:** smoked feta cheese; pan-fried fish with lentils; honey-soaked Greek doughnuts. **Details:** 10.30 pm; closed Sun.*

Redmond's SW14 £ 37 ★

170 Upper R'mond Rd West 8878 1922
*"Surprising, given the dull exterior and location" – you find a "friendly" welcome, "consistent" modern British cooking and a "well thought-out wine list" at this family-run Sheen venture, even if the feel is inescapably "suburban". / **Sample dishes:** salt cod with roast red peppers; beetroot risotto with Parmesan crisps; gingerbread pudding with rhubarb. **Details:** 10.30 pm; closed Sat L & Sun D; no Amex.*

Restaurant One-O-One SW1 £ 59 ★

William St, 101 Knightsbridge 7290 7101 1–3A
*"Initial apprehensions" – perhaps inspired by its roadside location and the silly staff uniforms – are well worth conquering at this "good-but-pricey" Knightsbridge hotel dining room, which offers some "exemplary cooking"; fish dishes are a speciality. / **Sample dishes:** red tuna carpaccio; Roasted scallops with spinach; apple, honey & goat's cheese parcel. **Details:** 10.30 pm.*

Rhodes in the Square SW1 £ 50 ★

Dolphin Sq, Chichester St 7798 6767 1–4C
*This "elegant", "well-spaced" and vaguely nautical dining room in the middle of a vast Pimlico apartment complex offers "creative", school-of-Gary-Rhodes, modern British cooking; sliding ratings, though, suggest it's cruising rather too comfortably. / **Sample dishes:** asparagus & Parmesan salad; pan-fried sea bass with roasted fennel; lemon & nutmeg brûlée. **Details:** 10 pm; closed Sat L & Sun D.*

Riva SW13 £ 38 ★

169 Church Rd, Barnes 8748 0434
*"Stunning" cooking makes Andrea Riva's "hard-to-get-to" Barnes establishment "arguably the best SW London Italian" for some reporters; as ever, though, the "what's-all-the-fuss-about?" contingent complains loudly of "over-fussy" cooking and a "dull" ambience. / **Sample dishes:** prosciutto & smoked sturgeon with apples; lobster & courgette risotto; lemon vodka sorbet. **Details:** 11 pm, Fri & Sat 11.30 pm, Sun 9.30 pm; closed Sat L.*

The River Café W6 £ 52 ★

Thames Whf, Rainville Rd 7381 8824
*This famous Hammersmith destination inspires passionate views, and supporters rave about the "exquisite" Italian cooking and the "fantastic-all-round" experience; the prices "really are outrageous", though, and the minority which says the place is "past it" grows every year. / **Sample dishes:** broad bean risotto; salt-baked salmon with linguini; chocolate Nemesis. **Details:** 9.30 pm; closed Sun D.*

Roussillon SW1 £ 43 ★★

16 St Barnabas St   7730 5550   4–2D

"Exceptionally good" results from an *"interesting and innovative"* Gallic menu are carving out a deserved reputation for this *"comfortable"* two-year old in a Pimlico backstreet; the setting is *"bland"* to some, *"enchanting"* to others. / **Sample dishes:** langoustines with grapefruit marmalade; grilled lamb with mint & olive purée; chocolate fondant. **Details:** www.roussillon.co.uk; 10.45 pm; closed Sat L & Sun; no smoking area.

Royal China SW15 £ 26 ★★

3 Chelverton Rd   8788 0907

The Putney cousin to the central Royal China chain (actually the original, now under different ownership) boasts a similar package, with a *"glitzy"* '70s setting and *"great dim sum"* the highlights. / **Sample dishes:** crispy spring rolls; seafood with fried noodles; fresh fruit. **Details:** 10.45 pm; no Visa, Mastercard or Switch; need 7+ to book for Sun L.

Royal China £ 29 ★★

40 Baker St, W1   7487 4688
13 Queensway, W2   7221 2535
68 Queen's Grove, NW8   7586 4280

"Dim sum to die for" – easily the best in town – and other *"really unusual"* dishes make it worth braving the queues to get in to these *"consistently excellent"* Chinese restaurants; their *"disco décor"* is *"so gross it's cool"*. / **Sample dishes:** prawn ball noodles in soup; fried spicy fish with lotus leaf rice; sweet egg yolk buns. **Details:** 10.45 pm, Fri & Sat 11.30 pm.

RSJ SE1 £ 33 ★

13a Coin St   7928 4554

The *"incredible collection of Loire wines"* adds lustre to this *"affordable and reliable"* South Bank fixture, whose modern British cooking *"can be very good on a good night"*; the setting is *"unpretentious"* – arguably to a fault. / **Sample dishes:** gazpacho; chicken pot au feu with winter vegetables; baked peaches. **Details:** 11 pm; closed Sat L & Sun.

Rules WC2 £ 45 Ⓐ

35 Maiden Ln   7836 5314   3–3D

Sure, it's a little *"touristy"*, but that doesn't stop London's oldest restaurant (1798) from being one of its most attractive, and a firm local favourite, especially for business; where else can you get *"good steak"*, *"the best game"* and *"rich-beyond-belief-fab sticky toffee pudding"*? / **Sample dishes:** scrambled eggs with smoked salmon; roast rib of beef; treacle sponge pudding. **Details:** www.rules.co.uk; 11.30 pm; no smoking.

S&P £ 30 ★

181 Fulham Rd, SW3   7351 5692
9 Beauchamp Pl, SW3   7581 8820

"Always consistent", this *"professionally run"* duo are a bit *"dull"*, but worth remembering for their *"tasty"* Thai fare and moderate prices. / **Sample dishes:** hot & spicy prawn soup; venison in green peppercorn sauce; lychees. **Details:** 10.30 pm; no smoking areas.

Saigon W1 £ 30 ★

45 Frith St   7437 7109   3–2A

"Fantastic" Vietnamese dishes – much better than you would expect given its tourist trap appearance – make this a worthy Soho survivor. / **Sample dishes:** Vietnamese spring rolls; stir-fried lamb in satay sauce; sweet sticky rice. **Details:** 11 pm; closed Sun; no Switch.

St John EC1 £ 38 𝔸★
26 St John St 7251 0848
"Try something different" – *"once the taste is acquired, there's just nowhere else"*, proclaim fans of this stark Smithfield ex-smokehouse, where the *"carnivore's heaven"* menu is *"terrific if you like tripe"*… but *"offal if you don't"*! / **Sample dishes:** smoked eel with pickles; pot-roasted Longhorn beef with wilted greens; Ecuadorian cheese platter. **Details:** www.stjohnrestaurant.co.uk; 11 pm; closed Sun.

Salloos SW1 £ 45 ★★
62-64 Kinnerton St 7235 4444 1–3A
"Pricey" but *"perfect"* cooking and generally *"engaging"* service reward those who seek out this long-established Belgravia mews Pakistani; its décor *"needs help"*, though. / **Sample dishes:** lamb chops; Karahi chicken; kulfi. **Value tip:** set weekday L £27(FP). **Details:** 11.15 pm; closed Sun.

The Salusbury NW6 £ 28 𝔸★
50-52 Salusbury Rd 7328 3286
With a cosy atmosphere somewhere between a coffee house and a pub, this *"lively newcomer to Queen's Park"* serves a *"good"*, simple Mediterranean menu. / **Sample dishes:** goat's cheese & aubergine ravioli; lamb shank with lemon & thyme; amaretto semifreddo. **Details:** 10.30 pm; closed Mon L; no Amex.

Sarkhel's SW18 £ 25 ★★
199 Replingham Rd 8870 1483
"Wonderful cooking from the ex-head chef of the Bombay Brasserie" – with *"distinct regional dishes"* – wins a wide following for Udit Sarkhel's Southfields venture; it doubled in size last year, but that's had little effect on the ratings. / **Sample dishes:** spicy fish skewers; chicken tikka with lemon & cashew nuts; kulfi. **Details:** 10.30 pm, Fri & Sat 11 pm; closed Mon, Tue & Thu; no Amex; no smoking area.

Savoy Grill WC2 £ 66 𝔸
Strand 7836 4343 3–3D
"Few places are as openly impressive" as this *"dated"* but *"immaculate"* power-lunching venue; its ratings are slipping, though, and the Anglo-French cooking (never the star attraction) is now no better than *"OK"*. / **Sample dishes:** hickory-smoked salmon salad; roast duck with fig Tatin & crispy vermicelli; burnt Cambridge cream. **Value tip:** pre-th. £41(FP). **Details:** www.savoy-group.co.uk; 11.15 pm; closed Sat L & Sun; jacket & tie required.

Scalini SW3 £ 42 𝔸★
1-3 Walton St 7225 2301 4–2C
"Fine" Italian food, a *"great"* and *"buzzy"* atmosphere and a *"trendy"* (*"Chelsea FC players"*) following ensure it's always *"lots of fun"* to visit this *"mad"* trattoria behind Harrods; *"take a fat wallet"*. / **Sample dishes:** tomato, Mozzarella & pesto ravioli; roast baby chicken with leeks; Belgian chocolate ice cream. **Details:** midnight.

Seashell NW1 £ 23 ★
49 Lisson Grove 7224 9000
Some think the *"atmosphere's still terrible, even after the renovation"*, but this eminent Marylebone chippy is once again staking a claim to providing *"the best fish and chips in London"*. / **Sample dishes:** melon; battered plaice & chips; apple pie. **Details:** 10.30 pm; closed Sun; no smoking area; no booking.

The Sequel SW4 £ 33 ★

75 Venn St   7622 4222

"Loud and slightly dishevelled (both staff and place)", this
Clapham curiosity is dominated by a big screen – a shame, as it
"distracts" from innovative cooking which can be "truly delicious".
/ **Sample dishes:** Penang noodle soup; shark steak with spiced crust;
chocolate brûlée. **Details:** 11 pm; closed weekday L.

Shanghai E8 £ 23 A★

41 Kingsland High St   7254 2878

The "best Chinese food in the East End" is claimed by fans of this
Dalston oriental, which occupies the "beautiful" tiled premises
of a famous former pie 'n' mash shop; weekend dim sum is
a particular draw. / **Sample dishes:** pan-fried vegetable dumplings;
Shanghai clams with rice; toffee apple. **Details:** 11 pm; no Amex.

J Sheekey WC2 £ 42 A★★

28-32 St Martins Ct   7240 2565   3–3B

"A super re-creation of an old favourite" – the Ivy/Caprice crew
have done it again with their "sleek", "refined" and "reasonably
priced" revamp of this Theatreland seafood parlour; let's hope
it survives the departure of the group's main men. / **Sample
dishes:** Belgian endive & gravadlax salad; seared scallops & baby squid with
leeks; steamed syrup sponge. **Value tip:** set weekday L £27(FP).
Details: midnight; closed Sat D & Sun D.

Shimla Pinks EC2 £ 32 A★

7-8 Bishopsgate Churchyard   7628 7888

"Imaginative Indian food" and an "interesting location", in a listed
City basement, make for consistent popularity of this impressively
furnished branch of Brum's most famous curry house. / **Sample
dishes:** charcoal-smoked aubergine; saffron chicken with cashews & rose
petals; iced Indian sweets. **Details:** www.shimlapinksgroup.co.uk; 9.30 pm;
closed Sat & Sun.

Shogun W1 £ 50 ★★

Adam's Rw   7493 1255   2–3A

Not only "a wide range of authentic dishes" (including "great
sushi"), but also the fact that "it actually has an atmosphere"
makes this "intimate" Mayfair basement many people's "best
Japanese"; there is the odd gripe that it's "over-rated". / **Sample
dishes:** spiced noodle salad; chicken teriyaki; Japanese ice cream.
Details: 11 pm; D only, closed Mon; no Switch.

Shree Krishna SW17 £ 21 ★

192-194 Tooting High St   8672 4250

"Take-your-breath-away-delicious" Indian dishes (many of them
vegetarian) at "very cheap" prices is still the general verdict
on this well-known Tooting veteran; a few do fret that it
"may be going downhill", however. / **Sample dishes:** lentil pancakes
with potato chutney; Malabar chicken with lemon rice; sweet coconut bread.
Details: www.sreekrishna.co.uk; 10.45 pm.

6 Clarendon Road W11 £ 33

6 Clarendon Rd   7727 3330

"Great effort is made" at this small, year-old "neighbourhood
restaurant" in Holland Park; the modern British menu offers
only a "modest" degree of choice, but it's "very well prepared".
/ **Sample dishes:** spinach & quail's egg tartlet; roast duck with green
peppercorns; strawberry summer pudding. **Details:** 10 pm; D only, closed Mon
& Sun; no Amex; no smoking area.

Smiths of Smithfield EC1   £ 35   𝔸

67-77 Charterhouse St   7236 6666
*The omens seem set fair at this "exciting", new
bar/brasserie/restaurant complex by Smithfield Market, where
the accent is on simple British cooking (with "good organic steak"
a highlight); the top-floor fine dining restaurant (formula price
£57) has an impressive open-air balcony.* / **Sample dishes:** *smoked
haddock with bacon & mustard; crispy pork belly with mash; lemon curd
parfait.* **Details:** *closed Sat L & Sun – café open all day, all week – fine dining
room closed Sat L.*

Sonny's SW13   £ 38   ★

94 Church Rd   8748 0393
*With its "relaxing" style and "good, well presented" modern
British food, this "great local" has always seemed a surprise
in "sleepy Barnes"; it is "not as reliably good as it used to be",
though, and there's an element of "hit and miss" to recent
reports.* / **Sample dishes:** *cured salmon with citrus salad; duck confit with
caramelised onions; buttermilk & vanilla bavarois.* **Details:** *11 pm; closed Sun
D.*

Sotheby's Café W1   £ 33   𝔸★

34 New Bond St   7293 5077   2–2C
*This "engaging" Mayfair auction-house café is a "class act",
and – even if its "corridor" setting affords "little privacy" – it
offers "wonderful" simple fare and a "very good wine list".*
/ **Sample dishes:** *grilled aubergine & black olive salad; salmon tartare with
cucumber & rocket salad; apricot & vanilla strudel.* **Details:** *L only; closed Sat
& Sun; no smoking.*

Le Soufflé W1   £ 59   ★

1 Hamilton Pl   7409 3131   2–4A
*"Stuffy atmosphere and dull décor detract from the food" at this
Mayfair dining room – a shame, as the "cooking, wines and
service are all good", and "Peter Kromberg knows how to cook
a soufflé".* / **Sample dishes:** *seared foie gras with baby figs; roast venison
with beetroot risotto & quinces; strawberry flambé with green peppercorns.*
Details: *www.interconti.com; 10.30 pm, Sat 11.15 pm; closed Mon, Sat L &
Sun D; no smoking area.*

Soulard N1   £ 28   𝔸★

113 Mortimer Rd   7254 1314
*"Authentic" French cooking and "a husband-and-wife team that
really makes you feel at home" mean it's "always a pleasure" to
visit this "cramped" but "charming" north Islington bistro.*
/ **Sample dishes:** *deep-fried goat's cheese with honey; lamb brochettes with
herb sauce; Montélimar nougat glacé.* **Details:** *10.30 pm; D only, closed Mon
& Sun; no Amex & no Switch.*

Soup Opera   £ 9   ★

2 Hanover St, W1   7629 0174
6 Market Pl, W1   7637 7882
17 Kingsway, WC2   7379 1333
Concourse Level, Cabot Pl East, E14   7513 0880
56-57 Cornhill, EC3   7621 0065
*"Consistent" and "really interesting" (if "slightly expensive") soups
and "friendly" service make it look as if this year-old chain may
be one with staying power.* / **Sample dishes:** *Greek salad; Thai green
chicken soup with foccacia; chocolate brownie.* **Details:** *www.soupopera.co.uk;
4 pm – W1 6 pm, Sat 5 pm; closed Sat & Sun – W1 branches closed Sun;
no credit cards; no smoking; no booking.*

constantly updated at www.hardens.com

SOUP Works   £ 9   ★
15 Moor St, W1   7734 7687
56 Goodge St, W1   7637 7687
9 D'Arblay St, W1   7439 7687
29 Monmouth St, WC2   7240 7687
"Just really good soup" – *"delicious"*, *"healthy"* and *"warming"* –
wins steady support for this *"quick and easy"* chain. / **Sample
dishes:** *Thai noodles; sausage & mash soup; fresh fruit salad.*
Details: *www.soupworks.co.uk; 7 pm, Sat 5 pm – WC2 8 pm – Moor St
11 pm, Fri & Sat midnight, Sun 6 pm; all except Moor St closed Sat D & Sun;
credit cards taken at WC2 & D'Arblay St only; no smoking; no booking.*

La Spiga W1   £ 34
84-86 Wardour St   7734 3444   2–2D
It's *"way too noisy and can get smoky"*, but *"they know how to
make a pizza"* at this *"cool"* Soho Italian; *"service can be a bit
inattentive"*. / **Sample dishes:** *three cheese ravioli; pizza with Mozzarella
& salami; baked blueberry cheesecake.* **Details:** *11 pm, Wed-Sat midnight.*

La Spighetta W1   £ 31   ★
43 Blandford St   7486 7340   1–1A
"Lovely pizzas" (and some *"inventive"* other dishes) make it
worth remembering this noisy Marylebone Italian; some think the
basement setting is *"nice"* – others liken it to a *"school canteen"*.
/ **Sample dishes:** *garlic & tomato bruschetta; spinach pasta with bolognese
sauce; cassata ice cream.* **Details:** *10.30 pm; closed Sun L; no smoking area.*

Spoon + W1   £ 75   𝔸
50 Berners St   7300 1444   2–1D
"How pretentious can you get?"; Ian Schrager's new *"hotspot"*
(*"wear your trendiest gear"*) north of Oxford Street charges
"extortionate" prices for the *"gimmicky"*, *"minimalist"*
conceptions of Parisian über-chef Alain Ducasse, and service is
appalling. / **Sample dishes:** *beef & green mango salad; roast veal with
truffle sauce & macaroni cheese; chocolate pizza.*

Springbok Café W4   £ 34   ★
42 Devonshire Rd   8742 3149
"The most unusual menu" – *"using ingredients I've never even
seen in South Africa"* – makes it *"well worth a repeat visit"* to
this *"strikingly friendly"* Chiswick spot; the simple setting, though,
is *"cramped and uncomfortable"*. / **Sample dishes:** *lamb skewers with
tomato salad; springbok fillet with 'kalkveld' potatoes; doughnuts with cold
spiced syrup.* **Details:** *www.springbokcafecuisine.com; 11 pm; closed Sun;
no Amex; no smoking area.*

The Square W1   £ 71   ★
6-10 Bruton St   7495 7100   2–2C
Phillip Howard's modern French cooking is *"sheer perfection"*,
say the many fans of this *"polished"* Mayfair dining room;
levels of dissatisfaction are on the rise, though – about the
cooking (*"ordinary"*), the service (*"overbearing"*) and, especially,
the *"stuffy"* atmosphere. / **Sample dishes:** *watercress soup with trout
canneloni; beef tournedos with foie gras & red wine sauce; blood orange soufflé.*
Value tip: *set weekday L £44(FP).* **Details:** *10.45 pm; closed Sat L & Sun L.*

Sri Siam W1   £ 33   ★
16 Old Compton St   7434 3544   3–2A
"The best Thai in the West End" (certainly as an all-rounder) –
this large and *"very reliable"* Soho oriental delivers *"good-quality"*
cooking in a *"lively"* setting. / **Sample dishes:** *chicken in tamarind
sauce; trout in banana leaf; ice cream.* **Details:** *11.15 pm; closed Sun L.*

Sri Siam City EC2   £ 32   ★

85 London Wall   7628 5772
"Nice Thai food, but not the best atmosphere"; this well-known basement, near Liverpool Street is an "always-reliable" City rendezvous, "both for business and socially". / *Sample* *dishes:* chicken wings with satay sauce; grilled steak with mint & lime dressing; banana tart. *Details:* www.srisiamcity.co.uk; 9.30 pm; closed Sat & Sun.

Sri Thai EC4   £ 30   ★

3 Queen Victoria St   7827 0202
"Consistently good" cooking – if, some say, of a rather "production-line" nature – endears this large and "wonderfully busy" City Thai to a wide-ranging following. / *Sample dishes:* beef satay; pad Thai with chicken & prawns; orange sorbet.
Details: www.srithai.co.uk; 8.30 pm; closed Sat & Sun.

St Moritz W1   £ 34   ★

161 Wardour St   7734 3324   2–1D
With its "back-to-the-slopes" feel, this "crowded" Soho chalet serves unexpectedly "interesting", "genuine" and "well-priced" food; surely those who gripe of service that's "too Swiss" are trying to have their fondue and eat it? / *Sample dishes:* smoked fish with horseradish & beetroot; Gruyère & tomato fondue; chocolate fondue with fruit. *Details:* 11.30 pm; closed Sat L & Sun.

Star of India SW5   £ 38   ★

154 Old Brompton Rd   7373 2901   4–2B
Famed for its "effusive" owner and "unique", camp décor, this "upscale" South Kensington Indian makes a "great place to take out-of-towners", and its "innovative" cooking can be "exceptional". / *Sample dishes:* paneer cheese & peppercorn samosa; fried mustard seed chicken with saffron rice; mango pudding.
Details: www.starofindia.co.uk; 11.45 pm.

Stephen Bull W1   £ 37   ★

5-7 Blandford St   7486 9696   1–1A
Stephen Bull has sold his two other outlets to focus on this, the original; its "innovative" modern British cooking is "consistently good", but service can be "coolly indifferent", and some find the "clinical" Marylebone premises as "devoid of atmosphere" as they are "full of suits". / *Sample dishes:* pressed ham terrine with chutneys; roast lamb with rosemary & garlic; chocolate brownie ice cream. *Details:* 10.30 pm; closed Sat L & Sun.

The Stepping Stone SW8   £ 35   Ⓐ★

123 Queenstown Rd   7622 0555
"Is there a better local in London?", ask regulars at this "charming" Battersea spot, where "imaginative" modern British cooking from an "ever-changing" menu is served by "friendly" staff. / *Sample dishes:* smoked trout salad; rack of lamb with roast potatoes; wild strawberry cheesecake. *Details:* 11 pm, Mon 10.30 pm; closed Sat L & Sun D; no Amex; no smoking area.

Sticky Fingers W8   £ 25

1a Phillimore Gdns   7938 5338   4–1A
"Kids love" this "dated" and "friendly" American diner in Kensington, where "good, meaty burgers" are the menu highlight; even some adults grudgingly admit it has a "great atmosphere". / *Sample dishes:* BBQ ribs; cheeseburger with bacon & fries; bread & butter pudding. *Details:* 11.30 pm.

constantly updated at www.hardens.com

The Sugar Club W1 £ 47 ★★

21 Warwick St 7437 7776 2–2D
"The best for inventive fusion", declare the many admirers of the *"very different and interesting"* cooking at Peter Gordon's *"chic"* minimalist establishment in Soho. / **Sample dishes:** griled scallops with sweet chilli sauce; pan-fried chicken with cornmeal mash; sesame meringue with Chantilly cream. **Details:** 11 pm; no smoking area.

Suntory SW1 £ 72

72 St James's St 7409 0201 2–4D
"Mouth-watering" delicacies inspire reverence for this imperious St James's Nipponese, long known as a place to take important visitors from Tokyo; it's *"annoyingly overpriced for a desperately dull experience"*, though, and service falls decidedly short of VIP standards. / **Sample dishes:** soft shell crab sushi rolls; Scotch steak with sesame & mustard sauce; sticky rice with pickled ginger. **Value tip:** set weekday L £39(FP). **Details:** 10 pm; closed Sun L; no children under 12.

Le Suquet SW3 £ 42 ★

104 Draycott Ave 7581 1785 4–2C
"More French than France", this *"cosy"* and *"old-fashioned"* Chelsea veteran offers *"delicious, simple fish"* and *"excellent fruits de mer"*, but *"mixed"* (and too often *"arrogant"*) service. / **Sample dishes:** seared scallop salad; Dover sole with spinach & crab; 'îles flottantes'. **Value tip:** set Sun L £24(FP). **Details:** 11.30 pm.

Sushi-Say NW2 £ 31 ★

33b Walm Ln 8459 7512
"Excellent sushi and other dishes" at *"reasonable prices"* justify quite a detour to this well-established family-run Willesden Green café. / **Sample dishes:** spinach with sesame sauce; chicken & egg sushi rolls; ice cream. **Value tip:** set weekday L £15(FP). **Details:** 10.30 pm; closed Mon, Tue-Fri D only, Sat & Sun open L & D.

Sweetings EC4 £ 38 🄰★

39 Queen Victoria St 7248 3062
"Old-fashioned simplicity" makes this *"cramped"* Victorian fish parlour *"utterly unbeatable"* for City traditionalists; you'd better *"arrive early or late"* if you want a table. / **Sample dishes:** eggs Benedict; grilled Dover sole with spinach; lemon tart. **Details:** L only; closed Sat & Sun; no credit cards; no booking.

Talad Thai SW15 £ 24 ★★

320 Upper Richmond Rd 8789 8084
You *"often have to queue"* at this *"down-to-earth"* Putney-fringe local (where eating is *"communal"*); *"you don't go looking for ambience, but great, cheap Thai food"*; BYO. / **Sample dishes:** vegetable spring rolls; red prawn curry & jasmine rice; green tea sorbet. **Details:** 10 pm; no credit cards; no smoking; no booking.

Tamarind W1 £ 44 🄰★★

20 Queen St 7629 3561 2–3B
"I didn't realise Indian food could taste so good" – this *"upmarket"* Mayfair basement presents *"a different angle"* on subcontinental cooking, with *"very interesting"* spicing and *"excellent presentation"*; service is *"gracious"*. / **Sample dishes:** vegetable kebabs with chilli dressing; Jon dory with crispy spinach; rasmalai (sweet curd cheese). **Value tip:** set weekday L £25(FP). **Details:** 11.30 pm; closed Sat L.

constantly updated at www.hardens.com

La Tante Claire SW1   £ 75
Wilton Pl   7823 2003   1–3A

For years, Pierre Koffmann ran London's best kitchen by far, and the "decline" since his move to Belgravia is "almost unbelievable"; "high prices" are charged for "average" food, served in a room with "all the atmosphere of a dentist's waiting room". / **Sample dishes:** *snail vol-au-vents with white bean ragoût; roast Pyrénées lamb with shallot compote; balsamic strawberries.* **Value tip:** *set weekday L £41(FP).* **Details:** *11 pm; closed Sat L & Sun; jacket required at D.*

Tartuf N1   £ 14   ★
88 Upper St   7288 0954

"The real thing", for budget diners, offering "quick, tasty and quirky" Alsatian pizzas and pancakes and "very pleasant" service. / **Sample dishes:** *potato salad; tarte flambée with mushrooms & salami; sweet chocolate tarte flambée.* **Details:** *midnight; no Amex.*

Tas SE1   £ 22   ★
33 The Cut   7928 2111

"Immensely popular and very cheap", this "bright, fun" Turkish yearling has deservedly made a big splash on the South Bank; it's "a great find after the Eye", and very convenient for the Old Vic. / **Sample dishes:** *grilled aubergine salad; stewed lamb shank with lentils & rice; baklava.* **Value tip:** *set weekday L £13(FP).* **Details:** *11.30 pm.*

Tate Modern, Level 7 Café SE1   £ 31   Ⓐ
Bankside   7401 5020

"Incredible views" – the best in town – make queuing less of a trial at the "busy, busy, busy" café atop London's sexiest new landmark; shame about the "appalling" service though, and that a great opportunity to showcase the 'best of British' has, so far at least, been missed. / **Sample dishes:** *Chinese noodle salad; battered haddock with chips & mushy peas; chocolate pie.* **Details:** *www.tate.org.uk; 5.30 pm, Fri & Sat 9.30 pm; closed D, Mon-Thu & Sun; no Amex; no smoking; no booking.*

Tatsuso EC2   £ 68   ★
32 Broadgate Circle   7638 5863

This City Japanese is still vaunted by many as "the best" in London – both for the teppan-yaki upstairs and "superb sushi" in the basement; growing outrage at the "extortionate" prices make it ever more one for "expense accounters only". / **Sample dishes:** *oyster mushroom soup with chicken dumplings; wild salmon teriyaki with noodles; roasted figs.* **Value tip:** *set weekday L £45(FP).* **Details:** *9.45 pm; closed Sat & Sun.*

Tawana W2   £ 26   ★
3 Westbourne Grove   7229 3785

A few paces from Queensway, this "friendly" Thai is always busy, thanks to its "good-value" cooking. / **Sample dishes:** *Thai fishcakes; green chicken curry & egg fried rice; ice cream.* **Details:** *11 pm.*

Teca W1   £ 36   ★
54 Brooks Mews   7495 4774   2–2B

This "chic" and "understated" Mayfair mews Italian is now in the hands of the Aubergine-Zafferano group, so it's no great surprise that this year saw more reports of "wonderful" food and "fabulous" service; it remains rather under-discovered. / **Sample dishes:** *beef carpaccio with asparagus; grilled swordfish with black olive tapenade; orange cake.* **Details:** *10.30 pm; closed Sat L & Sun.*

Tentazioni SE1 £ 40 ★
2 Mill St 7237 1100

"Refined" and "really interesting" cooking, an "excellent" wine list and "wonderful" service distinguish this Italian near Tower Bridge; its "understated" décor, though, tends to the "Spartan". / **Sample dishes:** broad beans & mushroom ravioli; crispy pork with lentils & spinach; panna cotta with raspberries. **Details:** www.tentazionirestaurant.co.uk; 11 pm; closed Mon L, Sat L & Sun.

Thai Bistro W4 £ 28 ★
99 Chiswick High Rd 8995 5774

It's "stark" and has "cramped" shared tables, but you get "simple, clean and tasty" cooking and "quick" service at this Chiswick Thai. / **Sample dishes:** Thai fishcakes; Mossaman duck curry & rice; ice cream. **Details:** 11 pm; closed Tue L & Thu L; no Amex; no smoking.

Thai on the River SW10 £ 37 A ★
15 Lots Rd 7351 1151 4–4B

"Insist on a river view" to get the best out of this "excellent" distant-Chelsea Thai; "it can be rather pricey, but the food is very good". / **Sample dishes:** spiced chicken with Thai spinach; mild beef curry with spring onions; steamed Thai coconut custard. **Details:** 11 pm, Fri & Sat 11.30 pm; closed Mon L & Sat L.

Thailand SE14 £ 28 ★★
15 Lewisham Way 8691 4040

"Authentic" Thai (in fact, Laotian) cooking makes it worth booking ahead for this "cosy" and "refreshingly friendly" Lewisham fixture – "if you survive the journey from the tube, the results are amazing". / **Sample dishes:** prawn satay; chicken & pumpkin with jasmice rice; green tea. **Value tip:** set weekday L £14(FP). **Details:** 10.30 pm; D only, closed Mon, Sat & Sun; no Amex; no smoking.

Toto's SW1 £ 42 A ★
Lennox Gardens Mews 7589 0075 4–2D

A "long-term favourite", this "charming" and "intimate" Italian behind Harrods – with its "beautiful" dining room and "attentive but discreet" service – goes from strength to strength. / **Sample dishes:** Mozzarella & tomato salad; spaghetti with clams; tiramisu. **Details:** 11.30 pm.

Two Brothers N3 £ 24 ★
297-303 Regent's Pk Rd 8346 0469

"Great fried fish" in "generous servings" guarantees a "loyal following" for this "bubbly" Finchley chippy. / **Sample dishes:** Arbroath smokies; cod & chips with fresh tartare sauce; apple pie. **Details:** 10.15 pm; closed Mon & Sun; no smoking area; bookings taken for L only.

Uli W11 £ 25 ★
16 All Saints Rd 7727 7511

"Interesting Asian food", "enthusiastic owners" and a cute rear garden make it worth discovering this simple and good-value oriental, in deepest Notting Hill. / **Sample dishes:** calamari; chicken with Thai basil & chilli; toffee bananas. **Details:** 11.15 pm; closed Mon L & Sun; no Amex.

Upper Street Fish Shop N1 £ 20 ★
324 Upper St 7359 1401

"Superior fish and chips" (and other "great" fishy fare), ensure continuing popularity for this "unpretentious", bistro-style Islington institution; BYO. / **Sample dishes:** fish soup with croutons; deep-fried cod & chips; fresh raspberry ice cream. **Details:** 10.15 pm; closed Mon L & Sun; no credit cards; no booking.

Vama SW10   £ 36   ★★
438 King's Rd   7351 4118   4–3B
"A pleasant surprise even though it's a bit out of the way", this "cosy, if slightly cramped" World's End nouvelle Indian is creating quite a buzz with its "memorable" cooking, that delivers "amazing, clean-tasting flavours". / **Sample dishes:** mushrooms stuffed with cheese & pomegranates; lamb with spinach & nutmeg; mango kulfi. **Details:** www.vama.co.uk; 11.30 pm, Sun 10 pm.

Viet Hoa E2   £ 21   ★
70-72 Kingsland Rd   7729 8293
Although "it feels like a student canteen", this "basic, but excellent" Shoreditch-fringe café has achieved quite a name for its "good, cheap" Vietnamese cooking. / **Sample dishes:** hot & sour soup; fragrant chicken with noodles; ice cream. **Details:** 11.30 pm; no Amex.

Vijay NW6   £ 20   ★★
49 Willesden Ln   7328 1087
"Great" south Indian food at "excellent" prices makes people seek out this "friendly" and "reliable" Kilburn spot. / **Sample dishes:** hot tamarind soup; chicken biriani; mango lassi. **Details:** 10.45 pm, Fri & Sat 11.45 pm; no Amex.

Vong SW1   £ 52   ★
Wilton Pl   7235 1010   1–3A
"Brilliant presentation" of "interesting" Thai/French fusion fare contributes to the "theatre" of dining at the "slick" and "minimalist" Belgravian outpost of top NYC chef Jean-Georges Vongerichten; as ever, it's "over-rated" in some people's book. / **Sample dishes:** lobster & Thai herb salad; roasted chicken & lemongrass with sweet rice; Valrhona chocolate cake. **Details:** 11.30 pm, Sat 10.30 pm; no smoking area.

Vrisaki N22   £ 24   𝔸★
73 Myddleton Rd   8889 8760
"The largest, best-value meze around" – you'll be hard-pushed to finish – are served at this huge and "popular" Greek, hidden behind a take-away "in an out-of-the-way Bounds Green location". / **Sample dishes:** calamari; grilled meat meze selection; amaretto cheesecake. **Details:** midnight; closed Sun; no Amex.

Wakaba NW3   £ 39   ★
122a Finchley Rd   7586 7960
"Fantastic sashimi and sushi" are the raison d'être of Mr Wakaba's fixture opposite Finchley Road tube; that the minimalist décor manifestly "needs some work" is ironic given that it is architecturally of some renown. / **Sample dishes:** soy bean soup; grilled salmon teriyaki; fresh fruit. **Value tip:** set Dinner £25(FP). **Details:** 10.45 pm; D only, closed Sun.

The Walmer Castle W11   £ 25   𝔸★
58 Ledbury Rd   7229 4620
"Very good Thai cooking, for a pub" is to be found in the "cosy" upstairs dining room of this "lively" Notting Hill boozer. / **Sample dishes:** chicken satay skewers; green Thai beef curry with rice; mango sorbet. **Details:** 11 pm.

The White Onion N1   £ 37   ★

297 Upper St   7359 3533

Many have "never had a bad night" at this "minimalist" Islington spot, and applaud "the best (and best value) modern British food" in the area; falling ratings, though, reflect more than a hint of "inconsistency" of late. / **Sample dishes:** crab salad with cucumber spaghetti; roast lamb with braised chickpeas & thyme; panna cotta with limoncello liqueur. **Details:** 11 pm; D only, Sun open L & D.

Wiltons SW1   £ 55   A★

55 Jermyn St   7629 9955   2–3C

"A Rolls-Royce experience in every way"; the "sheer power" of this "understated and urbane" St James's machine – with its "superb" fish and seafood and "charming, polished" service – makes it an outstanding, if not an especially economical, performer. / **Sample dishes:** smoked platter with salmon & eel; poached monkfish with spinach; steamed rhubarb sponge. **Value tip:** set Sun L £36(FP). **Details:** www.wiltons.co.uk; 10.30 pm; closed Sat; jacket & tie required.

Wolfe's WC2   £ 27

30 Gt Queen St   7831 4442   3–1D

It's "a reliable haunt", say fans of this genuinely American-style Covent Garden fixture, renowned in some quarters for "still serving London's best burger". / **Sample dishes:** gravadlax; char-grilled burger with blue cheese sauce; rhum baba. **Details:** www.wolfes-grill.com; 11.45 pm, Sun 8.45 pm.

Yoshino W1   £ 31   ★★

3 Piccadilly Pl   7287 6622   2–3D

This tiny and "unusual" café, near Piccadilly Circus, is "100% authentic, including the sign in Japanese outside" and well-liked for its "thoughtful set meals". / **Sample dishes:** deep-fried tofu; salmon tail sushi rolls; sorbet. **Details:** 9 pm; closed Sun; no smoking area.

Yum Yum N16   £ 24   A★

30 Stoke Newington Ch St   7254 6751

"Great food and service" help make this buzzing Stoke Newington favourite an "excellent" Thai all-rounder. / **Sample dishes:** chicken & coconut soup; chicken & papaya with sticky rice; pancakes with coconut ice cream. **Value tip:** set weekday L £14(FP). **Details:** 10.45 pm, Fri & Sat 11.15 pm.

Zafferano SW1   £ 47   A★★

16 Lowndes St   7235 5800   1–4A

"Up there with the best in Italy", this "impossible-to-book" Belgravian wins a huge following with its "wonderful" food and "attentive" service; the setting – which some find "cramped" and "uninspired" – is rather beside the point. / **Sample dishes:** beef carpaccio; roast trout with black olive paste; passion fruit ice cream. **Details:** 11 pm.

Zaika SW3   £ 39   A★★

257-259 Fulham Rd   7351 7823   4–2C

"Redefining the curry experience", this "sophisticated" Chelsea nouvelle Indian provides a "stylish" setting for "stunning" cooking, and has quickly acquired a huge following. / **Sample dishes:** Indian red onion & prawn risotto; pan-fried halibut with masala mash; chocolate samosas. **Details:** 10.45 pm; closed Sat L & Sun.

Zen Central W1 £ 50
20-22 Queen St 7629 8089 2–3B
"Great Chinese cooking" still attracts some to this grandly
minimalist Mayfair oriental; it can seem "overpriced" though,
nowadays, and its glory days are long gone. / **Sample dishes:** Peking
ravioli; crispy shredded beef with spring vegetables; toffee apples.
Details: 11.30 pm; no Amex.

Zen Garden W1 £ 42 ★
15-16 Berkeley St 7493 1381 2–3C
"Posh for a Chinese" and "expensive" too – hardly surprising,
just off Berkeley Square – this well-spaced restaurant offers some
"excellent" cooking; "fabulous dim sum" makes lunchtime visits
(relatively) "good value". / **Sample dishes:** smoked chicken; Dover sole
with Chinese greens; fresh mango pudding. **Details:** 11 pm; no trainers.

ZeNW3 NW3 £ 36 ★
83 Hampstead High St 7794 7863
Very '80s, glass-fronted Hampstead landmark, offering
a "sophisticated" Chinese formula that's generally held to be
"pricey but worth it". / **Sample dishes:** steamed shrimp dumplings;
'Zen Zen' chicken with rice; toffee bananas. **Details:** 11.15 pm.

Ziani SW3 £ 35 A★
45-47 Radnor Wk 7352 2698 4–3C
A "bubbly" Chelsea backstreet "old favourite", with "good",
"traditional" Italian cooking; it's "too noisy" and "too crowded"
for some, though, and its "attentive" service can seem rather
"in your face". / **Sample dishes:** liver & spinach salad; Venetian beef with
lemon vinaigrette; tiramisu. **Details:** 11.30 pm.

Zilli Fish W1 £ 43 ★
36-40 Brewer St 7734 8649 2–2D
It's "expensive" and "cramped", and the staff have a "bit of an
attitude", but this "buzzy" Soho "hang out" is "very popular with
media types"; on the culinary front, "very good-quality seafood"
is the key attraction. / **Sample dishes:** tuna carpaccio with Parmesan;
oriental fish with fresh vegetables; banana spring rolls.
Details: www.zillialdo.com; 11.45 pm.

LONDON
AREA OVERVIEWS
INDEXES
MAPS

CENTRAL

Soho, Covent Garden & Bloomsbury
(Parts of W1, all WC2 and WC1)

£60+	Savoy Grill	British, Traditional	𝔸
£50+	Asia de Cuba	East/West	𝔸
£40+	The Ivy	British, Modern	𝔸★
	Alastair Little	"	★
	Axis	"	★
	Bank	"	-
	Mezzo	"	-
	Rules	British, Traditional	𝔸
	L'Escargot	French	𝔸★
	The Criterion	"	𝔸
	The Admiralty	"	-
	The Sugar Club	East/West	★★
	J Sheekey	Fish & seafood	𝔸★★
	Zilli Fish	"	★
£35+	French House	British, Modern	𝔸★
	The Portrait	"	𝔸
	Incognico	French	𝔸★
	Mon Plaisir	"	𝔸★
	Le Palais du Jardin	"	𝔸
	Manzi's	Fish & seafood	★
	Joe Allen	American	𝔸
£30+	Andrew Edmunds	British, Modern	𝔸
	Italian Kitchen	Italian	-
	St Moritz	Swiss	★
	La Spiga	Pizza	-
	Fung Shing	Chinese	★★
	Malabar Junction	Indian	★
	Chiang Mai	Thai	★★
	Sri Siam	"	★
	Saigon	Vietnamese	★
£25+	Crivelli's Garden	French	-
	Il Forno	Italian	★
	Wolfe's	Burgers, etc	-
	Abeno	Japanese	𝔸★
	Melati	Malaysian	★
£20+	Mildreds	Vegetarian	𝔸★
	North Sea Fish	Fish & chips	★
	Gaby's	Middle Eastern	★
	Joy King Lau	Chinese	★
	Mr Kong	"	★
	Busaba Eathai	Thai	𝔸★

£15+	Bistro 1	Mediterranean	-
	Kulu Kulu	Japanese	★★
£5+	Fryer's Delight	Fish & chips	★
	Soup Opera	Soup	★
	Soup Works	"	★

Mayfair & St James's
(Parts of W1 and SW1)

£90+	Le Gavroche	French	★★
£70+	Connaught	British, Traditional	_A_
	The Square	French	★
	Dorchester, Oriental	Chinese	-
	Suntory	Japanese	
£60+	Dorchester Grill	British, Traditional	_A_
	cheznico	French	★
£50+	Rhodes in the Sq	British, Modern	★
	Wiltons	British, Traditional	_A_ ★
	Pétrus	French	_A_ ★★
	Mirabelle	"	_A_ ★
	L'Oranger	"	_A_ ★
	Le Soufflé	"	★
	Nobu	East/West	_A_ ★★
	Zen Central	Chinese	-
	Shogun	Japanese	★★
£40+	Le Caprice	British, Modern	_A_ ★
	Quaglino's	"	-
	Diverso	Italian	★
	Bentley's	Fish & seafood	★
	The Orient	Chinese	★
	Zen Garden	"	★
	Tamarind	Indian	_A_ ★★
	Matsuri	Japanese	★★
£35+	The Marquis	British, Modern	★
	Teca	Italian	★
	Al Sultan	Lebanese	★
	Al Hamra	"	-
	Cassia Oriental	Pan-Asian	-
£30+	Sotheby's Café	British, Modern	_A_ ★
	Boudin Blanc	French	_A_
	Al Duca	Italian	★
	Gaucho Grill	Steaks & grills	_A_ ★
	Yoshino	Japanese	★★
£25+	Hard Rock Café	Burgers, etc	_A_
	China House	Chinese	_A_

	Rasa	*Indian*	★★
£5+	Soup Opera	*Soup*	★

Fitzrovia & Marylebone
(Part of W1)

£70+	Pied à Terre	*French*	★
	Spoon +	*International*	𝔸
£40+	Ozer	*Turkish*	★
	Defune	*Japanese*	★★
£35+	Stephen Bull	*British, Modern*	★
	Ibla	*Italian*	★
	Maroush	*Lebanese*	★
	Rasa Samudra	*Indian*	★
£30+	Café Bagatelle	*French*	-
	La Spighetta	*Italian*	★
	Back to Basics	*Fish & seafood*	★★
£25+	Royal China	*Chinese*	★★
£5+	Soup Works	*Soup*	★

Belgravia, Victoria & Pimlico
(SW1, except St James's)

£70+	La Tante Claire	*French*	-
£50+	Foliage	*French*	★
	Restaurant One-O-One	"	★
	Isola	*Italian*	-
	Vong	*East/West*	★
£40+	Roussillon	*French*	★★
	La Poule au Pot	"	𝔸★
	Zafferano	*Italian*	𝔸★★
	Toto's	"	𝔸★
	Monte's	*Mediterranean*	-
	Ken Lo's Memories	*Chinese*	★
	Salloos	*Indian*	★★
£35+	Il Convivio	*Italian*	𝔸★
	Osteria d'Isola	"	-
£30+	Hunan	*Chinese*	★★
£25+	Blue Jade	*Thai*	★
£15+	Jenny Lo's	*Chinese*	★

WEST

**Chelsea, South Kensington,
Kensington, Earl's Court & Fulham
(SW3, SW5, SW6, SW7, SW10 & W8)**

£80+	Gordon Ramsay	French	Ⓐ★★
£60+	Aubergine	French	★
	Capital Hotel	"	★
	Bibendum	"	-
£50+	Clarke's	British, Modern	Ⓐ★★
	Monkeys	French	Ⓐ★
	Belvedere	"	Ⓐ
£40+	Launceston Place	British, Modern	Ⓐ★
	Bluebird	"	-
	Chezmax	French	Ⓐ★★
	Le Suquet	"	★
	Scalini	Italian	Ⓐ★
	Poissonnerie de l'Avenue	Fish & seafood	★★
	Blue Elephant	Thai	Ⓐ★
£35+	Goolies	British, Modern	Ⓐ★
	Kensington Place	"	-
	Monza	Italian	Ⓐ★
	Ziani	"	Ⓐ★
	L'Anis	Mediterranean	★★
	Chives	"	★★
	Cambio de Tercio	Spanish	Ⓐ★
	Maroush	Lebanese	★
	Phoenicia	"	-
	Good Earth	Chinese	★
	Zaika	Indian	Ⓐ★★
	Vama	"	★★
	Bombay Brasserie	"	Ⓐ★
	Chutney Mary	"	Ⓐ★
	Star of India	"	★
	Thai on the River	Thai	Ⓐ★
	Exhibition	"	★
£30+	Bibendum Oyster Bar	Fish & seafood	Ⓐ★★
	Mao Tai	Chinese	Ⓐ★
	Bangkok	Thai	★
	S&P Patara	"	★
£25+	Emile's	French	★
	Elistano	Italian	Ⓐ★
	Sticky Fingers	Burgers, etc	-
	Malabar	Indian	★
	Noor Jahan	"	★

	The Papaya Tree	*Thai*	★
	Itsu	*Japanese*	-
£20+	The Atlas	*Mediterranean*	A★
	Lomo	*Spanish*	A★

Notting Hill, Holland Park, Bayswater, North Kensington & Maida Vale (W2, W9, W10, W11)

£40+	Julie's	*British, Modern*	A
	Assaggi	*Italian*	A★★
	Bali Sugar	*East/West*	★
£35+	Alastair Little	*British, Modern*	★
	Mediterraneo	*Mediterranean*	A★
	Maroush	*Lebanese*	★
£30+	Brass. du Marché	*French*	A★
	6 Clarendon Road	*"*	-
	Osteria Basilico	*Italian*	A★
	Bombay Palace	*Indian*	A★★
	Inaho	*Japanese*	★★
£25+	The Cow	*British, Modern*	A★
	Mandarin Kitchen	*Chinese*	★★
	Royal China	*"*	★★
	Uli	*Pan-Asian*	★
	The Walmer Castle	*Thai*	A★
	Tawana	*"*	★
£20+	Ranoush	*Lebanese*	★★
£15+	Mandalay	*Burmese*	★
£5+	Lisboa Patisserie	*Sandwiches, cakes, etc*	★★

Hammersmith, Shepherd's Bush Chiswick & Olympia (W4, W5, W6, W12, W14)

£50+	The River Café	*Italian*	★
£40+	Cibo	*Italian*	★
	Grano	*"*	★
£35+	Chinon	*French*	★★
£30+	Parade	*British, Modern*	A★
	Popeseye	*Steaks & grills*	★
	Springbok Café	*South African*	★

£25+	The Havelock Tavern	British, Modern	★★
	The Gate	Vegetarian	A★★
	Esarn Kheaw	Thai	★★
	Thai Bistro	"	★
£20+	Blah! Blah! Blah!	Vegetarian	A★
	Latymers	Thai	★

NORTH

Hampstead, West Hampstead, St John's Wood, Regent's Park, Kilburn & Camden Town (NW postcodes)

£40+	Bradley's	British, Modern	★
	L'Aventure	French	A★★
	Oslo Court	"	★
£35+	Odette's	British, Modern	A★
	The New End	"	★
	ZeNW3	Chinese	★
	Wakaba	Japanese	★
£30+	The Black Truffle	Italian	★
	Gaucho Grill	Steaks & grills	A★
	Feng Shang	Chinese	A★
	Sushi-Say	Japanese	★
£25+	Pie2 Mash	British, Traditional	★
	Lemonia	Greek	A
	The Salusbury	Italian	A★
	Royal China	Chinese	★★
	Café Japan	Japanese	★
	Jin Kichi	"	★
£20+	Seashell	Fish & chips	★
	Laurent	Tunisian	★
	Vijay	Indian	★★
£15+	Geeta	"	★★

Islington, Highgate, Crouch End, Stoke Newington, Finsbury Park, Muswell Hill & Finchley (N postcodes)

£35+	Frederick's	British, Modern	A★
	The White Onion	"	★
£30+	Granita	British, Modern	★
	Kavanagh's	"	★
	The Real Greek	Greek	A★★

	Florians	*Italian*	🅰 ★
	Chez Liline	*Fish & seafood*	★★
£25+	Mesclun	*British, Modern*	🅰 ★
	Soulard	*French*	🅰 ★
	Metrogusto	*Italian*	🅰 ★
	Rasa	*Indian*	★★
£20+	Vrisaki	*Greek*	🅰 ★
	Two Brothers	*Fish & chips*	★
	Upper St Fish Shop	*"*	★
	Iznik	*Turkish*	🅰
	Yum Yum	*Thai*	🅰 ★
£10+	Tartuf	*Alsatian*	★
	Afghan Kitchen	*Afghani*	★

SOUTH

South Bank (SE1)

£60+	Le Pont de la Tour	*British, Modern*	-
£50+	Oxo Tower	*British, Modern*	🅰
£40+	Tentazioni	*Italian*	★
£30+	RSJ	*British, Modern*	★
	Tate Modern	*International*	🅰
	Bengal Clipper	*Indian*	★
£25+	The Apprentice	*British, Modern*	★
£20+	Konditor & Cook	*"*	★★
	Tas	*Turkish*	★
£15+	Pizzeria Castello	*Pizza*	★★

Battersea, Clapham, Wandsworth, Barnes, Putney, Brixton & Lewisham
(All postcodes south of the river except SE1)

£40+	Chez Bruce	*British, Modern*	🅰 ★★
£35+	The Glasshouse	*British, Modern*	🅰 ★★
	Ransome's Dock	*"*	🅰 ★
	The Stepping Stone	*"*	🅰 ★
	The Light House	*"*	★
	Redmond's	*"*	★
	Sonny's	*"*	★
	Riva	*Italian*	★

	Lobster Pot	*Fish & seafood*	★
£30+	Kennington Lane	*British, Modern*	A★
	Phoenix	"	★
	Enoteca Turi	*Italian*	A★
	Cantinetta Venegazzú	"	★
	Del Buongustaio	"	★
	The Sequel	*International*	★
	Moxon's	*Fish & seafood*	★★
	Popeseye	*Steaks & grills*	★
	La Pampa	*Argentinian*	A★
	Bombay Bicycle Club	*Indian*	A★
	Café Spice Namaste	"	A★
£25+	Rapscallion	*British, Modern*	A★
	Emile's	*French*	★
	Metrogusto	*Italian*	A★
	Cinnamon Cay	*East/West*	★
	Pizza Metro	*Pizza*	A★★
	Royal China	*Chinese*	★★
	Babur Brasserie	*Indian*	A★★
	Sarkhel's	"	★★
	Ma Goa	"	★
	Thailand	*Thai*	★★
	The Old School Thai	"	★
£20+	Le P'tit Normand	*French*	-
	Arancia	*Italian*	-
	Brady's	*Fish & chips*	★
	Indian Ocean	*Indian*	★
	Shree Krishna	"	★
	Talad Thai	*Thai*	★★
£15+	Kastoori	*Indian*	★★
	The Pepper Tree	*Thai*	★

EAST

Smithfield & Farringdon (EC1)

£40+	Bleeding Heart	*French*	A★
	Gaudi	*Spanish*	-
£35+	St John	*British, Modern*	A★
	Club Gascon	*French*	A★★
	Café du Marché	"	A★
	Alba	*Italian*	★
	Smiths of Smithfield	*Steaks & grills*	A
£30+	Home	*British, Modern*	A
	Moro	*Moroccan*	A★

£25+	Carnevale	*Vegetarian*	★
£20+	Fox & Anchor	*British, Traditional*	Ⓐ★
	The Eagle	*Mediterranean*	Ⓐ★

The City & East End
(All E and EC postcodes, except EC1)

£60+	Tatsuso	*Japanese*	★
£50+	City Rhodes	*British, Modern*	★
£40+	1 Lombard Street	*British, Modern*	-
	Prism	*"*	-
	Coq d'Argent	*French*	-
£35+	The Grapes	*Fish & seafood*	Ⓐ★
	Sweetings	*"*	Ⓐ★
£30+	The Light	*British, Modern*	Ⓐ★
	Gaucho Grill	*Steaks & grills*	Ⓐ★
	Imperial City	*Chinese*	Ⓐ★
	Café Spice Namaste	*Indian*	Ⓐ★
	Shimla Pinks	*"*	Ⓐ★
	Sri Siam City	*Thai*	★
	Sri Thai	*"*	★
£20+	The Place Below	*Vegetarian*	★
	Faulkner's	*Fish & chips*	★★
	Shanghai	*Chinese*	Ⓐ★
	K10	*Japanese*	★★
	Viet Hoa	*Vietnamese*	★
£15+	Arkansas Café	*Steaks & grills*	★
	Lahore Kebab House	*Indian*	★★
£5+	Soup Opera	*Soup*	★
£1+	Brick Lane Beigel Bake	*Sandwiches, cakes, etc*	★★

BREAKFAST
(with opening times)

Central
Bank *(7.30)*
Café Bagatelle *(10)*
Connaught *(7.30)*
Dorchester Grill *(7, Sun 7.30)*
Hard Rock Café *(8.30)*
Restaurant One-O-One *(7)*
Sotheby's Café *(9)*
Soup Opera: *Hanover St WI (7.30)*

West
Brass. du Marché *(10, Sun 11)*
Capital Hotel *(7, Sun 7.30)*
Kensington Place *(7.30)*
Lisboa Patisserie *(7.45)*
Ranoush *(8)*

North
Iznik *(Sat & Sun 9)*
Pie2 Mash *(10)*

South
Konditor & Cook *(8.30)*
Rapscallion *(9.15)*
Tate Modern *(10)*

East
Brick Lane Beigel Bake *(24 hr)*
Carnevale *(12)*
Coq d'Argent *(7.30)*
Fox & Anchor *(7)*
Gaucho Grill: *EC3 (7)*
1 Lombard Street *(7.30)*
Smiths of Smithfield *(café, 7)*
Soup Opera: *E14 (7)*

BRUNCH MENUS

Central
Bank
Le Caprice
Dorchester Grill
The Ivy
Joe Allen
Mirabelle
Restaurant One-O-One
The Sugar Club
Vong

West
Bluebird
Brass. du Marché
Capital Hotel
The Cow

North
Iznik
The White Onion

South
Cinnamon Cay
Phoenix
Le Pont de la Tour

Ransome's Dock
The Sequel
The Stepping Stone

East
Carnevale
Gaucho Grill: *EC3*
Smiths of Smithfield

BUSINESS

Central
Al Duca
Axis
Bank
Bentley's
Le Caprice
cheznico
Connaught
The Criterion
Diverso
Dorchester Grill
Dorchester, Oriental
L'Escargot
Foliage
Le Gavroche
The Ivy
Ken Lo's Memories
The Marquis
Mirabelle
Mon Plaisir
L'Oranger
Pétrus
Pied à Terre
Quaglino's
Restaurant One-O-One
Rhodes in the Sq
Rules
Savoy Grill
J Sheekey
Le Soufflé
The Square
Stephen Bull
The Sugar Club
Suntory
La Tante Claire
Vong
Wiltons
Zafferano
Zen Central

West
Aubergine
Bibendum
Bluebird
Capital Hotel
Clarke's
Gordon Ramsay
Launceston Place
Poissonnerie
   de l'Avenue

North
Frederick's
Odette's

South
Oxo Tower
Le Pont de la Tour
RSJ

East
Bleeding Heart
Café du Marché
City Rhodes
Coq d'Argent
Imperial City
Moro
1 Lombard Street
Prism
Sri Siam City
Sweetings
Tatsuso

BYO
(Bring your own wine)

Central
Fryer's Delight

West
Blah! Blah! Blah!

North
Upper St Fish Shop

South
Talad Thai

East
Faulkner's
Lahore Kebab House
The Place Below

CHILDREN
(h – high or special chairs
m – children's menu
p – children's portions
e – weekend entertainments
o – other facilities)

Central
Abeno *(hp)*
The Admiralty *(h)*
Al Hamra *(h)*
Al Sultan *(h)*
Alastair Little *(hm)*
Axis *(m)*
Back to Basics *(p)*
Bank *(hme)*
Bentley's *(h)*
Boudin Blanc *(h)*
Café Bagatelle *(p)*
Le Caprice *(hp)*
China House *(hpe)*
The Criterion *(h)*
Diverso *(h)*
Dorchester Grill *(hm)*
Dorchester, Oriental *(h)*
L'Escargot *(h)*
Foliage *(hm)*

Fung Shing *(h)*
Gaucho Grill: W1 *(h)*
Hard Rock Café *(hmo)*
Incognico *(h)*
Isola *(h)*
Italian Kitchen *(m)*
The Ivy *(hp)*
Joy King Lau *(h)*
Maroush: *all branches (p)*
Matsuri *(m)*
Mezzo *(h)*
Nobu *(h)*
Osteria d'Isola *(h)*
Quaglino's *(hm)*
Restaurant One-O-One *(h)*
Royal China: *all branches (hm)*
Rules *(h)*
Savoy Grill *(h)*
Le Soufflé *(hp)*
Soup Opera: *Hanover St W1 (h)*
La Spiga *(hp)*
La Spighetta *(hp)*
Tamarind *(h)*
Teca *(h)*
Vong *(h)*
Wolfe's *(hm)*
Zafferano *(hp)*
Zen Central *(h)*
Zen Garden *(ho)*

West
Alastair Little W11 *(hp)*
Assaggi *(p)*
Belvedere *(h)*
Blah! Blah! Blah! *(p)*
Blue Elephant *(he)*
Bluebird *(hmo)*
Bombay Brasserie *(h)*
Bombay Palace *(hp)*
Brass. du Marché *(hp)*
Chutney Mary *(m)*
Exhibition *(p)*
The Gate *(h)*
Goolies *(p)*
The Havelock Tavern *(hp)*
Itsu *(p)*
Julie's *(ho)*
Malabar *(hp)*
Mandalay *(p)*
Mandarin Kitchen *(h)*
Maroush: *all branches (p)*
Mediterraneo *(h)*
Parade *(e)*
Phoenicia *(h)*
The River Café *(hp)*
Royal China: *all branches (hm)*
Scalini *(h)*
Sticky Fingers *(hme)*
Vama *(hp)*
The Walmer Castle *(h)*

North
Florians *(hp)*
Frederick's *(hm)*
Kavanagh's *(p)*

Laurent *(p)*
Mesclun *(hp)*
Pie2 Mash *(p)*
Royal China: all branches *(hm)*
The Salusbury *(hm)*
Seashell *(hm)*
Two Brothers *(m)*
Upper St Fish Shop *(h)*
Vijay *(h)*
Yum Yum *(h)*
ZeNW3 *(h)*

South
Babur Brasserie *(h)*
Bengal Clipper *(h)*
Brady's *(p)*
Café Spice Namaste: all branches *(hp)*
Cantinetta Venegazzú *(hp)*
Chez Bruce *(h)*
Cinnamon Cay *(hm)*
Del Buongustaio *(p)*
Kastoori *(p)*
The Light House *(h)*
Lobster Pot *(p)*
Metrogusto: SW8 *(hp)*
The Old School Thai *(h)*
The Pepper Tree *(hp)*
Phoenix *(h)*
Pizza Metro *(h)*
Pizzeria Castello *(h)*
Le Pont de la Tour *(h)*
Ransome's Dock *(hp)*
Redmond's *(m)*
Riva *(hm)*
Sarkhel's *(h)*
The Sequel *(hm)*
Sonny's *(h)*
The Stepping Stone *(hmo)*
Tate Modern *(hpo)*
Tentazioni *(h)*

East
Café Spice Namaste: all branches *(hp)*
Carnevale *(p)*
Faulkner's *(hm)*
Gaucho Grill: EC3 *(h)*
Gaudi *(p)*
St John *(h)*
Shanghai *(h)*
Smiths of Smithfield *(hp)*
Viet Hoa *(h)*

ENTERTAINMENT
(Check times before you go)

Central
Le Caprice
(pianist, nightly, and at L)
China House
(family entertainment, Sun L)
The Criterion
(magician, Wed-Sat)
Foliage
(jazz, Mon-Sat)

Mezzo
(music, all week)
Quaglino's
(jazz, nightly in bar; pianist at L)
Le Soufflé
(string trio, Sun L)

West
Bluebird
(pianist, nightly)
Bombay Brasserie
(pianist & singer, nightly)
Cambio de Tercio
(guitarist, Wed)
Chutney Mary
(jazz, Sun L)
Maroush: W2
(music & dancing, nightly)
Star of India
(singer & jazz pianist, Wed & Thu)

South
Tas
(music, nightly)

East
Café du Marché
(pianist, nightly)
Coq d'Argent
(pianist, nightly & Sun L)
The Light
(DJ, Thu-Sat)
1 Lombard Street
(jazz, Wed night)
Sri Siam City
(music, Thu night)
Sri Thai
(music, Wed)

LATE
(open till midnight or later as shown; may be earlier Sunday)

Central
Asia de Cuba *(Midnight, 1 am Sat)*
Le Caprice
Gaucho Grill: W1 *(not Sun)*
Hard Rock Café *(12.30 am, Fri & Sat 1 am)*
Incognico
The Ivy
Joe Allen *(12.45 am)*
Maroush: W1 *(1 am)*
Melati *(Fri & Sat 12.30 am)*
Mezzo *(Mon-Wed midnight, Thu-Sat 1 am (crustacea till 3 am))*
Mr Kong *(2.45 am)*
Quaglino's *(Midnight, Fri & Sat 1 am)*
Rasa Samudra
J Sheekey
Soup Works: Moor St W1 *(midnight, Fri & Sat)*
La Spiga *(Wed-Sat midnight)*

West
Bombay Brasserie
Maroush: W2 *(2 am)*; SW3 *(5 am)*
Ranoush *(3 am)*
Scalini

North

Gaucho Grill: *NW3 (not Sun)*
Rasa: *N16 (Fri & Sat only)*
Tartuf
Vrisaki

South
Ransome's Dock *(Midnight, Sat)*

East
Brick Lane Beigel Bake *(24 hours)*

NO-SMOKING AREAS
(* completely no smoking)

Central
Abeno
The Admiralty*
Busaba Eathai*
Café Bagatelle*
China House
Connaught*
Crivelli's Garden*
Hard Rock Café
Ibla
Joe Allen
Kulu Kulu*
Malabar Junction
Mildreds*
Mirabelle
Nobu
The Orient
Osteria d'Isola
The Portrait*
Rasa: *all branches**
Rasa Samudra
Roussillon
Rules*
Sotheby's Café*
Le Soufflé
La Spighetta
The Sugar Club
Vong
Yoshino

West
Bali Sugar
Bombay Palace
Chutney Mary
Itsu*
Mandalay*
Mao Tai
The Papaya Tree
Phoenicia
S&P Patara: *Beauchamp Pl SW3*
6 Clarendon Road
Springbok Café
Thai Bistro*

North
Café Japan
Frederick's
Pie2 Mash
Rasa: *all branches**
Seashell

Two Brothers

South
The Apprentice
Babur Brasserie
The Light House
Metrogusto: *SW8*
The Old School Thai
The Pepper Tree
Sarkhel's
The Stepping Stone
Talad Thai*
Tate Modern*
Thailand*

East
Arkansas Café*
Brick Lane Beigel Bake*
Faulkner's
Home
K10*
The Place Below*

OUTSIDE TABLES
(* particularly recommended)

Central
Al Hamra*
Al Sultan
Back to Basics
Boudin Blanc*
Hard Rock Café
Mirabelle*
Ozer
Le Palais du Jardin
La Poule au Pot
Soup Opera: *Hanover St W1*
La Spighetta
Toto's*
Wolfe's
Zilli Fish

West
Alastair Little W11
The Atlas*
Bali Sugar*
Belvedere
Bibendum Oyster Bar
Bombay Brasserie
Bombay Palace
Brass. du Marché
Chinon
Chives
Elistano
Emile's: *SW6*
The Gate*
The Havelock Tavern
Julie's
Latymers
Lisboa Patisserie
Mediterraneo
Monza*
Osteria Basilico
The River Café*
Thai on the River*

Uli
Vama

North
L'Aventure*
The Black Truffle
Florians
Frederick's*
Gaucho Grill: NW3
Kavanagh's
Lemonia
North Sea Fish
Odette's
Pie2 Mash
The Real Greek
The Salusbury
Soulard
Tartuf

South
Arancia
Babur Brasserie
Café Spice Namaste: SW11
Cantinetta Venegazzú*
Cinnamon Cay
Kennington Lane
Oxo Tower*
Phoenix
Pizza Metro
Le Pont de la Tour*
Popeseye: SW15
Ransome's Dock*
Rapscallion
Riva
RSJ
The Sequel

East
Arkansas Café
Bleeding Heart*
Carnevale*
Coq d'Argent*
The Eagle
The Light
Moro
The Place Below*
Shimla Pinks
Smiths of Smithfield

ROMANTIC

Central
The Admiralty
Andrew Edmunds
Boudin Blanc
Le Caprice
Connaught
The Criterion
French House
Le Gavroche
Ibla
The Ivy
Joe Allen
Mirabelle
Mon Plaisir

L'Oranger
La Poule au Pot
Salloos
Savoy Grill
Shogun
Toto's

West
Aubergine
Belvedere
Bibendum
Blue Elephant
Chezmax
Clarke's
The Cow
Grano
Julie's
Launceston Place
Mediterraneo
Monkeys
Scalini
Le Suquet
Zaika

North
L'Aventure
Bradley's
Frederick's
Odette's
Oslo Court

South
Arancia
Chez Bruce
The Glasshouse
Oxo Tower
RSJ

East
Bleeding Heart
Café du Marché

ROOMS WITH A VIEW

Central
The Admiralty
Crivelli's Garden
The Portrait

West
Belvedere
Thai on the River

South
Oxo Tower
Le Pont de la Tour
Tate Modern

East
Coq d'Argent
Smiths of Smithfield

MAP I – WEST END OVERVIEW

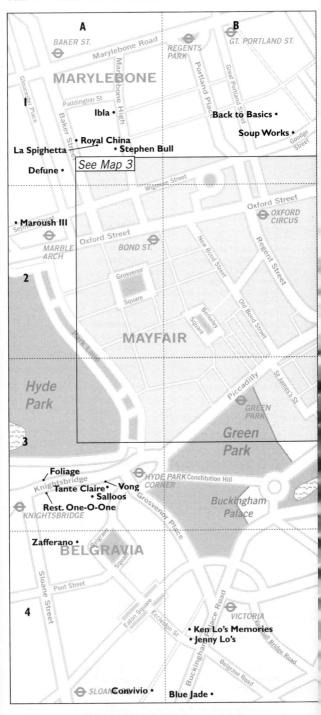

MAP I – WEST END OVERVIEW

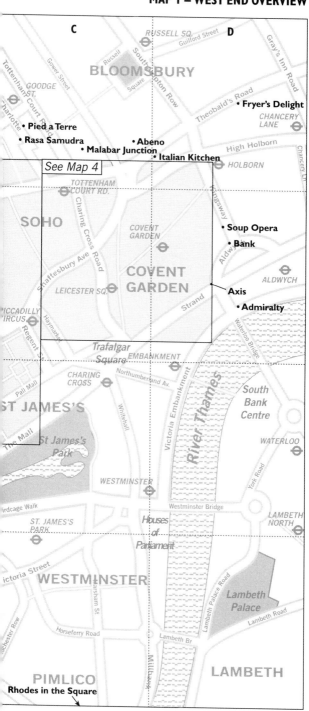

MAP 2 – MAYFAIR, ST JAMES'S & WEST SOHO

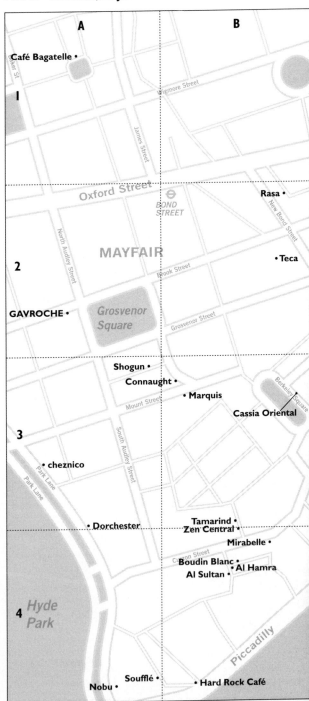

MAP 2 – MAYFAIR, ST JAMES'S & WEST SOHO

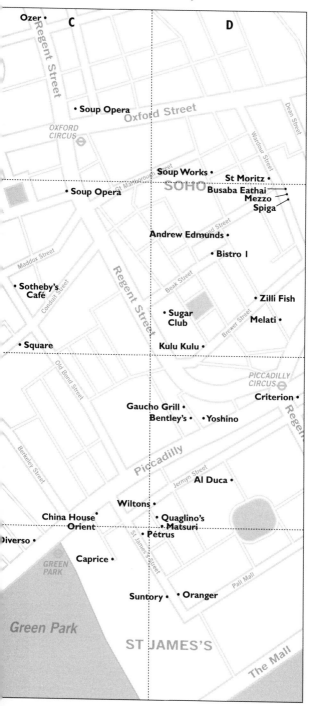

MAP 3 – EAST SOHO, CHINATOWN & COVENT GARDEN

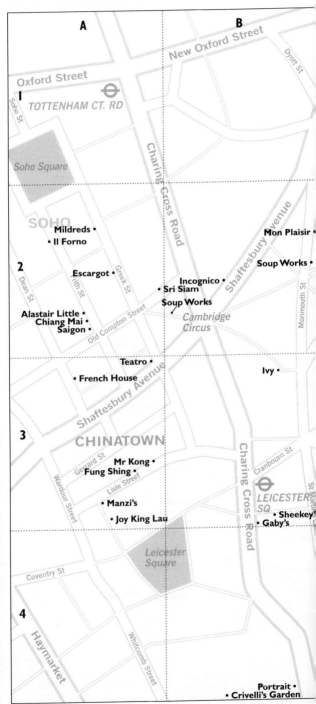

MAP 3 – EAST SOHO, CHINATOWN & COVENT GARDEN

MAP 4 – KNIGHTSBRIDGE, CHELSEA & SOUTH KENSINGTON

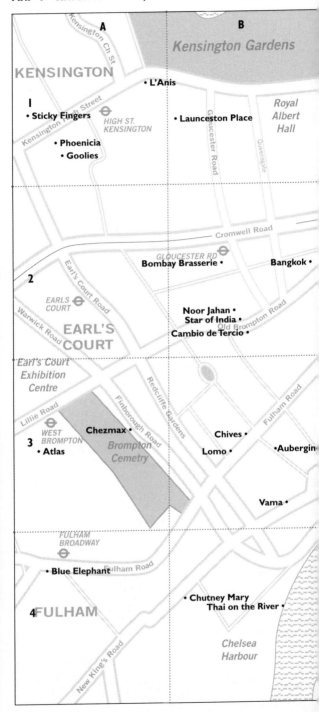

A

B

Kensington Ch St

Kensington Gardens

KENSINGTON

Royal Albert Hall

1

• Sticky Fingers

High Street

HIGH ST. KENSINGTON

Kensington High Street

• L'Anis

Gloucester Road

Queensgate

• Launceston Place

• Phoenicia

• Goolies

Cromwell Road

GLOUCESTER RD

Bombay Brasserie •

Bangkok •

2

Earl's Court Road

EARLS COURT

Warwick Road

EARL'S COURT

Noor Jahan •

Star of India •

Cambio de Tercio •

Old Brompton Road

Redcliffe Gardens

Fulham Road

Earl's Court Exhibition Centre

Lillie Road

WEST BROMPTON

Chezmax •

Finborough Road

Brompton Cemetery

Chives •

Lomo •

•Aubergin

3

• Atlas

Vama •

FULHAM BROADWAY

Fulham Road

• Blue Elephant

4 FULHAM

• Chutney Mary

Thai on the River •

Chelsea Harbour

New King's Road

MAP 4 – KNIGHTSBRIDGE, CHELSEA & SOUTH KENSINGTON

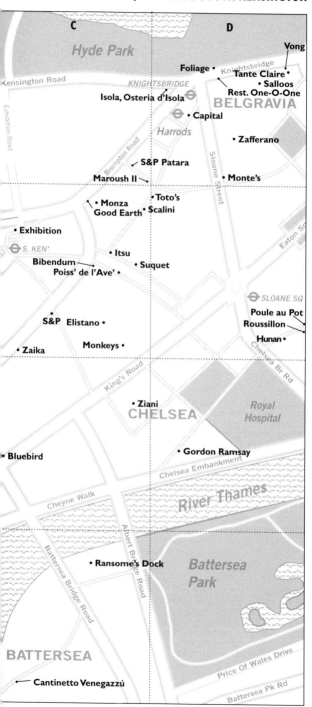

Hyde Park

Kensington Road

KNIGHTSBRIDGE

Knightsbridge

Vong •

Foliage •

Tante Claire •
• Salloos
Rest. One-O-One

Isola, Osteria d'Isola ⊖

BELGRAVIA

⊖ • Capital

Harrods

• Zafferano

Brompton Road

• S&P Patara

Maroush II

Sloane Street

• Monte's

• Monza
Good Earth • • Toto's
• Scalini

Exhibition Road

• Exhibition

Eaton Sq

⊖ S. KEN'

• Itsu

Bibendum
Poiss' de l'Ave' •

• Suquet

⊖ SLOANE SQ

Poule au Pot
Roussillon

• Hunan •

• S&P Elistano •

Monkeys •

Chelsea Br Rd

• Zaika

King's Road

• Ziani

CHELSEA

*Royal
Hospital*

• Bluebird

• Gordon Ramsay

Chelsea Embankment

Cheyne Walk

River Thames

Albert Bridge Road

• Ransome's Dock

*Battersea
Park*

Battersea Bridge Road

BATTERSEA

Cantinetto Venegazzú

Price Of Wales Drive

Battersea Pk Rd

UK & EIRE
SURVEY RESULTS
& TOP SCORERS

PLACES PEOPLE TALK ABOUT

Restaurants outside London mentioned most frequently in the survey (last year's position shown in brackets):

1	Yang Sing *(6)*	*Manchester*
2	Manoir aux Quat' Saisons *(1)*	*Great Milton, Oxon*
3	Mumtaz Paan House *(-)*	*Bradford*
4	Le Petit Blanc *(3)*	*Oxford*
5	Chaing Mai *(16)*	*Oxford*
6	Browns *(9)*	*Oxford*
7	Terre à Terre *(16)*	*Brighton*
8	Waterside Inn *(4)*	*Bray, Berks*
9	Seafood Restaurant *(2)*	*Padstow, Cornwall*
10	The Angel *(7)*	*Hetton, N Yorks*
11	Simply Heathcotes *(14)*	*Manchester*
12	Chung Ying Garden *(-)*	*Birmingham*
13	Pacific *(-)*	*Manchester*
14=	Chiang Rai *(-)*	*Manchester*
14=	Shimla Pinks *(13)*	*Birmingham*
16	Le Petit Blanc *(-)*	*Birmingham*
17	Walnut Tree *(5)*	*Llandewi Skirrid, Mon'shire*
18	The Crown *(16)*	*Southwold, Suffolk*
19=	The Lime Tree *(-)*	*Manchester*
19=	Tampopo *(-)*	*Manchester*

TOP SCORERS

All restaurants whose food rating is ★★; plus restaurants whose price is £50+ with a food rating of ★:

£100+ Le Manoir aux Quat' Saisons *(Great Milton)* ★

£90+ Altnaharrie Inn *(Ullapool)* ★★A
Waterside Inn *(Bray)* ★

£70+ Gidleigh Park *(Chagford)* ★★
Lucknam Park *(Colerne)* ★A
Patrick Guilbaud *(Dublin)* ★
Thorntons *(Dublin)* ★

£60+ Lettonie *(Bath)* ★★A
Winteringham Fields *(Winteringham)* ★★A
Harry's Place *(Great Gonerby)* ★★
Hambleton Hall *(Hambleton)* ★A
Midsummer House *(Cambridge)* ★
Old Vicarage *(Ridgeway)* ★
Vineyard at Stockcross *(Stockcross)* ★

£50+ Fischers at Baslow Hall *(Baslow)* ★★A
Horn of Plenty *(Gulworthy)* ★★A
Michael's Nook *(Grasmere)* ★★A
Sharrow Bay *(Ullswater)* ★★A
One Paston Place *(Brighton)* ★★
Chavignol *(Chipping Norton)* ★★
Croque en Bouche *(Malvern Wells)* ★★
Airds Hotel *(Port Appin)* ★A
Auberge du Lac *(Lemsford)* ★A
Charlton House *(Shepton Mallet)* ★A
Kinnaird House *(Dunkeld)* ★A
Lords of the Manor *(Upper Slaughter)* ★A
Old Beams *(Waterhouses)* ★A
One Devonshire Gardens *(Glasgow)* ★A
Sheen Falls Lodge *(Kenmare)* ★A
Summer Lodge *(Evershot)* ★A
Carved Angel *(Dartmouth)* ★
Champignon Sauvage *(Cheltenham)* ★
Number One *(Edinburgh)* ★
Old Chesil Rectory *(Winchester)* ★
Pool Court at 42 *(Leeds)* ★
Seafood Restaurant *(Padstow)* ★

£40+ Ballymaloe Hotel *(Shanagarry)* ★★A
Bodidris Hall Hotel *(Llandegla)* ★★A
Fairyhill *(Reynoldston)* ★★A
Summer Isles *(Achiltibuie)* ★★A
Three Chimneys *(Dunvegan)* ★★A
Markwicks *(Bristol)* ★★
Restaurant Martin Wishart *(Edinburgh)* ★★

TOP SCORERS

	Three Lions *(Stuckton)*	★★
	Walnut Tree *(Abergavenny)*	★★
	La Potinière *(Gullane)*	★★
	La Terrasse *(Sandgate)*	★★
	Le Gallois *(Cardiff)*	★★
	Ivory Tower *(Cork)*	★★
£30+	Blue Lion *(East Witton)*	★★A
	Chaing Mai *(Oxford)*	★★A
	Inn at Whitewell *(Clitheroe)*	★★A
	McCoys at the Tontine *(Staddlebridge)*	★★A
	Merchant House *(Ludlow)*	★★A
	Mr Underhill's *(Ludlow)*	★★A
	Nantyffin Cider Mill *(Crickhowell)*	★★A
	Plas Bodegroes *(Pwllheli)*	★★A
	Rococo *(Kings Lynn)*	★★A
	Star Inn *(Harome)*	★★A
	The Crab & Lobster *(Asenby)*	★★A
	The Lime Tree *(Manchester)*	★★A
	22 Mill Street *(Chagford)*	★★
	Aldens *(Belfast)*	★★
	Foresters Arms *(Carlton)*	★★
	Gingerman *(Brighton)*	★★
	Nutter's *(Cheesden)*	★★
	Rowan Tree *(Askrigg)*	★★
	Three Main Street *(Fishguard)*	★★
	White Hart *(Lydgate)*	★★
	Yang Sing *(Manchester)*	★★
£25+	Mother India *(Glasgow)*	★★A
	Ostrich Inn *(Newland)*	★★A
	Air Organic *(Glasgow)*	★★
	Demuths *(Bath)*	★★
	Drum & Monkey *(Harrogate)*	★★
	Palmiro *(Manchester)*	★★
	Spread Eagle *(Sawley)*	★★
	Terre à Terre *(Brighton)*	★★
	The Bell Inn *(Horndon on the Hill)*	★★
	The Punch Bowl *(Crosthwaite)*	★★
£20+	Glasnost *(Bristol)*	★★A
	Nobody Inn *(Doddiscombsleigh)*	★★A
	Magpie Café *(Whitby)*	★★
	Siam Thai *(Birmingham)*	★★
£15+	Fuji Hiro *(Leeds)*	★★
	Great Kathmandu *(Manchester)*	★★
	Mumtaz Paan House *(Bradford)*	★★
	Rajput *(Harrogate)*	★★
£10+	Gurkha Grill *(Manchester)*	★★

UK & EIRE
DIRECTORY

ABERDEEN, ABERDEEN CITY
9–2D

Royal Thai £ 26 ★

29 Crown Ter AB11 1HP (01224) 212922
*"Authentic south east Asian cooking" (particularly the "fantastic banquet") wins high praise from locals and visitors alike at this well-established oriental. / **Sample dishes:** chicken satay; scallops & prawns; fruit salad. **Details:** off Crown St; 10.30 pm; closed Sun L.*

Sawadee £ 25

16-17 Bon Accord Cr AB11 6AB (01224) 582828
*"Charming" service and "beautifully presented" Thai cooking, makes this central oriental a place of more than 'ethnic' appeal in this under-served city. / **Sample dishes:** Thai fishcakes; chicken chow mein; coconut ice cream. **Details:** 11 pm; closed Sat & Sun; no smoking area.*

ABERDYFI, GWYNEDD
4–3C

Penhelig Arms £ 26 A★

LL35 0LT (01654) 767215
*A location a stone's throw from the shore is only part of the appeal of this large, lively old inn; located on the main drag through a small seaside resort, it provides some "interesting" food and "perfectly kept beers". / **Sample dishes:** warm goat's cheese salad; seared tuna steak with aioli; apricot tart. **Value tip:** set 3-crs Sun L £13.50. **Details:** 9 pm; no Amex; no smoking in dining room. **Accommodation:** 10 rooms, from £69.*

ABERGAVENNY, MONMOUTHSHIRE
2–1A

Walnut Tree £ 43 ★★

Llandewi Skirrid NP7 8AW (01873) 852797
*"It surpassed our high expectations" – Franco Taruschio's "exquisite", "honest" Italian cooking maintains the "unbeatable" position of his 37-year-old fixture as "the best restaurant in Wales"; the food's the thing, though, and some do feel a little "crammed in" at these "casual and relaxed" pub-conversion premises. / **Sample dishes:** avocado, Mozzarella & tomato salad; tagliatelle with cream & asparagus spears; Italian chocolate mousse. **Details:** 3m NE of Abergavenny on B4521; 10.15 pm; closed Mon & Sun; no credit cards.*

ABERKENFIG, BRIDGEND
1–1D

New Garden £ 24

40-42 Pandy Rd CF32 9PP (01656) 724361
*There's "always an enjoyable evening" to be had at this "entertaining" Chinese, where "a pianist and a stream" contribute to the ambience. / **Sample dishes:** spare ribs; crispy beef with egg fried rice; toffee bananas. **Details:** 1.5m from M4, J36; 11 pm; closed Sun D.*

ABERSOCH, GWYNEDD
4–2C

Porth Tocyn Hotel £ 36 A★

LL53 7BU (01758) 713303
*A "superb location" – a little outside the town, and with lovely views – is just one of the attractions of the dining room at the Fletcher-Brewers' half-century-old seaside hotel; "good produce" (with the cheeseboard especially commended) and "well-trained staff" also make a major contribution. / **Sample dishes:** quail with apricot stuffing; herb-crusted sea trout with sautéed asparagus; chocolate cherry cheesecake. **Value tip:** set 3-crs Sun L £18. **Details:** 2m S of Abersoch - follow blue road signs with bed symbol; 9.30 pm; closed mid Nov to Easter; no Amex; no smoking; children: 7+ at D. **Accommodation:** 17 rooms, from £65.50.*

Summer Isles   £ 42   𝔸★★
IV26 2YG   (01854) 622282

"Unbelievable in such a remote location" – this "high-class,
family-run hotel by the sea" is "remarkably good"; the "freshness
of the produce and the originality of the preparation" are nothing
short of a "revelation", and there are "dreamy" views (towards
the islands after which the hotel is named). / **Sample dishes:** grilled
turbot with herb pesto; carpaccio of Aberdeen Angus beef; bread & butter
pudding. **Details:** 25m N of Ullapool on A835; 8 pm; no Amex; no smoking
in dining room; booking essential; children: 6+. **Accommodation:** 13 rooms,
from £98.

Rose Cottage Inn   £ 23   ★
BN26 6UW   (01323) 870377

"They know more about fish than Jacques Cousteau" at this
"real old pub" – a "beautifully located" 16th-century beamed inn
on the edge of the South Downs, which is universally praised for
its seafood and other "traditional" English dishes. / **Sample
dishes:** deep-fried prawns in filo pastry; char-grilled shellfish salad; meringue
with summer berries. **Details:** off A27 nr Drusillas Park; 9 pm; closed Sun D;
no Amex; no smoking.

Café 152   £ 27   ★
152 High St IP15 5AX   (01728) 454152

It's "more than just a local bistro", say supporters of this
"imaginative but unpretentious" spot, which offers "good
cooking" in a "busy but relaxing setting". / **Sample dishes:**
duck confit & spiced pears; char-grilled swordfish with salsa; nectarine tarte
Tatin. **Details:** follow signs off A12; 10 pm (9 pm in winter); 10pm in summer,
9pm in winter, closed Tue (& Mon in winter); no Amex; no smoking area;
children: before 8 pm only.

Lighthouse   £ 25   ★
77 High St IP15 5AU   (01728) 453377

"Book to avoid disappointment" (and downstairs, if you can) –
Peter and Sarah Hill's "bistro-style" establishment is "still the
most fashionable restaurant" in town, thanks to its "beautiful fish
cooked to perfection" and its "friendly and attentive service".
/ **Sample dishes:** warm salad of scallops & bacon; Dover sole in lemon
& butter; bread & butter pudding. **Details:** on High St, by cinema; 10 pm;
no Amex.

Regatta   £ 26   ★
171 High St IP15 5AN   (01728) 452011

A "regularly-changing menu" of "freshly prepared" food
(specialising in fish and seafood) and "a warm welcome to all,
children included" win consistent praise for this seaside spot.
/ **Sample dishes:** smoked prawns with dipping sauce; Dover sole with new
potatoes & salad; fudge ice cream. **Value tip:** set 2-crs pre-theatre £8.
Details: 10 pm; closed Wed, Nov-Mar; no smoking area.

ALDFORD, CHESHIRE

The Grosvenor Arms £ 27

Chester Rd CH3 6HJ (01244) 620228

"A lovely rural setting" and *"good-quality pub food"* in *"large portions"* earn unanimously positive reports for this popular inn, near the gates of the Duke of Westminster's estate. / **Sample dishes:** mushrooms in cream & mustard sauce; garlic chicken with mushroom risotto; glazed lemon tart. **Details:** 6m S of Chester on B5130; 10 pm; children: 14+ after 6 pm.

ALLOWAY BY AYR, SOUTH AYRSHIRE

Brig O'Doon House Hotel £ 27 A★

Murdochs Ln KA7 4PQ (01292) 442466

In the *"beautiful surroundings"* of Burns's birthplace, a *"wide selection"* of *"excellent"* dishes is *"professionally served"* at this hidden-away fixture; though the style is traditional, some find the overall approach *"surprisingly modern for this part of the world"*. / **Sample dishes:** smoked haddock & dill potato cake; Cajun-spiced chicken with pilau rice; sticky toffee pudding. **Details:** 10 mins from Prestwick Airport, 45 mins from Glasgow Airport; 9 pm; no smoking in dining room. **Accommodation:** 5 rooms, from £100.

ALTRINCHAM, GREATER MANCHESTER

French Restaurant £ 25

25 The Downs WA14 2QD (0161) 941 3355

"Easy-going, with reliable and decent food", this *"comfortable"* suburban restaurant *"maintains high standards at reasonable prices"*. / **Sample dishes:** king prawns in creole sauce; peppered steak with French fries; crème brûlée. **Details:** 10.30 pm; D only, ex Sun open L & D.

Juniper £ 49 ★

21 The Downs WA14 2QD (0161) 929 4008

"Exquisite" cooking makes this foodie five-year old the top French restaurant in the Manchester area; some find the setting *"too casual"* though – an odd inversion of the usual problem for places on the Michelin trail! / **Sample dishes:** grilled scallops with cherry tomatoes & Parma ham; roast cod with thyme & cucumber; trio of blackberry desserts. **Details:** 10 pm; closed Mon L, Sat L & Sun.

AMBERLEY, WEST SUSSEX

Amberley Castle £ 60 A

BN18 9ND (01798) 831992

"A serious mismatch between form and substance" diminishes support for this *"amazing"*, *"baronially splendid"* castle – all agree it's *"a great venue"*, but some encounter *"poor food and service"*. / **Sample dishes:** braised ham hocks & foie gras terrine; roast guinea fowl with Belgian endive tart; iced Grand Marnier soufflé. **Value tip:** set 2-crs L £12.50. **Details:** N of Arundel on B2139; 9.30 pm; jacket & tie; no smoking; booking: max 8; children: 12+. **Accommodation:** 15 rooms, from £145.

AMBLESIDE, CUMBRIA

Drunken Duck £ 28

Barngates LA22 0NG (01539) 436347

"Gorgeous Lakeland views" and a *"fantastic interior"* have won a *"great name"* for this *"pub and brewery with a restaurant attached"*; it serves *"wholesome"* pub food, prepared *"to a high standard"*. / **Sample dishes:** chicken with sugar snap peas; quail stuffed with mushrooms & prune risotto; lemon torte with spiced oranges. **Details:** 3m from Ambleside, towards Hawkshead; 9 pm; no smoking. **Accommodation:** 11 rooms, from £90 (£65 weekdays).

The Glasshouse £ 32 Ⓐ

Rydal Rd LA22 9AN (01539) 432137

This "smart, restored mill in the heart of the town" – complete with working water wheel – offers a "fantastic" environment; "imaginative" cooking that's "good value" too (particularly at lunch) has won it a strong reputation (although some regulars endured the occasional "awful" experience this year). / **Sample dishes:** deep–fried duck cakes; seared tuna niçoise; chocolate truffle. **Details:** behind Little Bridge House; 10 pm; no Amex; no smoking.

Zeffirelli's £ 21

Compston Rd LA22 9DN (01539) 433845

It's "joined to a cinema", so you can plan a whole evening around a visit to this "wholefood vegetarian", which is always "busy", thanks to the "inventive topped" pizzas and other moderately-priced fare. / **Sample dishes:** polenta with black olive & chilli tapenade; pasta with roasted red peppers & Mascarpone; tiramisu. **Details:** 9.45 pm; D only; no Amex; no smoking.

AMERSHAM, BUCKINGHAMSHIRE 3–2A

Famous Fish £ 28

11 Market Sq HP7 0DF (01494) 728665

It may be "noisy and crowded", but this "fun and different" spot in Old Amersham owes its increasing popularity to its "excellent fresh fish". / **Sample dishes:** prawn kebabs; Cajun cod; crème brûlée. **Details:** in Old Amersham; 10 pm; closed Sun; no smoking; booking essential.

Gilbey's £ 28

1 Market Sq HP7 0DF (01494) 727242

"Reasonably priced wines" (from a "wonderful" list), "attractively served food" and "prompt and unobtrusive service" help make this town-centre bistro a very popular local destination. / **Sample dishes:** smoked fishcakes with basil aioli; roast chicken supreme with Parma ham spaghetti; lemon tart. **Details:** in Old Amersham (1m from Amersham), 5m N of M40, J2; 9.45 pm.

Santhi £ 22 Ⓐ

16 Hill Ave HP6 5BW (01494) 432621

With its "subtle lighting, fountain and trees", this glitzy Indian, near the Metropolitan line station, is a "popular" destination on account of its "well-presented", "reasonably-priced" grub. / **Details:** take A40 to A413 towards Amersham; 10.45 pm; no smoking area.

ANSTRUTHER, FIFE 9–4D

Cellar £ 39 Ⓐ★

24 East Gn KY10 3AA (01333) 310378

"Talented" and "imaginative" fish and seafood cooking makes Peter & Susan Jukes's "relaxed" restaurant of long standing – in the cellar of a 17th-century stone house, behind the Scottish Fisheries museum – a deservedly "well-known" destination. / **Sample dishes:** haddock omelette; roast lobster with herb & garlic butter; crème brûlée. **Details:** in the harbour area; 9.30 pm; closed Mon & Tue L (& Sun in winter); no smoking; children: 8+.

constantly updated at www.hardens.com

Applecross Inn £ 24 ★

Shore St IV54 8LR (01520) 744262

"Fabulous lobster and other fresh seafood" served practically "at the water's edge" rewards those who seek out Judith Fish's (yes, really) inaccessible inn, at the end of one of Scotland's most picturesque drives. / **Sample dishes:** haggis flambéed in Drambuie; king scallops with crispy bacon & garlic; raspberry crannachan. **Details:** off A896, S of Shieldaig; 9 pm; no Amex & no Switch; no smoking. **Accommodation:** 7 rooms, from £50.

Underscar Manor £ 46 A★

CA12 4PH (01768) 775000

"Excellent standards, and you can watch the squirrels perform while you eat" – reports on this "relaxed" country house hotel dining room are all suffused with a "happy" glow, particularly where the "unflashy and unformulaic" modern British cooking is concerned. / **Sample dishes:** wild mushroom risotto with asparagus; braised lamb with soft polenta; lemon tart. **Details:** on A66, 17m W of M6, J40; 8.30 pm; jacket required; no smoking; children: 12+. **Accommodation:** 11 rooms, from £170, incl D.

The Thatched Tavern £ 28

Cheapside Rd SL5 7QG (01344) 620874

For "pleasant, informal dining", this part-thatched 17th-century building, with its "un-mucked-about-with home-cooking", is one of the few choices around this affluent town (perhaps explaining why some find it a little "overpriced"); it continues to generate the odd report of "rude" service. / **Sample dishes:** pan-fried salmon with lemon & herb risotto; roast lamb with mint & rosemary; apple tart & cream. **Value tip:** set 3-crs Sun L £19.50. **Details:** 10 pm.

The Crab & Lobster £ 35 A★★

Dishforth Rd YO7 3QL (01845) 577286

This "incredible" thatched tavern is certainly "not your average pub", and it has a huge following for its "delicious" cooking ("outstanding seafood" in particular) and also its "bizarre" but "lovely" bric-à-brac-filled setting; conditions are "cramped", though, and service can be "slow". / **Sample dishes:** monkfish tortilla; smoked haddock florentine; chocolate torte. **Value tip:** set 4-crs D £22.00 . **Details:** at the junction of Asenby Rd and Topcliffe Rd; 9.30 pm; no smoking in dining room. **Accommodation:** 11 rooms, from £100.

The King's Arms £ 39 A

Market Pl DL8 3HQ (01969) 650258

"Great log fires" contribute to a very "cosy" feeling at this "olde worlde" pub ('The Drovers' in 'All Creatures Great & Small'); the cooking has generally been good but, owing to a recent chef-change, we've left it unrated. / **Sample dishes:** spicy salmon fish cakes; chicken & cheese wrapped in smoked bacon; sticky toffee pudding. **Details:** 9 pm; no Amex; no smoking; children: 12+. **Accommodation:** 11 rooms, from £79.

Rowan Tree £ 31 ★★

Market Pl EH3 9JU (01969) 650536

This "tiny" restaurant (22 seats) is run by a "caring husband-and-wife team"; Mr Wylie's "exciting combinations of ingredients" create "the most memorable evening" and one that doesn't cost the earth. / *Sample dishes:* avocado salad with roasted cashews; lamb on parsnip mash with garlic toast; lemon porridge with raspberries. *Value tip:* 5-crs set D £22.95. *Details:* 4m from Aysgarth faults; 8.30 pm; D only, closed Mon & Sun; no credit cards; no smoking until coffee.

ASTBURY, CHESHIRE 5–3B

Pecks £ 36 ★

Newcastle Rd CW12 4SB (01260) 275161

The combination of a BYO wine policy and a set-price monthly-changing menu of "robust" dishes make this "high-quality" destination one where budgets can be assured. / *Sample dishes:* split pea & mint soup; braised lamb shank with red wine sauce; rum & raisin cheesecake. *Details:* off A34; 8 pm (one sitting only); D only, closed Mon & Sun; no smoking until coffee; booking essential.

AYLESBURY, BUCKINGHAMSHIRE 3–2A

Hartwell House £ 52 🄰

Oxford Rd HP17 8NL (01296) 747444

This part-Jacobean country house set in parkland undoubtedly offers a "beautiful" and "impressive" location; its modern British cooking, however, "does not do justice to the magnificent setting". / *Sample dishes:* char-grilled smoked salmon with fennel; caramelised shallot tart with roasted vegetables; hot chocolate soufflé. *Value tip:* set 2/3-crs L £22/£29. *Details:* 2m W of Aylesbury on A418; 9.45 pm; no Amex; jacket & tie; no smoking in dining room; children: 8+. *Accommodation:* 46 rooms, from £215.

BAKEWELL, DERBYSHIRE 5–2C

Renaissance £ 30 🄰★

Bath St DE45 1BX (01629) 812687

The "brilliant" cooking "echoes the origins of the Norman chef/patron" at this "very pleasant" restaurant, in a converted barn. / *Sample dishes:* lemon salmon with basil sauce; pan-fried scallop salad; crêpes Suzette. *Details:* in Bakewell town centre; 9.30 pm; closed Mon & Sun D; no Amex; no smoking.

BALTIMORE, COUNTY CORK, *EIRE* 10–4A

The Customs House IR £ 27 ★

(028) 20200

"Good" Mediterranean-influenced cooking (with fresh fish the speciality) and a "pleasant" atmosphere win praise for Susan Holland and Ian Parr's restaurant, on the road down to the harbour. / *Sample dishes:* seafood plate; turbot in lemon & olive oil; organic plum & almond tart. *Details:* 10 pm; D only, Wed-Sun; closed Nov-Easter; no credit cards; no smoking; booking: max 6; children: 6+.

BANBURY, OXFORDSHIRE 2–1D

Thai Orchid £ 24 🄰★

56 Northbar St OX16 0TL (01295) 270 833

"Tasty" Thai cooking, "sweet staff" and a "romantic conservatory" setting is an all-round package that has won a wide following for this "exotic" spot by Headington Park. / *Sample dishes:* chicken satay; Thai green chicken curry; chocolate sponge with spiced rum. *Details:* next to St Marys church; 10.30 pm; closed Sat L; no smoking area.

BANGOR, COUNTY DOWN

Shanks £ 45 ★

150 Crawfordsburn Rd BT19 1GB (028) 9185 3313

"Dazzling flavour combinations" along with modern (Conran) design and general "attention to detail" make this a golf club-house dining room with a difference. / **Sample dishes:** grilled lamb fillet with Mediterranean vegetables; steamed brill with leeks, mushrooms & truffle oil; fig puff with lavender ice cream. **Value tip:** set 2-crs L £14.95. **Details:** A2 to Bangor, follow signs for The Blackwood; 10 pm; closed Mon, Sat L & Sun.

BANGOR, GWYNEDD

The Fat Cat Café Bar £ 20

161 High St LL57 1NU (01248) 370445

"A varied and regularly-changing menu" and "consistent standards" of food and service make this "very relaxing" bar and café a local favourite. / **Sample dishes:** Mexican nachos; Fat Cat burger with French fries; Devonshire flan with custard. **Details:** nr Cathedral; 10 pm; closed Sun D; no smoking area; children: discouraged.

BARNARD GATE, OXFORDSHIRE

The Boot Inn £ 29

OX8 6XE (01865) 881231

"Themed around celebrities' footwear" (which some think rather "naff"), this refurbished free house is consistently praised for its "excellent", rather "rustic" cooking. / **Sample dishes:** salmon & crab fishcakes; lamb shank with root vegetable mash; sticky toffee pudding with fudge sauce. **Details:** off A40 between Eynsham & Witney; 9.30 pm; no smoking.

BARTON UPON HUMBER, NORTH LINCOLNSHIRE

Rafters £ 25

24 High St DN18 5PD (01652) 660669

This "small and cosy" market town restaurant comes "highly recommended" by locals for its "attentive, without being intrusive" service, and its "amazing – at the price" English cooking. / **Sample dishes:** grilled goat's cheese with pesto; pan-fried venison with wild mushrooms; meringue & marzipan tower. **Details:** 10 pm; closed Mon & Sun D; smoking in bar area only.

BASINGSTOKE, HAMPSHIRE

Hees Chinese £ 26

23 Westminster Hs RG21 7LS (01256) 464410

It may be quite "small" and "basic", but this "authentic" Chinese restaurant is worth knowing about in this thinly provided area. / **Sample dishes:** crispy seaweed; beef & green peppers in black bean sauce; lychees. **Details:** next to library; 9.30 pm; closed Sun L; children: 6+.

BASLOW, DERBYSHIRE

Fischers at Baslow Hall £ 52 𝔸★★

Calver Rd DE45 1RR (01246) 583259

"All the best elements of a country house hotel" – including "wonderful" cooking, "attentive" service and a "lovely rural setting" – make this Edwardian Gothic pile generally one of the North's most "perfect" venues; there is a minority, though, for whom "it does not live up to its reputation". / **Sample dishes:** roast scallops on ratatouille; roast saddle of lamb with rosemary jus; selection of mini desserts. **Details:** on A623 Stockport Rd, 0.5m past village church; 9.30 pm; closed Sun D; jacket at D; no smoking; children: 12+ after 7 pm. **Accommodation:** 6 rooms, from £100.

George Inn   £ 23

Mill Ln BA2 6TR   (01225) 425079
With its canalside location, this "magnificent old building" makes a good destination "summer and winter"; it offers "real English food" in a "real English pub" environment. / Sample dishes: no starters; salmon with leek & Parmesan risotto; chocolate cake. Details: off Warrinster Road; 9.30 pm; no credit cards; no smoking area; no booking Sun or after 9 pm; children: 14+ in bar.

BATH, BATH & NE SOMERSET   2–2B

Relative to its population, Bath has – thanks to the huge number of affluent residents and visitors – the largest concentration of restaurants in the UK. Many of them may dispense dull tourist fare, but there are also enough good places to provide a variety of interesting meals over a visit lasting several days.

Lettonie has now emerged as one of England's top culinary destinations. Among the other restaurants where the refinement of the cooking might be said to begin to match the city's architecture are the *Olive Tree* and the *Moody Goose*. Pleasant, mid-range places include a notable veggie (*Demuths*), quite a buzzy Cal/Ital (the *Firehouse Rotisserie*), a couple of good Thais (*Mai Thai* and *Sukhothai*), and this year saw the welcome re-opening of the *Hole in the Wall*.

Browns   £ 27

Old Police Station, Orange Grove BA1 1LP
(01225) 461199
Those who like "the usual Browns stuff" – "fans, plants, a wooden floor" – report that the Bath branch of this English brasserie chain is "as expected"; no surprise, then, that the food is "uninspiring" and "variable". / Sample dishes: roasted red peppers; lamb steak with garlic mash; sticky toffee pudding. Value tip: £5 2-crs weekday pre-theatre menu. Details: nr Pulteney Bridge; 11.30 pm; no smoking area; booking: max 8 at weekends.

Clos du Roy   £ 34

1 Seven Dials, Saw Close BA1 1EN   (01225) 444450
Some do report "French food with flair" at this long-established (and, some think, rather "tacky") venue near the Theatre Royal; set menus can offer good value, but standards generally are "below par". / Sample dishes: seafood bisque with anchovy crostini; roast quail stuffed with apricots; iced nougat terrine. Value tip: set 2/3-crs L & pre-theatre £10.95/£13.95, 3-crs Sun L £12.95. Details: 9.30 pm, Fri & Sat 10.30 pm.

Demuths   £ 25   ★★

2 North Parade Pas BA1 1NX   (01225) 446059
"Fantastically varied and delicious veggie food" (with "heavenly puddings" too) makes this "chilled" and "classy" fixture many reporters' "best place in Bath for a lunch or a light supper" – carnivores included. / Sample dishes: Vietnamese spring rolls; Thai green curry; vegan chocolate fudge cake. Details: off Abbey Green; 10 pm; no Amex; no smoking; booking: max 4, Fri & Sat.

Eastern Eye £ 20

8a Quiet St BA1 2JS (01225) 422323

*Reporters agree that this is a consistently "authentic" Indian restaurant, but opinions differ on its spacious new setting – some say it's "lovely", but for others it actually "detracts" from the dining experience. / **Sample dishes:** chicken tikka; spicy fried chicken with Indian cheese sauce; kulfi. **Details:** off Milsom St; 11 pm; no smoking area.*

Firehouse Rotisserie £ 29 ★

2 John St BA1 2JL (01225) 482070

*This "fun", "Californian-style" bistro has an agreeable setting, and its unusual "Cajun grills and pizza" menu is achieved to standards which are well above-average. / **Sample dishes:** Chinese chicken salad; chicken with lemon, thyme & garlic mash; chocolate pecan pie. **Details:** between Milsom St and Queen St; 11 pm; closed Sun.*

Green Street Seafood Café £ 34

6 Green St BA1 2JY (01225) 448707

*On a good day, you get "lovely fresh fish" at this "modern" dining room "over a fish and seafood shop"; there are a number of reports of bad days, however, from people who found it "very over-rated". / **Sample dishes:** grilled sea scallops; mixed fish with saffron & garlic butter; lemon crème brûlée. **Details:** 10 pm; closed Mon & Sun.*

Hole in the Wall £ 34 Ⓐ

16 George St BA1 2EN (01225) 425242

*Relaunched after a period of closure, this venerable "atmospheric cellar" – now decked out in more modern style – remains a "classy, yet friendly" fixture serving a "consistently high-standard" brasserie menu. / **Sample dishes:** warm scallop, bacon & pesto salad; guinea fowl with beetroot & garlic sauce; caramelised pears with coffee ice cream. **Value tip:** 2-crs set L £8. **Details:** 10 pm; closed Sun; no smoking area.*

The Hop Pole £ 25

7 Albion Buildings, Upper Bristol Rd BA1 3AR (01225) 446327

*This "newly reopened pub" of a couple of years standing is "very popular with families and couples", who are attracted by its "limited but good-value" menu, its "great beer" and its "lovely" garden. / **Sample dishes:** goat's cheese with Mediterranean vegetables; tuna steak with new potatoes; bread & butter pudding. **Details:** opp Victoria Park; 9 pm; closed Sun D.*

Lettonie £ 65 Ⓐ★★

35 Kelston Rd BA1 3QH (01225) 446676

*"Forget the overdraft"; for a "perfect treat", Martin and Siân Blunos's "sumptuous" city-fringe mansion, with its "fantastic" cooking, hits the very summit of achievement for the great majority of reporters – one must acknowledge, however, that there's a vociferous (if small) minority which "just can't understand the fuss". / **Sample dishes:** scrambled duck egg & caviar blinis; honey-glazed pork with rich port sauce; chocolate tart with banana ice cream. **Value tip:** set 2-crs L £15. **Details:** 2m W of Bath on A431; 9 pm; closed Mon & Sun; no smoking. **Accommodation:** 4 rooms, from £95.*

Mai Thai £ 21 ★

6 Pierrepont St BA1 1LB (01225) 445557

*"An extensive menu" of dishes that are "full of flavour" attract many positive reports from locals for this "very friendly" Thai; it's a "reasonably priced" place that's "good for a big group". / **Sample dishes:** chicken satay; Thai green chicken curry; banana fritters with ice cream. **Details:** nr Porsche garage; 10.30 pm, Fri & Sat 10.45 pm; children: 9+.*

Moody Goose £ 39 ★
74 Kingsmead Sq BA1 2AB (01225) 466688
Three years in business and this "sedate", but "relaxed and unpretentious", basement venture has settled into a "reliable" stride; Stephen Shore's "beautifully presented" cooking demonstrates "some unusual touches". / **Sample dishes:** scallop tempura with sweet & sour sauce; roast pigeon with foie gras; bitter chocolate & pistachio mousse. **Value tip:** set 2/3-crs L £12/£16. **Details:** down hill from Theatre Royal; 10 pm; closed Sun; no smoking in dining room.

No 5 Bistro £ 33 Ⓐ
5 Argyle St BA2 4BA (01225) 444499
An "old-favourite" of a bistro, near the Pulteney Bridge; the "Anglo-French" cooking doesn't set the world on fire, but fans say it's a "special" place, thanks to its "nice atmosphere" and "good-value" prices ("aided, during the week, by the BYO policy"). / **Sample dishes:** scallop parcels with langoustine bisque; lamb with wild mushroom & Dijon mustard sauce; almond & walnut tart. **Details:** nr Pulteney Bridge; 10 pm, Fri 10.30 pm, Sat 11 pm; closed Mon L & Sun; no smoking.

Olive Tree
Queensberry Hotel £ 38 ★
Russel St BA1 2QF (01225) 447928
"Imaginative" Mediterranean cooking that's "always spot-on" makes this well-known dining room a "favourite eating and watering hole" for its many fans, even if does have a basement setting that's a mite "bland" and "sedate". / **Sample dishes:** scallops with couscous & hollandaise; grilled Cornish lobster with herbs & lemon; raspberry mousse with roast peaches. **Value tip:** set 2/3-crs L £12.50/£14.50. **Details:** nr Assembly Rooms; 10 pm; closed Sun L; no Amex & no Switch; no smoking. **Accommodation:** 29 rooms, from £135.

Rajpoot £ 24
Argyle St BA2 4BA (01225) 466833
The entrance gives little hint of the "ornate" décor of this "mysterious" basement "warren", near the Pulteney Bridge; its "range of delicious Indian dishes" has a big local reputation, but not all readers are persuaded that it's justified. / **Sample dishes:** samosas; chicken mughli; ice cream. **Value tip:** set 3-crs L £6.95. **Details:** 11 pm, Fri & Sat 11.30 pm.

Richmond Arms £ 24 ★
7 Richmond Pl BA1 5PZ (01225) 316725
"Refreshingly different food and atmosphere" are winning new interest in the Cunninghams' Lansdown pub ("more a casual eaterie"), which offers a "varied" menu with a Pacific bias. / **Sample dishes:** Thai fishcakes with chilli peanuts; kangaroo steak with wasabi & ginger sauce; moist orange cake. **Details:** 1m from centre; 8.30 pm, Fri & Sat 9 pm; closed Mon & Sun D; children: 14+.

Sukhothai £ 21 ★
90a Walcot St BA1 5BG (01225) 462463
"The best Thai food outside of Bangkok" (well Bristol, perhaps) wins strong applause from Avon and beyond for this oriental ten-year-old. / **Sample dishes:** chicken satay; Thai green curry; banana fritters. **Details:** 10.30 pm; closed Sun; no smoking area.

constantly updated at www.hardens.com 99

Tilley's Bistro   **£ 29**

3 North Parade Pas BA1 1NX (01225) 484200
Thanks to its "friendly" service and "fresh" cooking, this "small" continental bistro in the heart of the town remains "very popular". / **Sample dishes:** *crab St Malo; pork with Roquefort dressing; clotted cream cheesecake.* **Details:** *10.50 pm; closed Sun L; no Amex; no smoking area.*

Woods   **£ 30**

9-13 Alfred St BA1 2QX (01225) 314812
It's "somewhat ordinary" nowadays and service is "haphazard", but this fixture of over two decades' standing remains one of the city's best known establishments; "good-value lunches" and other set meals are the best bets. / **Sample dishes:** *goat's cheese & apple filo parcel; poached sea bass with wilted spinach; rich amaretto & chocolate torte.* **Value tip:** *set 2-crs L £8.* **Details:** *opp Assembly Rooms; 11 pm; closed Sun D; no Switch.*

BAWTRY, SOUTH YORKSHIRE   5–2D

China Rose   **£ 30**

16 South Parade DN10 6JH (01302) 710461
"A local favourite in the region"; this "large" and "plush" Chinese "may not be cheap", but it offers "consistently good" service and cooking that's "always reliable". / **Sample dishes:** *spare ribs; beef with spring onions & ginger; wine ice-cream.* **Details:** *10.30 pm; no smoking in dining room.*

BEACONSFIELD, BUCKINGHAMSHIRE   3–2A

Leigh House   **£ 30**

53 Wycombe End HP9 1LX (01494) 676348
"A good Chinese, with a touch of class" – it's a "smart" and "friendly" place, and the only reservation is that it can seem a bit "pricey". / **Sample dishes:** *sesame prawn toast; spicy lemon prawns with rice; toffee apples.* **Details:** *10 pm; no smoking area.*

BEAUMARIS, ISLE OF ANGLESEY   4–1C

Ye Olde Bull's Head   **£ 38**   ★

Castle St LL58 8AP (01248) 810329
With its newly-opened brasserie, this historic coaching inn remains a "very enjoyable" stopping-off point for today's traveller; it offers "very enjoyable" and "varied" modern cooking in "good-size portions", both here and in the restaurant. / **Sample dishes:** *air-dried beef with Parmesan shavings; sea bass with basil & orange butter sauce; walnut & stem ginger parfait.* **Details:** *9.30 pm; closed Sun; no smoking; children: 7+.* **Accommodation:** *15 rooms, from £81.*

BEETHAM, CUMBRIA   7–4D

The Wheatsheaf   **£ 26**   ★

LA7 7AL (01539) 562123
"Traditional but up-to-date", this "rural" pub has been "updated without losing its charm", and its "modern" and "interesting" cooking is unanimously approved. / **Sample dishes:** *Roquefort & red plum bruschetta; roast cod with olive oil mash; white chocolate brûlée.* **Details:** *5m N of A6, J35; 9 pm; no Amex; no smoking.* **Accommodation:** *6 rooms, from £50.*

Aldens　　　　　£ 33　　★★
229 Upper Newtownards Rd BT4 3JF   (028) 9065 0079
Who would have guessed this emerging three-year-old used to be a supermarket? – "superb" and "imaginative" modern cooking, "attentive" service and a "lovely", "unstuffy" atmosphere are beginning to make quite a name for the place. / **Sample dishes:** *pan-fried scallops with samphire; rib-eye steak with black pudding; cracked black pepper meringues.* **Details:** *2m from Stormont Buildings; 10 pm, Fri & Sat 11 pm; closed Sat L & Sun; no smoking area.*

Bengal Brasserie　　　　　£ 22　　★
339-341 Ormeau Rd BT7 3GL   (028) 9064 7516
"The best Indian in Belfast" is universally praised for its "delicately spiced" cooking, its "well mannered" service and its "relaxed" atmosphere. / **Sample dishes:** *chicken pakora; chicken tikka masala; ice cream.* **Details:** *11 pm; closed Sun D; no Amex; children: 5+.*

Cayenne　　　　　£ 35
7 Lesley Hs, Shaftesbury Sq BT27 7DB   (028) 9033 1532
Rarely are new 'famous-name'-backed restaurants as dismally received by reporters as TV celeb' Paul Rankin's "funky", "Asian/fusion" relaunch of the once-celebrated Roscoff; "service and quality have nose-dived since the change". / **Sample dishes:** *salt & chilli squid; chicken with avocado & black bean salsa; dark chocolate brownie.* **Value tip:** *set 2/3-crs set L £14.50/£17.50.* **Details:** *nr Botanic Railway Station; 11.15 pm; closed Sat L & Sun; no smoking area.*

Deane's　　　　　£ 33　　★
34-40 Howard St BT1 6PE   (028) 9056 0000
"Busy, bustling" – and, in truth, slightly brassy – this city-centre brasserie offers "really tasty" food that's "well presented" and "quickly served"; enthusiasts judge the results in the fine dining room above (refurbished in late-2000, formula price £50) as "among the best in the UK". / **Sample dishes:** *seafood risotto with lemongrass; duck with spiced pasta & chilli oil; chocolate truffle cake.* **Details:** *nr Grand Opera House; 9.30 pm; closed Sun; no smoking area.*

Nick's Warehouse　　　　　£ 30　　★
35 Hill St BT1 2LB   (028) 9043 9690
For its many fans, this "first, and still best" of Belfast's 'new wave' eateries wins consistent popularity with its "good food given basic treatment"; the "relaxed", "wine-bar part is often full", but upstairs (lunchtime and Saturday night only) there's a more spacious restaurant, suitable for business. / **Sample dishes:** *red lentil & carrot soup; red snapper with vegetable confit; crème brûlée.* **Details:** *behind St Anne's Cathedral, near Waring St; 10 pm; closed Mon D, Sat L & Sun; children: before 9 pm only.*

Suwanna Thai　　　　　£ 24　　★
117 Great Victoria St BT2 7AH   (028) 9043 9007
"Fabulous Thai food" and "impeccable" "traditional" service make this small BYO spot a big local hit. / **Sample dishes:** *Thai bread; Thai green king prawn curry; summer pudding.* **Details:** *10.30 pm, Fri & Sat 11 pm; D only, closed Sun; no Amex; no smoking; bookings taken Mon-Thu only.*

Welcome Chinese　　　　　£ 25　　★
22 Stramills Rd BT9 5AA   (028) 9038 1359
"Chinese waiters with Belfast accents" serve "very good food" at this "solid", "elegant" and "relaxing" oriental. / **Sample dishes:** *BBQ spare ribs; sweet & sour chicken; baked Alaska.* **Details:** *10.45 pm; closed Sat L & Sun L.*

BERKSWELL, WARWICKSHIRE

5–4C

Bear Inn £ 25 ★

Spencer Ln CV7 7BB (01676) 533202
"A big pub that doesn't take bookings, but produces some of the best pub food in the area"; with its "low ceilings and log fires", many find it quite a "stylish" place too. / **Sample dishes:** *fishcakes; minted lamb with lime sauce; gypsy caramel tart.* **Details:** *10 pm; no booking; children: 14+.*

BEVERLEY, EAST RIDING OF YORKSHIRE

6–1A

Wednesdays £ 28 ★

8 Wednesday Mkt HU17 0DH (01482) 869727
"Unfussy dining" (with "good fish specials") and "friendly staff" make this "minimalistic" restaurant highly popular with the locals. / **Sample dishes:** *crispy duck & bacon salad; mixed fish gratin; coconut crème brûlée.* **Details:** *nr Beverley Minster; 9.30 pm; closed Sun L; no Amex; children: 4+ at D.*

BILBOROUGH, NORTH YORKSHIRE

5–1D

Three Hares £ 28

Main St YO23 3PH (01937) 832128
The atmosphere strikes some as a trifle "stuffy", but a "daring" and "reasonably priced" menu commands support for this "busy" pub near York. / **Sample dishes:** *twice-baked Roquefort soufflé; steak with crisp Parmesan polenta; Mascarpone & coffee cheesecake with almond biscotti.* **Details:** *9.15 pm; closed Mon & Sun D; no smoking.*

BIRCHOVER, DERBYSHIRE

5–3C

Druid Inn £ 24

Main St DE4 2BL (01629) 650302
A "massive range" of dishes (including for vegetarians) is to be had from the "enormous blackboard menus" of this "beautiful ivy-covered pub"; portions, likewise, are "huge". / **Sample dishes:** *Buxton blue cheese with apricots; pheasant & venison casserole; brandy snap ice cream.* **Details:** *NE of Ashbourne off B5056; 9 pm; no smoking area; children: 10+.*

BIRDLIP, GLOUCESTERSHIRE

2–2C

Kingshead House £ 39 ★

GL4 8JH (01452) 862299
The cooking is "always reliable", and sometimes comes "with an inventive twist", at the Knock family's "well-run small restaurant"; a "good wine list" is a feature. / **Details:** *off A417; 9.45 pm; closed Mon, Sat L & Sun; no Switch; no smoking during D; children: 9+.* **Accommodation:** *1 room, at about £70.*

BIRKENHEAD, MERSEYSIDE

5–2A

Capitol £ 26 ★

24 Argyle St CH41 6AE (0151) 647 9212
"The many awards for the cooking are deserved", say advocates of this "friendly" Chinese, who praise its "consistently good food" and "efficient" service. / **Sample dishes:** *spare ribs; sweet & sour pork; toffee apples.* **Details:** *11 pm; no smoking area.*

Culinarily speaking, England's second city is slowly beginning to show some signs of life. The first major brasserie, *Le Petit Blanc*, has passed its first anniversary, and it has now been joined by an offshoot of London's *Bank*. It remains the case, however, that the only really satisfactory, central restaurant is the rather glitzy *San Carlo* (or, for a lighter meal, the new *Ikon Café* makes a useful rendezvous).

Brum's greatest culinary claim to fame is still its balti houses, which cluster in the inner suburbs of Moseley and Sparkbrook. For the visitor, they offer an interesting experience which is at least cheap (especially as you take your own booze). We've listed a few of the best examples. The city's most celebrated ethnic restaurant is a minimalist modern Indian, *Shimla Pinks*, though fame does not equate to quality. There is also a Chinatown, but here only the *Chung Ying* duo really stand out.

Those looking for a dinner with a touch of grandeur might like to consider a trip to Sutton Coldfield, where the oldest moated manor-house in England, *New Hall*, offers a venue of some charm. Closer to the centre, *Jonathans* offers an experience whose Victorian aspects some find captivating.

Adils   £ 12   ★
148-150 Stoney Ln B12 8AJ   (0121) 449 0335
"Basic surroundings, but fresh-tasting, individual cooking" make this *"scruffy"* but *"friendly"* balti house *"one of the first and still the best"* for a number of reporters; BYO. / **Sample dishes:** chicken tikka; tropical balti; kulfi. **Details:** 3m from city centre on A41; 12.30 am; no smoking area.

Bank   £ 32
4 Brindley Place B1 2JB   (0121) 633 4466
London's Bank is one of the capital's better very large brasseries, so expectations of its new Brummie branch were high; some have indeed hailed it as "a superb modern dining experience", but there's a deafening flood of complaints from those who find the whole approach "sterile" and "superficial".
/ **Sample dishes:** foie gras with truffle sauce; confit of duck with red cabbage & salsa verde; sticky toffee pudding. **Details:** 11 pm, Fri & Sat 11.30 pm ; closed Sun D; no smoking area.

Beau Thai   £ 28   ★
761 Olde Lode Ln B92 8JE   (0121) 743 5355
"Authentic" Thai cooking and *"attentive"* service from *"congenial hosts"* win a large local following for this small Solihull Thai.
/ **Sample dishes:** king prawns in filo pastry; beef with chilli & basil; fresh fruit. **Details:** 10 pm; closed Mon L, Sat L & Sun; no smoking area.

California Pizza Factory   £ 21
42-44 High St B17 9NE   (0121) 428 2636
"Funky", *"family-friendly"* and *"quite cheap"* – it's no surprise that this *"cheerful"* pizzeria is a popular Harborne stand-by.
/ **Sample dishes:** Chinese chicken salad; pizza Cajun calzone; Oreo cookie cheesecake. **Value tip:** set 3-crs early eve £6.95. **Details:** nr Botanical Gardens, next to Marks & Spencer; 10.45 pm; no Amex; no smoking area.

Chez Jules £ 20 ★

5a Ethel St, off New St B2 4BG (0121) 633 4664

"Tasty filling meals" – and *"three courses for under a tenner"* too – have made this Gallic canteen a consistently popular destination; many reporters recommend the place *"for an excellent night out"*, even though the décor is decidedly *"unpretentious"*. / **Sample dishes:** moules marinière; rib-eye steak with cracked black pepper; crème brûlée. **Value tip:** set 2-crs L £5.90. **Details:** off New Street; 11 pm; closed Sun; no smoking area.

Chez Julien £ 30

1036-1044 Stratford Rd B90 4EE (0121) 744 7232

"Very good lunches" are a highlight of this bourgeois Gallic restaurant (whose *"quality interior"* hides behind an *"unprepossessing façade"*); the place is useful as a refuge from the nearby NEC. / **Sample dishes:** sautéed wild mushrooms; fillet steak with 'maitre d'hotel' sauce; crème brûlée. **Value tip:** set 3-crs L £10, set 3-crs D £13.50. **Details:** nr M42, J4; 10.30 pm; closed Sat L & Sun.

Chung Ying Garden £ 27 ★

17 Thorp St B5 4AT (0121) 666 6622

"The number of local Chinese people populating this restaurant speaks volumes"; this huge and *"busy"*, but *"friendly"* Chinatown emporium serves an *"enormous"* range of *"tasty and filling"* fare (*"excellent dim sum"* in particular); the formula at its nearby sister establishment, the Chung Ying (16-18 Wrottesley St, tel 622 5669) is broadly similar. / **Sample dishes:** spare ribs; beef Cantonese style; ice cream. **Details:** next to Hippodrome Theatre; 11.30 pm; no smoking.

52 Degrees North £ 32

Arcadian Centre, Hurst St B5 4TD (0121) 622 5269

As restaurants go, this trendy global/fusion spot is a real love-it-or-hate-it experience – fans laud *"inventive"* cooking served in an ambience that's *"cool without being posey"*, whereas others complain of a *"totally over-rated"* place where *"our cold, bland food matched the décor nicely"*; as a bar alone, few dispute its good points. / **Sample dishes:** Thai fishcakes; chicken kebabs with couscous; sloe gin pears & brandy snaps. **Details:** opp Hippodrome Theatre; 10.30 pm; D only; children: discouraged.

Giovanni's £ 28

27 Poplar Rd B14 7AA (0121) 443 2391

This Italian near Highbury Park offers *"solid cooking"*; it's best known for its *"very good choice of fish"*. / **Sample dishes:** fish lasagne; chicken in tomato & rosemary sauce; tiramisu. **Value tip:** set 3-crs L £11.80. **Details:** off A435, opp Cross Guns pub; 10.30 pm; closed Mon & Sun.

Henry Wong £ 26 ★

283 High St, Harborne B17 9QH (0121) 427 9799

"A true rose among thorns" – for its many admirers, this is *"the best Chinese in town"*; sited in *"remarkable"* former bank premises in *"old Birmingham"* (ie Harborne), it offers *"high-quality food in good measures"*. / **Sample dishes:** spring rolls & prawn toast; crispy Peking duck with pancakes; toffee bananas. **Details:** close to Bengal Hall; 11 pm; closed Sun; no Amex.

constantly updated at www.hardens.com

Ikon Café   £ 19   ★

Ikon Gallery, B1 2HS   (0121) 248 3226

"Authentic tapas" and *"paella par excellence"* are served in the *"stylish and suave"* surroundings of this city-centre art gallery café; it has quickly attracted a strong following. / **Sample dishes:** calamari; chicken in white white & garlic; ice cream. **Details:** off Broad St; 10.30 pm; closed Mon & Sun D; no Amex; no smoking area; children: before 9 pm only.

Imran's   £ 17

264-266 Ladypool Rd B12 8JU   (0121) 449 6440

"Naans the size of the table, and lots of fresh herbs" make this long-established Sparkbrook balti house *"still No. 1"*, for some reporters; others, though, find it *"rather over-rated"*; BYO. / **Sample dishes:** tandoori chicken; meat & vegetable balti; kulfi. **Details:** opp Training & Development Centre; midnight; no smoking area.

Jonathans   £ 36

16-24 Wolverhampton Rd B68 OLH   (0121) 429 3757

This *"Brummie local hero"* is perhaps best known for the Victorian charms of its décor; many reporters are disappointed by its *"overpriced"* cooking (*"smothered in rich sauces"*), however, and there are those for whom the setting is simply *"kitsch"*. / **Sample dishes:** warm goat's cheese salad; pork bangers & mash; apricot & walnut roly-poly. **Details:** on junction with Hagley Road; 10 pm; closed Sun D; no jeans; no smoking area. **Accommodation:** 48 rooms, from £88.

Jyoti   £ 18   ★

569-571 Stratford Rd B11 4LS   (0121) 766 7199

"Brilliant and so cheap!"; this BYO Sparkhill Gujerati wins numerous hearty endorsements for its vegetarian fare. / **Sample dishes:** vegetable samosas; aubergine curry with pilau rice; kulfi. **Details:** on A34, right opp Lloyds Bank; 9.15 pm; closed Mon, Tue L & Wed L; no Amex; no smoking.

K2   £ 19   ★

107 Alcester Rd B13 8DD   (0121) 449 3883

"Pleasant surroundings and different dishes" makes a winning formula for this *"cosy"* Kashmiri, which offers *"accommodating"* service and quality cooking. / **Sample dishes:** vegetable samosas & onion bhajis; lamb masala & rice; kulfi. **Details:** 2m S of town centre; 11 pm; D only; no Amex & no Switch; no smoking area.

Kabibish   £ 20

29 Woodbridge Rd B13 8EH   (0121) 449 5556

A *"better than average"* Kashmiri, in *"trendy"* Moseley, offering *"solid"* and *"reliable"* dishes, which include an *"interesting"* vegetarian selection. / **Sample dishes:** tandoori fish; chicken masala & coriander naan; pistachio kulfi. **Details:** 11.15 pm; closed Sun D.

Left Bank   £ 39

79 Broad St B15 1AH   (0121) 643 4464

"Good modern European food" is still in short supply in these parts, and some do hail this leading city-centre exponent of the style – housed in a converted banking hall – as a *"fashionable"* venue; unfortunately, though, the approach just strikes some reporters as *"pretentious"*. / **Sample dishes:** langoustine ravioli with shellfish vinaigrette; roast pigeon with cabbage & lentils; trio of brûlées: vanilla, lavender & lemon. **Details:** nr Symphony Hall; 10 pm; closed Sat L & Sun.

constantly updated at www.hardens.com

Maharaja £ 21 ★
23 Hurst St B5 4SA (0121) 622 2641
"I've been going for 20 years and it's always very good" – this
"old-favourite" city-centre spot offers *"consistently the best
conventional Indian food in Brum"*. / **Sample dishes:** onion bhaji;
spiced chicken in yoghurt; kulfi. **Details:** nr Hippodrome; 11 pm; closed Sun.

Le Petit Blanc £ 32
9 Brindley Place B1 2HS (0121) 633 7333
*In the latest offshoot of Raymond Blanc's brasserie chain,
Birmingham has the semblance of a "slick and professional"
modern brasserie; the level of achievement, however – on a par
with its Oxford and Cheltenham siblings – is "only so-so".*
/ **Sample dishes:** garlic & wilted rocket risotto; wild mushroom & spinach
ravioli; strawberry soup & strawberry sorbet. **Details:** facing Ikon Gallery;
11.30 pm; no smoking area.

Rajdoot £ 23 A★
12-22 Albert St B4 7UD (0121) 643 8749
"One of the classier curry houses", this *"friendly"* and
"unhurried" central establishment offers *"high-quality fish and
fowl dishes"*, *"well presented"*, and *"at a reasonable price"*.
/ **Sample dishes:** fish tikka; chicken tikka masala; gulab jaman (Indian
sweets). **Details:** nr Marks and Spencer; 11.15 pm; closed Sat L & Sun.

Restaurant Gilmore £ 33
27 Warstone Ln B18 6JQ (0121) 233 3655
*"It's quietly established itself as the leading Birmingham eating
experience"*, say advocates of Paul and Denise Gilmore's
"discreet" and *"intimate"* restaurant in Hockley's Jewellery
Quarter; competition is hardly intense, though, and the place
doesn't convince all the locals, some of whom think it *"expensive
for what it is"*. / **Sample dishes:** grilled smoked haddock with chive mash;
Scottish beef with black pudding & oyster mushrooms; glazed berries with
passion fruit sherbert. **Value tip:** set 2/3-crs L £12.50/£15.50. **Details:** 400
yds from clock tower; 9.30 pm; closed Mon, Sat L & Sun; no smoking area.

Royal Naim £ 16 ★
417-419 Stratford Rd B11 4JZ (0121) 766 7849
*An "excellent" Sparkhill choice, offering "basic balti, brilliantly
cooked, well presented and cheap"; BYO.* / **Sample dishes:** chicken
tikka; lamb balti; kulfi. **Details:** 2 mins from city centre on A34; midnight.

San Carlo £ 32 A★
4 Temple St B2 5BN (0121) 633 0251
In central Birmingham, "this busy Italian stands out" – a glitzy
trattoria with *"outstanding"* service and a *"delicious and tasty
range of dishes"*. / **Sample dishes:** marinated linguini; pan-fried chicken
& prawns in white wine; coffee & vanilla ice cream. **Details:** behind Cathedral;
10.45 pm; children: 5+.

Shimla Pinks £ 27
214 Broad St B15 1AY (0121) 633 0366
*"Balti goes Beverly Hills"; a "very modern setting" distinguishes
Brum's best-known curry house, and some find its high prices
"worth it for the people-watching and the arty atmosphere";
"arrogant waiting staff" however, strengthen the hand of those
who say the place is "overhyped" and "overpriced".* / **Sample
dishes:** jumbo king prawns; cumin chicken with spinach & cheese; kulfi.
Details: nr Symphony Hall; 11 pm; closed Sat L & Sun L.

Siam Thai £ 25 ★★

7a High St B14 7BB (0121) 444 0906

"Excellent authentic Thai food" is "cooked to order by a Thai grandmother" at this "very personal and individual spot, which is rather "like eating in someone's living room". / **Sample dishes:** Thai chicken satay; king prawn green curry; Thai custard. **Details:** 10.30 pm; D only, closed Mon & Sun; no Amex; booking essential.

BISHOP'S CASTLE, SHROPSHIRE 5–4A

Three Tuns £ 22 Ⓐ

Salop St SY9 5BW (01588) 638797

"A good range" of beers brewed on site complements some very "fresh", traditional cooking at this "genuine old pub". / **Sample dishes:** mixed seafood salad; beef in ale with celeriac mash; apple crumble with cinnamon cream. **Details:** 9 pm, Fri & Sun 9.30 pm; closed Sun D Oct-Easter; no smoking in dining room. **Accommodation:** 4 rooms, from £75.

BISHOPS TACHBROOK, WARWICKSHIRE 5–4C

Mallory Court £ 55

Harbury Ln CV33 9QB (01926) 330214

"Superbly located", luxury country house hotel where Allan Holland's cooking can be "very good"; some, though, do find the overall style of the place rather "heavy" and "pretentious". / **Sample dishes:** lobster salad with crispy bacon; roast pigeon with pickled cabbage & salsify; hot raspberry soufflé. **Value tip:** set 2/3-crs L £21/£28. **Details:** 2m S of Leamington Spa, off B4087; 10 pm, Sat 10.30 pm; no smoking in dining room; children: 9+. **Accommodation:** 18 rooms, from £185.

BISPHAM GREEN, LANCASHIRE 5–1A

Eagle & Child £ 22 Ⓐ★

Maltkiln Ln L40 3SG (01257) 462297

"Home-cooked, imaginative food in good portions" wins a fair number of recommendations for this red brick pub, whose old-fashioned themed interior creates a "good atmosphere"; there's a "fine selection of ales" too. / **Sample dishes:** deep–fried goat's cheese; toasted chicken & red pepper panini; sticky toffee pudding. **Details:** M6, J27 ; 8.15 pm; no Amex; no smoking area.

BLACKPOOL, LANCASHIRE 5–1A

September Brasserie £ 31 ★

15-17 Queen St FY1 1PU (01253) 623282

"Very good and, in the area, outstanding"; this small first-floor restaurant is "a pleasant surprise", offering "uncomplicated but exquisitely prepared fresh food" at "fair prices"; service is "delightful" too. / **Sample dishes:** rillettes of duck; chicken in blackcurrant sauce; white chocolate crème brûlée. **Details:** just past North Pier, opp Senate House; 10 pm; closed Mon & Sun.

BLOCKLEY, GLOUCESTERSHIRE 2–1C

Crown Hotel £ 32

High St GL56 9EX (01386) 700245

"It gets very crowded" at this "lovely" 15th-century coaching inn, whose blackboard menu offers a good range of "tasty" choices; change may be afoot, however, as a new régime was installed shortly after the survey closed. / **Sample dishes:** crispy duck confit with red cabbage marmalade; Moroccan spiced lamb with couscous; chocolate tart & chocolate ice-cream. **Details:** off A44 between Moreton-in-Marsh & Broadway; 10 pm; no Amex; no smoking; children: 10+. **Accommodation:** 21 rooms, from £99.

Church House Inn £ 21

Church St SK10 5PY (01625) 574014
"Cosy and quaint, and with roaring fires" this "olde worlde" boozer offers "copious" and "freshly prepared" food. / **Sample dishes:** garlic mushrooms; steak diane in Dijon mustard sauce; hot almond tart. **Details:** close to Strickley Hall Hotel; 9.30 pm; no Amex; no booking for main bar. **Accommodation:** 5 rooms, from £45.

Devonshire Arms £ 48

Grassington Rd BD23 6AJ (01756) 710441
The ambitious dining room of this imposing coaching inn has not impressed reporters and many complain of a "pretentious" place where "rude" staff serve "dreadful" cooking; a new chef arrived in February 2000, however, so let's hope for more favourable reports next year. / **Sample dishes:** goat's cheese with red onion marmalade; pan-roasted beef with red wine gravy; iced white chocolate nougatine. **Details:** on A59, 5m NE of Skipton; 9.30 pm; D only, ex Sun open L & D; no smoking. **Accommodation:** 41 rooms, from £165.

Strawberry Duck £ 17   A★

Overshores Rd, Turton BL7 OLU (01204) 852013
Duck is indeed served "with strawberry sauce" at this popular boozer, on the Pennines-fringe – a "very traditional and cosy" place, which is widely praised. / **Sample dishes:** deep-fried tiger prawns; slow-roasted lamb shank; sticky toffee pudding. **Details:** 100 yds from Entwistle railway station; 9.30 pm, Sat 10 pm; no Amex. **Accommodation:** 4 rooms, from £45.

Spice Box £ 26   A★

152 High St LS23 6BW (01937) 842 558
This may seem just a "friendly, inexpensive local restaurant" in "cosy" shop-conversion premises, but chef-patron Karl Mainey's "inventive" and "beautifully presented" cooking is "well worth a detour", and all his crew "try hard"; the place "gets booked up weeks ahead". / **Sample dishes:** pan-fried crab cakes; tandoori chicken with lime & lemon rice; apple & caramel tart. **Details:** 2 mins from A1; 9.30 pm; closed Mon L & Sun; no smoking.

Eastwell Manor £ 46

Eastwell Pk TN25 4HR (01233) 213000
No one doubts that this "classy" country house hotel has a "lovely" setting in splendid gardens; some categorise the cooking in its dining room as "exceptional", but it disappoints some, and there are those who dismiss it as "a waste of time". / **Sample dishes:** goat's cheese mousse with red onion dressing; pan-fried plaice with capers, parsley & lemon; apple & calvados cheesecake. **Value tip:** set 2-crs L £10. **Details:** 3m N of Ashford on A251; 10 pm; closed Sun D; no jeans; no smoking in dining room. **Accommodation:** 62 rooms, from £190.

BOURNEMOUTH, DORSET

2–4C

Ocean Palace £ 25 ★

8 Priory Rd BH2 5DG (01202) 559127

"Good and sociable", this Chinese restaurant near the
International Centre benefits from "a lovely airy conservatory".
/ **Sample dishes:** vegetable dumplings; chicken chow mein; ice cream.
Details: 11 pm.

BOWNESS, CUMBRIA

7–3D

Miller Howe £ 48 A★

Rayrigg Rd LA23 1EY (01539) 442536

It has been somewhat "modernised" under new ownership, but –
for almost all reporters – "stunning food and the sun setting over
the lake" remains as compelling a combination as ever at this
"delightfully decadent" country house hotel dining room; the
"theatrical" presentation "enhances the all-round experience".
/ **Sample dishes:** white bean & onion soup; pan-fried cod with aubergines;
lavender panna cotta. **Value tip:** set 3-crs L £15 (Sun £18.50). **Details:** on
A592 between Windermere & Bowness; 8 pm; no smoking; children: 8+.
Accommodation: 12 rooms, from £160, incl D.

Porthole £ 33 A★

3 Ash St LA23 3EB (01539) 442793

The Berton family's long-established town-centre fixture has
a "great local reputation" on account of its "exceptionally
friendly service" and its Mediterranean-influenced cooking that's
"second to none". / **Sample dishes:** red onion tarte tatin; salmon with
herb crust & béarnaise sauce; raspberry pavlova. **Details:** 10.30 pm; closed
Tue & Sat L.

BRADFORD ON AVON, WILTSHIRE

2–2B

Thai Barn £ 25

24 Bridge St BA15 1BY (01225) 866443

The setting – curiously, given the name – is "rather cramped",
but local fans are unanimous in their praise for this "wonderful"
Thai in the centre of town. / **Sample dishes:** prawn fishcakes; Thai
chicken green curry; baked Thai custard. **Value tip:** set 2/3-crs set
L £6.95/£7.95. **Details:** opp Bridge St car park; 10.30 pm; closed Mon & Tue
L; no Amex; no smoking area.

BRADFORD, WEST YORKSHIRE

5–1C

Aagrah £ 23 ★

483 Bradford Rd LS28 8ED (01274) 668818

"Slightly upmarket" from the general run of curry houses, this
"fun" and "comfortable" establishment typifies the attractions of
this well-established, seven-strong group; its "consistently good,
fresh food", includes a number of Kashmiri specialities. / **Sample
dishes:** chicken tikka; chicken & coconut curry; kulfi. **Details:** 7m S of York on
A64; 11.30 pm, Fri & Sat midnight; D only; no smoking area.

Akbars Balti £ 11 A★

1276-1278 Leeds Rd BD3 8LF (01274) 773311

"You need to book a month in advance!", claim fans of what
some say is "the best Indian in Bradford" – it "impresses
everyone", thanks to its "superb" cooking (with "excellent meat
and veggie dishes, and huge naans"), "wonderful" service and
"holiday" atmosphere. / **Sample dishes:** fish pakoras; chicken tikka
& keema balti; carrot halva. **Details:** 12.30 am; D only; no credit cards;
no smoking.

constantly updated at www.hardens.com

Bombay Brasserie £ 18 A★

1 Simes St, off Westgate BD1 3RB (01274) 737564
With its "splendorous décor" and its "top-class" curries, this former chapel – "now converted in OTT style" – "stands out", "even in Bradford". / **Sample dishes:** *lamb, fish & onion tandoori; Bombay lamb with pilau rice; pistachio kulfi.* **Details:** *11 pm; D only; no Amex; no smoking area.*

Karachi £ 11 ★

15-17 Neal St BD5 0BX (01274) 732015
"Splendid curries and excellent value" win many fans for this "utilitarian" and "cutlery-free" zone, where "you struggle to spend £10 for two"; BYO. / **Sample dishes:** *samosas; chicken curry; gulab jaman (Indian sweets).* **Details:** *nr ice skating rink off Little Horton Lane; 1 am; cash only.*

Kashmir £ 11 ★

27 Morley St BD7 1AG (01274) 726513
The "oldest curry house in Bradford" is still "reliably good", and it's "always busy"; you may get "no table cloths, no cutlery and have to bring your own booze", but then "two can eat for under a tenner". / **Sample dishes:** *mushroom bhaji; chicken Kashmiri; rasmalai (cream cheese dessert).* **Details:** *nr Alhambra Theatre; 3 am; no Amex; no smoking area.*

Mumtaz Paan House £ 18 ★★

Great Harton Rd BD7 3HS (01274) 571861
"It has to be magic to be the best in Bradford", and the "simple" Pakistani food "beautifully cooked" and at "very reasonable prices" wins this large curry house a vast following, which even the prohibition on alcohol does does nothing to quell! / **Sample dishes:** *chicken samosa; chicken tikka masala; ice cream.* **Details:** *nr Alhambra Theatre & Photographic Museum; 1 am; no smoking area.*

Nawaab £ 26 ★

32 Manor Rw BD1 4QE (01274) 720371
"It may not be the cheapest or the most authentic place in town", but they "treat you royally" at this relatively smart bank-conversion which – thanks to its "tasty" and "light" curries – is some people's top choice in this curry capital. / **Sample dishes:** *tandoori platter; Nirali special; kulfi.* **Details:** *nr the station; 11 pm; no smoking area.*

Ring O'Bells £ 11 ★

18 Bolton Rd BD1 4DA (01274) 721643
"Is it a pub or a restaurant?" – who knows, but what's clear is that the "gourmet dishes at very reasonable prices" are good enough to keep the place "very, very busy". / **Sample dishes:** *green salad; tuna & sweetcorn melt; no puddings.* **Details:** *nr Foster Square; L only; closed Sat & Sun; no credit cards; no booking; children: not at D.*

BRANSCOMBE, DEVON 2–4A

Masons Arms £ 30 A

Main St EX12 3DJ (01297) 680300
It's the "charming nature" of this "lovely old pub" which is its key attraction, though the "varied" and "substantial" food is quite "OK" too; service "means well", but can be "disorganised". / **Sample dishes:** *deep-fried goat's cheese in beer batter; baked sea bass; spiced apple & sultana flan.* **Details:** *8.45 pm; D only; no smoking; children: 10+.* **Accommodation:** *22 rooms, from £44.*

The Fat Duck   £ 68

1 High St SL6 2AQ   (01628) 580333
*The singular culinary style of Heston Blumenthal's "starkly" converted pub continues to sharply divide reporters – cooking which is "committed", "bold" and even "astonishing" to the converted, just seems "a chef's indulgence" to sceptics; all, however, agree that the place is "expensive". / **Sample dishes:** crab millefeuille with roasted foie gras; salt-crusted veal sweetbreads; rich chocolate cake. **Value tip:** set 3-crs L £23.50. **Details:** 2 miles off M4 J8/9 nr Maidenhead; 9.30 pm, Sat 10 pm; closed Mon & Sun D; no smoking area.*

Fish   £ 30   ★

Old Mill Ln SL6 2BG   (01628) 781111
*"Well-kept real ale" is still on offer here, but the place is "more a restaurant than a pub" nowadays, and – thanks to its "excellent" fish dishes – it "continues to live up to its reputation". / **Sample dishes:** Cornish crab with avocado & dill; poached salmon with saffron mash; chocolate truffle cake. **Details:** 9.15 pm; closed Mon & Sun D; no smoking area; children: 12+ at D.*

Waterside Inn   £ 98   ★

Ferry Rd SL6 2AT   (01628) 620691
*"Still a great experience, especially in the summer" – Michel Roux's long-established Thames-sider is widely praised for "masterful" cooking, "unimprovable" service and a "top location"; a perceptible minority leaves "strangely disappointed", though – some "expected more at the price", and others found it rather "stiff" and reverential ("I felt we were expected to burst into applause"). / **Sample dishes:** crab & langoustine gâteau with caviar; lamb with grain mustard, puff pastry & mushrooms; warm raspberry soufflé. **Value tip:** set 3-crs L Wed-Sat £32. **Details:** off A308 between Windsor & Maidenhead; 10 pm; closed Mon & Tue L (& Sun D, Oct-Apr); children: 12+. **Accommodation:** 9 rooms, from £150.*

The Malt Shovel   £ 18   🄰★

HG3 3BX   (01423) 862929
*"Hard to better in Yorkshire", this popular local occupies a "delightful" converted barn and is "always packed" on account of its "well kept" ales and "good and varied" menu. / **Sample dishes:** seafood salad; fish stew with summer vegetables; sticky toffee pudding. **Details:** off A61, N of Harrogate; 9 pm; closed Mon & Sun D; no credit cards; no booking.*

Riverside   £ 34   ★

West Bay DT6 4EZ   (01308) 422011
*"Outstanding fish and seafood" and a "good wine list" make this "comfortable and informal" café of over thirty years standing an "unbeatable" destination on a "relaxed summer evening". / **Sample dishes:** hot shellfish with chilli sauce; roast brill with crispy spinach & sorrel sauce; coconut rice pudding with mango. **Details:** in centre of West Bay; 9 pm; closed Mon & Sun D; no Amex; smoking discouraged.*

In the diversity of its culinary scene, 'London by the Sea' mimics the capital, though most establishments are comparatively modest in scale. The selection below includes good but quite inexpensive Lebanese, Indian, Thai and Chinese options. Veggies are particularly well served, with the leader of the pack, *Terre à Terre*, being probably the UK's best no-meat restaurant.

In *One Paston Place*, the town has a restaurant of more than local interest. The cooking of a former chef there may be enjoyed at the popular *Gingerman*, whose relatively modest pricing has won it an enthusiastic following. *Quentin's* is a reliable destination.

Al Duomo   £ 17

7 Pavilion Building BN1 1EE   (01273) 326741
"Italy in Brighton", say regulars at this "buzzy" budget spot near the Royal Pavilion, known particularly for its "fab pizzas"; it's generally a "reliable" place, though slip-ups are not unknown. / **Sample dishes:** calamari; margarita pizza; tiramisu. **Details:** 11 pm.

Ashoka   £ 17   ★

95-97 Church Rd BN3 2BA   (01273) 736463
"Well-spiced food in generous portions" and "good waiters" are the stock-in-trade of this "reliable and long-established" Indian, near Hove Town Hall. / **Sample dishes:** lamb kebab; sweet & spicy chicken with pilau rice; gulab jaman (Indian sweets). **Details:** 11.45 pm; no smoking area.

Aumthong Thai   £ 24   ★

60 Western Rd BN3 1JD   (01273) 773922
"The best soups in the world" are particularly enthusiastically endorsed by the local fan club of this "friendly" Thai restaurant in Hove. / **Sample dishes:** spicy prawn cakes; Thai green chicken curry; Thai coconut flan. **Details:** 10.30 pm; closed Mon.

Basketmakers Arms   £ 14   ★

12 Gloucester Rd BN1 4AD   (01273) 689006
"Home-made burgers to die for" and other "top value pub grub" – with "fine ales too" – help make this spot near the railway station an "oasis" for refugees from Saturday shopping. / **Sample dishes:** no starters; herby beefburger with chips; chocolate tart. **Details:** 8.30 pm; closed Sat D & Sun D; no booking; children: before 8 pm only.

Black Chapati   £ 30

12 Circus Pde, New England Rd BN1 4GW
(01273) 699011
"Occasional outbursts from the kitchen" liven up this "café-like" backstreet destination, which has long had a name for its "interesting" Indian-meets-European cooking; the place is "far too cramped", though, and the feeling that it's "not very welcoming" is not uncommon. / **Sample dishes:** grilled mackerel with crispy noodles; five-spice duck with Chinese sausage; Turkish coffee ice-cream. **Details:** 1m N of seafront; 10 pm; D only, closed Mon & Sun; smoking discouraged; booking: max 8.

Bombay Aloo £ 13 ★

39 Ship St BN1 1AB (01273) 771089

"All you can eat for £4.95" exclaim the numerous delighted fans of this *"scrumptious"* vegetarian *"curry buffet"* – an *"interestingly decorated"* place, with *"cheerful"* service. / **Sample dishes:** onion bhaji; mixed vegetable curry with garlic naan; Indian rice pudding. **Value tip:** £4.95 for eat as much as you like buffet. **Details:** 11 pm; no Amex & no Switch; no smoking area; need 6+ to book; children: under 8s eat free.

Browns £ 27

314 Duke Street BN1 1AH (01273) 323501

It's still an *"old favourite"* for many on accounts of its *"nice environment"* and *"good standard fare"*, but – as with the rest of this famous English brasserie chain – its outpost in The Lanes has *"lost some character"* and the *"food is not what it was"*. / **Sample dishes:** traditional fish soup; steak, mushroom & Guinness pie; summer pudding. **Details:** 11.30 pm; no smoking area.

Chilka House £ 15 ★

69 St James St BN2 1PJ (01273) 677085

This *"good, basic Indian"* has something of a name for its *"wide choice of regional cuisine"* – *"top fish and Goan delights"* are specialities. / **Sample dishes:** lamb kofta; Goan curry; home-made ice cream. **Details:** 10 pm; D only; no Switch.

China Garden £ 16 ★

88-90 Preston St BN1 2HG (01273) 325124

Thanks to its *"delicious"*, *"freshly-cooked"* food and *"great dim sum"* (at lunchtimes), this *"classy"* Chinese is an *"always reliable"* recommendation, and one of the most popular places in town. / **Sample dishes:** aromatic duck pancakes; sizzling Cantonese steak; toffee apples. **Details:** on seafront nr Grand Hotel & Metropole; 11 pm.

Cripes! £ 20

7 Victoria Rd BN1 3FS (01273) 327878

"It's amazing what you can do with pancakes"; this *"laid-back"* Breton spot is *"an old friend"* for some reporters – *"intimate"*, *"cosy"* or even *"decadent"*. / **Sample dishes:** dressed salad; spinach & cheese crepe; chocolate brownie. **Details:** nr Powis Square; 11.30 pm; closed Mon; no smoking area; booking: max 16.

Donatello £ 20

1-3 Brighton Pl BN1 1HJ (01273) 775477

This *"rather over-popular"* town-centre Italian is undoubtedly *"cheap"*, but many reporters find that insufficient compensation for its *"unexciting"* cooking and its *"fast and furious"* (*"conveyor-belt"*) service. / **Sample dishes:** Mozzarella, avocado & tomato salad; breaded chicken with tomato spaghetti; tiramisu. **Details:** 11.30 pm; no smoking area.

English's £ 35

29-31 East St BN1 1HL (01273) 327980

It may be *"unique and quaint"*, but this seafood institution in the Lanes gives an overwhelming impression of *"trading on its name and heritage"* – it attracts far too many complaints of *"tasteless"* dishes, *"appalling"* service and *"rip-off"* prices. / **Sample dishes:** squid in provençal sauce with seaweed; swordfish steak with oyster mushrooms; steamed lemon sponge. **Value tip:** set 2-crs L £7.95. **Details:** 10 pm.

Food for Friends £ 16

17-18 Prince Albert St BN1 1HF (01273) 202310

"Recently extended and beautified", this veggie near the Town Hall inspires a lot of feedback; the view that *"for quick and wholesome food, it can't be bettered"* prevails, but a number of critics decry *"dreary"* results and *"poor service"*. / **Sample dishes:** pea & mint soup; cheese strudel with roasted garlic sauce; banoffi pie. **Value tip:** set 2-crs L £3.95. **Details:** 10 pm; no Amex; no smoking area.

La Fourchette £ 31

101 Western Rd BN3 36H (01273) 722556

For its fans, this Gallic two-year-old is already "the best in Brighton" — an *"exciting"* venture with *"fresh"* and *"subtle"* cooking (*"especially seafood"*); even some supporters find it *"overpriced"*, though, and there are numerous complaints regarding *"surly"* service and *"overcrowding"* in a *"noisy"* setting some find plain *"hideous"*. / **Sample dishes:** quail ravioli; confit of duck with fresh vegetables; bitter chocolate tart. **Details:** 10.30 pm; closed Mon L & Sun.

Gars £ 27

19 Prince Albert St BN1 1HF (01273) 321321

"Bustly and fast-moving", this *"upbeat"* Chinese near the seafront remains one of Brighton's most popular orientals on account of its *"friendly"* service and *"reliably good"* chow. / **Sample dishes:** spare ribs, chicken satay & sesame prawns; crispy aromatic duck with pancakes; banana fritters. **Value tip:** set 2-crs L & Sun L £5.95, set 3-crs early eve £10.95. **Details:** beside the Lanes, nr seafront; 11 pm; children: 7+ after 7 pm.

The George £ 21 ★

5 Trafalgar St BN1 4EQ (01273) 681055

"Huge portions" of *"robust"* vegetarian fare make this *"innovative"* pub hugely popular — *"the Sunday nut roasts are great"*, but may require a *"longish wait"*. / **Sample dishes:** tomato & basil soup; wild mushroom fricassée; tarte Tatin. **Details:** close to railway station; 9.30 pm, Fri-Sun 8 pm; no booking Fri-Sun.

Gingerman £ 30 ★★

21a Norfolk Square BN1 2PD (01273) 326688

"Imaginative, precise and flavoursome cooking" — from a *"bright young chef"*, who trained at One Paston Place — makes it worth seeking out this *"small"* (*"cramped"*) and *"friendly"* Lanes restaurant; it *"provides excellent value for money, in some style"* — *"if you can get a booking"*, that is. / **Sample dishes:** crab, tomato & avocado salad; squab pigeon with celeriac purée; orange & saffron crème brûlée. **Value tip:** set 2/3-crs weekday L £12.95/£14.95. **Details:** off Norfolk Square; 10 pm; closed Mon & Sun.

Havana £ 35

33 Duke St BN1 1AG (01273) 773388

If it's true that "the staff change every week", it may explain the perennial lack of consistency in reports on this "nice-looking", "child-friendly" Lanes restaurant; on a good day, you might have a *"perfect"* meal with *"exciting"* modern British cooking — on a bad one, a *"disgraceful"* experience in a place *"with ideas above its station"*. / **Sample dishes:** fish terrine with chestnut sauce; chicken with mash & parsley sauce; iced caramel & praline parfait. **Details:** 10.15 pm, Fri & Sat 10.45 pm; booking: max 14 at weekends; children: 6+ after 6pm; no children in cocktail lounge.

Kambi £ 20

107 Western Rd BN1 2AA   (01273) 327934

This "fun" Lebanese restaurant, near Hove seafront, offers "interesting" and "well-prepared" food, and its BYO policy helps make it a "good-value" destination. / **Sample dishes:** meze; mixed grill; halva. **Details:** 11.30 pm; no Switch.

One Paston Place £ 51 ★★

1 Paston Pl BN2 1HA   (01273) 606933

"Brighton's best restaurant by far" – this Kempstown townhouse, near the seafront, is a "very friendly" place which serves "beautifully executed", quite "rich" modern French food. / **Sample dishes:** scallops & langoustines; rabbit with artichoke mash; blackberries & raspberries with biscuits. **Value tip:** set 2/3-crs L £14.50/£16.50. **Details:** between the pier and the marina; 9.45 pm; closed Mon & Sun; children: 2+.

Quentin's £ 30 ★

42 Western Rd BN3 1JD   (01273) 822734

"Creative twists on simple dishes" using "quality ingredients" win general praise for Quentin Fitch's "small" and "enthusiastic" Hove venture. / **Sample dishes:** black pudding soufflé; sea bass in lemon & butter sauce; apple pie with lavender ice cream. **Value tip:** set 2-crs L £9.95. **Details:** 9.30 pm; closed Mon, Sat L & Sun.

Regency £ 17 ★

131 Kings Rd BN1 2HH   (01273) 325014

"Eat here, and you know you are by the sea" – this "top seafront chippy" is in "cheerful, traditional style", and serves "massive portions" of "exceptionally fresh fish". / **Sample dishes:** deep-fried calamari; haddock & chips; tiramisu. **Details:** opp West Pier; 11 pm; no smoking area. **Accommodation:** 25 rooms, from £40.

Saucy £ 26 ★

8a Church Rd BN3 2FL   (01273) 324080

"It fills a niche locally", say early reporters on this "laid back" Hove restaurant, who hail "brilliant" modern British cooking and a "pleasant", "relaxed" atmosphere. / **Sample dishes:** 'Saucy' fish cakes; bangers & mash; crêpes Suzette. **Details:** 10.30 pm; no Amex.

Strand £ 28 ★

6 Little East St BN1 1HT   (01273) 747096

"Well-presented and creative global cuisine" (from a "varying" menu, with "lots of vegetarian and fish dishes") makes this "relaxed" and "friendly" spot near the Royal Pavilion is a popular local recommendation. / **Sample dishes:** Thai fishcakes; five-spiced rack of lamb; lemon & Mascarpone tart. **Details:** 10 pm; closed Mon L.

Terre à Terre £ 29 ★★

71 East St BN1 1NQ   (01273) 729 051

Arguably the best veggie in the UK, this "fun" Lanes fixture, decked out in vibrant modern style, produces an "excellent variety" of "beautifully presented" dishes with "strong and distinctive flavours"; it's "so popular you must book ahead". / **Sample dishes:** smoked noodle salad; mushroom 'saltimbocca'; blasted bananas & passion fruit. **Details:** 10.30 pm; closed Mon L; no smoking area.

Trogs £ 28
124 Kings Rd BN1 2FA   (01273) 204655
"High-quality" veggie fare, served "nouvelle cuisine"-style, generally makes this basement restaurant (with a "sunny courtyard") a very reliable destination; some "slapdash" meals were recorded this year though. / **Sample dishes:** Caribbean vegetables in rum sauce; Mexican mole with re-fried beans; bitter chocolate tart. **Details:** opp West Pier, by Metropole Hotel; 9.30 pm; no smoking.

Tsing Tao £ 23
33 Preston St BN1 2HP   (01273) 202708
"Excellent-quality dim sum and a good variety on main menu" help make this seafront fixture near the West Pier the place "where the Chinese eat in Brighton". / **Sample dishes:** mixed hor d'oeuvres; aromatic duck; green tea sorbet. **Details:** on seafront nr West Pier; 10.30 pm; children: 10+ at D.

BRINKWORTH, WILTSHIRE 2–2C
The Three Crowns £ 27 ★
The Street SN15 5AF   (01666) 510366
"Adventurous choices for a pub" (including "ostrich, kangaroo and crocodile") help make this hostelry, not far from the M4, "very popular" with those thereabouts; beware – "the locals have the advantage of knowing the best arrival times". / **Sample dishes:** no starters; salmon, monkfish & mussels in Pernod sauce; sticky toffee pudding. **Details:** between Malmesbury and Wootton Bassett on village green; 9.30 pm; no smoking area; no booking.

BRISTOL, CITY OF BRISTOL 2–2B

Bristol has a well-developed restaurant scene. The top end of the market is dominated by two names – *Harveys* and the cheaper but better *Markwicks*. At a slightly lower price-point, the recent *Hotel du Vin et Bistro* has been a welcome addition. Other relatively recent arrivals of note – such as *Glasnost*, the *Primrose Café* and *Tico Tico* – are eclectic going on wacky, but seem none the worse for that. Among the more established places, *Bell's Diner* and *Red Snapper* continue to put in respectable performances.

An unwelcome corollary of the relatively developed local restaurant market is that a number of establishments already seem to have passed through the 'civilisation' phase, and to have embraced 'decadence'. The *River Station* – when it opened, one of the most exciting new restaurants in the country outside London – will, if it continues to slide, join *Byzantium* and the *Glass Boat* in giving the impression of believing that interesting décor or a view is a satisfactory substitute for the provision of quality food and service.

Especially for a port, ethnic restaurants seem rather under-represented, though there are a number of Indians of some note.

Anthem £ 25 Ⓐ
27-29 St Michaels Hl BS2 8DZ   (0117) 929 2834
It's "a lovely place, with great service and sweet little rooms", say fans of this city-centre restaurant, where "imaginative" fusion dishes are the speciality. / **Sample dishes:** terrine of gravadlax & smoked trout; roast duck in star anise & plum sauce; chocolate truffle terrine. **Details:** 10.30 pm; D only, closed Mon & Sun; no Amex.

Belgo £ 26

The Old Granary, Queen Charlotte St BS1 4SB (0117) 905 8000

As at the London originals, "go for the beer, not the food" is the best advice on this "entertaining" Belgian joint; arguably "you can't go wrong with mussels and chips" (the linchpin of the menu) but it's all "a tad expensive". / **Sample dishes:** lobster soup; mussels in Dijon mustard & cream sauce; waffles with Belgian chocolate sauce. **Details:** 11 pm.

Bell's Diner £ 29 ★

1 York Rd BS6 5QB (0117) 924 0357

This "delightful small restaurant" is an "informal", "neighbourhood" favourite offering "thoughtful" cooking (including "a good range of fish and vegetarian options"); after many years in business it's "still a force to be reckoned with", but some find it "less enjoyable" than it was. / **Sample dishes:** grilled squid & chorizo salad; barbecued duck with figs & rocket; peach melba soufflé. **Details:** by Acton St, off A38; 10.30 pm; closed Mon L, Sat L & Sun D; no smoking.

Boston Tea Party £ 19 Ἰ

75 Park St BS1 5PF (0117) 929 8601

This "coffee shop with comfortable sofas and a pretty heated garden" may not have any great culinary ambition, but it's a "lively" and "colourful" place "which makes you forget you're in rainy Bristol". / **Sample dishes:** home-made soup; Thai fishcakes; rum & raisin cheesecake. **Details:** 10 pm, Sun 7 pm, Mon 6 pm; closed Mon D; no smoking.

Browns £ 27

38 Queens Rd BS8 1RE (0117) 930 4777

It may occupy a "fantastic and prominently-situated building", but this huge and "noisy" branch of Bass's English brasserie chain offers the "bland" and "overpriced" fare which has sadly become its hallmark. / **Sample dishes:** duck liver parfait; steak, mushroom & Guinness pie; lemon tart. **Value tip:** set 2-crs pre-theatre £5. **Details:** next to Museum; 11.30 pm; no smoking area.

Brunel Raj £ 18

Waterloo St BS8 4BT (0117) 973 2641

"Consistently good cooking" from a "very large menu" attracts consistent praise from regulars at this "friendly" Clifton Indian. / **Sample dishes:** fish tikka; chicken tikka masala; kulfi. **Details:** 11 pm.

Budokan £ 22 Ἰ★

31 Colston St BS1 (0117) 914 1488

"Modern minimalist decor, interesting food, and a good atmosphere" have made this "excellent-value" central two-year old, with its "Pan-Asian" menu, a big local hit. / **Sample dishes:** Thai fishcakes; Thai green curry; no puddings. **Details:** 5 mins walk from city centre; 11 pm; closed Sun; no Amex; no smoking; booking: min 10.

Byzantium £ 36

2 Port Wall Ln BS1 6NB (0117) 922 1883

"The atmosphere may seem fabulous on arrival", but this opulently furnished venue can sometimes offer "overpriced and boring" food and "forgetful" service – to a degree that some think the place "a disgrace". / **Sample dishes:** mixed hor d'oeuvres; pan-fried mullet with shallots & capers; chocolate cake. **Value tip:** 1-crs meal £10.50. **Details:** nr Temple Meads, opp St Mary's Redcliffe church; 11 pm; D only, closed Sun; no smoking area.

Ganges £ 23

368 Gloucester Rd BS7 8TP (0117) 924 5234

From the outside, this peripherally-located Indian looks very ordinary, but some of the locals say that "good service differentiates it from others", and its cooking is "consistent". / **Sample dishes:** tandoori trout; chicken tikka masala; kulfi. **Details:** on A38, 2m from town centre; 11.30 pm.

Glasnost £ 24 A★★

1 William St BS3 4TU (0117) 972 0938

"Quirky" and "vibrant", this small backstreet venture is carving out an excellent reputation locally with its "consistently fantastic" eclectic cooking (which might extend all the way from "beautifully-cooked kangaroo" to "good vegetarian options"). / **Sample dishes:** mushrooms stuffed with Stilton; pork in Parma ham with peach compote; chocolate & praline soufflé. **Details:** 10 pm; D only, closed Mon & Sun; no Amex.

The Glass Boat £ 34

Welsh Back BS1 4SB (0117) 929 0704

You're "paying for the great location" of this moored boat; otherwise – with its "mediocre" cooking, "uninspiring" environment, and sometimes "arrogant" service – it can be "as disappointing as it is expensive". / **Sample dishes:** roast beef, bean sprout & water chestnut salad; pan-fried grey mullet with cucumber tagliatelle; chocolate & walnut brownie. **Value tip:** set 2-crs L £10.95. **Details:** below Bristol Bridge, 10 mins from Temple Meads; 9.30 pm; closed Sat L & Sun; no smoking area.

Harveys £ 55

12 Denmark St BS1 5DQ (0117) 927 5034

"Classic" or plain "unimaginative"? – reports on this long-established cellar-restaurant remain rather mixed; most find "first-class" cooking in a "unique setting", though reports of "disappointing" or "stuffy" experiences are too numerous to ignore; as you would hope in place owned by the famous sherry shippers, though, the enormous list is an attraction in itself. / **Sample dishes:** smoked salmon millefeuille; pan-fried beef with bacon & stuffed potatoes; spiced crème brûlée. **Value tip:** set 2/3-crs L £14.95/£17.95. **Details:** 9.30 pm; no Switch; no smoking at D.

Hope & Anchor £ 22 A

38 Jacobs Wells Rd (0117) 929 2987

"Everything a pub should be" – this "brilliant" and hugely popular institution wins universal praise for its "massive portions" of "cheap, wholesome" scoff, its "fine range of beers" and its "magical garden". / **Details:** 1.5m from city centre; 9 pm; no credit cards; no booking.

Hotel du Vin et Bistro £ 35 A★

The Sugar Hs, Narrow Lewins Mead BS1 2NU (0117) 925 5577

Housed in the "historic" Sugar House building, this most recent member of the mini-hotel group is "better than Tunbridge Wells or Winchester" (perhaps reflecting a rather greater level of local competition); it's roundly praised for its "French/rustic modern food", "brilliant staff" and "great atmosphere". / **Sample dishes:** skate roulade with lemongrass dressing; pan-fried calves liver & bacon with mash; rice pudding with raspberries. **Details:** 9.45 pm; booking essential in bistro. **Accommodation:** 40 rooms, from £99.

Hullaballoos £ 26

85 Park St BS1 5PJ (0117) 907 7540

"The food is good and the BYO policy keeps costs down", say fans of this "bright", "lively" and "noisy" outpost of an expanding group; there are numerous critics who do find the food "very production line", though. / **Sample dishes:** Thai fishcakes with mango salsa; chicken with mushroom, bacon & sherry sauce; banoffi & butterscotch pie. **Details:** nr University buildings; 10.30 pm; closed Sun D.

Johns £ 23

27 Midland Rd BS2 0JT (0117) 955 0333

"Thai food from an English chef" (and with "English puds" too) is a bit of an oddity, yet John Wright's "relaxed" fixture of over twenty years' standing generally "delivers the goods". / **Sample dishes:** marinated deep-fried prawns; red wine & oyster sauce beef curry; blueberry crème brûlée. **Value tip:** 3-crs set menu is for groups of 10+ only. **Details:** nr Evening Post building; 10 pm; D only, closed Mon; no Amex; no smoking.

Markwicks £ 41 ★★

43 Corn St BS1 1HT (0117) 926 2658

"Intense" but "well balanced" flavours characterise Stephen Markwick's "top-class", "classic-rustic" Gallic fare; it's "a pity the place has no windows" though – perhaps unsurprising in a converted bank vault! – and some do find the smart setting a trifle "restrained and formal"; notable wine list. / **Sample dishes:** smoked eel with potato pancakes; roast lamb with truffle mash & ceps; caramelised tapioca tart. **Value tip:** set 2/3-crs L £14.50/£17.50. **Details:** 10 pm; closed Mon, Sat L & Sun; smoking discouraged.

Melbournes £ 29

74 Park St BS1 5JX (0117) 922 6996

The "BYO option" is a key part of the appeal of this dated-looking French fixture, in the centre of town; some locals find it a "relaxed and excellent" place for a budget meal. / **Sample dishes:** pork & bacon terrine in red wine; chicken stuffed with Somerset brie & basil jus; baked pecan cheesecake. **Details:** nr University; 10.30 pm; D only, closed Sun.

Mud Dock £ 30 Ⓐ

40 The Grove BS1 4RB (0117) 934 9734

"Down-to-earth" cooking and "superb views over the docks" help create a "lively" atmosphere at this elevated café (above a large cycling shop); service, though, can be just appalling. / **Sample dishes:** deep-fried halloumi with sweet chilli sauce; chicken in mustard, honey & ginger sauce; banoffi pie. **Details:** close to the Industrial Museum & Arnold Finney gallery; 10 pm; closed Mon D; no smoking area; booking: max 8, Sat & Sun .

Over The Moon £ 23

117 St George's Rd BS1 5UW (0117) 927 2653

The "fusion" cooking at this "happy" and "cheerful" (if rather "cramped") modern British bistro pleases most, if not all reporters; it's a "friendly" place, though, and quite "original" too. / **Sample dishes:** honey & citrus home-cured salmon; roast chicken stuffed with cream cheese; fresh lemon tart. **Details:** nr Cathedral; 10.30 pm; closed Sat L & Sun; no Amex.

Primrose Café £ 25 𝔸★

1 Boyces Ave BS8 4AA (0117) 946 6577

"Wondrous" fish cooking has created quite a name locally for this "lovely", "zany" little place; during the day, it does "terrific sarnies" and "great cakes" too. / *Sample dishes:* pumpkin tortellini & sage butter sauce; char-grilled sea bass with salsa verde; treacle pudding & liquorice ice cream. *Details:* close to suspension bridge; 9.30 pm; closed Mon D, Tue D, Wed D & Sun D; no Amex; no smoking area; evening bookings only.

Quartier Vert £ 32

85 Whiteladies Rd BS8 2NT (0117) 973 4482

Though ownership remains unchanged, the adoption of a new name – it was formerly Rocinantes – has unsettled reports on this "trendy but ethical" (all-organic) Cliftonian; it's the tapas-style dishes served in the bar which attract most attention, but on these – as on all aspects of the operation – reports have become very mixed. / *Sample dishes:* courgette & rosemary soup; fish soup with red mullet, langoustines & clams; cheesecake with summer berries. *Value tip:* set 2-crs L & Sun L £10.95. *Details:* 10.30 pm.

Rajdoot £ 24

83 Park St BS1 5PJ (0117) 926 8033

It's "classier than average" – and many approve the cooking too – but this long-established "upmarket" Indian strikes some as "a bit subdued" nowadays. / *Sample dishes:* chicken tikka shish kebab; chicken Bombay & pilau rice; kulfi. *Value tip:* two other set menu dinners 3crs £14 / £19.95 with coffee. *Details:* nr University; 11.15 pm; closed Sat L & Sun L.

Red Snapper £ 31 ★

1 Chandos Rd BS6 6PG (0117) 973 7999

Most reporters "can't fault" the "lovely seafood and relaxed atmosphere" of this simply-decorated shop-conversion, near Clifton; one or two, though, find the place "cold" rather than "cosy" and "expected more, given the place's glowing reputation". / *Sample dishes:* marinated anchovy & samphire salad; pan-fried John Dory with capers & fennel; mango & muscat crème brûlée. *Value tip:* set 2/3-crs L & Sun L £10.50/£14. *Details:* on M32, follow signs to BRI Hospital then Redland; 10 pm; closed Mon L & Sun D.

The River Station £ 35

The Grove BS1 4RB (0117) 914 4434

After a promising start, this architecturally "impressive" three-year-old, with the "best setting in Bristol" (a stylishly-converted river police station), is beginning to rely on its location; even fans say the modern cooking "doesn't always come off", and "poor and unhelpful" service "ruined" the experiences of a number of reporters. / *Sample dishes:* seared scallops in red wine & vanilla sauce; roast partridge, bubble & squeak & quinces; sticky toffee pudding. *Value tip:* set 2/3-crs L (in bar) £11.75/£13.75 (Sun L £13.75/£15). *Details:* nr St Mary's Redcliffe Church; 10.30 pm, Fri & Sat 11 pm; closed Sat L; no Amex; no smoking area; no booking for deli bar.

Severnshed £ 23

The Grove, Harbourside BS1 4RB (0117) 925 1212

"Quality food, simply presented with no fuss" makes this "Middle-Eastern-influenced" organic restaurant very popular with some reporters, and they praise its "relaxing atmosphere" and waterside location; others complain of "a long wait" for an "overpriced and tasteless" meal, served in a "low-key" setting. / *Sample dishes:* wheat salad; monkfish with charmoula; baked cheesecake. *Details:* 10.30 pm; no smoking.

Teohs £ 19 ★

28-34 Lower Ashley Rd BS2 9NP (0117) 907 1191

*"It's a fantastic place offering a multiplicity of eastern delights",
say supporters of this "lively", "canteen-style" oriental newcomer,
located a little way from the centre; it has quickly acquired a big
local following.* / **Sample dishes:** *fishcakes & noodles with spicy sauce; king
prawns with fried Thai rice sticks; ice cream.* **Details:** *100 yds on left from
M32, J3; 10.30 pm; closed Mon; no smoking.*

Thai Classic £ 21

87 Whiteladies Rd BS8 2NT (0117) 973 8930

*"Authentic", "beautifully presented" cooking offering "very tasty
Thai and Malaysian options" helps make this "intimate",
if "predictable", Clifton fixture one of the city's most popular
orientals.* / **Sample dishes:** *Thai fishcakes with dipping sauce; steamed fish
& king prawns; mango & sticky rice.* **Details:** *opp Bank of Scotland near the
ABC cinema; 11.30 pm; no smoking area.*

Tico Tico £ 30 ★

24 Alma Vale Rd BS8 2HY (0117) 923 8700

*The "truly worldwide influences" on the cooking at this Clifton
shop-conversion produce some "interesting combinations",
and the results are generally hailed as "first-class".* / **Sample
dishes:** *pumpkin & fennel risotto with fried sage; sea bass in rice paper with
Thai spices; cherry & chocolate mousse cake.* **Details:** *off Whiteladies Road;
10 pm; closed Mon D & Sun; no Amex.*

BRITWELL SALOME, OXFORDSHIRE 2–2D

The Goose £ 37

OX9 5LG (01491) 612304

*Opinions divide on this gentrified pub whose chef-patron used
to cook for the Prince of Wales; for some, it's a "lovely" place
with a "great countryside location" and "excellent" food – for
a vociferous minority, though, it's "totally overpriced and
overhyped".* / **Sample dishes:** *mussel broth with Thai spices; halibut with
leeks & sun-dried tomato pesto; iced banana parfait.* **Details:** *M40, J6 nr
Watlington; 9 pm; closed Mon & Sun D; no Amex; no smoking.*

BROAD HAVEN, PEMBROKESHIRE 4–4B

Druidstone Hotel £ 24 𝔸

Druid Haven SA62 3NE (01437) 781221

*"Beautifully located" in a clifftop position, and with "great views",
Rod and Jane Bell's "informal family hotel" has a loyal fan club
who praise its International cooking, particularly the "top bar
snacks".* / **Sample dishes:** *baked avocado with Stilton; vegetable enchilada
with Monterey Jack cheese; Tia Maria & chocolate tiramisu.* **Details:** *from
B4341 at Broad Haven turn right, then left after1.5m; 9.30 pm; D only Mon-
Sat, L only Sun (reduced opening before & after Christmas).*
Accommodation: *9 self-catering cottage rooms, from £28.50.*

BROADHEMBURY, DEVON 2–4A

Drewe Arms £ 35 𝔸★

EX14 3NF (01404) 841267

*"Exceptional seafood", "very fresh vegetables" and "superb
puddings" are culinary highlights at this consistently excellent
16th-century village inn; it's "small but full of character".* / **Sample
dishes:** *mixed seafood selection; grilled turbot with hollandaise; bread pudding
with whisky butter sauce.* **Details:** *5m from M5, J28, on A373 to Honiton;
9.45 pm; closed Sun D; no Amex; no smoking.*

Lygon Arms £ 56 Ὢ

High St WR12 7DU (01386) 852255
"Tops for olde worlde charm", the Savoy Group's Elizabethan
outpost in the Cotswolds makes a "wonderful venue for
a weekend of luxury and gourmet food"; it's "not cheap",
of course, and some inevitably dismiss its picture book charms as
a "cliché". / **Sample dishes:** grilled sea scallops with pickled cucumber;
aubergine with veal sweetbreads; chocolate crème brûlée & pistachio cookies.
Details: just off A44; 9.15 pm; no smoking; children: 8+.
Accommodation: 65 rooms, from £155.

Simply Poussin £ 34

The Courtyard, Brookley Rd SO42 7RB (01590) 623063
The Aitkens have shifted their long-established restaurant to
nearby Lyndhurst; the family retain ownership of this site which
under their management now aims to offer a simpler, cheaper
menu in a more informal environment. / **Sample dishes:** grilled
seafood with spicy sauce; sautéed beef with rosemary & red wine sauce; hot
passion fruit sorbet. **Details:** behind Bestsellers Bookshop; 9 pm; closed Mon
& Sun; no smoking; children: 8+.

Moghul £ 24

142 Connaught Rd GU24 0AS (01483) 472610
A "good range of dishes" (with much for veggies) makes it
worth knowing about this "decent" local Indian; service may be
"friendly", but it can also be "amateurish" and "slow". / **Sample
dishes:** butterfly king prawns; chicken tikka with pilau rice; honey ice cream.
Details: 5m from centre; 11.15 pm; D only, closed Mon.

Buck Inn £ 29 ★

BD23 5JA (01756) 760228
"Log fires" help impart a "very friendly" ambience to this
"village inn by the village green"; it offers "fantastic food in an
area where you're much more likely to find basic pub fayre".
/ **Sample dishes:** sea bass with roasted red peppers; smoked chicken with
port & thyme jus; crème brûlée. **Details:** take B6265 then B6160 from
Skipton; 9 pm, Fri-Sun 9.30 pm; no Amex; no smoking. **Accommodation:** 14
rooms, from £72.

Lamb at Buckland £ 35

Lamb Ln SN7 8QN (01367) 870484
This "may not be a great pub for pub-like atmosphere", but it's
the "imaginative and well-prepared" cooking here which makes
the place "worth a detour". / **Sample dishes:** grilled goat's cheese with
bacon; warm spiced chicken salad; sticky toffee pudding. **Details:** on A420
between Uxford & Swindon; 9.30 pm; no smoking. **Accommodation:** 4
rooms, from £37.50.

The Lamb   £ 37   A

Sheep St OX18 4LR   (01993) 823155

*"Long may it remain unchanged"; this "small, lively country pub"
in the Cotswolds is a "timeless gem", with a "pretty garden" for
the summer and "log fires" for the winter; the traditional-style
menu is "cooked well", with "brilliant puddings" a highlight.*
/ **Sample dishes:** grilled tiger prawns; Gressingham duck with ginger chutney;
raspberry crème brûlée. **Value tip:** set 3-crs Sun L £20 (including Buck's Fizz).
Details: 9 pm; D only, ex Sun open L & D; no Amex; no smoking.
Accommodation: 15 rooms, from £115.

David Woolley's   £ 29   ★

78 Main St LS29 7BT   (01943) 864602

*Even one reporter who thought Darren Pickup's "original" menu
on the "weird" side rated the modern British cooking as
"first-class" at this well-established restaurant; it's "not overly
expensive", either, and complemented by a "good wine list".*
/ **Sample dishes:** cheese & smoked haddock soufflé; lamb with leeks & spiced
celeriac chips; warm treacle & orange tart. **Details:** 10 pm; closed Sun;
no Amex; no smoking area.

Fishes   £ 29

Market Pl PE31 8HE   (01328) 738588

*A long-established and "really down-to-earth" spot, offering
"good fish", a "decent wine list" and "competent and friendly
service".* / **Sample dishes:** crab soup; skate wings with capers, butter
& lemon; chocolate mousse. **Value tip:** set 2/3-crs L £11.25/£12.75 (Sun
£11.70/£14.75). **Details:** 9 pm, Sat 9.30 pm; closed Mon & Sun L;
no smoking; need 5+ to book; children: not at D.

Hoste Arms   £ 31

The Green PE31 8HD   (01328) 738777

*Many still say this "carefully renovated old inn" offers
"wonderful", "well balanced" menus (including "excellent fresh
fish") at "reasonable prices"; however a growing minority –
perhaps less susceptible to its "Chelsea-on-Sea" charms (though
the coast is, in truth, a few miles away) – find it "not as good as
expected".* / **Sample dishes:** salmon & chilli fishcakes; halibut with Waldorf
salad & beetroot dressing; chocolate & nut brownie. **Details:** 6m W of Wells-
next-the-Sea; 9 pm; no Amex; no smoking area. **Accommodation:** 28 rooms,
from £64.

Red Lion   £ 31   A

BD23 6BU   (01756) 720204

*With its "log fires and panelled bar", this 16th-century building in
"an idyllic Dales village" and "beautifully located by the river
Wharfe" has a "very comfortable", "traditional country inn"
atmosphere; the menu offers a "wide range" of "gourmet" pub
fare.* / **Sample dishes:** fishcakes with salad leaves; roast chicken with winter
vegetables; chocolate sponge. **Details:** 9.30 pm; D only, ex Sun open L & D;
no smoking.

BURPHAM, WEST SUSSEX

3–4A

George & Dragon £ 38
BN18 9RR (01903) 883131
"Beautifully sited in the South Downs", this "good traditional English pub/restaurant" is a popular destination; perhaps that's why a hint of "complacency" occasionally emerges. / **Sample dishes:** roast sea scallop & rocket salad; steak with foie gras pâté & truffle jus; hot chocolate fondant. **Details:** 3m from Arundel station; 9.30 pm; closed Mon-Sat L & Sun D.

BUSHEY, HERTFORDSHIRE

3–2A

St James £ 35
30 High St WD2 3DN (020) 8950 2480
"London-quality food and presentation in the suburbs" wins local praise for this trendy modern spot, even if some visiting metropolitan types find it "quite expensive, for the area". / **Sample dishes:** tiger prawn, chicken & bacon salad; char-grilled tuna with ratatouille; Toblerone cheesecake. **Details:** opp St James Church; 9.45 pm; closed Sun; no smoking area.

CADNAM, HAMPSHIRE

2–3C

White Hart £ 28 ★
Old Romsey Rd SO40 2NP (023) 8081 2277
"Restaurant-standard cooking and presentation" and a "relaxed atmosphere" make Shirley & Peter Palmer's New Forest pub a place worth remembering. / **Sample dishes:** dressed crab with Mediterranean sauce; guinea fowl stuffed with couscous; crêpes Suzette. **Value tip:** 1-crs Sun L £8.95. **Details:** signposted off M27, J1; 9.30 pm; no Amex; no smoking area; booking advisable.

CALVER, DERBYSHIRE

5–2C

Chequers £ 24 Ⓐ
Froggatt Edge, Hope Valley S32 3ZJ (01433) 630231
This "hillside gastropub" welcomes walkers with "great log fires" and quite an "interesting" traditional menu. / **Sample dishes:** smoked duck with gooseberry chutney; baked salmon with Thai vegetables; marble chocolate cheesecake. **Details:** on road between Sheffield & Bakewell; 9 pm; no Amex; no smoking area. **Accommodation:** 6 rooms, from £64.

CAMBRIDGE, CAMBRIDGESHIRE

3–1B

Browns £ 27
23 Trumpington St CB2 1QA (01223) 461655
Some say it's "at least reliable and generally OK", but this "energetic" outpost of Bass's English brasserie chain has "gone downhill" – just like the rest of 'em; still, the dearth of local competition makes it one of the busiest places in town. / **Sample dishes:** roast red peppers; char-grilled lamb steak; crème brûlée. **Details:** opp Fitzwilliam Museum; 11.30 pm; no smoking area.

The Bun Shop £ 19
1 King St CB1 1LH (01223) 366866
"Honest", "well-priced food" in "sizeable portions" makes this pub near Sidney Sussex College worth knowing about in this disappointing and "overpriced" city. / **Sample dishes:** chicken liver pâté; chicken supreme with citrus sauce; sherry trifle with cream. **Details:** next to Sidney Sussex College; 9.30 pm.

Curry Queen £18

106 Mill Rd CB1 2BD (01223) 351027
*Even those who nominate this as "Cambridge's best Indian"
admit it offers "no surprises"; it is "consistent", though,
and service is "friendly". / **Sample dishes:** onion bhaji; chicken tikka
masala; kulfi. **Details:** midnight; no Switch.*

Dojo £16 ★

1-2 Millers Yd, Mill Ln CB2 1RQ (01223) 363471
*"Cambridge's first noodle bar" offers "excellent" and "authentic"
dishes in "big portions"; it's quite a small place, so it's no great
surprise that it has rapidly become "overcrowded". / **Sample
dishes:** tempura prawns with teriyaki sauce; prawn dumplings with pad Thai;
no puddings. **Details:** off Clanlington St; 10.45 pm; no Amex; no smoking;
no booking.*

Free Press £16 Ⓐ

Prospect Rw CB1 1DU (01223) 368337
*This "great smoke-free pub" – one of the more atmospheric in
town – is a "welcoming" place, popular for its "quality
home-cooking". / **Sample dishes:** curried tuna chowder; gammon with
bubble & squeak; apple & blackcurrant crumble. **Details:** in Parkers Peace;
9 pm; closed Sun D; no Amex; no smoking.*

Loch Fyne Oyster Bar £34

37 Trumpington St CB2 1QY (01223) 362433
*Perhaps it is "a breath of fresh air for Cambridge" (not saying too
much), but though some do praise the "excellent range of fish" at
this year-old venture – loosely linked with the famous Scottish
establishment – far too many say it's "nothing like its parent";
"poor service" figures prominently in many reports. / **Sample
dishes:** gravadlax with mustard sauce; halibut with pesto & thyme mash;
raspberry crannachan. **Details:** opp Fitzwilliam Museum; 10 pm;
no smoking in dining room.*

Maharaja £17

9-13 Castle St CB3 0AH (01223) 358399
*"A good range of curries" and "efficient" service are well received
by regulars at this long-established Indian. / **Sample dishes:** chicken
& lamb tikka; chicken jalfrezi; banana fritters. **Details:** midnight; no Switch.*

Michels Brasserie £33

21-24 Northampton St CB3 0AD (01223) 353110
*The food may be "unoriginal and bland", but some still quite like
the "cosy" ambience of this original branch of what is now an
undistinguished chain; set lunches offer "excellent value".
/ **Sample dishes:** pan-fried tiger prawns; roast Welsh lamb; hazelnut
& chocolate bread & butter pudding. **Value tip:** set 2/3-crs L £6.95/£8.45.
Details: close to A1303; 10 pm; no smoking area.*

Midsummer House £60 ★

Midsummer Common CB4 1HA (01223) 369299
*"The current chef has worked wonders"; Daniel Clifford seems to
have banished the previously erratic cooking at "the best
restaurant in Cambridge" – a "delightful Victorian villa" with an
"idyllic setting in a walled garden by the river"; for rather too
many, though, the place's "good potential" is marred by incidents
of "shoddy" and "snotty" service and a "pretentious" attitude.
/ **Sample dishes:** seared scallops with white truffle purée; pigs trotter stuffed
with sweetbreads & morels; chocolate pithiviers with kumquats. **Value tip:** set
2/3-crs L £13.50/£18.50. **Details:** facing University Boathouse; 9.45 pm;
closed Mon, Sat L & Sun D; no jeans; no smoking.*

Peking Restaurant   £ 28   ★

21 Burlieth St CB1 1DG (01223) 354755

"Despite the dodgy décor this place is great (if expensive)" – one reporter speaks for all about this oriental near the Grafton Centre. / **Sample dishes:** chicken satay; Peking duck with pancakes; toffee apples. **Details:** nr Grafton Centre; 10 pm; no credit cards; no smoking area.

Sala Thong   £ 21

35 Newnham Rd CB3 9EY (01223) 323178

"Family-run, small and friendly", this *"solid"* Thai restaurant has quite a following; some find choice *"limited"*, though, and feel that the place is *"a little expensive"* for what it is. / **Sample dishes:** spring rolls; Thai green chicken curry; steamed banana & coconut cream. **Value tip:** set 2-crs early eve £6.50. **Details:** nr mill pond; 9.45 pm; closed Mon; no Amex & no Switch; no smoking.

22 Chesterton Road   £ 34

22 Chesterton Rd CB4 3AX (01223) 351880

There are *"only a few tables"* in the *"intimate"* dining room of this Edwardian house; the modern British menu is quite *"limited"* too, and, though results can be *"wonderful"* and there's a *"good wine selection"*, some do find the place *"expensive"* for what it is. / **Sample dishes:** brochettes of fish with hollandaise sauce; roast lamb with mint & parsley jus; prune tart & praline ice-cream. **Details:** 9.45 pm; D only, closed Mon & Sun; no smoking during D; children: 12+.

Venue   £ 38   𝔸★

66 Regent St CB2 1DP (01223) 367333

A *"fresh approach"* in stodgy old Cantabrigia; this two-year old *"excellent jazz venue"* wins strong praise from the locals for its *"great take on modern British cooking"* and *"fun"* atmosphere. / **Sample dishes:** goat's cheese antipasti; roast duck with olive oil & garlic mash; dark chocolate truffle cake. **Value tip:** set 2-crs pre-theatre £14.50. **Details:** 11 pm; D only; no Amex; no smoking area; no booking.

Wrestlers Pub   £ 18   ★

337 Newmarket Rd CB5 8JE (01223) 566553

"It's not a very posh pub", but *"authentic"*, and *"reasonably priced"* Thai cooking *"makes up for"* the *"rather cheerless"* surroundings of this *"spit and sawdust"* boozer. / **Sample dishes:** prawn crackers; pork in oyster sauce with egg fried noodles; hot bananas, jack fruit & pineapple. **Details:** opp new shopping precinct on Newmarket Rd; 9 pm; no food served on Sunday; no Amex.

CANTERBURY, KENT   3–3D

Augustines   £ 30   ★

1-2 Longport CT1 1PE (01227) 453063

"Stylish food at reasonable prices" – *"all home-cooked"* – is beginning to make a name for Tom and Robert Grimer's small French restaurant; fans say it delivers a *"friendly"* package of *"very high quality"*. / **Sample dishes:** ravioli of skate; roast lamb with redcurrant sauce; lemon tart with raspberry coulis. **Value tip:** 3crs L £8.95. **Details:** nr the Cathedral; 9.30 pm; closed Mon & Sun D; no smoking; booking: max 7; children: no babies.

Cafe des Amis   £ 27   𝔸

95 St Dunstan's St CT2 8AA (01227) 464 390

"A salsa vibrancy" adds zing to this *"fun"* and *"noisy"* hang-out, which offers *"surprisingly good Mexican nosh"* at *"reasonable prices"*. / **Sample dishes:** pan-fried king prawns with garlic; crispy duck burger & mash; pineapple tarte Tatin. **Details:** by Westgate Towers; 10 pm; no smoking area; booking: max 6, Fri & Sat.

Bryn Tyrch £ 21 ★
LL24 0EL (01690) 720223
"Excellent vegetarian food for walkers and climbers" is provided
by this pub in the Snowdonia National Park; it offers *"great views
from the beer-garden"*. / **Sample dishes:** *beer-battered courgettes; carrot,
courgette & lentil pie; bread & butter pudding.* **Details:** *on A5; 9 pm;
no smoking area.* **Accommodation:** *15 rooms, from £19.50.*

CARDIFF, CARDIFF 2–2A

Though it now at last boasts – in Canton's emerging *Gallois* –
a restaurant of some note, what remains striking about
Cardiff's quality restaurant scene is how little of it there is
(idigenous or ethnic).

In the centre, the most notable venture – the enormous
complex which includes *La Brasserie* and *Le Monde* –
succeeds to be what it sets out to be, but its ambitions are
not great. Tides, at the newly-opened St David's Hotel had
the potential to be the destination restaurant the city so
badly needs, but sadly seems to have been on the ebb since
day one.

Down on the the Waterfront, *Woods Brasserie* is the only
destination of note.

Armless Dragon £ 26
97 Wyeverne Rd CF2 4BG (029) 2038 2357
*This cosy backstreet bistro changed hands last year, taking on
a more modern style of cooking; some report "excellent,
innovative" cooking under the new régime, but for a worrying
number of old fans the place is a "former favourite" for whom
the change is nothing short of "a tragedy".* / **Sample dishes:** *goat's
cheese; roast lamb with Mediterranean vegetables; crème brûlée.* **Details:** *off
Salsbury Road; 9.30 pm, Sat 10.30 pm; closed Mon & Sun; no Amex;
no smoking in dining room.*

La Brasserie £ 30
60 St Mary St CF10 1FE (029) 2037 2164
*"An enormous range of freshly cooked, high-quality
ingredients" – you choose them yourself, from the buffet –
is a "straightforward" formula that has made Benigno Martinez's
"vast" and rambling city-centre complex one of Cardiff's best-
known eating places.* / **Sample dishes:** *pint of shrimps; sea bass in lemon
& butter; amaretto mousse.* **Details:** *nr Marriott Hotel; midnight; closed Sun;
no booking.*

Le Cassoulet £ 34
5 Romilly Cr CF11 9NP (029) 2022 1905
*The appeal of this long-established local favourite in Canton
has always been rather traditional; while fans say it still offers
"delicious" and "authentic" Gallic cuisine, for dissenters it's
getting "over-reverent" and "overpriced".* / **Sample dishes:** *wild
mushroom & potato tartlet; confit & pan-fried duck with poached figs;
chocolate marquise.* **Value tip:** *set 2/3-crs L £11.50/£13.50.* **Details:** *10
mins drive W of city centre; 10 pm; closed Mon & Sun.*

Le Gallois **£ 40** ★★

6-10 Romilly Cr CF11 9NR (029) 2034 1264

"Getting better on each visit", this *"superb, unpretentious French restaurant"*, established only a couple of years ago by Graham and Ann Jones, is already *"the best in Cardiff"*; *"it can be a little noisy when it's full – it usually is"*. / *Sample dishes:* roasted foie gras with wild mushroom risotto; roast sea bass with aubergine fritters; crème brûlée. *Value tip:* set 2/3-crs L £10.95/£12.95. *Details:* 1.5m W of Cardiff Castle; 10.30 pm; closed Mon & Sun.

The Greenhouse Café **£ 22** ★

38 Woodville Rd CF24 4EB (029) 2023 5731

Even some local carnivores recommend Ian Young's "vegetarian and seafood café" near the University – it offers a "restricted but versatile" selection of "amazing" dishes, and in "large portions". / *Sample dishes:* roasted vegetables with saffron mayonnaise; spinach cannelloni with walnut sauce; plum & almond tart. *Details:* nr Cardiff University; 10.30 pm; D only, closed Mon & Sun; no Amex.

Happy Gathering **£ 25**

233 Cowbridge Rd East CF11 9AL (029) 2039 7531

"Like a mausoleum when empty, but a fiesta when full"; it's just as well that this *"huge"* establishment – thought by some to be *"the best Chinese in South Wales"* – is *"very popular"*. / *Sample dishes:* chicken satay & crispy seaweed; steamed duck in orange sauce; crispy toffee banana. *Details:* nr the Castle; 10.45 pm.

King Balti **£ 22**

131 Albany Rd CF24 3NS (029) 2048 2890

"American-style service and Indian food" may seem an odd combination, but it wins a very broad following for this *"eccentric"* BYO diner – the city's *"favourite place to eat curry"*. / *Sample dishes:* spiced potatoes with fresh chillies; King Balti speciality chicken 'taka-taka'; Indian ice cream. *Details:* off Newport Road; 11.45 pm; D only; no smoking area.

Le Monde **£ 30**

62 St Mary St CF1 1FE (029) 2038 7376

"Easily the best of the group" – the posher upstairs bit of the complex incorporating La Brasserie and Champers has more of a fish emphasis; it's essentially the same package and at best the food is *"simple and very good"*, but some feel results betray the fact that the cooking is *"by cooks, not chefs"*. / *Sample dishes:* moules marinière; fillet steak with peppercorn sauce; Welsh cheeses. *Details:* midnight; closed Sun; no booking; children: 10+.

Noble House **£ 23**

9-11 St. Davids Hs, Wood St CF1 4ER (029) 2038 8430

"Good food and good value" commend this *"authentic"* Chinese to its local fan club. / *Sample dishes:* beef & chicken satay; crispy duck with fried rice; lemon sorbet. *Value tip:* set 3-crs vegetarian menu £14. *Details:* next to the Millennium stadium; 11 pm.

Tides
St David's Hotel & Spa **£ 37**

Havannah St CF10 5SD (029) 2031 3018

The dining room of this swanky new hotel may have "lovely views across the bay", but has had a less than rapturous reception – "if the rooms are of the same quality as the restaurant, it should have two stars, not five". / *Sample dishes:* goat's cheese soufflé; Brecon venison with two pepper sauce; Welsh whisky parfait. *Value tip:* 3-crs brunch £23. *Details:* M4, J33 then A4232 for 9m, exit by Techniquest & follow signs; 10.30 pm; no jeans or trainers; no smoking area. *Accommodation:* 132 rooms, from £170.

Woods Brasserie £ 38 ★

Pilotage Building, Stuart St CF10 5BW (029) 2049 2400

This "unpretentious" and "good-value" Cardiff Bay spot is one of the few places in the Welsh capital serving "good modern food", and has décor to match. / **Sample dishes:** Thai fishcakes with dipping sauce; grilled Dover sole with chive butter; Eton mess with strawberries. **Details:** in the Inner Harbour; 10 pm; closed Mon & Sun.

CARLTON, NORTH YORKSHIRE 8–4B

Foresters Arms £ 35 ★★

DL8 4BB (01969) 640272

"Unbelievable" food (with "brilliant fish" a speciality) wins rave reviews for this "tiny" 16th-century inn – "superbly located" out in the wilds – from all who comment on it. / **Sample dishes:** smoked fish & mussel chowder; sea bream with onion mash; baked lemon & almond tart. **Details:** in Coverdale, off A684, 5m from Leyburn; 9.30 pm; closed Mon, Tue L & Sun D; no Amex; no smoking area; children: 12+. **Accommodation:** 3 rooms, from £75.

CARTERWAY HEADS, NORTHUMBERLAND 8–3B

Manor House £ 24 ★

DH8 9LX (01207) 255268

A "convivial and welcoming landlord" contributes to the "warm" atmosphere of this "pub with a restaurant attached"; "consistently-good" cooking comes "very reasonably priced". / **Sample dishes:** warm salad of smoked bacon & mushrooms; pork with leeks & juniper sauce; ginger cake. **Details:** A68 just past turn-off for Shotley Bridge; 9.30 pm; no smoking area; children: 9+ at D. **Accommodation:** 4 rooms, from £55.

CARTMEL FELL, CUMBRIA 7–4D

Masons Arms £ 23 Ⓐ★

Strawberry Bank LA11 6NW (01539) 568486

The view from this "inspiring country pub/inn/micro-brewery" is "not to be forgotten", and it offers "wholesome, home-cooked food" and "terrific beers" in a "snug" setting. / **Sample dishes:** local baby shrimp salad; spare ribs with blackcurrant sauce; butterscotch crumble. **Details:** W from Bowland Bridge, off A5074; 8.45 pm; need 12+ to book. **Accommodation:** 6 rooms, from £140 for 3 nights.

CASTLETON, DERBYSHIRE 5–2C

Castle Inn £ 20 ★

Castle St S33 8WG (01433) 620578

"Good, veggie choices" are amongst the "fantastic value" fare that wins widespread praise for this "relaxing" old hotel, in the heart of the Peak District. / **Sample dishes:** field mushrooms with garlic toast; butterfly chicken with tomato risotto; toffee bread & butter pudding. **Details:** 10 pm; no booking. **Accommodation:** 9 rooms, from £50.

George Hotel £ 20 Ⓐ★

Castle St S33 8WG (01433) 620238

"Excellent everything" – "good, traditional countryside fare", "very helpful staff" and a "good range of beers" – wins unanimous approval for this characterful pub/restaurant. / **Sample dishes:** confit of crispy duck with plum sauce; roast lamb with garlic potato patties & shallots; crème brûlée. **Details:** 16m from Sheffield on A625 to Peak District; 10 pm; no Amex.

Creel Inn £ 23 Ⓐ ★

AB39 2UL (01569) 750254

This "cosy inn" has a "stunning clifftop fishing village location" and its "generous" portions of "superb local seafood and farm produce" win strong local support. / **Sample dishes:** fishcakes; halibut in lemon & butter sauce; ice cream. **Details:** 9.30 pm; closed Tue; no Amex; no smoking. **Accommodation:** 2 rooms, from £40.

Caunton Beck £ 30

Main St Caunton NG23 6AB (01636) 636793

It may "not be up to the standard of the Wig & Mitre", but this rural offshoot of the esteemed Lincoln establishment is an "enjoyable" place nonetheless, whose "al fresco" dining possibilities come particularly recommended. / **Sample dishes:** baked Swiss cheese soufflé; fillet steak with bacon & potato cakes; raspberry Mascarpone crème brûlée. **Value tip:** set 2/3-crs L £8/£11. **Details:** 6m NW of Newark past British Sugar factory on A616; 10 pm; no smoking.

Brockencote Hall £ 41 Ⓐ

DY10 4PY (01562) 777876

This "lovely", elegant country house, complete with its own lake, offers "the height of old-fashioned luxury"; the "excellent all-round" formula included some "great" Gallic cooking under the former chef – let's hope new arrival Jerome Barbencon maintains standards. / **Sample dishes:** ravioli of guinea fowl; rare seared tuna with lemon risotto; chocolate croustillant. **Details:** on A448 between Kidderminster & Bromsgrove, just outside village; 9.30 pm; no smoking. **Accommodation:** 17 rooms, from £135.

Gidleigh Park £ 78 ★★

TQ13 8HH (01647) 432367

"A quality treat in deepest Dartmoor"; with its "faultless" French cooking and "lovely country house ambience", Kay and Paul Henderson's famous hotel (set in landscaped gardens on the fringe of the moor) approaches the "heavenly" for most reporters; abandon any images of olde worlde charm, though – the style is comfortable 'Stockbroker Tudor'. / **Sample dishes:** roast scallops with aubergine caviar; beef with roasted shallots; hot raspberry soufflé. **Value tip:** set 2-crs L £22. **Details:** from Chagford, right at Lloyds Bank, take right fork to end of lane; 9 pm; no Amex; no smoking; children: 7+ at D. **Accommodation:** 15 rooms, from £370, incl D.

22 Mill Street £ 36 ★★

22 Mill St TQ13 8AW (01647) 432244

"A delightfully refreshing find in the middle of nowhere"; Duncan Walker used to cook at the famous hotel just down the lane from this "small" and "friendly" village venture, and his "exquisite and exciting cooking" exhibits "Gidleigh Park standards at half the price". / **Sample dishes:** seared tuna with anchovy & quail's egg salad; roast squab pigeon with puréed peas; chocolate & raspberry tart. **Value tip:** set 3-crs L £17. **Details:** from Chagford, right at Lloyds Bank, 150 yds on left; 9 pm; closed Mon L, Tue L & Sun; no Amex; no smoking area; children: 14+. **Accommodation:** 2 rooms, from £45.

Greenhead House £ 40   *A* ★

84 Burncross Rd S35 1SF (0114) 246 9004

"Personal attention to every detail" and "beautiful" cooking are among the features which make Neil & Anne Allen's "comfortable" and "welcoming" house (which has a charming walled garden) a firm favourite for reporters locally. / **Sample dishes:** *baked goat's cheese tartlet; roast lamb with leek strudel; warm damson & apple pie.* **Value tip:** *set 2-crs set L £10.* **Details:** *1m from M1, J35; 9 pm; closed Mon, Tue, Wed L, Sat L & Sun; no smoking; children: 5+.*

Thornbury Hall Rasoi £ 23   *A* ★

Lockwood Rd ST10 2DH (01538) 750831

A "sumptuous" setting "straight out of the Raj" sets the tone at Mr & Mrs Siddique's "individual" Indian, whose "top-quality" cooking includes an "interesting vegetarian selection". / **Sample dishes:** *chicken & lamb kebabs with chickpeas; Thornbury chicken; halva.* **Details:** *nr Alton Towers; 10 pm; no Amex; booking essential at weekends.*

Nutter's £ 38   ★★

Edenfield Rd OL12 7TY (01706) 650167

TV-chef syndrome seems little in evidence at Andrew Nutter's "wonderful", "family-run" pub-conversion, where "super" food is "beautifully presented" by "unobtrusive but attentive" staff; the "wild moorland location adds to the ambience". / **Sample dishes:** *crispy black pudding wontons; lamb in wild mushroom crust with tomato jus; banana Tatin with Mascarpone.* **Value tip:** *set 3-crs Sun L £19.95.* **Details:** *between Edenfield and Nordon on A680; 9.30 pm; closed Tue; no smoking.*

Siam Cottage £ 26

44 Moulsham St CM2 OHY (01245) 352245

It may have "low-key atmosphere and décor", but "the best Thai in town" is certainly a "useful"-enough place. / **Sample dishes:** *spring rolls; chicken with cashew nuts; ice cream.* **Details:** *10.30 pm; closed Sun L; no Amex.*

Champignon Sauvage £ 51   ★

24-26 Suffolk Rd GL50 2AQ (01242) 573449

"Extremely subtle and refined" Gallic cooking – with "excellent use of fine ingredients" – makes a visit to David and Helen Everitt-Matthias's small and "friendly" dining room a "memorable" experience; it's "extremely reliable and consistent". / **Sample dishes:** *roasted foie gras & quinces; pork with home-made black pudding; fig tarte Tatin with spiced bread ice cream.* **Value tip:** *set 2/3-crs D (Tue-Fri only) £16.50/£19.95.* **Details:** *on A40 to Oxford, nr Boys' College; 9.15 pm; closed Mon & Sun; no smoking before 10.30 pm.*

Daffodil   **£ 24**   A

18-20 Suffolk Parade GL50 2AE (01242) 700055

"A waste of potential"; the only sure reason to visit this
"idiosyncratic" venture is "to soak up this former cinema's
Art Deco architecture" which creates a "super atmosphere" –
you dine watching the kitchen operate where the screen used to
be; the cooking is no more than "adequate" and service often
"fumbling". / *Sample dishes:* wild mushrooms in garlic; medallions of pork
with apple confit; chocolate cake. *Details: just off Suffolk Square; 10.30 pm;
closed Sun; no smoking area.*

Mayflower   **£ 26**   ★

32-34 Clarence St GL50 3NX (01242) 522426

"Light and tasty" cooking (with "good vegetarian options") makes
Mr and Mrs Kong's "traditional, good-quality" Chinese of long
standing a consistently popular destination. / *Sample
dishes:* deep–fried prawn rolls; Szechuan chicken; toffee bananas.
Details: between bus station & Boots; 10 pm; closed Sun L.

Le Petit Blanc   **£ 32**

Queen's Hotel, Promenade GL50 1NN (01242) 266800

It has fans who proclaim its "great food" and "London
atmosphere", but almost as many reporters find fault with this
town-centre brasserie – is the association with Raymond Blanc
really supposed to be sufficient compensation for "very average"
cooking and sometimes "off-hand" service? / *Sample dishes:* deep-
fried goat's cheese with tomato chutney; pan-fried calves liver & onions;
'floating island' dessert. *Details: in Montpellier; 10.30 pm;
no smoking in dining room.*

Ruby   **£ 27**   ★

52 Suffolk Rd GL50 2AQ (01242) 250909

"Cheltenham's foremost Chinese restaurant", say fans, is
a consistent spot, delivering "above-average Cantonese cooking"
and notably "charming" service. / *Sample dishes:* crispy aromatic
duck; stir-fried monkfish; toffee bananas. *Details: nr Cheltenham Boys College;
11.30 pm; no smoking area.*

Storyteller   **£ 28**   A

11 North Pl GL50 4DW (01242) 250343

"Daring" interior design and "interesting" fusion cooking are
beginning to create quite a name for this "cool" spot as
a "good-value and fun place to eat". / *Sample dishes:* bacon & prawn
quesadillas; seafood platter with vegetables; chocolate mousse cake.
Details: 10 pm.

CHESTER, CHESHIRE   5–2A

Albion Inn   **£ 18**   A

Park St CH1 1RN (01244) 340345

"Pub grub of a high standard" – and in "monster" portions too –
helps make this "idiosyncratic", "olde worlde" pub, a short walk
from the Newgate, a popular destination. / *Sample dishes:* no
starters; braised liver & onions; bread & butter pudding. *Details: between
Eastgate clock & the river; 8 pm; closed Mon D; no credit cards; booking: need
6+ to book; children: discouraged.*

Arkle
Chester Grosvenor Hotel £ 61

Eastgate CH1 1LT (01244) 324024

*Some find the dining room of this grand city-centre hotel an "elegant" affair, and it's long had a reputation for its cooking; "at the price, you expect something special", though, and rather too many reporters don't find it. / **Sample dishes:** scallops with cauliflower cream & truffle oil; turbot with mushroom tortellini & Madeira jus; coconut truffle with spiced Thai syrup. **Value tip:** set 2/3-crs L £20/£25. **Details:** by the Eastgate Clock; 9.30 pm; closed Mon & Sun; jacket & tie; no smoking. **Accommodation:** 85 rooms, from £195.*

Blue Bell £ 35 Ⓐ

Northgate St CH1 2HQ (01244) 317758

*This "lovely", "traditional" pub, near the Northgate, wins praise from all over the country with its "good all-round, and reasonably priced" cooking and its "crowded and friendly" setting. / **Sample dishes:** Toulouse sausage pancake; lemon sole stuffed with salmon & spinach; chocolate truffle cheesecake. **Details:** 9.45 pm; no Amex; no smoking.*

The Fat Cat Café Bar £ 20 Ⓐ

85 Watergate St CH1 2LF (01244) 316100

*A "busy, young atmosphere" and a menu which offers "something for everyone" make this outpost of a mini-chain a "relaxed and good-value" choice in an under-provided city. / **Sample dishes:** Mexican nachos; Fat Cat burger with French fries; Devonshire flan with custard. **Details:** follow signs to the racecourse; 10 pm; closed Sun D; no smoking area; children: discouraged.*

Francs £ 23

14 Cuppin St CH1 2BN (01244) 317952

*"French provincial food of good quality" has made this "reasonably priced" bistro a "bustling", hugely popular stand-by in an under-provided city; "excellent prix-fixe menus" (at lunch and early-evening) are a particular hit. / **Sample dishes:** garlic mushrooms; chicken & Mozzarella in tomato sauce; summer fruits. **Details:** just off Bridge St; 11 pm; no smoking.*

CHICHESTER, WEST SUSSEX 3–4A

Comme Ça £ 29 Ⓐ★

67 Broyle Rd BO19 4BD (01243) 788724

*"Imaginative" Anglo-French food, "amiable" service and "lovely surroundings" make this "excellent small dining room", in a converted pub, a top local recommendation. / **Sample dishes:** eggs Benedict; salmon in lemon & butter sauce; summer pudding. **Value tip:** set 2-crs L £15.95. **Details:** 0.5m N of city centre; 10.30 pm; closed Mon & Sun D; no smoking area.*

CHIDHAM, WEST SUSSEX 3–4A

Old House at Home £ 27 Ⓐ

Cot Ln TO18 8SU (01243) 572477

*The "great eccentric landlord" "truly does create a home-from-home sort of feeling" at this "unpretentious" inn, whose "delicious pub food is better than at many restaurants". / **Sample dishes:** crab with beanshoot salad; lamb shank with fresh vegetables; Belgian chocolate torte. **Details:** 9.30 pm; booking: max 6 at weekends.*

constantly updated at www.hardens.com 133

White Horse £ 35

High St PO18 9HX (01243) 535219
This South Downs pub is known for "the best wine cellar in the South", and has a wine list running to several hundred bins; it offers "excellent bar snacks" to complement the vino. / **Sample dishes:** *calves liver salad; sea bass in lemon & butter; cheese & biscuits.* **Value tip:** *set 2-crs Sun L £14.* **Details:** *8m NW of Chichester on B2141; 10 pm; closed Sun D; no smoking area.* **Accommodation:** *5 rooms, from £70.*

Griffins Head £ 25 ★

CT3 1PS (01304) 840325
This "lovely", medieval country inn is "reliably above average", and offers a "great" traditional menu of "freshly cooked pub food". / **Sample dishes:** *warm salad of brie & bacon; liver & bacon with mash; raspberry & almond tart.* **Details:** *3m outside Wingham, 10 mins from A2 to Dover; 9.30 pm; closed Sun D; children: 10+.*

Sir Charles Napier £ 38 Ⓐ

Spriggs Alley OX9 4BX (01494) 483011
With its "beautiful setting in the Chilterns", this "family-run", "Bohemian-chic" fixture is, say fans, well "worth the trek", thanks to its "delightfully relaxed" atmosphere and "interesting" cooking; it also has a fair number of critics, though, who find the attitude "snobby" and the culinary style "pretentious". / **Sample dishes:** *wild mushroom risotto; roast partridge with rosti potatoes & grapes; vanilla crème brûlée.* **Value tip:** *set 2-crs L £14.50.* **Details:** *M40, J6 into Chinnor, turn right at roundabout; 10 pm; closed Mon & Sun D; no smoking area; children: 6+ at D.*

Eight Bells £ 29

Church St GL55 6JG (01386) 840371
"Good and inventive pub food" is served in a "lovely olde worlde setting" at this "friendly" 14th-century stone pub, in a charming Cotswolds village. / **Sample dishes:** *hot cheese fritters with mustard mayonnaise; pan-fried beef with smoked bacon & croutons; lemon & lime tarts.* **Details:** *9 pm, Fri & Sat 9.30 pm; no smoking area.* **Accommodation:** *6 rooms, from £60.*

Chavignol £ 55 ★★

7 Horsefair OX7 5AL (01608) 644490
Marcus Ashenford's "amazing" cooking – with "excellent" presentation and a "great wine list" too – creates practically unanimous satisfaction with this "tiny" year-old "tea-room-turned-restaurant", on the town's market square. / **Sample dishes:** *smoked haddock with chives; sautéed turkey in a cream & citrus sauce; pan-fried peaches with ice cream.* **Value tip:** *set 3-crs L £25.* **Details:** *9.45 pm; closed Mon & Sun; no smoking.*

CHOBHAM, SURREY

Quails £ 31

1 Bagshot Rd GU24 8BP (01276) 858491

Occupying a neo-Georgian building in the centre of the town, this is a "quietly restrained" spot; most find the modern British cooking "imaginative" and "reasonably priced", but not everyone is convinced. / **Sample dishes:** *char-grilled smoked salmon with basil oil; monkfish & king prawn risotto with mango salsa; chocolate pudding with saffron ice cream.* **Value tip:** *set 2/3-crs set L £11.95/14.95.* **Details:** *2m SE of M3, J3; 9.30 pm; closed Mon, Sat L & Sun.*

CHURCH HANBOROUGH, OXFORDSHIRE

Hand & Shears £ 30

OX8 8AB (01993) 883337

With its large rear conservatory restaurant, this agreeable pub, a short drive from Oxford, makes a good place "to chill out"; it serves an unexceptional but perfectly adequate International menu. / **Sample dishes:** *Caesar salad; aromatic duck with fresh vegetables; crème brûlée.* **Details:** *follow signs from A40; 9 pm; no smoking.*

CLACHAN, ARGYLL & BUTE

Loch Fyne Oyster Bar £ 27 𝔸★

PA26 8BL (01499) 600236

"Superb fresh seafood" – "cooked simply but well" – and "wonderful views" have won some fame for this isolated but "friendly" spot (which has inspired the creation of a national chain, under separate ownership); book ahead to ensure dinner-time opening. / **Sample dishes:** *oysters; shellfish platter; banoffi pie.* **Details:** *10m E of Inveraray on A83; 8.30 pm; Nov-Mar D only; no smoking area.*

CLAVERING, ESSEX

The Cricketers £ 28 𝔸★

Wicken Rd CB11 4QT (01799) 550442

This "true country pub" – where, indeed, "you can sit outside and watch the cricket" – serves an "imaginative" and "regularly-changing" menu of "good wholesome cooking". / **Sample dishes:** *tuna in nori seaweed; steak, kidney & ale pie; chocolate cheesecake.* **Details:** *on B1038 between Newport & Buntingford; 9.45 pm; closed Sun D; smoking in bar only.* **Accommodation:** *8 rooms, from £90.*

CLAYGATE, SURREY

Le Petit Pierrot £ 30 ★

4 The Parade KT10 0NU (01372) 465105

This "great little restaurant" is run by a French husband-and-wife team in shop-conversion premises; it provides an "intimate" setting – "don't take noisy friends" – in which to enjoy "good food at a reasonable price". / **Sample dishes:** *crab parcels; calves liver with raspberry vinegar; crème brûlée.* **Details:** *nr station; 9.30 pm; closed Sat L & Sun; children: 8+.*

CLENT, WORCESTERSHIRE

The Fountain Inn £ 25 ★

Adams HI DY9 9PU (01562) 883286

This "pleasant beamed pub" – now a couple of years into its present ownership – is beginning to make quite a name for its eclectic "restaurant-quality" cooking. / **Sample dishes:** *deep-fried chicken liver paté filo parcels; fillet steak with French fries & salad; crème brûlée.* **Details:** *9.30 pm; no Amex; no smoking area.*

CLEOBURY MORTIMER, SHROPSHIRE 5–4B

Spice Empire £ 17 ★

17 High St DY14 8DG (01299) 270419
With its "wonderful combinations of spices", this "innovative,
high-quality" Indian comes as "something of a surprise, in this
small Shropshire town". / **Sample dishes:** spiced potato samosas; chicken
tikka; banana fritters. **Details:** 11 pm; closed Mon.

CLEVEDON, NORTH SOMERSET 2–2A

Junior Poon £ 31 ★

16 Hill Rd BS21 7NZ (01275) 341900
"Smart", "friendly" and "consistently good" – local fans find no
flaws in this "high-quality" pier-side Chinese. / **Sample
dishes:** blackened tiger prawns in garlic butter sauce; Peking aromatic duck;
lychee fritters. **Details:** nr Clevedon Pier; 10 pm; D only, closed Sun; no jeans
or trainers.

CLIPSHAM, RUTLAND 6–4A

Olive Branch £ 28 🅐★

Main St LE15 7SH (01780) 410355
"Worth a major detour" says a (London) reporter regarding this
"excellent new gastropub" – a "beautiful" building, where you get
"Hambleton Hall cooking at pub prices" (and the chef did indeed
formerly cook there). / **Sample dishes:** baked goat's cheese with crushed
nuts; sea bream with saffron tagliatelle; bread & butter pudding. **Details:** 2
miles off the A1; 9.30 pm; closed Mon & Sun D; no Amex.

CLITHEROE, LANCASHIRE 5–1B

Inn at Whitewell £ 33 🅐★★

Forest of Bowland BD7 3AT (01200) 448222
"Stunning food in a stunning location" – overlooking the River
Hodder, in the Forest of Bowland – wins amazingly consistent
praise for this famous and secluded "refuge from the modern
world"; those wanting a "lovely and romantic" weekend should
book about six months ahead. / **Sample dishes:** warm smoked haddock
tartlet; roast Bowland lamb; passion fruit cake. **Details:** nr Bruwsholme Hall;
9.30 pm; bar meals only at L. **Accommodation:** 17 rooms, from £80.

CLYTHA, MONMOUTHSHIRE 2–2A

Clytha Arms £ 33 ★

NP7 9BW (01873) 840206
Andrew Canning's "nice, small pub and restaurant" (with rooms)
comes "highly recommended" for its "lovingly produced" menu;
"the seafood is especially good, as is the selection of beers".
/ **Sample dishes:** laverbread with bacon & cockles; monkfish with ham
& leeks; Sauternes cream with spiced prunes. **Value tip:** set 3-crs Sun
L £14.95. **Details:** on Old Abergavenny Road; 9.30 pm; closed Mon D & Sun
D; no smoking. **Accommodation:** 4 rooms, from £50.

COBHAM, SURREY 3–3A

La Capanna £ 36

48 High St KT11 3EF (01932) 862121
"I thought I'd gone back to the '70s in a time-machine!" – even
some who say this "crowded" Italian is "still good" agree that the
whole approach could now "do with a freshening up". / **Sample
dishes:** fresh crab salad; veal & scallops in cream & mushroom sauce;
profiteroles. **Value tip:** set 3-crs L £14.95. **Details:** 10.45 pm; closed Sat L

Cricketers £ 37

Downside Common Rd KT11 4NX (01932) 862105

"Get there early if you don't want to stand"; "the queues themselves are an indication" of the "good pub food and beer" served at this "busy" boozer. / Sample dishes: smoked haddock & salmon with poached egg; roast lamb with garlic & rosemary; fresh cheesecake. Details: 2m from Cobham High St; 10 pm; no smoking area.

COCKERMOUTH, CUMBRIA 7–3C

Quince & Medlar £ 22 A★

13 Castlegate CA13 9EU (01900) 823579

"Vegetarian cuisine of superb quality" – and from an "innovative" menu too – makes it well worth seeking out the panelled dining room of Colin and Louisa Le Voi's Georgian house. / Sample dishes: poached pear with pickled walnuts; Stilton & celeriac crown; rich chocolate cake. Details: next to Cockermouth Castle; 9.30 pm; D only, closed Mon & Sun; no Amex & no Switch; no smoking; children: 5+.

COLCHESTER, ESSEX 3–2C

Warehouse £ 23

12 Chapel Street North CO2 7AT (01206) 765656

"A change of ownership has seen standards slip all round" at this formerly popular bistro – the food is now "poor" and "overpriced", and portions are "very small". / Sample dishes: crispy duck rolls; pork roulade; almond tart. Value tip: 4-crs L £7.95, 5-crs D £14.95. Details: nr St Johns St; 10 pm; closed Sun D; no Amex; no smoking area.

COLERNE, WILTSHIRE 2–2B

Lucknam Park £ 70 A★

SN14 8AZ (01225) 742777

You wouldn't expect the dining-room of a "fabulous small Georgian manor, converted to an hotel, within a stud farm" to be especially cheap, and it isn't – feedback is consistent, however, that a visit here is "worth it". / Sample dishes: roast quail salad with truffle ravioli; pan-fried sea bass with roasted vegetables; trio of chocolate mousses. Value tip: set 3-crs Sun L £25. Details: 6m NE of Bath, 10 mins from M4 J17; 9.30 pm; D only, ex Sun open L & D; jacket & tie; no smoking; children: 12+ at D. Accommodation: 41 rooms, from £190.

COLN ST ALDWYNS, GLOUCESTERSHIRE 2–2C

New Inn at Coln £ 38 ★

GL7 5AN (01285) 750651

"A hidden gem, whisper it only to your closest friends" – this "archetypal village pub with open fires, good beer" and a "pretty" location also offers a "consistently high standard" of "gourmet-style" food. / Sample dishes: pan-fried salmon with buttered noodles; lamb with lentils & rosemary jus; pancakes with plums & kirsh. Details: off B4425 between Cirencester to Burford road, 2 miles SW of Bibury; 9 pm, Fri & Sat 9.30 pm; no smoking; children: 10+. Accommodation: 14 rooms, from £80.

COLSTON BASSET, NOTTINGHAMSHIRE 5–3D

Martins Arms Inn £ 38 A

School Ln NG12 3FD (01949) 81361

This "beautiful and unspoilt country pub" enjoys "an idyllic setting"; its "varied" cooking makes it "a trusty favourite" for many reporters, but critics find quality "inconsistent" and prices "OTT". / Sample dishes: roasted asparagus & Parma ham fettuccine; duck with sweet potato pancakes & tamarind sauce; white chocolate marquise. Details: 2 miles off A46; 9.30 pm; closed Sun D; no Amex; children: 14+.

COMPTON, SURREY

Withies £ 37 𝔸

Withies Ln GU3 1JA (01483) 421158

It's "not always consistent", but on a good day this "fabulous", beamed building (a former pub) offers "good", "traditional" cooking; "dining outside in summer is a delight". / **Sample dishes:** seafood platter; duck with cranberry sauce; bread & butter pudding. **Details:** 10 pm; closed Sun D; booking essential.

CONSTANTINE, CORNWALL

1–4B

Trengilly Wartha Inn £ 34

Nancenoy TR11 5RP (01326) 340332

"A real find" in a remote rural location, this "very busy country pub" (with "a pleasant garden") proffers an "excellent variety" of dishes "both exotic and homely"; occasional disappointments were reported this year, though. / **Sample dishes:** char-grilled red mullet with Thai broth; roast lamb glazed with honey & rosemary; banana tart & cream. **Details:** 1m outside village; 9.30 pm; D only. **Accommodation:** 8 rooms, from £70.

COOKHAM, WINDSOR & MAIDENHEAD

3–3A

Bel & The Dragon £ 35

High St SL6 9SQ (01628) 521263

This "sympathetic make-over of a 15th-century inn" offers some "original" modern British dishes that "work well"; "friendly and efficient" service contributes to the favourable overall impression. / **Sample dishes:** baked mushrooms with aubergine & goat's cheese; haddock with spinach & potato cakes; sticky toffee pudding. **Details:** opp Stanley Spencer art gallery; 9.45 pm.

CORBRIDGE, NORTHUMBERLAND

8–2B

The Valley £ 27 ★

Old Station Hs NE45 5AY (01434) 633434

"First class" applies to eating rather than rail travel these days at this converted station, now home to "a wonderful non-traditional Indian restaurant"; it wins an appreciative more-than-local following with its "top-notch" cooking, its "attentive" and "humorous" service and its "tasteful" décor. / **Sample dishes:** onion bhaji; chicken tikka masala; pineapple paradise. **Details:** 10.30 pm; D only, closed Sun; no smoking area.

CORK, COUNTY CORK, EIRE

10–4B

Delhi Palace IR £ 25 ★

5 Washington St (021) 427 6227

"Always very good, if expensive" – "if you favour Indian, you will not be disappointed" at this well-established fixture. / **Sample dishes:** vegetable samosas; chicken masala; ice cream. **Details:** across the road from the Cineplex; 11.30 pm; D only.

Ivory Tower IR £ 40 ★★

Exchange Buildings, 35 Princes St (021) 227 4665

"Exquisite", "incredibly imaginative" eclectic cooking makes it worth seeking out Seamus O'Connell's "very different" restaurant; it has a "relaxed" New Age atmosphere – "far out, man". / **Sample dishes:** carpaccio of wood pigeon; wild boar & suckling pig in sherry sauce; dark chocolate & praline cake. **Details:** 10 pm; no Amex & no Switch.

CORSCOMBE, DORSET 2–4B

Fox Inn £ 26 A★

DT2 0NS (01935) 891330

"Super pub grub" ("using great local produce") and a 'chocolate box' "tranquil setting" combine to make this thatched 17th-century pub an "an absolute gem". / **Sample dishes:** warm salad of local scallops; venison with vodka & damson sauce; sticky toffee pudding. **Details:** at bottom of hill on road to Halstock, or five miles off A37; 9 pm, Fri & Sat 9.30 pm; no smoking area. **Accommodation:** 3 rooms, from £65.

CORSE LAWN, GLOUCESTERSHIRE 2–1B

Corse Lawn Hotel £ 38 ★

GL19 4LZ (01452) 780771

The Hine family's "friendly" and "relaxing" country house hotel has both a restaurant and a bistro; reporters find both "very good". / **Sample dishes:** wild mushroom pancake; pan-fried guinea fowl with split peas; poached fruits with vanilla cream. **Value tip:** set 2/3-crs L £14.95/£16.95 (Sun £17.95). **Details:** 5m SW of Tewkesbury on B4211; 9.30 pm; no smoking. **Accommodation:** 19 rooms, from £120.

COVENTRY, WEST MIDLANDS 5–4C

Browns £ 15 A★

Earl St CV1 2RU (024) 7622 1100

The "best veggie in Coventry" offers "hot and tasty food, buffet-style", and "loads of choice" too; "nice service and atmosphere" complete a package that provides some respite in this gastronomic wasteland. / **Sample dishes:** no starters; grilled fish & marlin kebabs; triple chocolate cheesecake. **Details:** next to Coventry Cathedral; 10.30 pm; no Amex; no smoking area; children: discouraged.

COXWOLD, NORTH YORKSHIRE 8–4C

Fauconberg Arms £ 23 A★

YO61 4AD (01347) 868214

"A good range of dishes", "well presented", is just part of the attraction of this "good, traditional inn", beautifully situated in the Hambleton Hills. / **Sample dishes:** smoked chicken, apple & pine nut salad; minted Yorkshire lamb; meringue with raspberries & peaches. **Details:** 8:30 pm; closed Mon D in winter; no Amex & no Switch. **Accommodation:** 4 rooms, from £55.

CRASTER, NORTHUMBERLAND 8–1B

Jolly Fisherman £ 10 ★

NE66 3TR (01665) 576461

"Great crab sandwiches" and "good fresh salmon" are among highlights of the traditional fare served at this popular inn. / **Sample dishes:** crab bisque; kipper pâté with salad; rhubarb crumble. **Details:** nr Dunstanburgh Castle; 10 pm; no credit cards.

CREIGAU, CARDIFF 2–2A

Caesars Arms £ 28

Cardiff Rd CF4 8NN (029) 2089 0486

"Fish fresh from the slab" – "best when cooked simply" – is the highlight on the menu at this brasserie-cum-pub; it's under the same ownership as Cardiff's Le Monde. / **Sample dishes:** Cajun fishcakes; venison in redcurrant & brandy sauce; raspberry pavlova. **Value tip:** set 2-crs L £5 (Sun £6.95). **Details:** beyond Creigau, past golf club; 10.30 pm; closed Sun D.

The Bear £ 30 A★

High St NP8 1BW (01873) 810408

"Just right for winter fill-ups"; with its "relaxed and welcoming traditional ambience", this glorious coaching inn, on the marketplace, is "worth a detour" for its "really tasty, high-quality food" ("superb lamb", "home-made pies", and so on); it makes "a great place to eat and drink in, or to stay". / **Sample dishes:** smoked haddock with minted peas; fillet steak with artichoke ravioli & spinach purée; port parfait with strawberries. **Details:** NW of Abergavenny on A40; 9.30 pm; D only, ex Sun L only; no smoking in bar; children: 7+. **Accommodation:** 34 rooms, from £65.

Nantyffin Cider Mill £ 31 A★★

Brecon Rd NP8 1SG (01873) 810775

"London-chic meets Welsh-traditional" at this "memorable" mill-conversion; its "location and ambience never fail to impress", and neither does the "interesting and imaginative" cooking (featuring "local venison, pheasant and salmon"), washed down with "an eclectic selection of beers, wines and ciders". / **Sample dishes:** char-grilled marinated squid; roast Old Spot pork with colcannon & cider mustard; autumn fruit clafoutis. **Details:** on A40 between Brecon & Crickhowell; 9.30 pm; closed Mon; no smoking area.

The Punch Bowl £ 28 ★★

LA8 8HR (01539) 568237

"Superb, imaginative" cooking and a "pleasant rural setting" combine to make Steven and Marjorie Doherty's "relaxed" and "unpretentious" gastropub an "excellent-value" choice for many reporters. / **Sample dishes:** goat's cheese niçoise; braised oxtails with garlic mash; warm chocolate Nemesis. **Value tip:** set 2/3-crs set weekday L £8/£10.95. **Details:** off A5074 towards Bowness, turn right after Lyth Hotel; 9 pm; closed Sun D (& Mon, Oct-Mar); no Amex; no smoking. **Accommodation:** 3 rooms, from £55 (£97.50 incl D).

Banana Leaf £ 16 ★

7 Lower Addiscombe Rd CR0 6BQ (020) 8688 0297

"Really good vegetarian Indian food" (with "beautiful use of spices") and "exceptional" service win a widespread fan club for this spot near East Croydon station. / **Sample dishes:** chicken pakora; chicken korma; gulab jaman (Indian sweets). **Details:** nr East Croydon station; 11 pm.

Bear & Ragged Staff £ 22

Appleton Rd OX2 9QH (01865) 862329

It's a shame that "amateurish" service and "poor" food can hit the wrong note at this 14th-century pub – its pretty location just outside Oxford makes it a place quite frequently commented on by reporters. / **Sample dishes:** deep-fried stuffed jalapeno chillies; monkfish & cod brochettes; sticky toffee & banana pudding. **Value tip:** set 3-crs Sun L £6.95. **Details:** up Cumnor Hill, right at Vine pub, left after post office; 9.30 pm.

Ostlers Close £ 40 ★

25 Bonnygate KY15 4BU (01334) 655574

Twenty years old this year, James & Amanda Graham's small fixture – entered from a small alleyway – "deserves its accolades", avers the small but enthusiastic fan club who applaud its "homely", but "marvellously prepared" traditional cuisine. / Sample dishes: duck liver with caramelised onions; local seafood with lobster sauce; trio of chocolate desserts. Details: 9.30 pm; closed Mon, Wed L, Thu L & Sun; no smoking; children: 6+.

The Peat Inn £ 40

KY15 5LH (01334) 840206

"Food to compete with anything London's culinary celebrities can offer" has for decades made the Wilsons' understated coaching inn conversion a notable destination; however, though most reporters still find it "close to perfection", some complain it's "living on its reputation". / Sample dishes: crab dressed with yoghurt & lime; cassoulet of pork, lamb & duck with white beans; banana cake with coconut parfait. Value tip: set 3-crs L £19.50. Details: at junction of B940 & B941, SW of St Andrews; 9.30 pm; closed Mon & Sun; no smoking. Accommodation: 8 rooms, from £145.

Travellers Rest £ 30 ★

DL11 7HU (01833) 621225

"French touches", "enthusiastic owners" and "original recipes" help distinguish François & Anne Morillon's "friendly" and "comfortable" country pub/restaurant. / Sample dishes: grilled black pudding with smoked trout mousse; seafood platter; apple tart & ice cream. Details: 8m N of Scotch Corner on A66; 9.30 pm; closed Sun; no Amex; booking essential at weekends.

Cott Inn £ 30 Ⓐ

TQ9 6HE (01803) 863777

"Great country pub atmosphere" and "good home cooking" ensure that it's "always an enjoyable experience" to visit this "beautiful" 14th-century inn. / Sample dishes: grilled baby squid with chilli jam; duck with chestnuts & cranberries; pear & banana crumble. Details: straight up hill from mini-roundabout by Cider Press Centre; 9.30 pm; no smoking. Accommodation: 6 rooms, from £65.

Carved Angel £ 55 ★

2 South Embankment TQ6 9BH (01803) 832465

"Good, but not as memorable as it was"; though devotees still applaud the "best, fresh materials, cooked with respect" at this "warm and unpretentious" harbourside dining room, there is a general feeling that it's "lost its edge since Joyce Molyneux retired". / Sample dishes: crab & avocado mousse; duck with foie gras & muscat grapes; chocolate harlequin. Details: opp passenger ferry pontoon; 9.30 pm; closed Mon L & Sun D; no smoking; children: not at D.

Le Talbooth   £ 42   🅰★

Gun Hill CO7 6HP   (01206) 323150
It's a "great" and "unhurried" experience to visit this "lovely"
timber-frame house, run by the Milsom family for almost fifty
years now, in its "beautiful" Constable Country location; the
cooking has not been a great strength in recent years, but there
were many more reports of "superb" results this year. / **Sample
dishes:** twice-baked cheese soufflé; saddle of peppered venison; warm
chocolate ganache tart. **Value tip:** set 2/3-crs weekday L £17/£19.50.
Details: 5m N of Colchester on A12, take B1029 towards Dedham; 9.30 pm;
closed Sun D in winter. **Accommodation:** 10 rooms, from £150.

Rams Head Inn   £ 25   🅰★

OL3 5UN   (01457) 874802
"Imaginative presentation of traditional dishes", "excellent wines",
"wonderful beers", "friendly" service … – praise for this Pennines
"ex-pub" is consistent, and it offers "lovely" views too. / **Sample
dishes:** breaded goat's cheese with basil dressing; fillet steak with cream
& whisky sauce; crème brûlée. **Value tip:** pre-theatre is for one course only,
also a Xmas party special offer 2crs £13.95/3crs £16.95. **Details:** 2m from
M63, J22 towards Oldham; 10 pm, Sun 8.30 pm; closed Mon L; no Amex;
no smoking area.

Darleys on the River   £ 37   ★

Darley Abbey Mill DE22 1DZ   (01332) 364987
Set "next to the river and a weir", this modern conversion of an
old mill generally wins praise for its "excellent" modern British
cooking and "friendly" service; the setting, perhaps surprisingly,
can "lack atmosphere". / **Sample dishes:** cauliflower & coconut soup;
caramelised duck with oriental vegetables; frangipane & raspberry tart. **Value
tip:** set 2/3-crs set L & Sun L £12.50/£14.50. **Details:** 2m N of city centre by
River Derwent; 10 pm; closed Sun D; no smoking.

West Riding Licensed
Refreshment Rooms   £ 14   ★

Railway Station, Wellington Rd WFB 1HF   (01924) 459193
Neither British Rail nor its successors ever achieved this! –
"a wide range of food and beer" (including "good veggie
options"), "reasonable prices" and "friendly staff" are among the
attractions which make this railway station-turned-pub a very
popular local terminus. / **Sample dishes:** vegetable soup & roll; beef in
beer & parsnip mash; steamed sponge & custard. **Details:** in old waiting room
of railway station; 9 pm; no credit cards; no smoking area.

Copperfield   £ 35   ★

49-53 Buxton Old Rd SX12 2RW   (01663) 764333
"Reasonably-priced grub in big helpings" makes it "worth the
journey" to this village restaurant; it has been "consistently good
over 20 years". / **Sample dishes:** salad niçoise; sea bass with tomato
& basil; Manchester pudding. **Details:** off A6; 9.30 pm; closed Mon & Sun D;
no Amex & no Switch.

DODDISCOMBSLEIGH, DEVON

Nobody Inn £ 24   A★★

EX6 7PS (01647) 252394

"Do mention the steak and kidney pudding, it's exceptional" is typical of endorsements for the food at this *"charming"* *"epitome"* of a 15th-century pub, in the middle of nowhere; its *"encyclopaedia-size wine list"* (over 1000 bins), *"excellent"* local cheeses (over 50 varieties) and *"freshly-caught trout (to be ordered in advance)"* all attract glowing reviews. / **Sample dishes:** trout pâté; lamb casserole with pineapple & apricot; syrup sponge & custard. **Details:** off A38 at Haldon Hill (signed Dunchidrock) & follow signs; 9 pm; closed Mon & Sun; no smoking area; children: 14+. **Accommodation:** 7 rooms, from £55.

DOGMERSFIELD, HAMPSHIRE

Queen's Head £ 24   ★

Pilcot Ln RG27 8SY (01252) 613531

"Even the Directory Enquiries ladies, in Scotland, had heard of this place!" – the *"very cosmopolitan and inexpensive"* cooking at this small pub is obviously gathering quite a following. / **Sample dishes:** avocado prawns; surf 'n' turf; treacle sponge. **Details:** off A287 between Barnham & Odiham; 9 pm; closed Mon.

DONCASTER, SOUTH YORKSHIRE

Hamiltons £ 26   A★

Carr House Rd DN4 5HP (01302) 760770

You don't find many places *"reminiscent of dining in a French château"* in this neck of the woods, but it is not just *"an oasis in a gastronomic desert"* that this *"superior"* venue wins its spurs – it offers *"London quality at Yorkshire prices"*. / **Sample dishes:** pan-roasted scallops with raisins; peppered lamb with lentils; toffee apple charlotte. **Details:** off M18 on A18; 9.45 pm; closed Sat L & Sun D. **Accommodation:** 4 rooms, from £70.

Indus £ 24

24-26 Silver St DN1 1HQ (01302) 810800

"It's big and busy, but the food is of constant quality", say supporters of this Indian *"stalwart"*, *"in business for over a quarter of a century"*. / **Sample dishes:** spare wings; king prawn tandoori; kulfi. **Details:** 11.30 pm; closed Sun L; no smoking area.

DORCHESTER, DORSET

Mock Turtle £ 25

34 High West St DT1 1UP (01305) 264011

This converted rectory attracted few reports this year; such as they are confirm it as a *"very friendly"* place capable of *"excellent"* results. / **Sample dishes:** king scallops provençale; lamb with roasted red peppers & olive oil; crème brûlée & strawberries. **Details:** 9.30 pm; closed Mon L, Sat L & Sun; no smoking area; no bookings after 9:30 pm.

DORKING, SURREY

Partners £ 42   A

2-4 West St RH4 1BL (01306) 882826

Sentiment on this beamed medieval building – located *"in the local 'Antiques' street"* – has become rather mixed; some say it offers *"beautifully-cooked"* dishes in an *"attractive"* setting, whereas for doubters the performance is *"elaborate, but surprisingly indifferent"*. / **Sample dishes:** whole quail; calves liver & black pudding with mash; apple & calvados brioche. **Value tip:** set 2-crs L £14.50. **Details:** 10 pm; closed Sun; no smoking area.

constantly updated at www.hardens.com 143

Reflecting the success of the Irish economy, Dublin has emerged strongly as a restaurant centre over recent years. In keeping with a longer-term history which until recently involved more emigration than immigration, however, ethnic restaurants are by-and-large incidental to the city's appeal (not, as in London, fundamental to it). All restaurants of real note cook in some variation of the European tradition, with more traditional establishments being heavily French-influenced.

Since last year, *Patrick Guilbaud* has overtaken rival *Peacock Alley* as the best restaurant in town, rather by default. *Thorntons*, *Jacob's Ladder* and the *Mermaid Café* have maintained their appeal, while the place for traditional grandeur remains *Le Coq Hardi*.

As everywhere, reporters' favourites tend not to be places where the emphasis is solely on the food. The atmospheric *La Stampa* is a top tip for a Big Night Out. *Roly's Bistro* is fashionable Dublin's smart, everyday brasserie. Hipsters head for U2's über-trendy *Clarence Hotel*.

Temple Bar is the best known touristy area, but – like London's Covent Garden – you will generally eat better and more cheaply elsewhere.

(UK readers who habitually rely on a Switch card, should note that you cannot use it in the Republic.)

Café Mao   **IR £ 27**   ★
2-3 Chatham Rw D2 (01) 670 4899
"Lively, youthful and good fun", this *"buzzy"* café, off Grafton Street, offers *"Asian/fusion"* cooking in an *"urban/cosmopolitan"* setting. / *Sample dishes:* chilli squid; lemongrass & chilli tiger prawns; passion fruit syllabub. **Details:** just off Grafton St & St Stephen's Green; 11 pm; no Amex & no Switch; no booking.

Clarence Hotel (Tea Rooms)   **IR £ 44**   𝔸★
6-8 Wellington Quay D2 (01) 670 7766
"Decadence with style" characterises the *"cool"* dining hall of the *"friendly hotel owned by U2"*; most reporters find it *"difficult to fault"* the *"trendy, well-presented dishes"*, though others say that the cooking's *"good, not inspired"*, considering the prices. / **Sample dishes:** deep–fried oysters & crab mayonnaise; roast lamb with white onion purée; lemon curd ice cream. **Details:** down from O'Connell Bridge, opp New Millennium Bridge; 10.45 pm; closed Sat L; no Switch; no smoking area. **Accommodation:** 50 rooms, from IR £185.

Cooke's Café   **IR £ 42**   𝔸
12 South William Street D2 (01) 679 0536
This *"modern Italian/Irish"* café has a *"funky"* ambience, and some followers of fashion say its offers a *"consistently excellent"* experience; there is some feeling, though, that *"for the price, it could be better"*. / **Sample dishes:** fried calamari; grilled chicken with Mediterranean vegetables; chocolate pecan tart with bourbon ice cream. **Details:** 11 pm; no Switch; no smoking area.

Le Coq Hardi   IR £ 60   𝔸

35 Pembroke Rd D4   (01) 668 9070
It's "fabulous for a celebration", say devotees of John and
Catherine Howard's "beautiful" Ballsbridge Georgian house, who
approve its grand, traditional French cooking and extensive cellar;
it's now nearing its quarter century, so comments that it's "good,
but not what it used to be" are perhaps inevitable. / **Sample
dishes:** smoked haddock & cheese tart; chicken stuffed with apple & ham;
vanilla crème brûlée. **Value tip:** 5-crs L £24.50. **Details:** nr Lansdowne Park;
10.30 pm; closed Sat L & Sun; no Switch.

L'Ecrivain   IR £ 49

109 Lower Baggot St D2   (01) 661 1919
After a major refurbishment, Derry & Sally Anne Clarke's
well-known establishment has expanded and adopted a more
modern style; limited feedback is somewhat mixed, with one
mishap ("average at best") amongst more favourable reports of
a "lovely and airy" setting, "excellent value wine" and "great",
"well-judged" modern Irish food. / **Sample dishes:** deep-fried Dublin
prawns in pastry; rack of lamb, with carrot & parsnip purée; summer berry
truffle. **Value tip:** set 2/3-crs L £15/£18. **Details:** opp Bank of Ireland;
11 pm; closed Sat L & Sun; no Switch; no smoking area.

Eden   IR £ 33

Meeting House Sq D2   (01) 670 5372
"A cut above the standard, rowdy Temple Bar offerings" –
especially in terms of its cool design – this "smoothly-run"
café/restaurant by the Olympia Theatre attracts consistent praise
for its "professional" approach; "make sure you get a table
downstairs". / **Sample dishes:** Arbroath smokies; pan-fried organic lamb's
liver & kidney; crème brûlée with peanut butter cookies. **Details:** nr Olympia
Theatre; 10.30 pm; no Switch.

Elephant & Castle   IR £ 31   𝔸

18 Temple Bar D2   (01) 679 3121
This characterful, relaxed and friendly Temple Bar diner is
a "breakfast/brunch location" par excellence, and at any time of
day – useful "in a city in which it's not always easy to get up in
the morning!" / **Sample dishes:** chicken wings; beefburger with cheese
& chips; carrot cake. **Details:** 11.30 pm; no Switch; no smoking area;
no booking.

Jacob's Ladder   IR £ 39   ★

4-5 Nassau Street D2   (01) 670 3865
Service can be "erratic", but Adrian Roche's "imaginative,
modern cooking" at his ambitious first-floor venture, overlooking
the grounds of Trinity College, is "always good". / **Sample
dishes:** shellfish & salmon sausage; roast duck with bok choy; warm chocolate
fondant. **Details:** beside Trinity College; 10 pm; closed Mon & Sun; no Switch;
no smoking area.

Juice   IR £ 24

73-83 South Great Georges St D2   (01) 475 7856
A "good-value" vegetarian café, to the north of Temple Bar;
it's "ideal for a snack on the run". / **Sample dishes:** bruschetta;
Szechuan vegetables with fried rice; tiramisu. **Details:** opp Globe pub;
11.30 pm; no Switch; no smoking area.

constantly updated at www.hardens.com

King Sitric   IR £ 48

East Pier, Howth   (01) 832 5235

*Overlooking the harbour of this picturesque Dublin suburb
located at the end of the DART, this long-established, recently
refurbished seafood restaurant is known for serving "the best
fish" (but also serves some "excellent game"); one or two
complain that it is "overpraised and overpriced". / **Sample
dishes:** prawn tempura with noodles & soy sauce; roast monkfish with forest
mushrooms; meringue Sitric. **Details:** 10.30 pm; closed Sun D; no Switch.
Accommodation: 8 rooms, from IR £90.*

Mermaid Café   IR £ 38   ★

69-70 Dame Street D2   (01) 670 8236

*The setting is a touch "austere", and "could perhaps be
upgraded", but nonetheless this "professional" restaurant, on the
fringe of Temple Bar provides a "relaxed" environment in which
to enjoy some "great-value" modern European cooking. / **Sample
dishes:** crab cakes with pecan mayonnaise; roast duck with black pudding
& pearl barley risotto; pecan pie with maple ice cream. **Details:** nr Olympia
Theatre; 11 pm, Sun 9 pm; no Amex & no Switch; no smoking area.*

101 Talbot Street   IR £ 27   ★

100-102 Talbot St D1   (01) 874 5011

*Even those who say the setting, just off O'Connell Street, is
"not very pretty", think this quirky venue's Middle
Eastern-influenced cooking is "attractively original", and the
place is "always crowded". / **Sample dishes:** smoked haddock & leek
flan; spinach pancakes with broccoli, tomato & olives; white chocolate & Bailey's
cheesecake. **Details:** nr Abbey Theatre; 10.45 pm; D only, closed Sun;
no Switch; no smoking area.*

Patrick Guilbaud   IR £ 78   ★

Merrion Hotel, 21 Upper Merrion St D2   (01) 676 4192

*This "airy, church-like temple to fine French/Irish food" is
"simply the best restaurant in Dublin" in many people's book;
perhaps inevitably, others find the whole approach – over 2000
choices on the wine list, for example – "a bit over the top".
/ **Sample dishes:** foie gras; duck with crispy salad; crème brûlée. **Value
tip:** set 2-crs L £22. **Details:** opp government buildings; 10.15 pm; closed
Mon & Sun; no Switch; no smoking area.*

Peacock Alley   IR £ 72

Fitzwilliam Hotel, 119 St Stephen's Grn D2   (01) 677 0708

*Either reporters were serially unlucky, or standards have
plummeted at Conrad Gallagher's once-exemplary flagship
venture – "Michelin star my hat", "over-rated", "don't bother";
something, perhaps, to do with distraction caused by opening an
offshoot in London's West End, rumoured as we go to press?
/ **Sample dishes:** sea scallops; pan-fried sole with black butter; lemon tart
with raspberry coulis. **Details:** next to Planet Hollywood; 10.30 pm; closed Sun
L; no Switch; no smoking area; children: 12+.*

Roly's Bistro   IR £ 36   Ⓐ★

7 Ballsbridge Ter D4   (01) 668 2611

*"Excellent and reasonably-priced" bistro/brasserie fare and
a "very friendly and relaxed" atmosphere ensure consistent
popularity for this Ballsbridge fixture, which – if not a particularly
foodie venue – is many a Dubliner's favourite all-rounder.
/ **Sample dishes:** duck spring rolls; roast lamb with honey & thyme sauce;
vanilla crème brûlée. **Value tip:** set 3-crs L £12.95. **Details:** nr American
Embassy; 9.45 pm; no Switch; no smoking area.*

La Stampa IR £ 44
35 Dawson St D2 (01) 677 8611
*For "a lively night out", this "wonderful" 19th-century building provides a "memorable" venue; cooking and service – though often praised – are less reliable attractions. / **Sample dishes:** foie gras with carrot confit; roast lamb with spices; panna cotta with roasted rhubarb. **Details:** off St Stephens Green; 11 pm; D only; no Switch; no smoking area.*

Thorntons IR £ 74 ★
1 Portobello Rd D8 (01) 454 9067
*In a slightly out-on-a-limb location to the north of the city centre, the Thorntons "lovely house, next to a canal" lives up to its eminent reputation for "delicious" classically-rooted cooking. / **Sample dishes:** sautéed foie gras & scallops; suckling pigs trotter with mash; warm chocolate tartlet with strawberries. **Details:** 2m S of city centre; 11 pm; closed Sun & Mon; D only Tue-Thu & Sat; no Switch; no smoking area.*

Wagamama IR £ 19 ★
South King St (01) 478 2152
*"As in London it's quick, reliable and healthy"; this stylish refectory 'ramen'-bar has successfully jumped across the Irish Sea and makes a useful place for a "reasonably-priced" (and "smoke-free") meal of noodles, noodles and more noodles. / **Sample dishes:** vegetable dumplings; chicken & noodles in a teriyaki sauce; no puddings. **Details:** opp Gaiety Theatre; 11 pm; no Switch; no smoking; no booking.*

DUNDRUM, COUNTY DOWN 10–2D

Bucks Head £ 27 𝔸★
77-79 Main St BT33 0LU (01396) 751868
*This may look just like a "quaint village inn", but supporters proclaim "a jewel of a restaurant" within, where "delicious" food is served in a "relaxed" setting; the latter features a conservatory and changing displays of art for sale. / **Sample dishes:** mussels & Thai salad; smoked haddock with grain mustard; bread & butter pudding. **Value tip:** set 3-crs Sun L £12.50. **Details:** 3m N of Newcastle; 9 pm; Oct-Mar, closed Mon; no smoking area.*

DUNGARVAN, COUNTY WATERFORD, *EIRE* 10–4C

The Tannery IR £ 37 ★
10 Quay St (058) 45420
*This converted tannery may be "out of the way", but fans say it's "well worth finding"; reports of the cooking are limited, but "excellent" fish dishes are a highlight. / **Sample dishes:** ravioli of smoked chicken; roast lamb with ratatouille & chick pea fritters; apple jelly with cider ice cream. **Details:** 10 pm; closed Mon & Sun; no Switch; no smoking; children: before 8.30 pm only.*

DUNHAM MASSEY, CHESHIRE 5–2B

Axe & Cleaver £ 26 ★
WA14 5RN (0161) 928 3391
*The "variety of innovative dishes" (with "excellent seasonal menus, including game") wins enthusiastic local support for this "cosy" haunt, which is "more a restaurant than a pub". / **Sample dishes:** crab & prawn thermidor; venison with juniper & garlic mash; Oreo cookie madness. **Details:** on A56 W of Altrincham, by Dunham Massey Deer Park; 9.45 pm; no smoking area; no booking.*

DUNKELD, PERTH & KINROSS

Kinnaird House £ 59 𝔸★

Kinnaird Estate PH8 0LB (01796) 482440

To dine in the "charming panelled dining room" of this "spectacular country house in beautiful scenery" is "an experience" – a "very expensive" one, admittedly, but one which, thanks to the "superb food and service", most judge "well worth the cost". / **Sample dishes:** red mullet with crab & herb salad; rack of lamb with spinach, potatoes & peas; prune & armagnac soufflé. **Value tip:** set 2-crs set L £19.50. **Details:** 8m NW of Dunfield, off A9 onto B898; 9.30 pm; closed Mon-Wed during Jan & Feb; no Amex & no Switch; jacket & tie; no smoking; children: 12+. **Accommodation:** 9 rooms, from £345.

DUNVEGAN, ISLE OF SKYE

Three Chimneys £ 44 𝔸★★

Colbost IV55 8ZT (01470) 511258

A "stupendous" location and "incredible" seafood – Shirley and Eddie Spear's converted crofter's cottage really is "outstanding"; it may be "a wee bit out of the way!", but "it's well worth the drive" ("if you're on Skye", that is). / **Sample dishes:** Skye crab risotto; grilled lamb with mash & port wine gravy; apple & apricot treacle tart. **Value tip:** set 2/3-crs L £12.95/£17.95. **Details:** 5m from Dunvegan Castle on B884 to Glendale; 9.30 pm; closed Sun L, closed mid Jan-mid Feb; no smoking. **Accommodation:** 6 rooms, from £160.

DUNWICH, SUFFOLK

The Ship £ 23 𝔸★

St James St IP17 3DT (01728) 648219

"Fish 'n' chips and Adnams bitter – what more do you need?", declare fans of this "lovely" pub, with its "charming" location in this seaside village; (the menu also encompasses other traditional dishes). / **Sample dishes:** Stilton & walnut pâté; herb sausages with buttered mash; bread & butter pudding. **Details:** 7m S of Southwold, follow signs from A12; 9.30 pm; no Amex; no smoking; no booking at L. **Accommodation:** 3 rooms, from £54.

DURHAM, COUNTY DURHAM

Bistro 21 £ 32 𝔸★

Aykley Heads Hs DH1 5TS (0191) 384 4354

This "converted riverside warehouse" is "charmingly informal, yet totally professional", and it's "hard to book", thanks to its "consistently good" Gallic fare and its "relaxed" atmosphere. / **Sample dishes:** chilli, cheese & spinach soufflé; barbecued salmon with Moroccan couscous; sticky toffee pudding. **Value tip:** set 2-crs L £12. **Details:** nr Durham Trinity School; 10.30 pm; closed Sun; no smoking.

Court Inn £ 17

Court Ln DH1 3AW (0191) 384 7350

"Incredibly cheap" and "filling" dishes ensure there's "always a crush of locals and students" at this "nice" modern pub – worth knowing about in this under-provided city. / **Sample dishes:** mushrooms baked in cheese; chicken with brie, bacon & eggy bread; sticky toffee pudding. **Details:** 10.30 pm; no credit cards; no smoking area.

Shaheens Indian Bistro £ 19 ★

The Old Post Office, 48 North Bailey DH1 3ET (0191) 386 0960

"Crazy" but "charming" service sets the tone at this popular Indian, whose "first-class" cooking achieves a more-than-local following. / **Sample dishes:** garlic mushrooms; chicken roghan josh; banana split. **Details:** 11 pm; closed Mon; no Amex & no Switch; no smoking area.

Duxford Lodge £ 35

Ickleton Rd CB2 4RU   (01223) 836444

Visitors to the nearby aircraft museum may be surprised by the "very professional" standards set at this hotel dining room, whose modern British cooking can be "superb". / **Sample dishes:** goat's cheese & spicy peach chutney; poached chicken stuffed with seafood mousse; orange soufflé pancakes. **Value tip:** set 2/3-crs set L £10/£14, set 3-crs Sun L £16.95. **Details:** off M11, J10 nr war memorial; 9.30 pm; closed Sat L; no smoking area. **Accommodation:** 15 rooms, from £85.

Mims £ 28

63 East Barnet Rd EN5 8RN   (020) 8449 2974

It's the local foodie hotspot, but this humble-looking Barnet café could use a shake-up; service is mediocre, and even those who say the 'Masterchef' cuisine is "excellent" grizzle about a menu which "changes too infrequently". / **Sample dishes:** deep-fried tomato & onion salad; roast duck with roast vegetables; banana crepes. **Details:** between Cockfosters & High Barnet; 11 pm; closed Mon; no Amex & no Switch; no smoking area.

Jolly Sportsman £ 29 ★

BN7 3BA   (01273) 890400

This "terrific pub/restaurant" (under the same ownership as Thackeray's House in Tunbridge Wells) may have "simple, rustic décor" but it has a great following for its "eclectic" but "unfussy" cooking. / **Sample dishes:** tiger prawn, saffron & chive risotto; roast guinea fowl with spinach & almonds; sticky toffee pudding. **Details:** N of Lewes; 9 pm, Fri & Sat 10 pm; closed Mon & Sun D; no Amex.

Gravetye Manor £ 60 Ⓐ

Vowels Ln RH19 4LJ   (01342) 810567

This "delightful" Elizabethan manor offers "the quintessential country house experience", and most still say it creates a "wonderful setting for excellent food"; there were more reports this year of "variable" cooking and "inattentive" service, though shortcomings "are invariably made up for by a visit to the garden". / **Sample dishes:** goat's cheese ravioli; wild salmon & crab with chive cream; pannettone with poached peaches. **Value tip:** set 3-crs L £27. **Details:** 2m outside Turner's Hill; 9.30 pm; no Amex; jacket & tie; no smoking; children: babies and children 7+ welcome. **Accommodation:** 18 rooms, from £175.

Drovers Inn £ 31

5 Bridge St EH40 3AG   (01620) 860298

"The chef aims high, and mostly succeeds" at this bistro-style dining room behind a pub, where traditional Scottish notions are realised in a way that's a touch more "imaginative" than you might expect. / **Sample dishes:** haggis tartlets; Drover's honey & ginger roast pork; rice pudding. **Details:** by A1; 9.30 pm; no smoking area.

Blue Lion   £ 32   𝔸★★

DL8 4SN   (01969) 624273

*With its beautiful Dales location, this "very upmarket",
"olde worlde" coaching inn makes an exceedingly popular
destination, not least on account of its "fantastic" food – "both in
the bar and in the restaurant". / **Sample dishes:** filo parcel with duck
& ginger; roast lamb with pesto mash; treacle sponge & custard.*
Details: *between Masham and Leyburn on A6108; 9.30 pm; no Amex.*
Accommodation: *12 rooms, from £69.*

EDINBURGH, CITY OF EDINBURGH   9–4C

The last year has seen important developments towards the
upper reaches of the market. Perhaps the most important is
that, in Leith's *Restaurant Martin Wishart*, Auld Reekie finally
has the standard-bearer it has long cried out for. At the
same time, the *Atrium* – long held out as the trendy place in
town – has sharpened up its act, and is at last beginning to
live up to the hype which has long enveloped it. Other
'modern' restaurants winning favourable mentions include
Ducks at Le Marche Noir and *36 Restaurant*.

Two of the biggest 'names' – the *Witchery by the Castle* and
the *Tower* – seem to rely on the attractions of their setting
and/or view for custom. The style of the Balmoral's grand
Number One limits its appeal mainly to expense-accounters
(except, perhaps, at lunch). For those wanting to dine well in
a setting with real character, therefore, the all-round
attractions of the *Vintners Rooms* are difficult to beat.

A lot of the mid-range places tend to be good and
comfortable but in a rather dated, traditional idiom (such as
Café St-Honoré, *Dubh Prais*, *Jacksons* and *Martins*. The
contrast presented by the *blue bar café* and by upmarket
deli-café *Valvona & Crolla* may account for what some might
say is their disproportionate popularity.

Leith has become well-known as a going-out destination, and
boasts a number of lively waterside bistros, such as *Fisher's*,
The Shore and *Skippers*. Though removed from the water's
edge by a short way, *(Fitz)Henry* is a destination worth
seeking out.

Thanks perhaps to the university and the large number of
younger visitors, there are a number of good less expensive
places, including a good number of vegetarians, such as *Bann
UK*, *Black Bo's*, *Henderson's* and the phenomenally popular
Indian *Kalpna*.

Ann Purna   £ 19

44-45 St Patrick's Sq EH8 9ET   (0131) 662 1807

*"All dishes are cooked to order by the proprietor's wife" at
this "smoke-free" vegetarian Indian – her "subtle" cooking and
the "friendly" welcome win affection for this somewhat
"unpromising"-looking café. / **Sample dishes:** mixed vegetable pakoras;
okra masala; gulab jaman (Indian sweets). **Value tip:** set 3-crs L £4.95.*
Details: *10.45 pm; closed Sat L & Sun L; no Amex & no Switch; no smoking;
children: 10+.* **Accommodation:** *7 rooms, from £50.*

constantly updated at www.hardens.com

Apartment £ 22

7-13 Barclay Pl EH10 4HN (0131) 228 6456

"Electric atmosphere" and *"abundant"* portions of *"quality fodder"* at *"extremely reasonable prices"* are hailed by supporters of this very *"trendy"* newcomer, some way out of the centre; *"much hyped but not up to expectations"*, say sceptics, who slam its *"confusing"* menu and *"unimpressive"* delivery. / **Sample dishes:** wild mushrooms with aubergine & sweet potato; spicy lamb meatballs with goat's cheese; lemon tart with raspberry coulis. **Details:** between Tollcross & Bruntsfield; 11 pm; no Amex; no smoking area.

The Atrium £ 37 ★

10 Cambridge St EH1 2ED (0131) 228 8882

There remain many who think that *"only in Edinburgh would such a pretentious place be so popular"*, but this much talked-about venue generated significantly more enthusiasm this year for its *"exciting"* and *"innovative"* modern British cooking and *"cool"* setting. / **Sample dishes:** scallops & crabs with glazed artichokes; roast pigeon with wilted spinach; warm autumn berries. **Details:** by the Usher Hall; 10 pm; closed Sat L & Sun.

Bann UK £ 25 🄰★

5 Hunter Sq EH1 1QW (0131) 226 1112

This *"designer-veggie"*, recently revamped, enjoys a charming Old Town location and is unanimously praised for its *"excellent selection of good-quality food"* and its *"terrific value"*. / **Sample dishes:** asparagus mousse with garlic polenta; roast pumpkin & spinach roulade; organic chocolate tart. **Details:** 11 pm; no smoking area.

Black Bo's £ 28 ★

57-61 Blackfriar's St EH1 1NB (0131) 557 6136

"Extremely imaginative", *"gourmet vegetarian"* cooking makes this *"cramped"* dining room (next to a busy bar) an undoubted culinary hit; *"catastrophically poor"* service, however, can take the edge off the experience. / **Sample dishes:** aubergine & smoked cheese pâté; mushrooms & madeira sauce in filo pastry; cheesecake. **Details:** off Royal Mile, 2nd on right after Crowne Plaza Hotel; 10.30 pm; D only, ex Fri & Sat open L & D; no Amex.

Bleu £ 23

36-38 Victoria St EH1 2GW (0131) 226 1900

"Noisy" bistro mini-chain (with other branches at 8 Union Street and 8 Gloucester Street) which, say fans, is a good *"cheap and cheerful"* option that's *"French, right down to the table-cloths"*; sceptics just think it's getting more and more *"mediocre and overpriced"*. / **Sample dishes:** calamari; seared tuna with shrimps; banana cheesecake. **Details:** 11 pm; no smoking area.

blue bar café £ 32 ★

10 Cambridge St EH1 2ED (0131) 221 1222

This *"light and bright bar/restaurant near the castle"* – the Atrium's less ambitious offshoot – remains a top trendy destination *"for good meals and snacks"*; it offers *"innovative food at very reasonable prices"*, in a setting some find *"cavernous and echoing"*. / **Sample dishes:** Dolcelatte, tomato & onion tart; chicken & mushroom risotto with black pudding; raspberry & banana crème brûlée. **Value tip:** set 2/3-crs set L £9/£12. **Details:** by the Usher Hall; 11 pm; closed Sun.

Le Café St-Honoré   £ 35   Ⓐ

34 NW Thistle Street Ln EH2 1EA   (0131) 226 2211
"A real French bistro in central Edinburgh"; this "well-run"
establishment, tucked away in the New Town, offers "consistent"
cooking, "nicely priced wines" and a "good atmosphere". / **Sample
dishes:** warm prawn, chorizo & scallop salad; shank of lamb with black
pudding; tarte Tatin. **Details:** between George St and Queen St; 10 pm; closed
Sat L & Sun; no smoking area.

La Cuisine d'Odile   £ 13   ★

13 Randolph Cr EH3 7TT   (0131) 225 5685
"Small and chic" basement restaurant "hidden away" in the
basement of the Institut Français where the cooking is as
"authentic" as you might hope; you can BYO for modest corkage.
/ **Sample dishes:** cream of sorrel soup; rabbit in a mustard sauce; choc'Odile.
Details: between Dean Bridge & Charlotte Square; L only; closed Mon & Sun.

Daniel's   £ 24

88 Commercial St EH6 6LX   (0131) 553 5933
"If you're not afraid of choucroute" (tarte flambé and other
hearty Alsatian fare), this "friendly" bistro near Leith's waterfront
has its fans; it doesn't do it for everyone, though, and some
report "plain" results. / **Sample dishes:** tarte flambé; duck confit with
spring greens; spicy ice cream terrine. **Value tip:** set 2/3-crs set
L £4.95/£5.95. **Details:** 10 pm; no Amex; no smoking area.

The Dial   £ 28   ★

44 George IV Bridge EH1 1EJ   (0131) 225 7179
This "innovative" Old Town basement is still praised for its
"individual service and modern style" and for its imaginative
modern Scottish cuisine; some think the décor looks "tatty"
though nowadays, and there's the odd "disappointing" result on
the food front. / **Sample dishes:** trout & parsley fishcakes; Scottish salmon
with citrus butter; white chocolate cheesecake. **Value tip:** set 3-crs L £7.95.
Details: on George IV Bridge Road off the Royal Mile; 11 pm.

Dubh Prais   £ 31   ★

123b High St EH1 1SG   (0131) 557 5732
This cosily-dated basement, off the Royal Mile, doesn't generate
a huge amount of feedback, but such as there is continues to
attest to the "mouthwatering" nature of its "traditional, but light"
Scottish cuisine, using "prime ingredients". / **Sample
dishes:** avocado, goat's cheese & tomato salad; chicken with gooseberry
& sage stuffing; butterscotch terrine. **Value tip:** set 2/3-crs L £7.50/£9.50.
Details: opp Holiday Inn; 10.30 pm; closed Mon, Sat L & Sun.

Ducks at Le Marche Noir   £ 35   ★

2-4 Eyre Pl EH3 5EP   (0131) 558 1608
A "friendly and informative host" sets the tone at Malcolm
Duck's emerging New Town success-story; it offers "quietly
accomplished" French cooking in an agreeably "informal" setting.
/ **Sample dishes:** seared pigeon salad; roast lamb with lentil casserole
& tomato butter; chocolate & marshmallow ice cream. **Details:** 10 pm, Sat
& Sun 10.30 pm; no Amex; no smoking area.

Fisher's Bistro   £ 27   ★

1 The Shore EH6 6QW   (0131) 554 5666
"Lovely seafood, beautifully served in an unpretentious
atmosphere" makes this "relaxed" bistro near the Leith
waterfront a universally popular recommendation. / **Sample
dishes:** sea bass with orange & lychee salsa; roast halibut with wild
mushrooms; pecan & chocolate pie with coconut sauce. **Details:** opp
Malmaison Hotel, on the shore in Leith; 10.30 pm.

constantly updated at www.hardens.com

(Fitz) Henry £ 40   A ★

19 Shore Pl EH6 6SW (0131) 555 6625

*Some reporters claim this "unusual" Leith warehouse-conversion as "Edinburgh's gastronomic highlight"; it comes "highly recommended" for its "interesting and very fresh" Gallic cooking and its "smooth and mellow service". / **Sample dishes:** goat's cheese & potato cake with fennel marmalade; stuffed squid with peppered butter beans; prune & apple pudding. **Value tip:** set 2/3-crs L £12/£16. **Details:** 10 pm, Fri & Sat 10.30 pm; closed Sun.*

Henderson's £ 18   ★

94 Hanover St EH2 1DR (0131) 225 2131

*After more than three decades in business, this "reliable", if dated basement buffet vegetarian near Princes Street "just keeps going" with its wide selection of "cheap" and "filling" dishes. / **Sample dishes:** broccoli & blue cheese soup; spinach & cashew nut lasagne; banoffi pie. **Details:** 10 pm; closed Sun; no smoking area.*

Indian Cavalry Club £ 27   ★

3 Atholl Pl EH3 8HP (0131) 228 3282

*"Refined" and "varied" modern Indian cuisine served in "elegant colonial surroundings" makes this popular subcontinental a "good all-rounder", and it has a wide following. / **Sample dishes:** mixed kebabs; lamb passanda; Indian ice cream. **Details:** between Caledonian Hotel & Haymarket Station; 11.30 pm; no smoking area.*

Indigo (yard) £ 28

7 Charlotte Ln EH2 4QZ (0131) 220 5603

*If you're eating, this noisy, trendy and intriguingly-designed bar/restaurant is "best for brunch or lunch" – its really more a place to hang out than a place to eat. / **Sample dishes:** goat's cheese & onion soufflé; Thai green chicken curry with jasmine rice; cheesecake. **Value tip:** set 3-crs D £15. **Details:** just off Queensferry St; 10 pm; no smoking area; children: 12+.*

Jacksons £ 35   ★

209 High St EH1 1PZ (0131) 225 1793

*"Tucked away down steep steps", this Royal Mile basement can seem "a real find" (though it does strike some as "a touch gloomy"); the "top-value set lunch" earns particular praise. / **Sample dishes:** haggis, neeps & tatties timbale; lamb with whisky mustard & brioche crust; crème brûlée with cinnamon shortbread. **Value tip:** set 2/3-crs L £7.50/£8.95. **Details:** on Royal Mile; 10.30 pm, Fri & Sat 11 pm.*

Kalpna £ 17   ★

2-3 St Patrick Sq EH8 9EZ (0131) 667 9890

*A "spectacular range of flavours and textures" reward visitors to this "exceptional" Gujerati vegetarian, whose "utilitarian" premises near the University belie the place's absolutely enormous following. / **Sample dishes:** vegetable pakora; okra masala; gulab jaman (Indian sweets). **Details:** 10.30 pm; closed Sat L & Sun; no Amex & no Switch; no smoking.*

Khushi's £ 13   ★

16 Drummond St EH8 9TX (0131) 556 8996

*"Don't be put off by the basic surroundings", this "studenty" BYO café near the university has been "family-run for 50 years", and it offers "simple and tasty Punjabi cooking" at notably "reasonable prices". / **Sample dishes:** deep-fried vegetable pakora; chicken curry; kulfi. **Details:** next to New Festival Theatre; 9 pm; closed Sun; no credit cards.*

Loon Fung   £ 25

2 Warriston Pl EH3 5LE   (0131) 556 1781
*This "popular" and "well-established" Canonmills Cantonese is
almost unanimously acclaimed "a classic quality restaurant";
a slight "lack of atmosphere" is the only real reservation.
/ **Sample dishes:** chicken & sweetcorn soup; beef in black bean sauce; ice
cream.* **Details:** *nr Botanical Gardens; 11.30 pm, Fri & Sat 12.30 am; closed
Sat L & Sun L.*

Malmaison   £ 28

1 Tower Place EH6 7DB   (0131) 468 5002
*The "chic" and "intimate" bistro of this "lovely" design-hotel on
the Leith waterfront "seems to have deteriorated" – there is now
a widespread feeling that it is "overpriced" and "pretentious".
/ **Sample dishes:** fishcakes with buttered spinach; smoked salmon blinis;
crème brûlée.* **Details:** *11 pm.* **Accommodation:** *60 rooms, from £110.*

The Marque   £ 34

19-21 Causewayside EH9 1QF   (0131) 466 6660
*This Southside two-year-old is an "efficient" place whose
"flavoursome" (and often quite meaty) cooking attracts fairly
consistent praise – especially from those who seek out the
"very good prix-fixe lunches" or the "cheap pre-theatre options".
/ **Sample dishes:** Caesar salad; baked sea bass with lentils; chocolate brownie
& fudge sauce.* **Value tip:** *set 2/3-crs L & pre-theatre £10/£12.50.* **Details:** *S
of Meadows, 15 mins from Princes Street; 10 pm, Fri & Sat 11 pm; closed
Mon; no smoking.*

Martins   £ 41   ★

70 Rose St, North Ln EH2 3DX   (0131) 225 3106
*It's certainly "not trendy", but that's part of the attraction of this
"fantastic small restaurant" in a New Town side street, which
offers "delicious" modern Scottish cooking; some find the pace of
a meal too "slow", but then the "unique" cheeseboard can "take
the owner 20 minutes to explain".* / **Sample dishes:** *monkfish with
bean & basil broth; roast guinea fowl with mash & black pudding; panna cotta
with iced berry parfait.* **Details:** *between Frederick St & Castle St; 10 pm;
closed Mon & Sun; closed 4 weeks at Christmas; no smoking; children: 7+.*

Number One   £ 53   ★

The Balmoral Hotel, 1 Princes St EH2 2EQ
(0131) 557 6727
*A "flat" ambience – thank to a setting that some feel "needs
a total overhaul" – discourages a wider following of this
well-reputed hotel basement dining room, where the culinary
"standards are set high and are maintained"; the "lunchtime set
menu is very good value". / **Sample dishes:** dressed crab salad; beef
with mushrooms in red wine sauce; Dutch cake & cream.* **Value tip:** *set 2-crs
L £18.* **Details:** *above Waverley Station; 10 pm, Thu–Sat 10.30 pm; closed
Sat L & Sun L; no smoking area.* **Accommodation:** *189 rooms, from £215.*

Pâtisserie Florentin   £ 10

8 St Giles St EH1 1PT   (0131) 225 6267
*What was, apparently, the first Gallic pâtisserie in Edinburgh,
near the Castle, is still a "useful" place, serving "delicious" cakes
and savoury snacks; there's also a Stockbridge branch at 5 NW
Circus Pl. / **Sample dishes:** home-made soup & bread; warm goat's cheese
salad; French chocolate truffle cake.* **Details:** *off Royal Mile, 200 metres from
Castle; 8 pm, Fri & Sat 9 pm; no credit cards; no smoking area; no booking.*

constantly updated at www.hardens.com   154

Le Petit Paris   £ 21   *A*

38-40 Grassmarket EH1 2JU   (0131) 226 2442

"Cheap and cheerful tasty food" and *"authentically French
service and ambience"* commend this aptly-named bistro, by the
Castle, to all who comment on it. / **Sample dishes:** *avocado & smoked
chicken salad; salmon in filo pastry with mange tout; orange & Cointreau
crepes.* **Details:** *11 pm; no Amex.*

Point Hotel Restaurant   £ 20   *A*

34 Bread St EH3 9AF   (0131) 221 5555

"The most classy cheap eat around" – the *"lovely"* dining room of
this *"stylish"* hotel impresses all who report on it with its
"good-value" menus. / **Sample dishes:** *snow crab & prawn salad; roast
duck with spring vegetables; strawberry tart with maple syrup.* **Details:** *2 mins
from Princes St, off Lothian Rd; 10 pm.*

Restaurant Martin Wishart   £ 40   ★★

54 The Shore EH6 6RA   (0131) 553 3557

Martin Wishart's *"stunningly creative cooking"* is *"the best
in Edinburgh by a long way"*, say the many fans of this
emerging star of the Leith waterfront, and his staff manage to be
*"zealous without being intrusive"; "go now, while the prices are
still reasonable"*. / **Sample dishes:** *crab & avocado salad; roast ham with
sautéed veal sweetbreads; armagnac parfait with fudge pears.* **Details:** *nr
Royal Yacht Britannia; 10 pm; closed Mon, Sat L & Sun; no Amex; no smoking
before 10 pm.*

Sept   £ 24

7 Old Fishmarket Close EH1 1RW   (0131) 225 5428

With a *"brilliant location"* down an atmospheric alley in the
Old Town, this slightly dated crêperie is liked for its *"great-value
prices"*; it's rather *"hit and miss"*, though, and some say
"standards have been dropping recently". / **Sample dishes:** *king
prawns; venison with roast vegetables; crème brûlée.* **Value tip:** *set 2/3-crs set
L £5/£6.* **Details:** *just off High St next to Cathedral; 10.30 pm, Fri 11.30 pm;
no smoking area.*

The Shore   £ 27   *A*

3-4 The Shore EH6 6QW   (0131) 553 5080

With its *"jazzy atmosphere"* and its dependable *"simple"*
seafood at *"affordable prices"*, this *"lovely", "casual"* bar and
restaurant remains a popular destination, near Leith's waterfront.
/ **Sample dishes:** *duck with Chinese spiced vegetables; grilled salmon fillet;
pear & plum tart.* **Details:** *10 pm; no smoking in dining room.*

Siam Erawan   £ 22   ★

48 Howe St EH3 6TH   (0131) 226 3675

The *"cave-like"* setting *"could be more inspiring"*, but *"staff are
friendly"* and the Thai cooking is *"lovely"* at this long-established
New Town basement. / **Sample dishes:** *crispy Thai pancakes with prawns
& coconut; Thai green chicken curry; banana fritters & coconut ice cream.*
Details: *10.45 pm; no Amex.*

Skippers   £ 30   *A*★

1a Dock Pl EH6 6UY   (0131) 554 1018

"Fishcakes to die (or kill) for" and *"perfect Dover sole"* are the
sort of dishes which make this *"quirky"* bistro a *"brilliant"* option;
it's reporters' favourite on Leith's waterfront. / **Sample dishes:** *grilled
sardines with Parmesan toast; sautéed scallops with smoked haddock risotto;
cheese & biscuits.* **Details:** *10 pm; closed Sun D.*

constantly updated at www.hardens.com   155

Stac Polly £ 38

29-33 Dublin St EH3 6NL (0131) 556 2231
*Haggis in filo pastry typifies the traditional-with-a-twist style at
this rather '80s New Town fixture (there is another branch at
8-10 Grindlay Street, tel 229 5405); fans say the food is
"superb" and like the "quiet and pleasant atmosphere" while to
others it's a tad "dowdy" and rather "expensive" for what it is.*
/ *Sample dishes: haggis filo parcels with plum sauce; pan-fried beef with
mushrooms in claret jus; iced raspberry crannachan parfait.*
Details: *10.30 pm; closed Sun L; no smoking area.*

Sukhothai £ 25 ★

23 Brougham Pl EH3 9JU (0131) 229 1531
*"Consistently good food" and "warm and friendly service" are the
hallmarks of this Tollcross Thai.* / *Sample dishes: spring rolls; Thai
green curry with coconut milk & aubergines; banana fritters.* ***Details:*** *nr Kings
Theatre; 10.30 pm; closed Tue L.*

Suruchi £ 25

14a Nicolson St EH8 9DH (0131) 556 6583
*"Serious Indian cooking" (with a hint of "Scottish fusion" thrown
in) ensures it's not just visitors to the nearby Festival Theatre who
seek out this "friendly" and "tastefully-decorated" spot.* / *Sample
dishes: chickpeas, potatoes & coriander in tangy sauce; chicken in lemongrass
& mustard seed sauce; kulfi.* ***Details:*** *opp Edinburgh Festival Theatre;
11.30 pm; closed Sun L; no Amex.*

Susies £ 15 ★

51-53 West Nicholson St EH8 9DB (0131) 667 8729
*"Really good veggie food" and "eccentric but friendly" service
make this "rustic", "cafeteria-style" spot, by the University,
a popular "cheap and cheerful" choice; licensed, but you can
BYO.* / *Sample dishes: spinach & chick pea soup; vegetable & tofu sweet
& sour stir-fry; almond & pear tart.* ***Details:*** *opp the University buildings opp
the Pear Tree pub; 9 pm; no credit cards; no smoking area; no booking.*

Thai Orchid £ 23 ★

44 Grindlay St EH3 9AP (0131) 228 4438
*"Great-tasting food" at "very reasonable prices" together with
"very helpful staff" are helping this small oriental off Lothian
Road "to go from strength to strength".* / *Sample dishes: chicken
satay; Thai green curry with chicken; sticky rice with mango.*
Details: *10.30 pm; closed Sat L & Sun L.*

36 Restaurant £ 39 ★

36 Great King St EH3 6QH (0131) 556 3636
*The "modern" and "minimalist" style of this hotel dining room
seems all the more striking in contrast to its elegant New Town
hotel setting; the cooking is quite "unusual", too, and makes deft
use of "fresh Scottish produce".* / *Sample dishes: tandoori chicken
terrine with mango; halibut with goat's cheese & parsley crust; hot orange
& mint soufflé.* ***Details:*** *between Dundas St & Drummond Place; 10 pm;
D only, ex Sun open L & D; no smoking.* ***Accommodation:*** *15 rooms,
from £245.*

Tinelli's £ 25

139 Easter Rd EH7 5QA (0131) 652 1932
*Though there is the odd gripe, locals continue to applaud
Giancarlo Tinelli's well-established neighbourhood fixture as
a "top-quality, authentic Italian family restaurant".* / *Sample
dishes: soup; roast veal with new potatoes; cassata.* ***Value tip:*** *set 2-crs L &
pre-theatre £8.95.* ***Details:*** *11 pm; closed Sun; no Switch.*

The Tower   **£ 38**

Museum of Scotland, Chambers St EH1 1JF
(0131) 225 3003
*The Atrium's year-old sibling on the top floor of the museum has
an "amazing view" over the castle; it's a particular shame, then,
about the "pretentious" and "overpriced" modern British cooking
and the "snooty" service. / **Sample dishes:** duck liver parfait; beef with
smoked garlic & mushroom broth; chocolate truffle torte. **Value tip:** set 2-crs
pre-theatre £12 (post-theatre £10.95). **Details:** at top of Museum of Scotland;
11 pm; no smoking.*

Valvona & Crolla   **£ 23**   ★

19 Elm Row EH7 4AA   (0131) 556 6066
*"It's worth the wait" for "the best Italian cooking in Scotland",
say the many devotees who regularly queue to enter the "lively"
café adjoining this "amazing foodie shop"; even some who
acknowledge the place's finer qualities, however, feel that prices
are a wee bit "high"; wines, however, come at shop prices plus
modest corkage (L £3, D £6). / **Sample dishes:** polenta with
Gorgonzola & Parmesan; roast poussin stuffed with lemon, garlic & rosemary;
chocolate cake & baked apricots. **Details:** at top of Leith Walk, 500m from
the Playhouse Theatre; 5 pm; closed Sun; no smoking.*

Vintners Rooms   **£ 40**   Ａ★

The Vaults, 87 Giles St EH6 6BZ   (0131) 554 6767
*"Lovely food" and the "historic" but "cosy" setting combine to
make this 17th-century Leith wine warehouse ("lit with candles
and chandeliers") Auld Reekie's top all-rounder, certainly for
those of a traditional bent; "take a cab, and allow plenty of time
– you won't want to leave". / **Sample dishes:** char-grilled scallops with
red pepper sauce; lamb with rosemary, onions & leeks; lavender crème brûlée.
Value tip: set 3-crs L £15. **Details:** 10.30 pm; closed Sun; closed first
2 weeks in Jan; no smoking in dining room.*

The Waterfront   **£ 27**   Ａ

1c Dock Pl EH6 6LU   (0131) 554 7427
*Prominently-located Leith docksider whose rambling, wine bar-like
interior offers a "mix of old world charm and modern
conservatory"; there is "a good selection of wine and beer" and
the cooking is "good if you think of it as pub food". / **Sample
dishes:** moules marinière; salmon & sole with saffron cream sauce; banoffi pie.
Details: close to Royal Yacht Britannia; 9.30 pm, Fri & Sat 10 pm;
no smoking area; children: 5+.*

The Witchery by the Castle   **£ 47**   Ａ

352 Castlehill, The Royal Mile EH1 2NF   (0131) 225 5613
*The extraordinary and "charming" Gothic-style setting near the
Castle may be "fantastic" – the most atmospheric in town by far
– but this long-established destination "relies on its reputation";
the Scottish cooking is "very average" and "overpriced",
and service can be "arrogant, inept and slow". / **Sample
dishes:** smoked duck with beetroot sorbet; Aberdeen Angus with smoked garlic
broth; dark chocolate torte. **Value tip:** set 2-crs L & pre-theatre £9.95.
Details: at the top of the Royal Mile; 11.30 pm. **Accommodation:** 2 rooms,
from £195.*

Tankerville Arms £ 24

15 The Village NE66 2TX (01665) 578444
A "wide choice" of "good pub food" commends this "comfortable" and "friendly" traditional pub to local reporters, and it's often very busy. / **Sample dishes:** chicken & saffron sausage with black pudding; roast sea bream with Thai vegetables; black cherry & almond tart. **Details:** off A1; 9 pm; no smoking in dining room.

Woolpack £ 25

The Green GU8 6HD (01252) 703106
A "brilliant location and a gorgeous garden" are the top attractions of this "enjoyable pub", where the traditional fare comes in "good portions". / **Sample dishes:** deep-fried Camembert with port & cranberries; chicken & ham pie; fruit pavlova. **Details:** 7m SW of Guildford, on village green; 9.45 pm; no Amex; no booking.

Old Fire Engine House £ 30

25 St Mary's St CB7 4ER (01353) 662582
A "good range of English dishes" has made this "lovely and informal" spot a popular destination for over 30 years; some note that "the menu doesn't seem to have changed in the last decade", or think the place stuck "in an old-fashioned rut". / **Sample dishes:** game terrine with crab apple jelly; roast English lamb with mint & lemon stuffing; syllabub. **Details:** nr Cathedral; 9 pm; closed Sun D; no Amex; no smoking area.

36 on the Quay £ 49 ★

47 South St PO10 7EG (01243) 375592
"Accomplished" cooking and an "excellent" seaside location make this "superb" restaurant a universally popular recommendation; it's certainly no bargain, though, and the occasional reporter complains that it's "full of business groups". / **Sample dishes:** pan-fried mullet with pesto; seared scallops with chicken & goose liver sausage; quartet of lemon desserts. **Value tip:** set 2/3-crs L £16.95/£19.95. **Details:** off A27 between Portsmouth & Chichester; 10 pm; closed Mon L, Sat L & Sun; no smoking in dining room; booking: max 15.

Epworth Tap £ 28

DN9 1EU (01427) 873333
The food is only somewhere between "good and simple" and "very average", but even critics say Helen Wynne's rustic wine bar of over 20 years standing is "redeemed by its excellent wines". / **Sample dishes:** smoked haddock with cucumber & chilli salsa; roast pork stuffed with apricots & sage; poached pears. **Details:** 3m from M180; 9 pm; D only, open Wed-Sat only; no smoking.

Good Earth £ 34

14-18 High St KT10 9RT (01372) 462489
"Thoroughly consistent over the last 20 years", this "above-average" Chinese – "both in quality and in cost" – "is a reliable performer, but then there's not a huge amount of local competition". / **Sample dishes:** spring rolls; vegetable chow mein; Chinese ice cream. **Details:** 11 pm.

Gilbey's   £ 30
82-83 High St SL4 6AF   (01753) 855182
The name may have changed – from the more explanatory Eton
Wine Bar – but the ownership of this "consistent" performer is
the same as ever; its "buzzy" atmosphere makes it an agreeable
rendezvous, either in the wine bar at the front or the
conservatory restaurant behind. / **Sample dishes:** Tatin of goat's cheese
& red onions; char-grilled squid; dark chocolate mousse with strawberries.
Details: 5 mins walk from Windsor Castle; 10.30 pm, Fri & Sat 11 pm.

Summer Lodge   £ 57   A ★
Summer Lodge DT2 0JR   (01935) 83424
It's "worth the drive into the depths of Dorset", says
a London-based fan of this "hidden gem" of a country house
hotel (which celebrated its twentieth anniversary this year);
it benefits from a "very civilised" setting (with a beautiful walled
garden) and most reporters find the cooking "fantastic". / **Sample
dishes:** grilled red mullet on herb couscous; beef with Swiss rosti & pan-fried
foie gras; hot praline soufflé. **Value tip:** set 2/3-crs L £12.50/£15.75.
Details: 12m NW of Dorchester on A37; 9.30 pm; jacket;
no smoking in dining room; children: 7+. **Accommodation:** 17 rooms,
from £165.

Wild Duck   £ 25   A
Drakes Island GK7 6BY   (01285) 770310
"A romantic country inn with hearty locals and equally hearty
food" is one reporter's summary of this "bustling", old inn, which
has a "lovely" village location; the menu is essentially traditional,
with the odd modern twist. / **Sample dishes:** fishcakes with salsa; rib-eye
steak; sticky toffee pudding. **Details:** 10 pm. **Accommodation:** 11 rooms,
from £75.

Brazz   £ 27
10-12 Palace Gate EX1 1JU   (01392) 252525
This "bright and shiny new eatery" – an offshoot of the Taunton
establishment – has so far attracted modest commentary; such
as there is concentrates on the fact that it's a "good, lively place",
with the cooking attracting little comment. / **Sample dishes:** club
sandwich terrine; smoked haddock kedgeree with poached egg; caramel
mousse with prunes. **Details:** off South St, opp White Hart Hotel; 10.30 pm,
Fri & Sat 11 pm.

Double Locks Pub   £ 20   A
Canal Banks, Alphington EX2 6LT   (01392) 256947
"A fantastic setting and an interesting and wide-ranging menu"
help make it "a real experience" to visit this "wonderful"
canalside pub; it's located near the centre of the town, and has
a "great beer garden". / **Sample dishes:** mushrooms & blue cheese on
toast; spinach pie; sticky toffee pudding. **Details:** through Marsh Barton
industrial estate, follow dead-end track over bridges to end of towpath;
10.30 pm; no Amex.

Lambs   **£ 31**

15 Lower North St EX4 3ET   (01392) 254269

This popular restaurant built quite a reputation (and won impressive rating from reporters) under its former owners, the Aldridges – lets hope that that the new owners, the Owens, can keep the flag flying. / Sample dishes: caramelised onion, leek & almond tart; Devon lamb with leek & potato mash; triple chocolate glory. Details: under Iron Bridge, 200m from Cathedral; 10 pm; closed Mon, Sat L & Sun; no smoking area.

Thai Orchid   **£ 29**

5 Cathedral Yd EX1 1HJ   (01392) 214215

"I've been to Thailand, and this is authentic", says one of the more vocal local fans of this "intimate" oriental, whose overall level of achievement is "unusual for Devon". / Sample dishes: hot & sour king prawn soup; Thai green chicken curry; Thai fresh fruit salad. Value tip: 30 minute 1crs lunch £5/ 2crs business lunch £9.50 with coffee/ regular 2crs lunch menu £7.50. Details: nr Exeter Cathedral; 10.30 pm; closed Sun; no Amex; booking advisable.

FAVERSHAM, KENT   3–3C

Read's   **£ 37**   ★

Mummery Court ME13 0EE   (01795) 535344

It may be housed in an "ugly" former supermarket, but the Pitchford family's long-established restaurant is "very comfortably furnished"; it "maintains very high standards of cooking" and a "good wine list", while service is "quietly courteous". / Sample dishes: oak-smoked haddock; roast lamb with wild mushrooms & pea purée; hot harlequin soufflé. Details: 2.5m SW of Faversham, by A2 & Brogdale Road; 9.30 pm; closed Mon & Sun.

FAWLEY, OXFORDSHIRE   2–2D

Walnut Tree   **£ 29**

RG9 6JE   (01491) 638360

A "wonderful", "rural" location – down a single track road – adds lustre to this "friendly" and "comfortable" pub, which serves some "novel" grub at "reasonable prices". / Sample dishes: salmon, asparagus & dill fishcakes; roast lamb with rosti potatoes; walnut & orange pudding with caramel sauce. Details: off A4153 between Marlow & Henley; 9.30 pm; no smoking area. Accommodation: 3 rooms, from £55.

FERRENSBY, NORTH YORKSHIRE   8–4B

General Tarleton   **£ 31**   ★

Boroughbridge Rd HG5 0QB   (01423) 340284

"Good food" – in "fabulous variety" and "Yorkshire portions" – makes it worth the deviation from the A1 to sample this roadside bar/restaurant (an offshoot of the illustrious Angel at Hetton); its atmosphere strikes some as "not quite wine bar, and not quite pub". / Sample dishes: smoked salmon tartare with lemon oil; roast lamb with ratatouille & red pepper jus; chocolate & banana bread & butter pudding. Details: 9.30 pm; D only, ex Sun when L only; no jeans; no smoking. Accommodation: 14 rooms, from £74.95.

FISHGUARD, PEMBROKESHIRE

4–4B

Three Main Street £ 38 ★★

3 Main St SA65 9HG (01348) 874275

"Innovative" and "consistently excellent" cooking, together with "relaxed" but "attentive" service, wins unanimous rave reviews for Inez Ford & Marian Evans's "small restaurant with rooms, overlooking the harbour"; it offers "good value for money" too. / **Sample dishes:** confit of guinea fowl with roast garlic; sea bass with braised fennel & butter sauce; orange & Grand Marnier jelly. **Details:** off town square on Newport to Cardigan road; 9 pm; closed Mon & Sun; no credit cards; no smoking in dining room. **Accommodation:** 3 rooms, from £60.

FLETCHING, EAST SUSSEX

3–4B

The Griffin Inn £ 30 ★

TN22 3SS (01825) 722890

"Well above-average pub food in an inn of character" – this "cosy" country pub wins a widespread following with its "imaginative" menu, "friendly" service and "nice big garden". / **Sample dishes:** gravadlax with lemon & fennel; char-grilled beef with red onion confit; summer fruit brûlée. **Details:** off A272; 9.30 pm; no smoking area. **Accommodation:** 8 rooms, from £65.

FORD, WILTSHIRE

2–2B

White Hart Inn £ 33

SN14 8RP (01249) 782213

Worth knowing about near historic Castle Coombe, this very fine old inn has a "beautiful country setting" – with a terrace by the River Bybrook – and offers a "good range" of "generous" dishes. / **Sample dishes:** beef carpaccio with Parmesan crisps; grilled cod on colcannon & buttered spinach; fig & honey Mascarpone tart. **Details:** on A420 between Chippenham & Bristol; 9.30 pm. **Accommodation:** 11 rooms, from £84.

FORT WILLIAM, HIGHLAND

9–3B

Crannog £ 35 Ⓐ★

Town Pier PH33 7NG (01397) 705589

The "great, fresh and fairly unfussy" seafood is highly rated at this "closely packed" venture; it occupies a "wonderful" converted smokehouse in an "idyllic location", overlooking Loch Linnhe. / **Sample dishes:** smoked salmon selection; fisherman's feast with dauphinoise potatoes; heather cream cheesecake. **Details:** 10 pm (9 pm Dec-Mar); no Amex; no smoking area.

Inverlochy Castle £ 58 Ⓐ

Torlundy PH33 6SN (01397) 702177

"Spectacular Highland surroundings" help make a visit to this splendid baronial pile a "fabulous" experience; the grandly traditional cooking may cost an arm and a leg, but it rarely disappoints. / **Sample dishes:** salmon with cucumber & yoghurt; roast veal with morel & madeira sauce; poached pears in puff pastry. **Details:** off A82; 9.15 pm; closed Jan-mid Feb; jacket & tie; no smoking; children: 12+. **Accommodation:** 17 rooms, from £250.

FOWLMERE, CAMBRIDGESHIRE

3–1B

Chequers £ 27 ★

SG8 7SR (01763) 208369

"A perfect example of a quality food-pub", the Rushtons' classic day-out-from-Cambridge destination offers "an excellent menu" ("with lots of fish") complemented by "a good wine list". / **Sample dishes:** smoked haddock & tomato in chive cream; sautéed turkey in citrus & tomato sauce; pan-fried peaches with amaretto. **Details:** on B1368 between Royston & Cambridge; 10 pm; no smoking area.

FRESSINGFIELD, SUFFOLK 3–1D

The Fox & Goose £ 32 ★

IP21 5PB (01379) 586247

Fans find "pure escapism" in a visit to this "long-time favourite" –
an old inn in the heart of rural Suffolk – whose hearty menu
(which includes "a good choice for vegetarians") is realised to
"consistently good" standards. / **Sample dishes:** grilled halloumi with
pitta bread; roast cod with garlic mash; sticky toffee pudding. **Value tip:** set
2/3-crs L £9.50/£12.50. **Details:** off A140; 9.30 pm; closed Mon & Tue;
no Amex; no smoking.

FRITHSDEN, HERTFORDSHIRE 3–2A

Alford Arms £ 29

HP1 3DD (01442) 864480

"Much improved under new owners", this "nice country pub"
offers "unusual" and "imaginative" cooking in a "traditional"
setting. / **Sample dishes:** poached salmon; pork stuffed with black pudding;
grilled figs with honey ice cream. **Details:** nr Ashridge College, by vineyard;
10 pm; booking: max 12.

FRODSHAM, CHESHIRE 5–2A

Netherton Hall £ 27 ★

Chester Rd WA6 6UL (01928) 732342

"Exceptionally good fish" is a highlight at this "stylish" and
"friendly" boozer, which offers "very good pub cooking (if at
restaurant prices)", with "real ale and live bands". / **Sample
dishes:** pork & duck terrine; chicken stuffed with Brie & Parma ham;
Cointreau & chocolate mousse. **Details:** 4m from Stanlon service station;
9 pm; no smoking area.

GANTS HILL, ESSEX 3–3B

Elephant Royale £ 30

579 Cranbrook Rd IG2 6JZ (020) 8551 7015

This suburban Thai is "well furnished", and local fans profess
themselves "intoxicated" by its "exotic" cooking. / **Sample
dishes:** chicken satay; sweet & sour king prawns; steamed banana with
coconut cream. **Details:** 11.45 pm; closed Mon.

GATESHEAD, TYNE & WEAR 8–2B

Last Days of the Raj £ 22 ★

Low Fell NE9 5HY (0191) 482 6494

An "excellent choice" of "good" and "plentiful" Indian cooking of
"high quality" combines with "cheerful" service to create quite
a name for this "traditional" Indian, conveniently located for
visitors to the Angel of the North. / **Sample dishes:** mixed kebab;
chicken masala; Italian cassata ice cream. **Value tip:** £43.95 or £44.95 five
courses and coffee. **Details:** 1m from Angel of the North statue; 11 pm;
no smoking area.

GIBRALTAR, BUCKINGHAMSHIRE 2–2D

Bottle & Glass £ 34

HP17 8TY (01296) 748488

"It may look like a pub from the outside, but in fact it's a
very good restaurant" – this "wonderfully English", thatched
establishment offers "quite a variety of dishes", with fish and
seafood the speciality. / **Sample dishes:** smoked pork with chutney; wok-
fried chilli prawns with ginger sauce; strawberry & raspberry shortcake.
Details: on A418 between Thame & Aylesbury; 9.15 pm; closed Sun D.

Glasgow has a diversified restaurant 'scene' in a way which, outside London, no other British city does, with quality establishments of many different types and at all price levels. It has distinguished traditional-style places (such as *City Merchant*), quirky favourites (*Café Gandolfi*, *Stravaigin*) and a very good choice of ethnic restaurants (especially Indians). It also boasts a couple of famous institutions – the Art Deco *Rogano's* and the much-cherished *Ubiquitous Chip* (both of which currently give the impression of being deeply mired in complacency) – and also, in *One Devonshire Gardens*, a top-end restaurant of real quality.

Glasgow is also one of the few cities outside London where the restaurant-scene is fast-changing enough that there is always some hot new place the locals are chattering about. Current tips include *Arthouse*, *Eurasia* and *Groucho St Judes*.

Those in search of Indian cooking are spoilt for choices (such as *Ashoka*, *Kama Sutra*, *Killermont Polo Club* and *Mother India*), and there are also good oriental restaurants at various price levels, places such as *Amber Regent*, *Ichiban* and *Thai Fountain*).

Air Organic £ 28 ★★
36 Kelvingrove G3 7SA (0141) 564 5200
"Fresh organic produce, smartly presented in a "bright" environment by enthusiastic, young staff" is a formula which *"never disappoints"* at this *"slick"* Kelvingrove spot; *"excellent Bento boxes"* figure among the selection of *"superb Asian and Eastern food"*. / **Sample dishes:** *roast tomato & Mozzarella crostini; beef fillet bento box; white chocolate & lemon cheesecake.* **Details:** *nr Kelvingrove art galleries ; 11 pm; no smoking area; booking: max 10 at weekends.*

Amber Regent £ 33 ★
50 West Regent St G2 2QZ (0141) 331 1655
"Great Chinese food" from a *"vast and bountiful menu"* combines with *"efficient"* service to make this *"luxurious"* spot a *"consistently good"* city-centre choice. / **Sample dishes:** *crab claws stuffed with prawns; barbecued duck with ginger & spring onions; apple tart.* **Value tip:** *half-price main courses Mon & Tue and Wed-Sat L.* **Details:** *500m from Central Station; 11 pm; closed Sun.*

Arthouse £ 33 Ⓐ★
129 Bath St G2 2SY (0141) 221 6789
This new hotel dining room is already "one of Glasgow's best"; it's shot to popularity with its "excellent food, especially fish", and its "stylish" but "laid-back" approach. / **Sample dishes:** *roast field mushrooms with Parmesan; char-grilled lamb cutlets; pineapple upside-down cake.*

Ashoka £ 25 ★

19 Ashton Ln G12 8SJ (0800) 454817

*The Ashoka group of Indian restaurants is indeed a shocker for poor old restaurant guide editors, as the original and, some would say, best 'branch' (108 Elderslie St, tel 0141-221 1761) is under different ownership from the rest of the chain (the leading branch of which is detailed above) – fortunately, almost all reports on all the establishments are of the "consistently good" variety. / **Sample dishes:** vegetable & fish pakoras; grilled chicken with coconut & chilli sauce; 'death by chocolate' cake. **Details:** behind Hillhead Underground station; midnight; closed Sun L.*

Babbity Bowster £ 26 Ⓐ

16-18 Blackfriar's St G1 1PE (0141) 552 5055

*"A good selection of Scottish food", "friendly" service and a "lively" but "always comfortable" ambience make this celebrated Merchant City pub a consistently popular choice. / **Sample dishes:** haggis; lamb with spinach & sorrel sauce; fresh fruit crepes. **Details:** 10 pm; closed Sat L & Sun.*

Bar Brel £ 24

Ashton Ln G12 8SG (0141) 342 4966

*"Sophisticated, yet hip and down-to-earth", this "Scottish/Belgian" hang out is particularly tipped for its "fantastic" moules and "wonderful" sausages. / **Sample dishes:** grilled polenta with goat's cheese; sausage & chips; Belgian waffles. **Details:** behind the University; 10.30 pm, Fri & Sat 11 pm.*

Buttery £ 50

652 Argyle St G3 8UF (0141) 221 8188

*With its comfortable, panelled interior, this clubby spot near the SECC is tailor-made for business; it's a shame that its current approach strikes the few reporters who comment on it as "dull" and "unimaginative". / **Sample dishes:** chicken with herb mousse & lentils; seared lamb with apricot Tatin; Scotch whisky tart with cinnamon custard. **Value tip:** set 2/3-crs L £14.95/£16.95. **Details:** under Kingston Bridge; 10.30 pm; closed Sat L & Sun; no smoking area.*

Café Gandolfi £ 25 Ⓐ★

64 Albion St G1 1NY (0141) 552 6813

*"It's worth a visit, just to see the furniture" at this "warm" and "woody" Merchant City favourite, where "consistently high-quality local produce is cooked simply, and served with a smile". / **Sample dishes:** cullen skink; smoked venison with potato dauphinoise; lemon tart. **Details:** nr Tron Theatre; 11.30 pm; no Amex; no smoking area.*

Café India £ 20

171 North St G3 7DA (0141) 248 3818

*It doesn't always hit the heights, but, for its many supporters, this "enormous cavern of a place" offers "really authentic" Indian cooking, which includes "particularly good vegetarian dishes". / **Sample dishes:** chicken pakora; spiced lamb with tomatoes; Indian sweets. **Details:** nr Charing Cross, next to Mitchell Library; midnight; no smoking area.*

Café Mao £ 25

84 Brunswick St G1 1ZZ (0141) 564 5161

*"Asian/Thai food with a twist" served in "bright", "trendy", "utilitarian" premises by "friendly" staff wins strong – if not universal – praise for this new "Scottish version of a trendy Dublin bar". / **Sample dishes:** fried fishcakes; lemongrass & chilli tiger prawns; frozen yoghurt. **Details:** close to George St; 11 pm; no Amex; no smoking area.*

City Merchant £ 31 A★

97-99 Candleriggs G1 1NP (0141) 553 1577

*"Faultless" fish and game are highlights from the "imaginative"
blackboard menus of this unpretentious institution, in the heart
of the Merchant City.* / **Sample dishes:** fish soup with parsley; salmon
& prawns with sesame noodles; Scottish clootie dumpling. **Value tip:** set 2/3-
crs L & pre-theatre £10.50/£12.75. **Details:** nr George Square; 11 pm; closed
Sun L; no smoking area.

Crème de la Crème £ 28

1071 Argyle St G3 8LZ (0141) 221 3222

"The name says it all", claim the many fans of the *"best Indian
buffet in town"*, served in a converted cinema in a rather desolate
area just south of the West End; *difficulty catching a waiter's eye
leaves some feeling "under-served".* / **Sample dishes:** fresh mussels;
Indian garlic chilli chicken; kulfi. **Details:** nr Scottish Exhibition Centre; 11 pm;
closed Sun L; no smoking area.

Eurasia £ 44 ★

150 St Vincent St G2 5NB (0141) 204 1150

*"It's worth starving yourself for a week – ambience, food and
wine all excel"*, says one of the many enthusiasts for the
European/Asian fusion fare at Ferrier Richardson's financial
district newcomer; *the experience doesn't always gel, though,
and one refusnik likens it to "eating in an airport waiting room,
and being served by students".* / **Sample dishes:** oriental hors
d'oeuvres; salmon with bok choy & prawn bouillon; trio of citrus desserts.
Details: 2 mins from George Square; 11 pm; closed Sat L & Sun.

Fusion £ 19 ★

41 Byres Rd G11 (0141) 339 3666

"It's worth the wait for a table", at this *"great"* year-old sushi-bar
in the West End; the *"different"* experience it offers is universally
praised. / **Sample dishes:** beef teriyaki; mixed vegetable & seafood tempura;
nut ice cream. **Details:** at very end of Byres Rd, at Dunbarton Road
intersection; 10 pm, Fri & Sat 11 pm; closed Sun L; no smoking.

Gamba £ 42 ★

225a West George St G2 2ND (0141) 572 0899

"Early promise has been maintained" at this *"stylish"* Milngavie
yearling, which offers *"serious seafood cooking"* (*"in a modern
and imaginative way"*), a *"very good wine list"* and *"intelligent"*
service. / **Sample dishes:** fish soup with crab & prawn dumplings; halibut
with prawns, asparagus & croutons; lemon & poppy seed cake. **Value tip:** set
2/3-crs L & early eve £10.95/£13.95. **Details:** 10.30 pm; closed Sun; children:
14+.

Groucho St Judes £ 28 A★

190 Bath St G2 4HG (0141) 352 8800

*Unlike its parent, the new offshoot of the trendy London media
club lets in the hoi polloi; early reports are very positive about the
"soothing" style, the "generous" and "delicious" cooking, and the
"friendly" service.* / **Sample dishes:** eggs in Parma ham with melted
Gorgonzola; grilled langoustines with ginger & parsley; raspberry & Mascarpone
tart. **Details:** 10.30 pm; closed Sun L. **Accommodation:** 6 rooms, from £95.

Ichiban £ 17 A★

50 Queen St G1 3DS (0141) 204 4200

"Everything tastes fabulous, and looks even better", says one
of the many enthusiastic local fans of the *"stupendous"
Japanese noodles"* served at this *"fun"* and *"funky"* bar.
/ **Sample dishes:** assorted sushi; salmon teriyaki bento box; green tea.
Details: 9.45 pm, Fri & Sat 10.45 pm; no smoking; no booking on weekends.

The Inn on the Green   £ 29   A

25 Greenhead St G40 IES   (0141) 554 0165
*The food may be slightly incidental, but a pianist and a blues
singer create "just the right atmosphere for an evening out with
friends"* at this Calton institution. / *Sample dishes: haggis filo parcels
with plum sauce; grilled oak-smoked salmon; pineapple, banana & butterscotch
pie. Value tip: set 2-crs L & early eve £5.95 (Sun £11.95). Details: 1m E of
city centre on London Rd; 9.30 pm. Accommodation: 18 rooms, from £75.*

Insomnia   £ 16

38-42 Woodlands Road G3 6UR   (0141) 564 1530
*The name says it all about this all-hours clubbers' delight of
a café near Kelvingrove Park, which serves simple snacks that
"taste good whenever".* / *Sample dishes: home-made soup; Casablanca
chicken; chocolate fudge cake. Details: nr Charing Cross; open 24 hrs.*

Kama Sutra   £ 27   A★

331 Sauchiehall St G2 3HW   (0141) 332 0055
*For a curry "away from the 10-pint crowd", this "modern and
chic" 'designer' Indian, opposite the Centre for Contemporary Art,
delivers a high level of satisfaction; cooking is "fresh and tasty"
and service is "friendly".* / *Sample dishes: samosas; chicken tikka; ice
cream. Value tip: 3-crs buffet lunch £5.95. Details: midnight; closed Sun L.*

Killermont Polo Club   £ 26   A★

2022 Maryhill Rd G20 0AB   (0141) 946 5412
*"Very different from the usual Indian"; the "idiosyncratic" theme
successfully creates an air of "faded elegance" around this pukka
Maryhill establishment whose "very good" and "different"
cooking and "top" service are universally praised.* / *Sample
dishes: prawn tikka; chicken stuffed with cheese & pomegranate; fruit pavlova.
Details: nr Maryhill Station; 10.30 pm; closed Sun L; jacket & tie;
no smoking area.*

Mitchell's   £ 25

157 North St G3 7DA   (0141) 204 4312
*This small and "brightly decorated" stand-by – which has a West
End offshoot at 35 Ashton Lane, tel 339 2220 – offers
"Scottish/bistro" cooking at moderate prices; some reports are
more enthusiastic than others.* / *Sample dishes: wood pigeon salad;
seafood & game specials; crème brûlée. Value tip: set 2/3-crs pre-theatre
£8.95/£10.95. Details: nr Charing Cross; 10.30 pm; closed Sat L & Sun;
children: 12+.*

Mother India   £ 27   A★★

28 Westminster Ter G3 7RU   (0141) 221 1663
*"Freshly made" and "flavoursome" dishes from a "short but
excellent" menu and "genuine and friendly" service make this
"lively" Indian reporters' top Glaswegian subcontinental –
no mean achievement in this curry-mad city; BYO.* / *Sample
dishes: spiced haddock; cumin chicken with courgettes; ice cream. Value
tip: set 3-crs L £6.95, (pre-theatre £8.95). Details: beside Kelvingrove Hotel;
10.30 pm, Fri & Sat 11 pm; closed Sun L; no Amex.*

Mr Singh's India   £ 23   ★

149 Elderslie St G3 7JR   (0141) 204 0186
*"Quality cooking" and the "no-rush, no-hurry" approach adopted
by its kilted waiters help make this Kelvingrove Park Indian
a "satisfying" destination.* / *Sample dishes: pan-fried prawns in garlic
& lime; South Indian garlic spiced chicken; toffee pudding. Value tip: 5-crs
menu £16.50. Details: on Charing Cross corner, nr art galleries; 11.30 pm.*

Nairns £ 42

13 Woodside Cr G3 7UP   (0141) 353 0707

Even some who say the food's "excellent" complain of the "pretentious" and "snobby" attitude of TV-chef Nick Nairn's "rather stark" Kelvingrove Park townhouse establishment; for many, the place is just "well below expectations – and his reputation – in every department". **Sample dishes:** *hot smoked salmon with avocado & mango salsa; char-grilled lamb with roasted vegetables; hot ginger treacle pudding.* **Value tip:** *set 2/3-crs L £9/£12 (Sun £18.50).* **Details:** *nr Charing Cross; 10 pm; closed Mon L & Sun; no smoking at D; children: 10+ at D.* **Accommodation:** *4 rooms, from £90.*

Number 16 £ 25   ★

16 Byres Rd G11 5JY   (0141) 339 2544

"Outstanding Scottish/French bistro cooking" that's "simple but refined" wins enthusiastic local endorsements for this "small and friendly" spot, near the Dumbarton Road. / **Sample dishes:** *pan-fried scallops; honey-roast duck with vegetables; chocolate tart.* **Value tip:** *pre-theatre menu available between 5.30-6.30.* **Details:** *close to Dumbarton Rd; 10 pm; closed Mon L, Tue L, Wed L, Thu L, Fri L & Sun; no Amex; no smoking until coffee.*

Oblomov West End £ 22

372-374 Great Western Rd G4 9HT   (0141) 339 9177

With its "basic" Eastern European menu, this West End bistro pleases its local fans who say its "brilliant value"; sceptics, though, find the food "very average". / **Sample dishes:** *blinis with sour cream & caviar; Budapest chicken casserole; Hungarian cheesecake.* **Details:** *11.45 pm; children: before 5 pm only.*

One Devonshire Gardens £ 55   A★

1 Devonshire Gardens G12 0UX   (0141) 339 2001

It's "an experience" to dine at this "lovely" Georgian townhouse-hotel, which is the grandest dining room in town, and just "excellent in every respect"; "let's hope it doesn't go off now that the group that owns it has changed hands". / **Sample dishes:** *smoked lobster with lime butter; roast venison with pickled red cabbage; banana soufflé with chocolate sauce.* **Details:** *1.5m from M8, J17; 9.45 pm; closed Sat L; no Switch; no smoking.* **Accommodation:** *27 rooms, from £130.*

Parmigiana £ 30   ★

447 Great Western Rd G12 8HH   (0141) 334 0686

Waiters who are "real Italians" contribute to the authenticity of Angelo and Sandro Giovanzzi's small trattoria on the western fringe of the city centre – "it goes on for ever, at the same high standards". / **Sample dishes:** *pasta with prawns & tomatoes; corn fed chicken with Mozzarella stuffing; poached pears with Mascarpone.* **Value tip:** *set 3-crs D £8.60.* **Details:** *at Kelvinbridge underground station; 11 pm; closed Sun.*

Puppet Theatre £ 43   A

11 Ruthven Ln G12 9BG   (0141) 339 8444

Everyone agrees that this "sumptuous" and "very intimate" series of rooms has a "wonderful ambience"; even some fans, though, admit the cooking can be "unpredictable" and a few find it "very disappointing, for the price". / **Sample dishes:** *fricassée of scallops & courgettes; pan-fried lamb with fennel & potato purée; orange flower & cardamom tart.* **Value tip:** *set 2/3-crs L £12.95/£14.50.* **Details:** *nr Ashton Lane; 10.30 pm; closed Mon & Sat L; no smoking area; children: 12+.*

constantly updated at www.hardens.com

Rogano £ 45

11 Exchange Pl G1 3AN (0141) 248 4055
This "famous, long-established oyster bar" has long been
a "stylish and elegant jewel in Glasgow's crown"; it's lost some
of its gleam of late, however – the "fine Art Deco" interior may
be as "splendid" as ever, but the food is "uninspiring", prices
are "high", and some find the experience plain "dull". / *Sample
dishes:* tuna & salmon sushi; seared trout & noodles with Thai curry sauce;
pear & peach tarte Tatin. *Value tip:* set 3-crs L & Sun L £16.50 (also cheaper
basement café). *Details:* off Buchanan St, opp Borders; 10.30 pm; no smoking
before 10 pm.

Sarti's £ 20 A★

121 Bath St G2 2SZ (0141) 204 0440
Many see this "cramped" and "always busy" Glasgow institution
as "the perfect Italian deli/restaurant"; it's family-run and the
food "tastes like family food"; ("this is the only place my Italian
mother will go for pizza", says one reporter). / *Sample
dishes:* stuffed mushrooms; penne ragu; tiramisu. *Details:* 11 pm;
no smoking area; no booking at L.

78 St Vincent £ 35

78 St Vincent's St G2 5UB (0141) 221 7710
This "impressive" city-centre venture is "always full", thanks in
part to some "imaginative" cooking; support is undermined,
though, by complaints of "overpricing", and by an attitude some
find "pretentious". / *Sample dishes:* smoked chicken, duck & ham terrine;
Scottish salmon in Parma ham with spinach; chocolate cheesecake with coffee
cream. *Value tip:* set 2/3-crs L £10.95/£13.95. *Details:* 2 mins from George
St; 10.30 pm, Fri & Sat 10.45 pm; closed Sun L; no smoking area.

Shish Mahal £ 23 ★

66-68 Park Rd G4 (0141) 339 8256
"The best naans in Scotland" figure among the "authentic"
and "unadorned" Indian fare on offer at this long-established
subcontinental; fans find it "revitalised" by its "stylish" renovation.
/ *Sample dishes:* chicken & cashew nut curry; chicken tikka masala; gulab
jaman (Indian sweets). *Details:* 11.30 pm; closed Sun L; no smoking area.

Stravaigin £ 34 ★

28 Gibson St G12 8NX (0141) 334 2665
Colin Clydesdale's "original and clever" cooking that's
"adventurous" but "unfussy" makes this "casual" and "friendly"
fixture, near the University, one of the most consistently popular
places in town; regulars often tip the "cheaper" bar over the
basement restaurant. / *Sample dishes:* oriental noodle salad with confit
duck; seared fish in Malaysian coconut broth; Belgian chocolate cake with
bananas. *Details:* 11 pm; closed Sun L; no smoking before 10 pm.

Thai Fountain £ 33 ★

2 Woodside Cr G3 7UL (0141) 332 1599
Glasgow's original and best Thai restaurant may be "a bit pricey",
but it delivers consistently "tasty" and "authentic" cooking; some
find its "smart" setting "slightly lacking in atmosphere". / *Sample
dishes:* chicken satay; crispy beef & egg fried rice; bananas in coconut milk.
Details: by Clydesdale Bank; 11 pm; closed Sun; children: 7+.

Thirteenth Note £ 21 ★

50-60 Kings St G1 5QT (0141) 553 1638
"A totally vegan pub, wow!"; this "studenty" spot serves
"great-value" grub and is a popular place to "chill out, meet and
eat". / *Sample dishes:* dolmades with Greek salad; red Thai curry with
jasmine rice; blueberry cake. *Details:* just off Argyle St at Trongate clock
tower; 10 pm; no Amex; children: 18+ after 6.30 pm.

The Tron Bar £ 25 🄰

63 Trongate G1 5HB   (0141) 552 8587
*Recent renovation has unsettled reports on this trendy local
favourite, in the Tron Theatre; most still confirm its "unusual and
inventive menu" and "excellent value for money", but there were
also complaints of "terrible" cooking and "sullen" service.*
/ **Sample dishes:** bruschetta with plum tomatoes; rib-eye steak with Parmesan
chips; chocolate tart with praline ice cream. **Value tip:** set 2-crs pre-theatre
£8.95. **Details:** 11 pm; closed Sun D if theatre is closed; no Amex;
no smoking area; children: before 8 pm only.

Two Fat Ladies £ 36

88 Dumbarton Rd G11 6NX   (0141) 339 1944
*"The banter between the chef and the waiter" can add spice to
a visit to this "tiny" fixture, where "nice fish dishes" are the
culinary highlight; (the place has never been related to the TV
duo, which it pre-dated).* / **Sample dishes:** pan-fried squid with garlic
salad; char-grilled scallops with coriander salsa; white chocolate terrine.
Details: 10 pm; closed Mon, Tue-Thu L & Sun L; no Amex.

Ubiquitous Chip £ 43

12 Ashton Ln G12 8SJ   (0141) 334 5007
*Thanks to its "lush" and very "charming" courtyard setting and
its "rich and savoury Scottish fare", this famous institution still
commands the affections of many reporters; what's much more
striking, however, is the very large proportion who are
disappointed by "rude" and "self-obsessed" service or by
"over-intricate", "over-cooked" and "overpriced" cuisine.* / **Sample
dishes:** salt cod & salmon with cauliflower cream; roast pigeon in bacon with
pearl barley risotto; Caledonian oatmeal ice cream. **Value tip:** set 3-crs Sun
L £16.60. **Details:** directly behind Hillhead underground; 11 pm.

Yes! £ 43

22 West Nile St G1 2PW   (0141) 221 8044
*With chef-patron Ferrier Richardson leaving to establish
nearby Eurasia, this once-eminent modern basement in the
city centre has lost its way; the setting was always a bit "bland",
but the same is increasingly true of the food, and there are also
complaints of "poor" service.* / **Sample dishes:** pan-fried scallops with
couscous & mango; roast guinea fowl with herb & bacon broth; crème brûlée.
Details: in centre between St. Vincent St & Gordon St; 10.30 pm; closed Sun.

GLENCULLEN, COUNTY DUBLIN, *EIRE*   10–3D

Johnnie Fox's Pub IR £ 36 🄰

(01) 295 5647
*"Peat fires" and "friendly and intelligent service" are major
selling-points of this very popular, "real Irish pub in the
Wicklow Hills"; the "fantastic seafood" for which the place is
known receives strong, if not quite universal, praise.* / **Sample
dishes:** mussels in white wine; lobster salad; Bailey's cheesecake. **Details:**
off N11; 10 pm; closed Sun L; no Amex; children: 18+ after 7 pm.

GOLCAR, WEST YORKSHIRE   5–1C

Weavers Shed £ 40 🄰★

Knowl Rd HD7 4AN   (01484) 654284
*Though one or two reporters say it "doesn't live up to its former
reputation", most find it "a real treat" to visit Steven Jackson's
"out-of-this-world" mill-conversion; it scores highly for its
"imaginative" dishes that "mix the modern and the traditional".*
/ **Sample dishes:** Thai prawn & squid salad; poached beef with peppercorn
sauce; apricot crumble. **Details:** 10 pm; closed Mon, Sat L & Sun.
Accommodation: 5 rooms, from £40.

GORING, BERKSHIRE
Leatherne Bottel   £ 38   2–2D   𝔸

Bridleway   RG8 OHS   (01491) 872667

The attractions of this rather idiosyncratic venture, with its "lovely Thames-side setting", seem to have withstood the sad death of owner Keith Read; chef Julia Storey still wins praise for her "tricky-sounding dishes that do actually work", but as ever some find the menu "overpriced" and service a touch "off-hand". / **Sample dishes:** *flat mushrooms on black olive toast; jasmine tea-smoked duck; sticky toffee pudding.* **Details:** *0.5m outside Goring on B4009; 9 pm; closed Sun D; children: 8+.*

GRAMPOUND, CORNWALL
Eastern Promise   £ 29   1–4B   ★

1 Moor View   TR2 4RT   (01726) 883033

"Excellent Chinese food" ("with lots of variety") comes served "with a broad Cornish accent" at Philip and Lisa Tse's "great local favourite". / **Sample dishes:** *crispy won-tons; chicken with cashew nuts; banana fritters.* **Details:** *between Truro & St Austell on A390; 10 pm; D only ex Wed open L & D; no smoking area; children: 3+.*

GRANGE MOOR, WEST YORKSHIRE
Kaye Arms   £ 28   5–1C

29 Wakefield Rd   WF4 4BG   (01924) 848385

"Good fish dishes" and "delicious puds" are menu highlights at this "friendly" and "consistently good" pub-turned-into-a-restaurant. / **Sample dishes:** *mushroom & bacon salad with mustard dressing; mature cheddar cheese soufflé; trio of sweets.* **Details:** *7m W of Wakefield on A642; 9.30 pm; no Amex; no smoking area; children: not at D.*

GRASMERE, CUMBRIA
Lancrigg Country House Hotel   £ 34   7–3D   ★

Easedale Rd   LA22 9QN   (01539) 435317

Unusually for an hotel, this "small" establishment, "stunningly-located" in the Easedale Valley, offers "wholesome, exclusively veggie produce" and a range of "organic wines". / **Sample dishes:** *Parmesan & pine kernel soufflé; chestnut, wild mushroom & cranberry tart; orange, sultana & pecan pudding.* **Details:** *off A591; 8 pm; D only (bar snacks at L); no smoking in dining room.* **Accommodation:** *12 rooms, from £100, incl D.*

Michael's Nook   £ 58   𝔸★★

LA22 9RQ   (01539) 435496

"Perfect location, perfect food"; the Giffords' long-established, "intimate" and "luxurious" country house hotel provokes practically unanimously positive reports for its "excellent" Gallic cooking and its "stunning wine list". / **Sample dishes:** *foie gras with Périgord duckling; roast lamb with herb crust; Bramley apple mousse.* **Details:** *A591 to Grasmere, turn right at Swan Hotel; 9 pm; jacket & tie; no smoking; children: 7+.* **Accommodation:** *14 rooms, from £135, incl D.*

GREAT DUNMOW, ESSEX
Starr   £ 34   3–2C

Market Pl   CM6 1AX   (01371) 874321

This "old inn in the market square" has been "cleverly extended", and fans say it's a "classy, but not intimidating" spot offering "consistently good" cooking; doubters, though, find its whole approach "rather pretentious". / **Sample dishes:** *fresh scallops & bacon; rack of lamb with garlic & rosemary parfait; steamed syrup pudding.* **Value tip:** *set 2-crs L £11.* **Details:** *M11, J8 then 7m E on A120; 9.30 pm; closed Sun D; no jeans; no smoking.* **Accommodation:** *8 rooms, from £100.*

Harry's Place £ 68 ★★

17 High St NG31 8JS (01476) 561780

*This family cottage dining room is "intimate" and "select" in
a way only a 10-seater could ever hope to be – book, or they just
won't have any food for you!; reporters unanimously proclaim
Harry Hallam's very personal, modern British cooking
"a revelation", and none begrudge its not inconsiderable cost.*
/ **Sample dishes:** smoked Scottish salmon; spring lamb with tarragon sauce;
prune & armagnac ice cream. **Details:** on B1174 1m N of Grantham;
9.30 pm; closed Mon & Sun; no Amex & no Switch; no smoking; booking
essential; children: 5+.

Le Manoir aux Quat' Saisons £101 ★

Church Rd OX44 7PD (01844) 278881

*Raymond Blanc's "awesome" modern French cuisine, service
"of the highest order" and a "near perfect" setting deliver
a "consummate all-round experience" for most visitors to this
manor house near Oxford; prices are, of course, "ridiculous" and
some find the venture now "commercialised" to an unacceptable
degree.* / **Sample dishes:** foie gras & quince terrine with balsamic jelly; roast
partridge with black pudding; caramelised pear brioche. **Value tip:** set 3-crs
L £42. **Details:** from M40, J7 take A329 to Great Milton; 10.15 pm;
no smoking; booking: max 8. **Accommodation:** 32 rooms, from £230.

Falkland Arms £ 23 Ⓐ★

The Green OX7 4DB (01608) 683653

*Thanks to its "charming village setting" and its "honest,
unpretentious English food" that's "promptly served", this "lively"
and "friendly" old pub is a universally popular recommendation.*
/ **Sample dishes:** grilled goat's cheese salad; slow-cooked lamb with rosemary
& garlic; fudge cheesecake. **Details:** A361 between Banbury & Chipping
Norton; 8 pm; closed Sun D; no smoking; children: 14+. **Accommodation:** 6
rooms, from £65.

White Hart £ 33 Ⓐ★

Pool St CO9 4HJ (01787) 237250

*"You really feel appreciated and cared for" at this
"exemplary country inn" (under the same ownership as the
Three Horseshoes at Madingley); the highlight is the "lovely",
"half-timbered" 15th-century setting, but the cooking –
"executed with care and style" – does not disappoint.* / **Sample
dishes:** wild mushroom tart; roast cod in pancetta with split pea purée; lemon
tart. **Value tip:** set 2/3-crs L £8.50/£12.25. **Details:** between Haverhill
& Halstead on A604; 9.30 pm; no smoking.

Café de Paris £ 34

35 Castle St GU1 3UQ (01483) 534896

*Some find that "genuine French cuisine" adds to this place's
charms as a venue for "good casual dining"; too many reporters,
though, leave "unimpressed" by either food or service.* / **Sample
dishes:** pan-fried scallops with aubergines & tomatoes; sea bream with red
peppers & coriander; floating islands. **Details:** 11 pm; closed Sun; booking:
max 20.

Cambio £ 35   A

10 Chapel St GU1 3UH (01483) 577702
In the "cottage setting" of this "civilised" and "friendly" spot,
the "modern Italian cooking" it offers seems all the more
"innovative". / **Sample dishes:** black lasagne with crab; salt-crusted sea
bass; strawberries in balsamic vinegar. **Value tip:** set 2-crs L £9.50.
Details: by Guildford Castle; 10.30 pm, Fri & Sat 11 pm; closed Sun, Mon
L and Sat L; no smoking in dining room.

Rum Wong £ 22

16-18 London Rd GU1 2AF (01483) 536092
It may be "very crowded" and "moderately expensive", but this
"old-favourite" Thai – with its "very fresh and authentic" cooking
– has a large and enthusiastic local fan club. / **Sample
dishes:** chicken & coconut soup; pad Thai; Thai ice cream.
Details: 10.45 pm; closed Mon; no Amex & no Switch; no smoking area.

GUISELEY, WEST YORKSHIRE 5–1C

Harry Ramsden's £ 17

White Cross LS20 8LZ (01943) 874641
"Fish and chips in traditional style, and all the better for it"
commend this de luxe chippy – the granddaddy of the chain –
to most reporters; even some fans, though, say the place "may
be past its peak". / **Sample dishes:** Yorkshire pudding with onion gravy;
haddock & chips; bread & butter pudding. **Details:** off A65; 10 pm; booking:
need 4+ to book.

GULLANE, EAST LOTHIAN 9–4D

La Potinière £ 46   ★★

Main St EH31 2AA (01620) 843214
"Hilary Brown is justly famous" for the "sublime" (no-choice)
menus at this "unpretentious" "treasure", outside Edinburgh,
where a visit is a "memorable" experience; David Brown presides
over the hefty wine list, and over the small dining room whose
ambience is "more 'provincial French' than France!" / **Sample
dishes:** crispy salmon with vierge sauce; honey-roast venison; lemon tart.
Details: 17m E of Edinburgh, off A198; 8 pm; closed Sun-Thu D, Fri L & Sat
L; no credit cards; no smoking.

GULWORTHY, DEVON 1–3C

Horn of Plenty £ 50   A★★

PL19 8JD (01822) 832528
"All-round professional competence" makes reporters feel
"very special" at this "fabulous" restaurant with rooms, which
occupies in a large, rural Victorian house with "fine" views of the
Tamar Valley; Peter Gorton's "fresh" and "imaginative" cooking
inspires almost unanimous applause. / **Sample dishes:** goat's cheese
& courgette salad; fillet steak with garlic & parsley soufflé; tuille biscuits & fruit
compote. **Value tip:** set (no choice) 3-crs Mon D £23.50. **Details:** 3m W of
Tavistock on A390; 9 pm; closed Mon L; no smoking; children: 13+.
Accommodation: 10 rooms, from £115.

HADDINGTON, EAST LOTHIAN 9–4D

Waterside Bistro £ 27

1-5 Nungate EH41 4BE (01620) 825674
This "really lovely waterside spot" seems to "suffer from its own
popularity"; the French cooking may be "reasonable", but prices
strike some as rather high, and service can be "slow" and
"amateurish". / **Details:** 17m E of Edinburgh, on A1; 10 pm.

HALIFAX, WEST YORKSHIRE 5–1C
Design House £ 31 ★
Dean Close HX3 5AX (01422) 383242
*Now back on better form, this "London-style" restaurant in
a minimalist mill-conversion offers generally "excellent" modern
British cooking in a "stylish" setting. / Sample dishes: pappardelle with
crab; sweet potato & prawn cakes; baked banana & almond tart. Value
tip: set 2/3-crs L £10.95/£14.95. Details: 0.5m from Halifax, towards Ceeps;
10 pm; closed Mon D, Sat L & Sun D.*

HAMBLETON, RUTLAND 5–4D
Hambleton Hall £ 65 A★
Hambleton LE15 8TH (01572) 756991
*"Magnificent food in a spectacular setting" makes Tim Hart's
"gorgeous" hotel, on a peninsula surrounded by Rutland Water,
"a real joy in every department" for most reporters; some note
that "it's not got the most relaxed atmosphere", though, and one
or two find the prices a little "crazy". / Sample dishes: poached
langoustines with tomato jus; honey-roast duck with stir-fried vegetables;
caramelised passion fruit tart. Details: 3m E of Oakham; 9.30 pm;
no smoking; children: 6. Accommodation: 17 rooms, from £195.*

HAMPTON HILL, SURREY 3–3A
Monsieur Max £40 ★★
133 High St TW12 1NJ (020) 8979 5546
*"Delightfully rich, succulent French fare" and "courteous,
knowledgeable and efficient" staff make it "worth the drive" to
Max Renzland's foodie mecca in Hampton Hill; "prices have
risen", but it still delivers "huge value". / Value tip: set 2-crs L £13.
Details: nr Teddington; 10.30 pm; closed Sat L; children: 8+.*

HANDFORTH, CHESHIRE 5–2B
Hilal Restaurant £ 20
90 Wilmslow Rd SK9 3ES (01625) 524942
*"A cut above the usual curry house", this "friendly" Indian offers
a "comprehensive menu, well cooked and served". / Sample
dishes: chicken tikka kebabs; chicken Dansak; mango, lychee & pineapple.
Details: 11 pm, Fri & Sat 11.30 pm; no Amex.*

HAROME, NORTH YORKSHIRE 8–4C
Star Inn £ 33 A★★
YO6 5JE (01439) 770397
*"Everything was a winner" is typical of the numerous reports on
Andrew and Jacquie Pern's "quaint, picturesque and very friendly"
14th-century inn, which some think houses "the best restaurant
in North Yorkshire"; the "outstanding" cooking "makes innovative
use of excellent local ingredients". / Sample dishes: grilled black
pudding with pan–fried foie gras; cod with blue Wensleydale & watercress
salad; ginger parkin with rhubarb ice cream. Details: 3m SE of Helmsley off
A170; 9.30 pm; closed Mon & Sun D; no Amex; no smoking.*

HARPENDEN, HERTFORDSHIRE 3–2A
Chef Peking £ 24
5-6 Church Green AL5 2TP (01582) 769358
*"All your favourite dishes, cooked to perfection" make this "basic
but reliable" Chinese an excellent local. / Sample dishes: spring rolls;
crispy duck & pancakes; toffee apples. Details: just off the High Rd;
10.45 pm; no Switch; no smoking area.*

Bettys £ 28   𝔸

1 Parliament St HG1 2QU (01423) 502746
"Like a '30s timewarp" – *"with frilly black and white clad
smiling waitresses"* – this *"absolute classic"* of a tearoom sails
serenely on; *"Yorkshire thrift has not inhibited the pricing"*,
but *"who cares? – the tea is wonderful"*. / **Sample dishes:** *Betty's
Yorkshire rarebit; Swiss rosti with bacon & raclette cheese; fresh cream
strawberry heart.* **Details:** *opp Cenotaph; 9 pm; no Amex & no Mastercard;
no smoking area; no booking.*

Drum & Monkey £ 27   ★★

5 Montpellier Gardens HG1 2TF (01423) 502650
"Excellent-value fresh fish" – lunchtime prices are *"incredible"* –
and *"superb"* seafood ensure there's always a *"lively"* atmosphere
in the *"cramped"* surroundings of this converted Victorian bar
and restaurant; *"arrive early for lunch"*, when there's no booking
in the bar (though you can reserve tables upstairs). / **Sample
dishes:** *langoustine salad; sea bass, prawns & monkfish in brandy sauce;
crème brûlée.* **Details:** *10.15 pm; closed Sun; no Amex; booking: max 8.*

Ganja £ 23   𝔸

34 Oxford St HG1 1PP (01423) 504475
Unusually *"stylish"* décor creates an interesting setting for this
"modern" subcontinental, whose *"delicately spiced"* cooking
intoxicates a small but vociferous band of addicts. / **Sample
dishes:** *onion bhaji; chicken curry; ice cream.* **Details:** *next to Palamon St;
midnight; D only; no Amex & no Switch; no smoking area.*

Rajput £ 17   ★★

11 Cheltenham Pde HG1 1DD (01423) 562113
"You rarely spend more than a tenner a head" at Perveen Khan's
"wonderful Indian", and his *"exceptional"*, *"home-made"* food is
"prepared with love and generosity". / **Sample dishes:** *chicken tikka;
chicken balti with pilau rice & naan bread; ice cream.* **Details:** *midnight;
D only; no Amex; children: 4+.*

Villu Toots £ 32

Balmoral Hotel, Franklin Mount HG1 5EJ (01423) 705805
"Consistently interesting" and *"dramatically-presented"* cooking
makes this *"minimalist"* spot stand out in these parts; for some
reporters, though, it *"tries too hard"* to be up-to-date. / **Sample
dishes:** *duck spring rolls with orange dressing; Caesar salad with chicken
& bacon; chocolate fondue.* **Details:** *off King's Rd; 10 pm; closed Sat L.*
Accommodation: *20 rooms, from £84.*

The Mermaid Café £ 19   ★

2 Rock-a-Nore Rd TN34 3DW (01424) 438100
"The best fish and chips anywhere" justify a visit to Tom &
Dryden Fennell's somewhat *"pokey"* beachside spot;
"excellent full English breakfasts" are a further attraction.
/ **Sample dishes:** *shell-on prawns with lemon mayonnaise; battered haddock
& chips; spotted dick & custard.* **Value tip:** *brunch at £4.50.*
Details: *7.30 pm; no credit cards; no bookings (except for D in winter).*

Sea Pebbles   £ 17   ★

348-352 Uxbridge Rd HA5 4HR   (020) 8428 0203

*"The best old-fashioned fish and chips you can find, in enormous portions" make this "the best chippy for miles". / **Sample dishes:** sweet marinated herrings; haddock fried in matzo meal with chips; apple pie with custard. **Details:** 9.45 pm; closed Mon L & Sun; no credit cards; no booking.*

Blue Strawberry   £ 33   𝔸★

The Street CM3 2DW   (01245) 381333

*The obscure location and beamed cottage setting belie the modern style and atmosphere of this rural bistro; "the food is always good", and service is friendly and efficient, so the place can get "fully booked, weeks in advance". / **Sample dishes:** fresh green salad; lamb shank with saffron & thyme risotto; passion fruit & apricot mousse. **Details:** 3m E of Chelmsford; 10 pm; closed Mon L, Sat L & Sun D.*

Weavers   £ 26   𝔸★

15 West Ln BD22 8DU   (01535) 643822

*"Quiet, cosy and extremely well run", Colin & Jane Rushworth's "long-term favourite" – in a row of old cottages – maintains "a high standard" of "tasty and homely" cooking. / **Sample dishes:** pear, Yorkshire blue cheese & crisp bacon salad; duck with stir fried greens & ginger sauce; chocolate & marshmallow brownie. **Details:** 1.5m W on B6142 from A629 close to Parsonage; 9 pm; D only, closed Mon & Sun; no smoking. **Accommodation:** 3 rooms, from £75.*

Jeremys at Bordehill   £ 34   ★

Balcombe Rd RH16 1XP   (01444) 441102

*This "small bar and restaurant" is "just as good" as the better known Jeremy's at the Crabtree (now closed) – by the standards of "friendly", "local" places, Jeremy Ashpool produces some "outstanding" results. / **Sample dishes:** tiger prawns & guacamole salad; pigeon with celeriac rosti & Madeira sauce; chocolate torte with cinnamon ice cream. **Details:** 15m S of M23, exit 10a; 9.30 pm; closed Mon & Sun D; no smoking.*

1086   £ 33

Hazlewood Castle Hotel, Paradise Ln LS24 9NJ
(01937) 535354

*The "pretty but pricey" dining room of this ancient building – mentioned in The Domesday Book, apparently – gets a rather mixed report; some describe "wonderful food in a wonderful setting", but others found that "surly" service contributed to an "uncomfortable" overall experience. / **Sample dishes:** honey-roast gammon with lentil purée; confit lamb with artichoke purée & roast fennel; raspberry soufflé with lemon cream. **Details:** signposted on the A64; 9.30 pm; D only, ex Sun L only; no smoking. **Accommodation:** 21 rooms, from £125.*

constantly updated at www.hardens.com

Café at All Saints £ 17 Ⓐ★

All Saints Church, High St HR4 9AA (01432) 370415
"Super-fresh vegetarian cooking" wins a chorus of praise for the café in this *"stunningly-converted medieval church"*. / **Sample dishes:** broccoli & Stilton soup; potato & onion gratin with cheese & broccoli; raspberry cheesecake. **Details:** nr Cathedral; L only; closed Sun; no smoking; no booking; children: 6+.

Dining Room £ 27 ★

10 Queens Rd KT12 5LS (01932) 231656
"Old English cooking at its best" – served in a setting *"like someone's front room"* – is praised for its *"consistency"* at this pleasant spot; don't miss the blackbird pie (whose ingredients are not as you might imagine). / **Sample dishes:** Gloucester cheese & ale mustard with toast soldiers; steak & kidney pudding with gravy; spotted dick & custard. **Details:** just off A3, by village green; 10.30 pm; closed Sat L & Sun D.

The Angel £ 37 ★

BD23 6LT (01756) 730263
It may be *"in the middle of nowhere"*, but this *"cosmopolitan"* Dales inn remains the UK's most popular country pub; occasionally *"slow"* service (largely caused by the legions of people served) is the only tangible gripe regarding an establishment which consistently serves *"exceptionally good"* traditional-ish food (in both bar and restaurant), and which maintains a large cellar of *"excellent"* wines. / **Sample dishes:** tomato & basil risotto; roast venison wrapped in Parma ham; strawberry brûlée crunch. **Value tip:** set 2/3-crs early-eve £12/£15. **Details:** 5m N of Skipton off B6265 at Rylstone; 9.30 pm; D only, ex Sun when L only; no smoking area.

King William IV £ 29 Ⓐ★

Chishill Rd SG8 8PW (01763) 838773
A *"licensee with personality"* creates a *"unique atmosphere"* at this *"friendly"* boozer, tucked up a steep lane; *"good vegetarian food is hard to find in pubs, but here it forms the best part of the menu"*. / **Sample dishes:** crispy duck tossed in raspberry vinaigrette; beef & mushrooms with herb dumplings; pancakes with golden syrup. **Details:** take A505 from M11 J10, for 4 miles; 10 pm; no Amex; no smoking area; children: 12+.

Hintlesham Hall £ 45

IP8 3NS (01473) 652334
This *"wonderful house"*, famous for its past association with Mr Robert Carrier, has *"the potential to be great"*; it misses its mark with reporters, though, a number of whom complain of *"mediocre"* cooking and *"prissy"* service. / **Sample dishes:** guinea fowl & peppercorn sausage; char-grilled lamb with roasted vegetables; chilled rhubarb soup. **Value tip:** set 3-crs weekday L £21. **Details:** 4m W of Ipswich on A1071; 9.30 pm; closed Sat L; jacket & tie; no smoking; no booking; children: 10+. **Accommodation:** 33 rooms, from £120.

HISTON, CAMBRIDGESHIRE

3–1B

Phoenix £ 24 ★

20 The Green CB4 4JA (01223) 233766

This "very popular restaurant, near the village green" offers Chinese cooking that's "expensive" by local standards; it's "worth it", though, as results are "always surprisingly good". / **Sample dishes:** pepper & salt squid; smoked chicken salad; ice cream. **Value tip:** set 2-crs L £6.50. **Details:** 10.30 pm; no Amex; no smoking area.

HOGNASTON, DERBYSHIRE

5–3C

Red Lion £ 28 ★

Main St DE6 1PR (01335) 370396

An "excellent standard" of "varied food" at "good prices" helps make this "pleasant country pub", in the heart of a small village, a very useful spot en route to the Peak District. / **Sample dishes:** smoked salmon pâté; tropical moontail sea bass; home-made panna cotta. **Details:** 9 pm; closed Mon L & Sun D; no Amex. **Accommodation:** 3 rooms, from £75.

HOLT, NORFOLK

6–3C

Yetman's £ 42 Ⓐ★

37 Norwich Rd NR25 6SA (01263) 713320

"A lady who can really cook and a guy with a superb knowledge of wines" is the setup at this "friendly restaurant in a small country town", where the "superb" modern British cooking makes use of "excellent, fresh local produce". / **Sample dishes:** char-grilled fish with red chilli jam; roast duck marinated in red wine; cinnamon, apple & quince pancakes. **Details:** on A148, 20m N of Norwich; 9.30 pm; D only, ex Sun open L & D, summer, closed Tue ; no smoking area.

HONLEY, WEST YORKSHIRE

5–2C

Mustard & Punch £ 27

6 Westgate HD7 2AA (01484) 662066

This "intimate modern British restaurant" is unanimously hailed by the locals for providing "cheap, cheerful and fun meals, served in simple surroundings" and for its general "care and attention to detail"; midweek menus, in particular, offer "excellent value". / **Sample dishes:** king prawn won tons; monkfish with lemon & butter sauce; white chocolate tart. **Value tip:** set 2-crs L £6.50. **Details:** 10 pm; closed Mon, Sat L & Sun; no Amex.

HORNDON ON THE HILL, ESSEX

3–3C

The Bell Inn £ 29 ★★

High Rd SS17 8LD (01375) 642463

This may just seem like a "very old pub", but it's "always full", thanks to its "exceptional" cooking, which offers an "original and interesting mix of flavours" – "it's such a cracking place, I always feel lucky to get a table". / **Sample dishes:** marinated prawn & tomato tart; braised beef with mustard mash; steamed apple pudding. **Details:** signposted off B1007, off A13; 10 pm; no smoking. **Accommodation:** 15 rooms, from £40.

HORTON, NORTHANTS

3–1A

French Partridge £ 34 ★

NN7 2AP (01604) 870033

"Traditional French cuisine, well executed" and a "good wine selection" have made this family-run spot a reliable destination for over a quarter of a century. / **Sample dishes:** potted shrimps; roast venison with port jus; panna cotta with peaches. **Details:** on B526 between Newport Pagnell & Northampton; 9 pm; D only, closed Mon & Sun; no credit cards; no smoking.

Knife & Cleaver £ 32

The Grove MK45 3LA (01234) 740387

*"Excellent pub/restaurant" food "justifies above-average prices"
and makes this converted tavern a popular local choice; a
"very pleasant terrace" is an added attraction. / **Sample
dishes:** deep–fried plaice & crab cakes; home-smoked duck with apple
& ginger; butterscotch pot with chocolate shortbread.* **Value tip:** *set 2/3-crs
L £12.95/£14.95.* **Details:** *off A6, 5m S of Bedford; 9.30 pm; closed Sat L &
Sun D; no smoking.* **Accommodation:** *9 rooms, from £49.*

Linos £ 26   🅐★

122 Market St CH47 3BH (0151) 632 1408

*The Galantini family's "wonderful" bistro has quite a name locally
for its "mouthwatering" French cooking and "superb" value; for
such a small place, it offers quite a show too – "Nigel will recite
the list of scrumptious desserts like a Shakespearean soliloquy".
/ **Sample dishes:** fresh duck & chicken livers with balsamic vinegar; Spanish-
style roast lamb with mash; coffee ice cream with chocolate wafers.*
Details: *3m from M53, J2 towards Hoylake; 9.45 pm; closed Mon & Sun.
Closed August for holidays; no Amex.*

Bradley's £ 30   ★

84 Fitzwilliam St HD1 5BB (01484) 516773

*"Thoughtful and imaginative" cooking that offers "exceptional
value for money" – especially at lunch – combines with "friendly"
service to make this a well-liked town-centre spot. / **Sample
dishes:** black pudding fritters with beetroot salsa; chicken & asparagus
wrapped in Parma ham; black cherry clafoutis.* **Value tip:** *set 3-crs D Mon-Fri
(& pre-theatre Sat) £14.50.* **Details:** *in town centre above the railway arches;
10 pm; closed Sat L & Sun; no Amex; no smoking area.*

Nawaab £ 22   ★

35 Westgate HD1 1NY (01484) 422775

*"Excellent food" served in a "kitsch" but "airy" setting makes this
"good-value" subcontinental "worth travelling for" – "not after
a few pubs, but for a celebration!" / **Sample dishes:** mixed tandoori;
Nirali special; kulfi.* **Details:** *between bus & railway stations; 11 pm, Fri & Sat
midnight; D only.*

Shabab £ 19   ★

2 Eastgate L52 7JL (0113) 246 8988

*"Friendly" and "attentive" service helps create a good impression
at this "pleasant" Indian of long standing – one of a small
Yorkshire chain; "everything is carefully prepared and very
satisfying". / **Sample dishes:** chicken tikka; chicken balti with peshwari
naan; kulfi.* **Value tip:** *£9.95 buffet between 6-9.30pm everyday.*
Details: *11.30 pm, Fri & Sat midnight; closed Sat L & Sun L.*

Cerutti's £ 27   ★

10 Nelson St HU1 1XE (01482) 328501

*With a "fantastic" location by the Humber, Tony Cerutti's "classic
fish restaurant" has put in over a quarter of a century's service of
producing "quality produce, exquisitely prepared"; his family also
run Cerutti's 2 in nearby Beverley (tel 01482 866700). / **Sample
dishes:** avocado, scallop & bacon salad; grilled halibut with garlic butter;
double chocolate torte.* **Value tip:** *set 3-crs menu for two people.*
Details: *follow signs to the fruit market; 9.30 pm; closed Sat L & Sun;
no Amex.*

Garden Palace £ 25

31 Lottingham Rd HU5 2PP (01482) 492475

"Forget you're in Hull at this luxurious Chinese"; it's an eminent place locally on account of its "good and tasty" cooking from a "varied" menu. / **Sample dishes:** Mongolian crispy lamb; roast Cantonese style duck; ice cream. **Details:** nr University; 10.45 pm; closed Sun L.

Hitchcocks £ 14 ★

1 Bishop Ln HU1 1PA (01482) 320233

"Booking is essential" – the place doesn't open otherwise – at Bruce Hitchcock's "unique" buffet vegetarian where "if you're the first to call you can determine the culinary theme for the evening"; a "relaxed" atmosphere and "excellent value for money" make the place a big hit locally. / **Sample dishes:** guacamole & bean dip; artichoke & Mozzarella pizza; pecan pie. **Details:** follow signs to Old Town; 10.30 pm; D only; booking essential; no credit cards.

HUNTINGDON, CAMBRIDGESHIRE 3–1B

Pheasant £ 32 ★

PE18 0RE (01832) 710241

An "innovative, frequently-changing menu", "a good selection of wines and beers" and "easy-going" staff are consistently well received at this popular thatched tavern (in the same group as Madingley's Three Horseshoes). / **Sample dishes:** gazpacho with garlic bread; pink sea bream with goat's cheese crostini; custard tart with nutmeg ice cream. **Details:** one mile south of A14 between Huntingdon and Kettering; 10 pm; no smoking area.

ILKLEY, WEST YORKSHIRE 5–1C

The Box Tree £ 43

35-37 Church St LS29 9DR (01943) 608484

This is one of the North's longest-established gastronomic destinations, and it still garners praise for its "very fine French cuisine" and "amazing wine list"; feedback was hugely mixed this year, however, with disappointment focussing on "inadequate", "nouvelle cuisine"-sized portions, and a "fussy" and "reverential" approach. / **Sample dishes:** scallops with lemon & butter sauce; lamb cutlet with roasted onions; chocolate harlequin. **Details:** on A65 near town centre; 9.30 pm; closed Mon & Sun D; no smoking in dining room.

IPSWICH, SUFFOLK 3–1D

Baipo £ 21

63 Upper Orwell St IP4 1HP (01473) 218402

"Super food is let down by the décor" at this well-liked town-centre Thai. / **Sample dishes:** chicken & sweetcorn in a pastry basket; red curried chicken stir-fry with egg fried rice; steamed banana in coconut milk. **Details:** 10.45 pm; closed Mon L & Sun.

The Galley £ 30

25 St Nicholas St IP1 1TW (01473) 281131

A "great mix of English and Turkish food" adds an "original" twist to this "traditional"-looking, family-run restaurant/wine bar; "the menu is a bit static, but always enjoyable". / **Sample dishes:** Scottish salmon & fresh herb fishcakes; chicken in Parma ham with tarragon pasta; caramel plums with toasted almonds. **Details:** 10 pm; closed Sun; no Amex; no smoking area.

Mortimer's on the Quay £ 26 ★

3 Wherry Quay IP4 1A5 (01473) 230225

It's "a lovely place for lunch in the summer" and offers a
"huge variety of fish all year", so it's no surprise that Ken
Ambler's "good-value" riverside establishment "usually seems to
be booked out". / **Sample dishes:** seafood gratin; steamed halibut; lemon
chiffon. **Details:** 9.15 pm; closed Sat L & Sun; no smoking area.

IVINGHOE, BUCKINGHAMSHIRE 3–2A

Kings Head £ 49

Station Rd LU7 9EB (01296) 668388

This well-established restaurant in an "old beamed building"
is "still an old favourite" – it's "expensive", but fans say it's
"worth it". / **Sample dishes:** seafood, bacon & smoked chicken salad;
Aylesbury duck with calvados sauce; bread & butter pudding. **Value tip:** set 3-
crs L £14.50. **Details:** 3m N of Tring on B489 to Dunstable; 9.30 pm; closed
Sun D; no smoking in dining room.

JERSEY, JERSEY

Jersey Pottery Restaurant £ 34 Ⓐ★

Gorey Village JE3 9EP (01534) 851119

"A fantastic 'conservatory' atmosphere" and "wonderful seafood"
are the prime attractions at this "pleasant" spot. / **Sample
dishes:** avocado with Jersey crab & coriander; Jersey lobster salad with prawns;
farmhouse cheeses. **Details:** signposted from St Helier; L only; closed Mon;
no smoking area.

Longueville Manor £ 53

Longueville Rd JE2 7WF (01534) 725501

The Channel Islands' generally acknowledged top spot "maintains
its standards of excellence and comfort"; it gets "so much
business trade" though, that it can seem a touch impersonal.
/ **Sample dishes:** grilled tuna, sardine & calamari salad; sea bass with baked
aubergines, scallops & sauce vierge; Longueville summer pudding. **Value
tip:** set 2/3-crs set L £18/£22. **Details:** 10.30 pm; no smoking area.
Accommodation: 32 rooms, from £210.

Village Bistro £ 32 Ⓐ★

Main Rd JE3 9EP (01534) 853429

An owner with "a passion for food" injects much life into this
"friendly local bistro", located in a converted chapel. / **Sample
dishes:** pan-fried scallops; pan-fried sea bass with scallops & spinach; warm
gingerbread pudding. **Value tip:** set 3-crs L £12.50 (Sun £14.50).
Details: signposted from St Helier, next to Post Office; 10 pm; closed Mon,
Tue L & Wed L.

JEVINGTON, EAST SUSSEX 3–4B

Hungry Monk £ 37 Ⓐ

BN26 5QF (01323) 482178

This "cosy" but "cramped" spot, with its "incredible location" in
converted Elizabethan cottages, is generally hailed for cooking
which is "as reliable as ever", though some do say the place
"lives on its reputation". / **Sample dishes:** gazpacho; Thai green curry
with squid, mussels & clams; lemon tart. **Details:** 5m W of Eastbourne;
9.30 pm; D only, ex Sun open L & D; no Amex; no smoking in dining room;
children: 5+.

Bosquet   £ 40   ★

97a Warwick Rd CV8 1HP   (01926) 852463

The "consistently splendid" Gallic cooking from the "inspired husband-and-wife team" here creates a marginally more enthusiastic following among reporters than for neighbouring Simpsons (but a rather smaller one); even fans, though, can find it a touch unatmospheric. / **Sample dishes:** squid stuffed with prawns; roast squab pigeon; blueberry & almond tart. **Details:** 10 pm; closed Mon & Sun, L on Sat.

Simpsons   £ 42   ★

101-103 Warwick Rd CV8 1HL   (01926) 864567

"Dependable and cosy", Andreas Antona's "imaginative" town-centre bistro is heartily endorsed by locals as a "good all-round" choice. / **Sample dishes:** seared foie gras; salmon in lemon & butter; chocolate parfait. **Value tip:** set 2-crs L £15. **Details:** 10 pm; closed Sat L & Sun; no smoking area.

Sheen Falls Lodge   IR £ 55   Ⓐ★

(064) 41600

"There's a waterfall outside the window" of the dining room of this Danish-owned hotel – whose ardent fan club hailed its "elegant" setting and "knowledgeable and friendly" staff; praise was also fulsome for Fergus Moore's "beautifully prepared and presented" French cooking – let's hope his colleague and successor Chris Farrell can keep up the good work. / **Sample dishes:** swordfish & celeriac cake with pancetta; roast pigeon on pumpkin purée with glazed apples; chocolate mousse & coffee crème brûlée. **Details:** follow signs for Glengariff from Kenmare Hotel; 9.30 pm; D only; no smoking area; children: 10+. **Accommodation:** 61 rooms, from IR £250.

King's Cliffe House Restaurant   £ 38   ★

31 West St PE8 6XB   (01780) 470172

Even those who find the atmosphere a touch "stilted" say the food – "from marinated olives to coffee and fudge" – is "outstanding" at this small restaurant in the heart of the village, and there's an "intriguing" wine list too; note the very restricted opening times. / **Sample dishes:** scallops with lentils & wild fennel; lamb with oyster mushrooms & Marsala wine; oranges in rosemary syrup. **Details:** 4m W of A1, close to A47; 9 pm; D only, open Wed-Sat only, closed 2 wks in spring & autumn; no credit cards; no smoking area.

Peacock   £ 23

Icknield St B38 0EH   (01564) 823232

"Close to Birmingham, but with a rural atmosphere", this popular pub offers "good traditional English food" ("from basic butties to game pie") in "large portions"; Sunday lunch is especially busy, and some feel that standards slip accordingly. / **Sample dishes:** chicken liver pâté; roast lamb with vegetables; bread & butter pudding. **Details:** 9.30 pm, Sun 7.30 pm.

Rococo   **£ 37**   𝔸★★

11 Saturday Marketplace PE30 5DQ   (01553) 771483
*Nick and Anne Anderson's "stylishly" decorated 17th-century
cottage provides a "wonderful" backdrop against which to
enjoy some "original and devastatingly delicious" modern cooking;
"great wines" and "very attentive" service contribute to "a real
treat" that's "excellent value" too. / **Sample dishes:** mushroom brioche
with duck's egg; steamed turbot with fondant potatoes; lemon tart with citrus
caramel. **Value tip:** set 2/3-crs set L £12.50/£14.50. **Details:** in Old Town,
opp St Margaret's Church; 9 pm, Fri & Sun 10 pm; closed Mon L & Sun;
no smoking area.*

The Cross   **£ 48**   ★

Tweed Mill Brae, Ardbroilach Rd PH21 1TC
(01540) 661166
*The Hadleys' "spacious" and "contemporary" hotel, in
a converted tweed mill, offers "well thought out and beautifully
prepared" modern Scottish cooking and a very "extensive,
non-French wine list". / **Sample dishes:** seafood salad; pan-fried beef with
wild mushrooms & madeira; pear & butterscotch tart. **Details:** head uphill on
Ardbroilach Rd, turn left into private drive after traffic lights; 8.30 pm; D only,
closed Tue; no Amex; no smoking; children: 8+. **Accommodation:** 9 rooms,
from £115.*

The Man Friday   **IR £ 35**   ★

Scilly   (021) 477 2260
*For a "splendid seafood surprise" or other "well prepared
gourmet fare", this "cosy" fixture overlooking the harbour is
unanimously approved. / **Sample dishes:** crab gratin; scallops & monkfish
with sun-dried tomatoes; strawberry crème brûlée. **Details:** just on sea front;
10.30 pm; D only, closed Sun; no Switch; no smoking area.*

Snooty Fox Hotel   **£ 24**

Main St LA6 2AH   (01524) 271308
*"Has it changed hands - it used to be so good?"; one
perspicacious reporter scents the cause of the changes that seem
to be diminishing the appeal of this elegant town-centre hostelry.
/ **Sample dishes:** Mozzarella salad; roast chicken with buttered carrots; lemon
parfait. **Details:** off A65, 6m from M6, J36; 10 pm; no smoking area.
Accommodation: 9 rooms, from £50.*

Talbot   **£ 29**   ★

WR6 5PH   (01886) 821235
*"Brewing its own beer and cider", this popular organic
microbrewery occupies an old pub by the River Teme; it serves
"plenty of food for little money" – that's "very tasty and
beautifully cooked" – with much of the produce "organic, from
their own garden". / **Sample dishes:** crab blinis; pork with creamy garlic
sauce & chips; sticky toffee pudding. **Details:** 9m from Worcester on A44;
9 pm.*

La Belle Epoque £ 31

King St WA16 6DT (01565) 633060

This splended art nouveau building was once regarded as a beacon in the North West's culinary scene; it "has gone downhill", though, now offering modestly ambitious brasserie cooking which "could be more exciting". / **Sample dishes:** Tuscan spring salad; sea bass with red onion, caper & olive salsa; apricot fritters with Cointreau mousse. **Details:** 1.5m from M6, J19; 10.30 pm; closed Sat L & Sun; no smoking area. **Accommodation:** 6 rooms, from £60.

LACOCK, WILTSHIRE 2–2C

At the Sign of the Angel £ 33 🄰★

6 Church St SN15 2LB (01249) 730230

"Superb food from an unusual menu in a quaint country setting" sums up the consistent feedback on the "intimate" dining room at this small hotel – part of a 14th-century house in a picturesque National Trust village. / **Sample dishes:** pan-fried lamb's kidneys; roast sirloin with Yorkshire pudding; home-made ice cream. **Details:** close to M4 , J17; 9 pm; closed Mon L. **Accommodation:** 10 rooms, from £99.

LANCASTER, LANCASHIRE 5–1A

Golden Dragon £ 16

11 George St LA1 1XQ (01524) 33100

The décor may be "old-fashioned", but this "relaxing" Chinese, is "the best" in the area, and its menu includes some "imaginative vegetarian dishes". / **Sample dishes:** chicken soup; Chinese chicken & stir-fried vegetables; chocolate bananas. **Details:** 11.45 pm, Fri & Sat 12.15 am; D only.

Simply French £ 23

27a, St Georges Quay LA1 1RD (01524) 843199

A "lovely quayside setting" and "tasty" cooking commend this "lively" bistro – whose Gallic menu "changes frequently" – to a number of local reporters. / **Sample dishes:** grilled goat's cheese with balsamic dressing; duck with coriander & ginger; almond crème brûlée. **Details:** 9.30 pm; closed Mon, Tue & Wed L; no Amex.

Sultan of Lancaster £ 19 🄰

Old church, Brock St LA1 1UU (01524) 61188

An "imaginatively converted former church" provides an "ornate", "spacious" and "relaxed" setting for this eminent Pakistani; its "wide variety of tasty food" wins wide support, even though the place is "an alcohol-free zone". / **Sample dishes:** BBQ chicken tikka; shish & onion kebabs; coconut supreme. **Details:** opp town hall; 11 pm; D only; no Amex; no smoking area.

LANGAR, NOTTINGHAMSHIRE 5–3D

Langar Hall £ 27 ★

NG13 9HG (01949) 860559

A "very welcoming and friendly" lady proprietor adds charm to a visit to this "idiosyncratic" Georgian house, "which always offers good food, service and atmosphere" – all of a relatively traditional nature. / **Sample dishes:** escabeche of red mullet; char-grilled Langar lamb; home-made ice cream. **Value tip:** set 2/3-crs L £7.50/£10. **Details:** off A52 between Nottingham & Grantham; 9.30 pm, Sat 10 pm; no smoking area. **Accommodation:** 10 rooms, from £90.

LANGHO, LANCASHIRE

Northcote Manor   **£ 49**   ★   5–1B

Northcote Rd   BB6 8BE   (01254) 240555

"Well-paced" and *"polite"* service delivers *"imaginative"* and *"beautifully prepared"* English cooking – *"with excellent use of tripe and black pudding"*, for those who can stomach it – in the dining room of this grand Ribble Valley country house hotel. / **Sample dishes:** black pudding & pink trout salad; lamb with couscous & pesto; bread & butter pudding. **Value tip:** set 3-crs L & Sun L £16. **Details:** M6, J31, follow signs for Skipton, left onto A59; 9.30 pm; closed Sat L; no smoking. **Accommodation:** 14 rooms, from £110.

LAPWORTH, WARWICKSHIRE

The Boot   **£ 29**   5–4C

Old Warwick Rd   B94 6JU   (01564) 782464

This well-known and *"vibrant"* canal-side pub has a *"great beer garden"*, and its *"imaginative"* menu selection offers *"something for everyone"*. / **Sample dishes:** crispy duck salad; roast rack of lamb; panna cotta with honeycomb. **Details:** off A34; 10 pm.

LAVENHAM, SUFFOLK

Great House   **£ 36**   𝔸★   3–1C

Market Pl   CO10 9QZ   (01787) 247431

"A little bit of France in the middle of Suffolk"; the Crépys' well-established fixture has a *"superb"* setting – a medieval house in the market square – and *"the food is usually very good"*. / **Sample dishes:** marinated tuna & smoked salmon tartare; calves liver with smoked bacon & mustard sauce; sticky toffee pudding. **Value tip:** set 2-crs L £9.95. **Details:** follow directions to Guildhall; 9.30 pm; closed Sun L & Mon, Oct-May; no smoking in dining room. **Accommodation:** 5 rooms, from £70.

LEEDS, WEST YORKSHIRE   5–1C

Thanks to its economic vitality, Leeds now has quite a number of upmarket restaurants. Few of them, as yet, maintain reliably impressive standards. For 'serious' cooking, the canalside *Pool Court at 42* is the leader. Competitors – most of which are also housed in converted canalside warehouses, not far from the railway station – are *Rascasse* and the (less ambitious) *Brasserie Forty Four* and *Leodis*.

The younger, trendier places, such as the seminal *Art's Bar*, tend to cluster in the Exchange Quarter (around the Corn Exchange).

Those in search of more exotic cuisines are well catered for. *Darbar*, an impressively-decorated and very central restaurant heads the cast of Indians, ably supported by *Aagrah* and *Hansa*. Rather unusually, there are also a couple of Japanese restaurants of some note (*Fuji Hiro* and *Shogun Teppanyaki*), as well as two Chineses (*Lucky Dragon* and *Maxi's*) and a Thai (*Sala Thai*).

Aagrah   **£ 23**   ★

Aberford Rd   LS25 1BA   (0113) 287 6606

This prominent subcontinental often gets *"very busy"* – hardly surprising, as numerous reports aver that it *"never fails to deliver"* providing *"fantastic food in a luxurious setting"*; *"nice"* service garners particular praise. / **Sample dishes:** chicken tikka; chicken achar; kulfi. **Details:** from A1 take A642 Aberford Rd to Garforth; 11.30 pm; D only; no smoking area.

Amigos £ 17 Ⓐ

70 Abbey Rd LS5 3JG (0113) 228 3737

"An ambience like you were in Spain" – *"no room to stick out your elbows, though"* – and *"scrummy"* and *"straightforward" tapas* has helped make this *"fun"* Headingley bar quite an institution; there's a new city-centre offshoot *"underneath railway arches"* in Kirkgate (tel 243 5477) which early reports say is *"just as good"*. / **Sample dishes:** spicy potatoes; chicken with garlic & wine; crème caramel. **Details:** on A65 in Kirkstall; 11 pm; no Amex.

Art's Bar (Café) £ 22 Ⓐ

42 Call Ln LS1 6DT (0113) 243 8243

"Cool and continental", this *"simple and relaxed"* bar/café remains a top *"trendy"* Exchange Quarter hang-out; the grub is *"reliable"*, and there are *"great cocktails"* too. / **Sample dishes:** marinated feta & Parma ham salad; asparagus, tarragon & Parmesan risotto; Belgian chocolate cake. **Details:** nr Corn Exchange; 11 pm; no Amex.

Bibis £ 31

Minerva Hs, 16 Greek St LS1 5RU (0113) 243 0905

This *"big"* and *"bustling"* '70s-survivor central Italian may be *"overcrowded"* and *"noisy"* – and *"still has waiters who come equipped with large black pepper-grinders"* – but it's a *"dependable"* place with a large following. / **Sample dishes:** pigeon foie gras terrine; devilled tiger prawns; chocolate & amaretto cake. **Details:** off Park Row ; 11.30 pm; no booking Sat.

Brasserie Forty Four £ 31

44 The Calls LS2 7EW (0113) 234 3232

"Consistently good" French cooking and a *"lovely canalside location"* commend this large brasserie to most reporters; even fans admit the *"stylish"* setting can feel *"subdued"*, though, and a minority finds it simply *"inhospitable"*. / **Sample dishes:** mussels with spinach & saffron; roast lamb with cumin; espresso & amaretto tart. **Value tip:** set 2-crs L £9.75. **Details:** 10.30 pm, Fri & Sat 11 pm; closed Sat L & Sun.

Bryan's £ 20

9 Weetwood Ln LS16 5LT (0113) 278 5679

Opinions divide on this Headlingley fixture, and though the majority declare that it *"still offers some of the best fish and chips in the North"*, there are also quite a few who think it *"used to be brilliant, but is now vastly over-rated"*. / **Sample dishes:** prawns in breadcrumbs; haddock & chips; custard tart. **Details:** nr Headingley cricket ground; 10 pm; no Amex; no smoking.

The Calls Grill £ 23

Calls Landing, 38 The Calls LS2 7EW (0113) 245 3870

"The beat-the-clock menus are undoubtedly fantastic value" at this long-established canalside fixture; reports of visits at other times range all the way from *"first-class"* to *"a school dinners experience"*. / **Sample dishes:** king prawn salad with wasabi & mango; char-grilled beef with béarnaise sauce; strawberries with champagne sorbet. **Details:** opp Tetleys brewery on waterfront; 10.30 pm, Thu-Sat 11 pm; closed Mon & Sun L; need 6+ to book Fri & Sat.

Casa Mia Trattoria £ 19 Ⓐ★

33 Harrogate Rd LS7 3PD (0113) 266 1269

"Authentic Italian food, served in a relaxed atmosphere" is making quite a name for this *"lively"* and *"unsophisticated"* family-run Chapel Allerton Italian; *"an amazing range of fresh fish"* is a highlight. / **Sample dishes:** seafood salad; chicken with cheese & mushroom sauce; tiramisu. **Details:** 10.30 pm; no Amex; no smoking; no booking.

Clockhouse Café £ 21 A★
16a Headingley Ln LS6 2AS (0113) 294 5464
"Superb East-meets-West cuisine", "friendly service" and a "very relaxed" atmosphere commend this "studenty" spot, which is a café by day and a bistro by night. / Sample dishes: red pepper & goat's cheese crostini; red snapper; banana & cinnamon crepes. Details: 10 pm, Fri & Sat 10.30 pm; no Amex.

Darbar £ 27 A★
16-17 Kirkgate LS1 6BY (0113) 246 0381
"This is a restaurant, not a curry house", and its "beautiful" and "opulent" décor and its "attentive" service impart "a great sense of occasion" to dining here; the menu offers a "good range" of dishes that "can't be faulted". / Sample dishes: onion bhaji; chicken balti with peshwari naan; gulab jaman (Indian sweets). Details: behind Marks & Spencer; midnight; closed Sun.

Flying Pizza £ 26
60a Street Ln LS8 2DQ (0113) 266 6501
This "bustling" Roundhay institution may still, for some, be "the place to be seen" in Leeds, but enthusiasm for its pizza-and-more menu was muted this year, and there were particular gripes that the "friendly and entertaining" service is "not as good if you haven't got a famous face". / Sample dishes: penne with crab; chicken in cream sauce with peppered vegetables; tiramisu. Details: just off A61, 3m N of city centre; 11.30 pm; no smoking area; no booking at D.

Fourth Floor Café £ 35
Harvey Nichols, 107-111 Briggate LS1 6AZ
(0113) 204 8000
"Rather similar to Knightsbridge, but with less cramp and hassle", Harvey Nics's top-floor restaurant is a "lively" venue for a "tasty and well presented lunch" in "chic" surroundings; "the terrace on a summer evening is an exceptional experience", but – as in SW1 – some can find the interior a touch "soulless". / Sample dishes: smoked cod & mussel ravioli; seared foie gras with potato & turnip gallete; passion fruit mousse. Value tip: set 2-crs L £13. Details: 10.30 pm; closed D (Sun-Wed); no smoking area.

Fuji Hiro £ 18 ★★
45 Wade Ln LS2 8NJ (0113) 243 9184
"Simple and authentic", this "minimalist" noodle bar offers "fantastically fresh" and "healthy" dishes in "huge" portions; "if this place was better located, business would go through the roof". / Sample dishes: gyoza dumplings; grilled seafood with glass noodles; no puddings. Details: 10 pm, Fri & Sat 11 pm; no credit cards; no smoking.

Hansa £ 19 ★
72-74 North St LS2 7PN (0113) 244 4408
The "freshly-cooked, vegetarian Gujerati food" here may come "from an all-female kitchen", but the place has little of the 'minority appeal' which that description might suggest, and it's a "relaxed" spot with a huge reputation. / Sample dishes: patra & banana bhaji; rice pancakes with spiced mixed vegetables; seero (Indian semolina). Details: 200 yds from Grand Theatre; 11 pm; closed Sun D; no Amex; no smoking area.

Leodis £ 35

Victoria Mill, Sovereign St LS1 4BJ (0113) 242 1010
This "busy" canalside brasserie is rather a love-it-or-hate-it
experience – fans speak of its "excellent cooking and top-class
service", whereas for detractors it just serves "overpriced,
poorly-cooked food" in a "snooty" and "unrelaxing" environment.
/ **Sample dishes:** foie gras terrine; chicken with wild mushrooms, truffles
& leeks; crème brûlée. **Value tip:** set 3-crs L & early eve £14.95. **Details:** nr
City Hilton Hotel; 10 pm, Fri & Sat 11 pm; closed Sat L & Sun.

Lucky Dragon £ 25 ★

Templar Ln LS2 7LP (0113) 245 0520
"Where Leeds's Chinese community meets and eats"; this "busy"
and "authentic" city-centre basement is consistently praised for its
"fresh" cooking and its "friendly" service. / **Sample dishes:** aromatic
duck pancakes; fillet steak Cantonese style; lychees. **Details:** behind Vicker
Lane; 11.30 pm.

Malmaison £ 30

Sovereign Quay LS1 1DQ (0113) 398 1000
Some say it has a "great atmosphere" and serves "innovative"
cooking, but – as at other locations of this design-hotel chain
nationwide – reports generally suggest a huge decline in the
standard of the brasserie cooking here. / **Sample dishes:** eggs
Benedict; fishcakes; crème brûlée. **Details:** nr central railway station;
10.30 pm. **Accommodation:** 100 rooms, from £99.

Maxi's £ 29 ★

6 Bingley St LS3 1LX (0113) 244 0552
This "massive", "bustling" warehouse-conversion on the
city-centre's western fringe may seem "slightly impersonal",
but it serves some "extremely tasty" Chinese cooking. / **Sample
dishes:** spare ribs in Peking sauce; sizzling steak with ginger & spring onions;
toffee bananas. **Details:** beyond Westgate; 11.30 pm.

New Jumbos £ 22

120-122 Wicker Ln LS2 7NL (0113) 245 8547
This long-established Chinese retains a wide following for its
"tasty and authentic" dishes, despite the fact that it's "not very
atmospheric". / **Sample dishes:** prawn toast; fillet steak with black bean
sauce; banana fritters. **Value tip:** all day 3-crs menu £14.50. **Details:** opp
Banningham pub; 11.45 pm; no smoking area.

Olive Tree £ 37

55 Rodley Ln LS13 1NG (0113) 256 9283
"Bouzuki evenings are best", say advocates of this "fun",
family-run Greek in a Victorian house on the city's main ring-road;
the occasional reporter finds expectations disappointed. / **Sample
dishes:** cheese pastries; moussaka; custard & raisin tart. **Details:** on ring road
(Rodley roundabout); 11 pm.

Pool Court at 42 £ 50 ★

42 The Calls LS2 7EW (0113) 244 4242
The cooking at the "small", "modernist" dining room, attached
to a canalside design-hotel, "can hit great heights", and service
is "attentive but unobtrusive"; for some it still seems a little
"lacking", though, with the "rather cold" setting attracting
particular complaint. / **Sample dishes:** smoked salmon with potato blinis
& caviar; fillet steak with seared foie gras; bitter chocolate & almond pithiviers.
Value tip: set 2/3-crs L £14.50/£19. **Details:** 200 yds from parish church;
10 pm, Fri & Sat 10.30 pm; closed Sat L & Sun; no smoking; children: no
babies.

Rajas   £ 16   ★

186 Roundhay Rd LS8 5PL   (0113) 248 0411

The setting of this Indian near Roundhay Park may be "a touch run-down", but Leeds regulars say the "clean", "fresh" and "tasty" cooking offers more than adequate compensation. / Sample dishes: chicken pakora; chicken balti; kulfi. Details: close to Roundhay Park; 10.30 pm; no Amex.

Rascasse   £ 40

Canal Whf, Water Ln LS11 5BB   (0113) 244 6611

The head chef left this well known and potentially "fabulous" canalside spot in April 2000 – too late for significant feedback on the kitchen under John Lyons; let's hope the new régime doesn't stop at brushing up the previously "ordinary" cooking, but also improves the "sniffy" service and sometimes "cold" atmosphere. / Sample dishes: veal sweetbreads with chanterelle mushrooms; John Dory with cockle & bacon cassoulet; trio of apple desserts. Value tip: set 2/3-crs L & early eve £14/£18. Details: off M621 J3, behind Granary Wharf; 10 pm, Fri & Sat 10.30 pm; closed Sat L & Sun.

Sala Thai   £ 22

Oakbank 13-17, Shaw Ln LS6 4DH   (0113) 278 8400

With its "plush" décor and its "subtle" and "flavoursome concoctions", this "excellent" Headingley Thai is a major local destination. / Sample dishes: chicken satay & spring rolls; chicken curry; banana in coconut milk. Details: just off Otley Rd, nr Arndale Centre; 10.30 pm; closed Sun; no smoking area.

Salvo's   £ 26   ★

115 Otley Rd LS6 3PX   (0113) 275 5017

"The late Salvo's two sons ensure continued excellence of kitchen and service" at this "delightful" Headingley Italian of a quarter century's standing; there's no evening booking, and the occasional disappointments seem to result from the fact that the place is just "too popular". / Sample dishes: roasted pepper, crab & bean salad; duck with pasta & caramelised red onions; crème brûlée. Value tip: set 2-crs L £5. Details: 2m N of University on A660; 10.45 pm, Fri & Sat 11 pm; closed Sun; no smoking area; no booking for D.

Sheesh Mahal   £ 16   ★

346-348 Kirkstall Rd LSD 2DS   (0113) 230 4161

"Cheap, very friendly and catering for all", this Indian by the Yorkshire TV centre has many fans for the "basic" but "consistently very good" dishes from its "original and extensive" menu. / Sample dishes: lamb balti tikka; shish kebab with vegetables; home-made ice cream. Details: next to Yorkshire TV centre; midnight; D only; no smoking area.

Shogun Teppanyaki   £ 31   🄰★

Unit V-W, Granary Whf LS1 4BN   (0113) 245 1856

"Good food and great fun" – this "unusual" modern Japanese combines teppan-yaki ("chefs cooking on a hot plate in front of you") with conveyor-belt sushi (pick what you like and then pay per plate); "the freshest ingredients" are used and "fantastic" results are proclaimed on all counts; "good noodle dishes" too. / Sample dishes: vegetable tempura with chilli dip; jumbo scallops; tempura ice cream. Value tip: set 5-crs L £12.95. Details: in arches under Leeds BR station; 10.30 pm; closed Mon & Sun D.

Sous le Nez en Ville   £ 24

Quebec House, Quebec St LS1 2HA   (0113) 244 0108
The "unbeatable" earlybird menu is the special attraction
at this "noisy", city-centre basement wine bar/restaurant;
its "comprehensive" wine list is also approved. / **Sample
dishes:** deep-fried Brie with mango & pepper chutney; roast sea bass stuffed
with fennel; dark chocolate parfait. **Details:** 100 yds from City Square; 10 pm;
closed Sun; no smoking.

Tasca   £ 23

4 Russell St LS1 5PT   (0113) 244 2205
"Busy, buzzing and with lots of tapas to choose from", this
"cramped" branch of an emerging chain is widely praised for its
"reliably good value". / **Sample dishes:** crispy pork in red wine sauce;
Valencian paella with chicken & seafood; dark chocolate truffle & ice cream.
Details: 10.30 pm; booking: need 8 to book.

Thai Siam   £ 22   ★

68 New Briggate LS1 6NU   (0113) 245 1608
The management has changed (and there has been
a refurbishment) at this "little gem" of a "tucked away" Thai;
chef Butham – who has won a disproportionate local following
for the place – remains, however, as do the standards of his
"consistent" and "very tasty" cooking. / **Sample dishes:** Thai
fishcakes; roast duck in Thai red curry sauce; Thai jasmine cake. **Details:** 100
yds from Grand Theatre; 11 pm; closed Mon & Sun L.

Whitelocks Luncheonette   £ 18   Ⓐ

Turk's Head Yard, off Briggate LS7 6H3   (0113) 245 3950
"Good, honest Yorkshire food and beer" help make this wonderful
period pub dining room a not-to-be-missed city-centre experience.
/ **Sample dishes:** soup; Moroccan lamb; treacle sponge. **Value tip:** set 3-crs
Sun L £8.95. **Details:** nr Marks & Spencer; 10 pm; children: 18+.

LEICESTER, LEICESTER CITY   5–4D

Bobby's   £ 17   ★

154 Belgrave Rd LE4 5AT   (0116) 266 0106
"Subtle and delicious" south Indian vegetarian fare at very
"good-value" prices makes "the cheapest, most authentic
café-style Indian in town" the most mentioned destination on the
famous 'Golden Mile'; neither décor nor service is anything to
write home about. / **Sample dishes:** deep-fried potato baskets; aubergine
stuffed with peanut & potato; caramelised ice cream. **Details:** 10.30 pm;
closed Mon; no Amex & no Switch; no smoking.

Case   £ 30

4-6 Hotel St LE1 5AW   (0116) 251 7675
"London-comes-to-Leicester", declare the many local fans of
this "stylish" and "airy" café-restaurant in St Martins, and they
proclaim its cooking as "gorgeous" and "creative"; out-of-towners
are more prone to find the dishes "artsy rather than tasty",
and the whole package a little "overpriced". / **Sample dishes:** wild
boar sausage with shallots; roast cod with buttered asparagus; trio of chocolate
mousse & coffee anglaise. **Details:** nr the Cathedral; 10.30 pm; closed Sun;
no smoking area.

Curry Fever   £ 25   ★

139 Belgrave Rd LE4 6AS   (0116) 266 2941
"They say the Indian cricket team ate here last year... 'nuff said!";
this small subcontinental café of over 20 years standing offers
"top-quality" cooking in a "lively" setting. / **Sample dishes:** samosas;
masala chicken; kulfi. **Details:** 0.5m from city centre; 11 pm; closed Mon.

Friends Tandoori   £ 20   ★

41-43 Belgrave Rd LE4 6AR   (0116) 266 8809

"Extensive research shows this to be consistently the best place in a highly competitive city for Indian food" – one curry-mad local's view is widely supported by numerous reports of the *"authentic"* cooking at this smart and *"friendly"* fixture, near the start of the 'Golden Mile'. / **Sample dishes:** kebabs; chicken Karahi; kulfi. **Details:** off Inner Ring; 11.30 pm; no smoking in dining room.

Stones   £ 26

29 Millstone Ln LE1 5JY   (0116) 291 0004

The Spanish-inspired dishes *"sound great on the menu"*, but the locals are divided on whether this *"original"* city-centre spot actually delivers – what is *"diverse"* and *"excellent"* to some is *"overhyped"* and *"expensive for what it is"* to others. / **Sample dishes:** sausages with honey & mustard; lamb chops with green beans; chocolate pudding. **Details:** 10.30 pm; closed Sun.

The Tiffin   £ 27

1 De Montford St LE1 7GE   (0116) 247 0420

You don't have to brave Leicester's curry quarter to visit this well-established Indian, long known as a somewhat more "upmarket" option than a trip to the Belgrave Road; it presents "quality" cooking, if perhaps not with quite the same emphasis on authenticity as its humbler peers. / **Sample dishes:** chicken tandoori kebabs; aubergine & tamarind curry; rasmalai (cream cheese dessert). **Details:** nr railway station; 10.45 pm; closed Sat L & Sun; no smoking.

Watsons   £ 28   ★

5-9 Upper Brown St LE1 5PE   (0116) 222 7770

"Imaginative and sophisticated food is much needed in Leicester", and this *"sophisticated"* yearling seems to be fitting the bill admirably; *"it can get very noisy when its busy"*. / **Sample dishes:** Parma ham, roast pear & rocket salad; roast sea bass with chorizo mash & tomatoes; vanilla crème brûlée. **Details:** next to Phoenix Art Theatre; 10.30 pm; closed Sun.

LEMSFORD, HERTFORDSHIRE   3–2B

Auberge du Lac   £ 58   Ⓐ★

Brocket Hall AL8 7XG   (01707) 368888

"Magnificent food served in beautiful surroundings" has (after only two years in business) made the Brocket Hall estate's *"superbly situated"* lakeside restaurant *"Hertfordshire's best"*; *"discreet"* service and an *"excellent"* wine list complete the winning package. / **Sample dishes:** lobster salad with leeks & asparagus; lamb in red wine sauce with creamy mash; lemon & lime soufflé with coconut sorbet. **Value tip:** set 3-crs L £25. **Details:** on B653 towards Harpenden; 10 pm; closed Mon & Sun D; no jeans. **Accommodation:** 16 rooms, from £150.

LEWDOWN, DEVON   1–3C

Lewtrenchard Manor   £ 41   Ⓐ★

EX20 4PN   (01566) 783256

Limited feedback was received this year on this beautiful Elizabethan house set in gorgeous countryside, where the last couple of years have seen changes of ownership and of chef; such reports as we received say it remains "good all round" and – for one local – "our current favourite in the area". / **Sample dishes:** smoked haddock & cucumber salad; stuffed guinea fowl with risotto; banana parfait. **Details:** off A30 between Okehampton to Launceston; 9 pm; jacket; no smoking in dining room; children: 8+. **Accommodation:** 9 rooms, from £110.

Thrales   **£ 30**
40-44 Tamworth St WS13 6JJ (01543) 255091
"Well-cooked food in generous portions" makes this "cosy"
and "intimate" town-centre restaurant a "consistently good
value-for-money" experience for most reporters, though the
odd "school dinners" experience is also recorded. / **Sample
dishes:** prawn & mushroom thermidor; Scotch beef with red wine reduction;
Soufflé. **Value tip:** set 2/3-crs set L £9.50/£10.50, set 3-crs D £11.95.
Details: 9.30 pm; closed Sun D.

LICKFOLD, WEST SUSSEX   3–4A

Lickfold Inn   **£ 33**   A★
GU28 9EY (01798) 861285
The name gives no hint of the Pacific Rim influence on the
"extensive" and "beautifully prepared" menu of this "friendly"
old pub "in the heart of the country"; it's also praised for its
"wonderful" ambience. / **Sample dishes:** pan-fried chorizo with
tomatoes; seared tuna with tomato, mango & chilli salsa; chocolate & almond
tart. **Details:** nr Petworth House; 9.30 pm.

LIDGATE, SUFFOLK   3–1C

Star Inn   **£ 29**   A★
CBY 9PP (01638) 500275
"Spanish food in a cosy country pub" may be an unusual formula,
but Hispanic fare "goes surprisingly well with ale", and local
reporters are unanimous in their praise for this "comfortable"
and "agreeable" venture. / **Sample dishes:** Mediterranean fish soup;
grilled hake with seasonal vegetables; blackberry & apple pie. **Details:** on
B1063 6m SE of Newmarket; 10 pm; closed Sun; no smoking.

LIFTON, DEVON   1–3C

Arundell Arms   **£ 40**   ★
Fore St PL16 0AA (01566) 784666
"Local produce at its best" is the watchword at the "comfortable"
dining room of this "traditional English country hotel restaurant",
on the River Tamar; as you would hope from an establishment
owned by a famous angler (and with 20 miles of the river at
guests' disposal), "good fish" is the highlight. / **Sample
dishes:** scallops & smoked salmon in pastry; roast lamb with honey
& rosemary; peaches with orange caramel sauce. **Value tip:** set 2/3-crs
L £17/£21. **Details:** 0.5m off A30, Lifton Down exit; 9.30 pm; no smoking.
Accommodation: 28 rooms, from £110.

LINCOLN, LINCOLNSHIRE   6–3A

Browns Pie Shop   **£ 27**   ★
33 Steep Hill LN2 1LU (01522) 527330
"Lovely pies" and "the best cheesecake ever" are highlights
among the "super home-cooked dishes" on offer at this
"inventive" and "consistent" spot, near the Cathedral. / **Sample
dishes:** fishcakes on lamb's lettuce; roast Lincoln red beef; Bailey's cheesecake.
Value tip: set 2-crs pre-theatre £5.95. **Details:** nr the Cathedral; 10 pm;
no smoking area.

Jew's House £ 34   Ⓐ★

15 The Strait LN2 1JD (01522) 524851

Entered via a splendid carved doorway, this well-established venture in one of Lincoln's oldest buildings provides a "calm and unhurried" setting in which to enjoy some "classy modern cooking" – "fresh ingredients, beautifully cooked and presented". **/ Sample dishes:** smoked salmon with pistachios; roast lamb with rosemary; tarte Tatin with calvados. **Value tip:** set 2/3-crs L £5/£10. **Details:** halfway down Steep Hill from Cathedral; 9.30 pm; closed Mon & Sun; no smoking.

The Wig & Mitre £ 35

30 Steep Hill LN2 1TL (01522) 535190

"Simply presented" cooking using "great ingredients" still generally carry the day at this "informal" and "welcoming" tavern, near the Cathedral; even a fan who thinks it's still "first rate" says its recent shift to neighbouring premises was "a shame" and there are those who think the place has "lost it". **/ Sample dishes:** chicken liver & smoked bacon pâté; bangers with mustard seed mash; custard tart with nutmeg ice cream. **Details:** between Cathedral & Castle; 11 pm; no smoking.

LINLITHGOW, WEST LOTHIAN 9–4C

Champany Inn £ 52

EH49 7LU (01506) 834532

Though even some fans say "it can be a little variable", the "best Scottish beef, served plain or with wonderful sauces" and "an enormous wine list" (with over 1,000 bins) is a formula which wins general approval at this well known "institution", half an hour outside Edinburgh; the "cheaper" adjoining 'Chop & Ale House' (formula price £30) serving "top quality" burgers is similarly praised. **/ Sample dishes:** roast quail with bacon & tarragon stuffing; porterhouse sirloin with sautéed potatoes; chocolate marquise. **Value tip:** set 2-crs L £16.75. **Details:** 2m NE of Linlithgow on junction of A904 & A803; 10 pm; closed Sat L & Sun; jacket & tie; children: 8+. **Accommodation:** 16 rooms, from £95 B&B for 2.

LITTLE SHELFORD, CAMBRIDGESHIRE 3–1B

Sycamore House £ 31   ★

1 Church St CB2 5HG (01223) 843396

Cooking "of very good quality" and wines which offer "very good value" win unanimous support for Michael & Susan Sharpe's "intimate" and "personal" restaurant, which deserves to be better known. **/ Sample dishes:** mushroom & hazelnut soup; grilled pigeon with shallots; brandy snap basket. **Details:** 1.5m from M11, J11 on A10 to Royston; 9 pm; D only, closed Mon & Sun; no Amex; no smoking; children: 12+.

LIVERPOOL, MERSEYSIDE 5–2A

Presumably reflecting its seafaring past, Liverpool has long boasted quite a number of Chinese restaurants, but until recently there was not much else to interest the visitor.

The city is, however, finally beginning to establish something of a more general restaurant culture, and now counts at least four restaurants aiming to provide quality European cooking (*Becher's Brook*, *Left Bank*, *60 Hope Street* and *Ziba*). It's no doubt symbolic that two of them are on Hope Street (which links the two cathedrals). For the moment, however, the most popular place in town remains the *Everyman Bistro*, which recently celebrated thirty years in business.

Becher's Brook £ 47   A

29a Hope St L1 9BQ (0151) 707 0005
"High-quality food" – "Gallic with a touch of orient" –
undoubtedly makes this "intimate" and "friendly" five-year old
a "special" Merseyside destination; the food rating is undercut
by those who find the place "a bit overpriced" or a touch
"pretentious", but the place's success has been such that an
offshoot opened, in Hamilton Square, shortly before we went to
press. / **Sample dishes:** king scallops & Waldorf salad; turbot with
caramelised onions; coconut & banana parfait. **Details:** between the
Cathedrals; 10 pm; closed Sat L & Sun; no smoking; children: 7+.

Casa Italia £ 19

40 Stanley St L1 6AL (0151) 227 5774
"Good salads and pastas, and great pizzas" – there's
a wood-burning stove – make this "old-style Italian" a "good
value-for-money choice". / **Sample dishes:** mixed antipasti; lasagne verdi;
tiramisu. **Details:** off Victoria St; 10 pm; closed Sun; no Amex; need 8+ to
book.

Everyman Bistro £ 17   A★

5-9 Hope St L1 9BH (0151) 708 9545
An "unbelievably varied menu" (including "brilliant veggie
options") of "well-prepared dishes" at "reasonable prices"
makes this "warm and friendly" self-service bistro, beneath the
Everyman Theatre, the Pool's best-known place to eat; it has
recently celebrated 30 years in business. / **Sample dishes:** soup with
herb foccacia; pork with Madeira mushrooms & rice; apricot & almond cobbler.
Value tip: set 2-crs pre-theatre £6.95. **Details:** midnight; closed Sun;
no Amex; no smoking area; booking sometimes restricted.

Far East £ 26

27-35 Berry St L1 9DF (0151) 709 3141
Located above an oriental supermarket, this "massive" restaurant
receives a further "authenticity" boost thanks to its "popularity
with the local Chinese population"; it serves an "extensive" menu,
with Sunday dim sum a top attraction. / **Sample dishes:** crispy duck
with plum sauce; garlic prawns; ice cream. **Details:** by church on Berry St;
11.15 pm; no smoking area.

Gulshan £ 25

544-548 Aigburth Rd L19 3QG (0151) 427 2273
"The best of a bad bunch where Liverpool's Indians are
concerned", this "plush" spot combines "ornate, almost kitsch"
décor with Indian cooking that "may not be gourmet, but lives up
to expectations"; bizarrely enough, the "fabulous ladies
lavatories" are widely reported to be "a main attraction".
/ **Sample dishes:** deep-fried prawns; chicken tikka masala; ice cream.
Details: on road to Liverpool airport; 10.45 pm; D only.

Jalons Wine Bar £ 22   A

473-475 Smithdown Rd L15 5AE (0151) 734 3984
Piano bar nights (Wednesdays and weekends) win particular
praise at this "atmospheric" joint; the cooking isn't an incidental
attraction, with particular praise for its "superb value set meals".
/ **Sample dishes:** crispy spring rolls; roast lamb with a red wine sauce;
strawberry cheesecake. **Value tip:** 2-crs D £13.95 (Fri & Sat- £15.95), 2-crs
pre-theatre £9.95. **Details:** 10 pm; D only; children: before 7 pm only.

Keiths Wine Bar £ 15   Ⓐ

107 Lark Ln L17 8UR (0151) 728 7688
*For "the Bohemian Liverpool experience", try this "buzzing" and "inexpensive" bistro, near Sefton Park, which has many admirers for its "fresh and home-made" dishes (with "superb" veggie options) and "good-value" wines. / **Sample dishes:** grilled halloumi with pitta bread; char-grilled Spanish chicken with rice; sticky toffee pudding.* **Details:** *11 pm; no Amex.*

Left Bank £ 32   ★

1 Church Rd L15 9EA (0151) 734 5040
*"Reservations are always necessary" at Danny Cannon's small and "very friendly" five-year-old; its "diverse" French menu and "great wine list" seem all the more "outstanding" in the absence of much in the way of local competition at this level. / **Sample dishes:** prawns in garlic butter; beef in red wine & cream sauce; crème brûlée.* **Details:** *off Penny Lane; 10 pm; closed Mon L & Sat L.*

Not Sushi £ 24   ★

Imperial Ct, Exchange Street East L2 3PH (0151) 236 0643
*"Quality, care and attention to detail" win a consistently good press for this modernistic, "good-value snack and sushi bar"; it offers "a mix of Thai and Indonesian dishes, as well as Japanese". / **Sample dishes:** salmon sushi; char-grilled chicken teriyaki with noodles; banana tempura.* **Details:** *nr Town Hall; 9.45 pm; closed Sun; no smoking area.*

Number 7 Café £ 22

7-11 Falkner St L8 7PU (0151) 709 9633
*"Tasty and filling well-cooked fare, and an art exhibition too" – this "multi-cultural" "café/deli/gallery", which offers "an excellent veggie selection as well as meat dishes", attracts wide-ranging support. / **Sample dishes:** Thai chicken soup; cheese & potato bake; ginger crumble.* **Details:** *nr Cathedral, between two churches; 9 pm; closed Sun D; no credit cards; no smoking area.*

Pod £ 30   Ⓐ★

137-139 Allerton Rd L18 2DD (0151) 724 2255
*A "great night out" atmosphere and "an excellent range of well-cooked tapas" make this "lively" bar quite a local hot spot; Sunday breakfast has "a huge following". / **Sample dishes:** chicken satay kebabs; fillet steak with Dolcelatte & red onions; sticky toffee pudding.* **Value tip:** *as is tapas is £25-30 for 4 dishes per person including wine, no "3-crs" format..* **Details:** *9.30 pm; no Amex.*

Siam Garden £ 23

607 Smithdown Rd L15 5AG (0151) 734 1471
*The décor of this Sefton Park Thai may be on the "dodgy" side, but its "tasty dishes at affordable prices" and its "attentive" service have made an instant local hit of this year-old oriental (whose business lunch gets a particular thumbs-up). / **Sample dishes:** Thai fishcakes; stir-fried chilli & garlic chicken; Thai ice cream.* **Details:** *11.45 pm; closed Sun L.*

60 Hope Street £ 27

60 Hope St L1 9B2 (0151) 707 6060
*For its fans, this "trendy" new restaurant is already the "best in the city", offering an "unusual" menu in "beautiful" surroundings; many find it "not as good as its reputation", though, and complain loudly of "bland" food and "dire" service. / **Sample dishes:** seared scallops with avocado & tomato; John Dory with papardelle & pesto cream; deep-fried jam sandwich with ice cream.* **Details:** *between two cathedrals; 10.30 pm; closed Mon & Sun; no Amex; no smoking area.*

Tai Pan £ 21 ★

WH Lung Building, Gt Howard St L5 9TX
(0151) 207 3888

"It must be authentic – all the Chinese community eats here",
say supporters of this "supermarket-sized" restaurant (it is,
indeed, located above an oriental supermarket); "excellent dim
sum" and "a huge range of vegetarian options" attract particular
praise. / **Sample dishes:** chicken satay; pork with green pepper in black
bean sauce; ice cream. **Value tip:** menus for two £18/£21/£25.
Details: 11.30 pm.

Tasca £ 23 Ⓐ

3 Queen Sq L1 1RH (0151) 709 7999

A particularly "lively" atmosphere commends this city-centre
branch of the "cheap" and "tasty" tapas bar chain, which offers
"good-quality food in good-size portions". / **Sample dishes:** crispy
pork in red wine sauce; Valencian paella with chicken & seafood; dark
chocolate truffle & ice cream. **Details:** 10.30 pm; booking: need 8 to book.

Yuet Ben £ 21 ★

1 Upper Duke St L1 9DU (0151) 709 5772

Terry Lim's smallish Chinatown fixture has been in business for
over thirty years, and it remains a popular regional destination
on account of its very "decent" grub (with "a good vegetarian
selection") and its "friendly" and "intimate" style. / **Sample
dishes:** Peking aromatic duck; chilli shredded beef; glazed Chinese toffee
apples. **Value tip:** set 2-crs L £10. **Details:** in Chinatown, facing Chinese
Arch; 11 pm; D only, closed Sun.

Ziba £ 33 ★

15 Berry St L1 9DF (0151) 708 8870

The ambitious cooking at this "stylish", modern city-centre
venture is often praised for its "thoughtful" and "subtle"
combinations (though the occasional refusnik finds it
"pretentious"); the "affordable fixed-price menus" win particular
praise. / **Sample dishes:** roasted scallops with lemon & butter; roast lamb
with olives with seasonal vegetables; poached peaches with cream. **Value tip:**
2/3-crs L & D £10.50/£13.50. **Details:** nr Chinatown; 10 pm; closed Sun;
no smoking area.

LLANBERIS, GWYNEDD 4–1C

Pete's Eats £ 9 Ⓐ★

40 High St LL55 (01286) 870358

"Big portions for active people" – Peter Norton's "cheap, cheerful
and colourful climbers' café" has an enormous following for its
"tasty", "simple" and "plentiful" home-made food, washed down
with "pints of tea" (it's unlicensed). / **Sample dishes:** carrot
& coriander soup; Greek spinach & cheese filo parcel; cheesecake. **Details:** in
large blue building; 8 pm; no smoking area.

LLANDEGLA, DENBIGHSHIRE 5–3A

Bodidris Hall Hotel £ 41 Ⓐ★★

LL11 3AL (01978) 790434

There was little feedback this year on this much applauded
medieval manor house; the superb views of the lakes and
snow-capped hills are presumably the same as ever, though,
and such limited commentary as there is indicates that the
modern British cooking is still "sublime". / **Sample dishes:** warm
pigeon & bacon salad; tournedos of beef with truffle sauce; roast pear
& almond tart. **Details:** on A5105 from Wrexham; 9 pm; no jeans;
no smoking; children: 18+ on Sat. **Accommodation:** 9 rooms, from £105.

Cawdor Arms £ 27

Rhosmaen St SA19 6EN (01558) 823500

"Tasty" cooking of a fairly traditional nature – beef, duck, trout, local cheeses – is provided at this tastefully-decorated Georgian coaching inn at the heart of a market town; the occasional misfire is not unknown. / Sample dishes: goat's cheese & herb tartlet; chicken with leeks, shallots & fondant potatoes; white chocolate & walnut tart. **Value tip:** *set 2/3-crs L £11.50/£13.50.* **Details:** *NE of Carmarthen, adjacent to A40 on main street; 9 pm; no smoking.* **Accommodation:** *17 rooms, from £60.*

Richards £ 33 ★

7 Church Walks LL30 2HD (01492) 877924

Richard Hendey's intimate ten-year-old venture is deservedly a "very popular local restaurant" in this atmospheric seaside town, and his "succulent" cooking and "good, sensibly-priced wines" receive nothing but praise. / Sample dishes: salad niçoise; roast duckling with potato rosti; chocolate cake. **Details:** *nr the pier; 11 pm; D only.*

Red Lion £ 22

LD8 2TN (01544) 350220

An old drovers' inn in the Hills of Radnor, known for its "reliable" cooking; let's hope any changes from its new régime – which postdated survey feedback – are for the better. / Sample dishes: toasted goat's cheese crostini; Welsh black beef with potatoes Anna; chocolate & brandy truffle terrine. **Details:** *off A44 between Cross Gates & New Radnor; 9.45 pm; closed Mon L; no Amex; no smoking area.* **Accommodation:** *5 rooms, from £45.50.*

Lake Country House £ 41 ★

LD4 4BS (01591) 620202

"Subtle" cooking and a "very good wine list" reward those who seek out the "large, traditional dining room" of this Edwardian house, set in 50 acres of parkland. / Sample dishes: terrine of venison; Welsh lamb with mint jelly; raspberry pudding. **Details:** *off A483 at Garth, follow signs; 9 pm; jacket & tie; no smoking; children: 7+.* **Accommodation:** *19 rooms, from £125.*

Bryn Howel Hotel £ 30

LL20 7UW (01978) 860331

With its fine views, this attractively-situated hotel dining room still wins praise for "superb" traditional cooking using "fresh local ingredients"; reports this year, however, were unusually mixed. / Sample dishes: fondue of melons; pan-fried Welsh beef with red pepper coulis; milk chocolate terrine. **Value tip:** *set 3-crs Sun L £14.90.* **Details:** *on A539 towards Ruabon; 9 pm; no smoking.* **Accommodation:** *36 rooms, from £95.*

Lake Vyrnwy Hotel   £ 38   A★

Lake Vyrnwy SY10 0LY (01691) 870692

"A great menu in a picturesque setting" makes this Victorian pile – built to house the engineers who built the huge reservoir it overlooks, and set in a large estate – a very popular destination. / **Sample dishes:** chicken & wild mushroom terrine; red mullet on saffron mash with braised fennel; dark chocolate tart with orange coulis. **Value tip:** set 3-crs L & Sun L £16.95. **Details:** on B4393 at SE end of Lake Vyrnwy; 9.15 pm; no jeans; no smoking. **Accommodation:** 35 rooms, from £99.

Griffin Inn   £ 27   A★

LD3 0UR (01874) 754241

This ancient inn is a *"friendly and welcoming spot, with roaring fires"*; its *"top-quality, home-made meals at reasonable prices"* – *"tasty soup"* and *"flavoursome beef"*, for example – are *"always reliable"*. / **Sample dishes:** hot smoked salmon salad; braised lamb shank with roasted garlic; treacle tart. **Details:** on A470; 9 pm; closed Sun D; no smoking area. **Accommodation:** 9 rooms, from £70.

Llangoed Hall   £ 55

LD3 0YP (01874) 754525

"Beautifully" sited on the River Wye, this country house hotel has a *"grand dining room"* truly decked out in Laura Ashley style (the house is owned by her family); *"imaginative dishes using Welsh produce"* win general but by no means unanimous support, and some find service *"patronising"*. / **Sample dishes:** caramelised scallops; tuna & sea bass chowder; crème brûlée. **Details:** 11m NW of Brecon on A470; 9.30 pm; jacket & tie; no smoking; children: 8+. **Accommodation:** 23 rooms, from £195.

Cameron House   £ 59

G83 8QZ (01389) 755565

Those who are suckers for *"ornate"* service – *"be queen for a day!"* – seem particularly susceptible to the *"spoiling"* charms of this grand lochside hotel; others are more inclined to find it *"pretentious and expensive"*. / **Sample dishes:** French onion soup with smoked bacon; seared sea bass with pineapple & polenta; white & dark chocolate parfait. **Details:** M8, cross over Erskine Bridge to A82, take roundabout to Crianlarich; 9.45 pm; closed Sat L & Sun L; jacket & tie; no smoking; children: 14+. **Accommodation:** 96 rooms, from £185.

Rockingham Arms   £ 42

52 Front St YO25 9SH (01430) 810607

"Friendly", family-run former pub with quite ambitious modern British cooking; fans say the *"fantastic"* food is *"not cheap, but worth every penny"*, though reports this year were rather mixed. / **Sample dishes:** poached pear, rocket & walnut salad; roast Scotch salmon with spinach; glazed cherry sabayon. **Details:** between Beverly & Gt Driffield on A164; 9.30 pm; D only, closed Mon & Sun; no Amex; children: 10+. **Accommodation:** 3 rooms, from £110.

Chapter One £ 37

Farnborough Common   BR6 8NF   (01689) 854848

An "interesting" and "varied" menu, "stylishly presented" in a modern setting, makes this "crowded" venture "better than anything else in the area by miles"; even so, culinary performance can be "average" and service a let-down. / **Sample dishes:** balottine of Scottish salmon & scallops; braised oxtail & pancetta with parsnip purée; warm apple charlotte & apple sorbet. **Value tip:** set 3-crs Sun L £16. **Details:** 2m E of Bromley on A21; 10.30 pm.

Angel £ 39

Bicester Rd   HP18 9EE   (01844) 208268

Styling itself the Angel Restaurant rather than the Angel Inn these days, this "tastefully restored", er, inn provides a "comfortable" and "friendly" setting in which to enjoy a "good selection of fish" and an "interesting" (if "limited") wine list. / **Sample dishes:** black pudding with bubble & squeak; Aylesbury pork with sage & apple mash; red berry trifle. **Value tip:** set 2/3-crs set L £12.95/£14.95. **Details:** 2m NW of Thame, off B4011; 10 pm; closed Sun D; no Amex; no smoking area. **Accommodation:** 3 rooms, from £65.

Mole & Chicken £ 30 Ⓐ

Easington   HP18 9EY   (01844) 208387

This picturesque pub near the top of a hill makes an especially "cosy" winter destination, and – thanks to its "tasty" cooking, "big" portions and "great" atmosphere – it can get "very busy"; it has recently come under new management. / **Sample dishes:** smoked chicken, avocado & bacon salad; shoulder of lamb; tiramisu. **Details:** follow signs from B4011 at Long Crendon; 9.45 pm.

Heathcote's £ 46

104-106 Higher Rd   PR3 3SY   (01772) 784969

"Good, but not brilliant" is still the tenor of too much feedback on the cottagey flagship of Paul Heathcote, the North West's leading chef; that's not to say that "exquisite" experiences from the hearty menu are never reported, but there are far too many complaints of "bland" cooking, and of somewhat "perfunctory" service. / **Sample dishes:** caramelised shallot tart with goat's cheese; Scottish lobster & asparagus with shellfish sauce; prune & armagnac soufflé. **Value tip:** set 3-crs L £16.50 (Sun L £22.50). **Details:** follow signs for Jeffrey Hill; 9.30 pm; closed Mon & Tue; no smoking.

Peat Spade Inn £ 28 Ⓐ★

SO20 6DR   (01264) 810612

"The best roast beef" and "delicious bread and butter pudding" typify the sort of dishes done best at this "absolutely consistent" Victorian pub in the Test Valley. / **Sample dishes:** smoked chicken mousse in prosciutto; roe deer fillet with mushroom sauce; poached Brazilian figs in muscat. **Details:** 9 pm; closed Mon & Sun D; no credit cards; no smoking area. **Accommodation:** 2 rooms, from £58.75.

LOUGHBOROUGH, LEICESTERSHIRE 5–3D
Thai House £ 25
5a, High St LE11 2PY (01509) 260030
*"Good-value" cooking makes this popular oriental an "always reliable" destination for its sizeable local fan club. / **Sample dishes:** spare ribs; Thai green curry; coconut roll. **Value tip:** 5-crs £15.95 inc coffee. **Details:** 10.45 pm.*

LOUGHTON, ESSEX 3–2B
Ne'als Brasserie £ 34
241 High Rd IG10 1AD (020) 8508 3443
*Most reports say that Neil Cohen's "starkly decorated" brasserie offers "very good food", if at "West End prices". / **Sample dishes:** Southern-fried snapper & Cromer crab cake; English lamb with garlic portobello mushrooms; New Orleans spiced bread & butter pudding. **Value tip:** set 2/3-crs Sun L £12.50/£15.50. **Details:** off M25, J26; 10 pm; closed Mon & Sun D; no Amex.*

LOW FELL, TYNE & WEAR 8–2B
Eslington Villa Hotel £ 29 🄰
8 Station Road NE9 6DR (0191) 487 6017
*"Modern, eclectic cooking in an elegant setting" has made this "hidden away" country house hotel quite a "local favourite"; let's hope their new chef can keep up the momentum. / **Sample dishes:** toasted muffin with mushrooms & bacon; seared yellow fin tuna; chocolate cherry mousse. **Details:** A1 exit for Team Valley Retail World, then left off Eastern Avenue; 9 pm, Fri & Sat 9.30 pm; closed Sat L & Sun D; no smoking. **Accommodation:** 18 rooms, from £50.*

LOWER ODDINGTON, GLOUCESTERSHIRE 2–1C
The Fox Inn £ 26 🄰★
GL5 0UR (01451) 870555
*"Excellent everything" earns numerous endorsements for this "hidden-away" Cotswolds "dream" of a pub, where "light and fresh cooking" is served in "tasteful" surroundings; it recently changed hands – the chef remains, however, and early reports suggest that the food is still "the same". / **Sample dishes:** smoked chicken & rocket salad; smoked haddock & Welsh rarebit; pear & ginger pudding. **Details:** on A436 nr Stow on the Wold; 10 pm; no Amex. **Accommodation:** 3 rooms, from £58.*

LOWER PEOVER, CHESHIRE 5–2B
Bells of Peover £ 35
The Cobbles WA16 9PZ (01565) 722269
*"Charmingly located", by the church in a "beautiful hamlet", this "characterful", "old country pub" is popular for its "good-quality grub". / **Sample dishes:** deep-fried Brie with redcurrant sauce; fillet steak & bacon stuffed with Stilton; sticky toffee pudding. **Details:** opp St Oswald's church, off B5081; 9 pm; children: 14+.*

LOWER SLAUGHTER, GLOUCESTERSHIRE 2–1C
Lower Slaughter Manor £ 72
GL54 2HP (01451) 820456
*On a good day, you can find "superb food" in the "serene" surroundings of this gracious Cotswold hotel; not all are 'wowed', though, and some find the package rather "expensive" for what it is. / **Sample dishes:** chicken mousse with truffles; honey-roast duck with five spice sauce; strawberry soufflé. **Value tip:** set 2/3-crs L £12.95/16.95. **Details:** 9.30 pm; no smoking; children: 10+. **Accommodation:** 16 rooms, from £150.*

Trout Inn £ 23 *A*

195 Godstow Rd OX2 8PN (01865) 302071

"Inspector Morse-fever" has now overtaken this "idyllically located" riverside pub, and – with its "long queues" and "slow service" – it now strikes some as a bit of a "tourist trap"; it's "still a favourite" for many, though, in spite of its iffy traditional fare. / **Sample dishes:** *chicken pâté; beef & bass ale pie; chocolate brownie cake.* **Details:** *2m from junction of A40 & A44, on river; 9 pm, Fri & Sat 9.30 pm; no Amex; no smoking area; no booking.*

LUDLOW, SHROPSHIRE 5–4A

The Cookhouse £ 27

Bromfield SY8 2JR (01584) 856565

"Thoughtful presentation" and "ample portions" are among the strengths of this bright bistro-cum-restaurant; situated just outside this culinarily exalted town, its style is a touch more contemporary than the norm. / **Sample dishes:** *fish soup; chicken stuffed with Gruyère & bacon; lemon tart.* **Value tip:** *set 3-crs Sun L £10.50.* **Details:** *2m N of Ludlow on A49 to Shrewsbury; 10 pm; no smoking area.*

Ego Café Bar £ 22

Quality Square SY8 1AR (01584) 878000

It has no great ambitions, but this "bustling" wine bar is a "nice", "unpretentious" place in the heart of town, and offers some relief for those who would prefer not to eat in a temple of gastronomy! / **Sample dishes:** *fresh tuna niçoise; seared salmon with pesto dressing; chocolate & brandy tart.* **Details:** *off Castle Square, through black & white timber arches; 9 pm; closed Fri D, Sat D & Sun; no Amex; no smoking upstairs; booking advisable.*

Hibiscus £ 46

17 Corve St SY8 1DA (01584) 872325

This oak-panelled dining room in a 17th-century coaching inn – formerly called Oaks Restaurant – is the site for the new solo venture of Claude Bosi, former chef of Overton Grange; he opened too late for much in the way of survey feedback (hence the lack of a rating), but his track record suggests this could be one to watch. / **Sample dishes:** *foie gras with liquorice; roast lamb with almond crust; roast peaches with hawthorn ice cream.* **Details:** *9.30 pm; closed Mon L, Tue L & Sun; no Amex; no smoking.*

Merchant House £ 38 *A★★*

Lower Corve St SY8 1DU (01584) 875438

"Shaun Hill is one of the very best chefs" in the British Isles and his "beautifully cooked, no-frills food" "more than lives up to the reputation of this foodie town" (for which his "peaceful" and "homely" establishment was initially largely responsible); if there are reservations, it is the somewhat "plain" setting and occasionally "distant" service. / **Sample dishes:** *artichoke hearts with mushroom stuffing; saddle of hare with goat's cheese gnocchi; raspberry crème brûlée.* **Details:** *next to Unicorn pub; 9 pm; closed Mon & Sun; no Amex & no Switch; no smoking in dining room.*

Mr Underhill's £ 37 *A★★*

Dinham Wier SY8 1EH (01584) 874431

Over its first couple of years, Chris and Judy Bradley's "very pleasant" and "relaxed" riverside establishment has put in an "excellent all-round" performance, with "fine, modern cooking" from an "imaginative" (no-choice) menu. / **Sample dishes:** *marinated wild smoked salmon; organic chicken & sage with balsamic sauce; rice pudding with apricots.* **Details:** *8.30 pm; closed Tue; no Amex; no smoking.* **Accommodation:** *6 rooms, from £75.*

Overton Grange £ 46

Hereford Rd SY8 4AD (01584) 874314

*Since the survey, a new chef has taken over at this well-known foodie destination; perhaps this change of régime will have provided an opportunity for the management to tackle the service ("overbearing"), the atmosphere ("dull") and the prices ("excessive"). / **Sample dishes:** quail & asparagus cannelloni; seared sea bass, roasted shallots & cep purée; chocolate cup with pistachio ice cream. **Details:** 9.30 pm; closed Mon L; no smoking area. **Accommodation:** 14 rooms, from £95.*

LYDGATE, GREATER MANCHESTER 5–2B

White Hart £ 30 ★★

51 Stockport Rd OL4 4JJ (01457) 872566

*"A pleasant new dining room" has been added to this "stylish" and hugely popular inn – combining bar, brasserie and restaurant – set high in the moors overlooking Oldham; "sausages to die for" (they also run Saddleworth Sausage Company) are the linchpin of the "fantastic" traditional menu. / **Sample dishes:** Saddleworth sausages; tempura of cod with minted potatoes; chocolate & almond tart. **Value tip:** set 2/3-crs L & early eve £9/£11.50 (Sun £13.50/£15.50). **Details:** 2m E of Oldham on A669, then A6050; 9.30 pm; no smoking area. **Accommodation:** 12 rooms, from £90.*

LYMINGTON, HAMPSHIRE 2–4C

The Old Bank House £ 31

68 High St SO41 9AL (01590) 671128

*A "restaurant-cum-wine bar" praised for its "well-prepared" and "tasty" Mediterranean cooking. / **Sample dishes:** smoked salmon muffin; salmon fishcakes; tarte Tatin. **Value tip:** set 2-crs L £7.95. **Details:** 9.30 pm; closed Sat L & Sun.*

LYNDHURST, HAMPSHIRE 2–4C

Le Poussin at Parkhill £ 45

Beaulieu Rd SO43 7FZ (023) 8028 2944

*In mid-2000, Alex & Caroline Aitkens moved their "expensive and quite formal" venture of long standing from Brockenhurst to this Georgian country house hotel; if past form is any guide, the food will see "the best local ingredients, superbly handled", but the occasional off-night will not be unknown. / **Sample dishes:** poussin, foie gras & prune terrine; roast, confit & pan-fried lamb with green beans; passion fruit soufflé. **Value tip:** set 2-crs L £15.50. **Details:** 9.30 pm.*

MADINGLEY, CAMBRIDGESHIRE 3–1B

Three Horseshoes £ 33 ★

CB3 8AB (01954) 210221

*"Still one of the best places to eat round Cambridge", this well-known pub in a "beautiful" village is "very tastefully" converted, and has a large conservatory dining room (or you can eat in the bar); some do find it "over-rated", but most praise the "reasonably priced and delicious" food and notably "excellent wine list". / **Sample dishes:** watermelon, feta & toasted pumpkin seed salad; roast monkfish with melted leeks & prawns; hot chocolate fondant. **Details:** 2m W of Cambridge, off A14 or M11, J13; 9.30 pm, Fri & Sat 10 pm; closed Sun D; no smoking area.*

Five Horseshoes   **£ 31**   Ⓐ

RG9 6EX   (01491) 641282

*Its location feels very "out of the way", but this Chilterns inn is only ten minutes drive from Henley, and it's often praised for its "great" atmosphere and "good" pub food; it gets very busy at weekends, especially in the summer when there's a regular BBQ. / **Sample dishes:** prawn & crab mornay; seafood plate; Oreo cookie cheesecake. **Value tip:** set 3-crs Sun L £14.95. **Details:** on B481 between Nettlebed & Watlington; 10 pm; no Amex.*

Croque en Bouche   **£ 53**   ★★

221 Wells Rd WR14 4HF   (01684) 565612

*Marion Jones may have "no TV, books or pretensions" to her name, but she is "a very serious chef" – "superlatives" abound for her "sublime, traditional cuisine", and husband Robin's "innovative" wine list (over 1,000 choices, but you can get a preview by post) is "exceptional" too; "don't be late" to these tiny shop-conversion premises, though, or "your welcome may be frosty". / **Sample dishes:** rabbit & mushroom croustade; roast Welsh marches lamb; cheesecake. **Details:** 2m S of Gt Malvern on A449; 9.30 pm; open only Thu-Sat, D only; no Amex; no smoking; booking: max 6.*

MANCHESTER, GREATER MANCHESTER   5–2B

When it comes to diversity of ethnic choice, only the capital beats Manchester. The cheerleader for the city's non-European restaurants is the *Yang Sing* – the country's best-known Chinese restaurant (and one of only a handful of 'destination' restaurants in cities outside London). Chinatown (to the east of Portland Street) offers a range of other good-quality oriental possibilities, including the *Little Yang Sing* and the new and much-mentioned *Pacific*. Continuing the oriental theme, the Thai *Chiang Rai* (in Didsbury) has a very large following, as does the stylish noodle bar *Tampopo*.

Fans of Indian cooking should not be disappointed either. Here the leading names are *Great Kathmandu* and *Gurkha Grill*, and there are also the multiple gaudy delights of Rusholme's 'street of a thousand curries' (a half-mile stretch of Wilmslow Road), whose more popular establishments are included in the listings below.

Vegetarians are well catered for, with *Green's*, the *Greenhouse* and *On The Eighth Day* among the leading names. Other minority tastes are also well represented and, in the Gay Village, the city has a feature which is unique. Reporters' leading choice here is, by a clear margin, *Velvet*.

All these strengths in diversity contrast starkly with the difficulty which the city centre has manifested in establishing a straight-down-the-line, quality non-ethnic restaurant culture. Thus, with the exception of the small and idiosyncratic *Market*, there are no mid-range places which are highly esteemed by reporters. The ambitious two-year-old *Lincoln* is closest to the mark, but it has a way to go. The other pretenders are simply second-rate – to emphasise the point, the past year has seen the (deserved) closure of Mash & Air, and the high-profile, 'gangster-Baroque'-style Reform (not listed below) was trading in receivership as we went to press.

Those who want to eat good-quality, non-ethnic food must therefore head a little way of out town to West Didsbury, where the excellent *Lime Tree* has established itself one of the country's very best brasseries, or to Whalley Range, where *Palmiro* looks set to establish a stellar reputation. For Gallic cooking of a high order, it's worth considering a short journey out of town to Altrincham's Juniper.

Cachumba £ 20

220 Burton Rd M20 2LW   (0161) 445 2479
"Authentic Asian grub" (but with *"striking English-style puds"*) makes this *"small"* and *"friendly"* BYO Vietnamese café in West Didsbury a unanimously popular recommendation. / **Sample dishes:** red coconut chicken curry; Thai king prawns with lemongrass; mango & berry crumble. **Details:** 9.30 pm; closed Sun L; no credit cards.

Café Pop £ 16 Ⓐ

34-36 Oldham St M1 1JN   (0161) 237 9688
"Fab", *"pure kitsch"* décor wins fans for this *"veggie greasy spoon"*; *"excellent breakfasts"* and *"great milkshakes"* are highlights from the all-day menu. / **Sample dishes:** soup of the day; all-day breakfast with veggie sausage; chocolate fudge brownie. **Details:** off Piccadilly Gardens; L only; no credit cards; no smoking area.

Casa Tapas £ 27 Ⓐ

704 Wilmslow Rd M20 2DW   (0161) 448 2515
A *"wide range of authentic food"*, *"friendly service"* and a *"very cosy"* setting complete with *"Spanish cartoon décor"* commend this ten-year old Rusholme tapas bar. / **Sample dishes:** king prawn kebabs; paella with chicken & shellfish; amaretto cake. **Details:** 11 pm.

Chiang Rai £ 27 ★

1st Floor, 762 Wilmslow Rd M20 2DR   (0161) 448 2277
"Yum yum"; focussing solely on its Didsbury branch has done nothing to diminish the appeal of Manchester's leading Thai – a *"spacious"*, *"clutter-free"* space, offering a *"wonderful"* choice of dishes realised to a *"highly consistent"* standard. / **Sample dishes:** spicy fishcakes; Thai green chicken curry; mango sorbet. **Value tip:** set 2/3-crs L/D £7/£9. **Details:** 10.30 pm; closed Mon, Sat L & Sun L; no smoking area.

Darbar £ 15

65-67 Wilmslow Rd M14 5TB   (0161) 224 4392
For many, this *"always original"* Rusholme subcontinental offers *"the best curry on the curry mile"* – *"it has a multiple-award-winning-chef, and it shows"*; there's no ignoring the large minority, though, which insists it's *"very, very average"*. / **Details:** 11.30 pm; no Amex; no smoking area.

Didsbury Brasserie £ 25

747 Wilmslow Rd M20 2RQ   (0161) 438 0064
*An "extensive menu" of "reasonably priced" French-inspired
cooking and a "nice setting, particularly in winter (with fires, etc)"
makes this self-explanatory place a "popular" local destination.*
/ **Sample dishes:** crostini; medallions of beef in pink peppercorn sauce;
strawberry shortcake. **Details:** 10 pm; no Amex; children: before 9 pm only.

Dimitri's £ 25 A★

1 Campfield Ave Arcade, Tonman St M3 4FN
(0161) 839 3319
*Thanks to its "atmospheric" location (in an arcade off
Deansgate) and the facility it affords to "sit outside in the
summer", this "cheap, and always cheerful" taverna is "lively
seven days a week"; "it's deservedly almost impossible to get
into", as service is "friendly" and the Greek/Mediterranean
cooking "does not disappoint".* / **Sample dishes:** pitta bread & Greek
dips; chicken kebabs with couscous; baklava. **Details:** nr Museum of Science
& Industry; 11.30 pm.

Dukes 92 £ 17 A★

19-25 Castle St M3 4LZ   (0161) 839 8646
*"Loads of bread and cheese" and other good, simple fare
("great soups and pâté", for example) is the recipe for success
at this "cool" and hugely popular riverside café/bar.* / **Sample
dishes:** soup of the day; gourmet open sandwich with French fries; hot fudge
cake. **Details:** 9 pm; no Amex.

El Rincon £ 24 A★

Longworth St, off St John's St M3 4BQ   (0161) 839 8819
*"Manchester's hidden gem", this "authentic" bar tucked away off
Deansgate is universally praised for its "wonderful" atmosphere,
its "well priced wines" and its tapas — they're "incredibly cheap
for the quality".* / **Sample dishes:** lobster bisque; chicken stuffed with
ricotta; apple pie. **Details:** off Deansgate; 11.30 pm.

Est Est Est £ 27

5 Ridgefield M2 6EG   (0161) 833 9400
*This eminent branch of a "lively" and brightly-decorated Italian
chain — prominent throughout the North West, and now national
in ambition — is "great for kids" and some tout it as a "reliable"
stand-by; it disappoints many reporters, though, with the
sometimes "terrible" service drawing particular flak.* / **Sample
dishes:** carpaccio of beef; chicken with pasta & spring vegetables; dark
chocolate mousse cake. **Details:** nr House of Fraser; 11 pm; no smoking area;
Fri & Sat, need 8+ to book.

Great Kathmandu £ 19 ★★

140 Burton Rd M20 1JQ   (0161) 434 6413
*"Consistently the best" of the Mancunian subcontinentals;
thanks to its "authentic dishes at great prices", this West
Didsbury Nepalese "tops Rusholme any day".* / **Sample dishes:**
chilli chicken; Nepalese mixed masala; kulfi. **Value tip:** set 3-crs L £5.95.
Details: off M20; midnight.

Green's £ 23 ★

43 Lapwing Ln M20 2NT   (0161) 434 4259
*Most reporters still find "exceptional food every time" — with "big
portions and subtle flavours" — at this "gourmet" BYO veggie café
in West Didsbury; this year, though, a few found it "overpriced"
or "lacking inspiration".* / **Sample dishes:** baked spinach & Parmesan
risotto; Indonesian curry with sweet potatoes & Asian greens; Mexican
chocolate pudding. **Value tip:** set 2-crs L £5 (Sun £8.50). **Details:** 4m S of
city centre; 10.30 pm; closed Mon L & Sat L; no Amex.

The Greenhouse £ 14
331 Great Western St M14 4AN   (0161) 224 0730
*There's a huge variety of veggie dishes and fair range of organic
wines served at this "friendly" Rusholme end-terrace; fans say
the grub's "brilliant", but misfires are not unknown. / **Sample
dishes:** meze (houmous, aubergines, dolmades); Greenhouse sweet & sour
pork; Drambuie cheesecake. **Details:** at junction of Great Western St
& Herald Grove; 9.30 pm; no credit cards; no smoking.*

The Grinch £ 22
5-7 Chapel Walks, off Cross St M2 1HN   (0161) 907 3210
*"A funny café-bar, with interesting food" and a "casual"
atmosphere; it maintains a disproportionately large fan club,
with the "special early-evening cheap offers (including wine)"
attracting particular comment. / **Sample dishes:** pizzas £5 & cocktails
grilled chicken Caesar salad; hot cheesecake. **Value tip:** pizzas £5 & cocktails
£2.50, 5 pm-7 pm every day. **Details:** 10.30 pm; no smoking area.*

Gurkha Grill £ 12 ★★
198 Burton Rd M20 1LH   (0161) 445 3461
*"Exceptional food at reasonable prices" – and with "lots of dishes
you won't find elsewhere" – together with "very friendly service"
win numerous bouquets for this "excellent Nepalese curry
house", even if some think its "converted end terrace" premises
in Didsbury a touch on the "grotty" side. / **Sample dishes:** shish
kebab; chicken tikka masala; ice cream. **Details:** 11.30 pm, Fri & Sat
12.30 am; D only; no Amex.*

Lal Haweli £ 18 ★
68-72 Wilmslow Rd M14   (0161) 248 9700
*"Authentic" dishes (including Pakistani and Nepalese specialities)
win high marks from devotees of this "friendly" Rusholme Indian.
/ **Sample dishes:** chicken tikka; chicken madras; kulfi. **Details:** 2 am;
no smoking area.*

Lemongrass £ 25 ★
19 Cobson St M20 3HE   (0161) 434 2345
*This Withington Thai may be a "quirky little venue", but it has
a disproportionately large following for its "huge" range of
"fantastic" dishes, and its "friendly" service; "BYO helps make it
a cheaper night out". / **Sample dishes:** fishcakes; Thai green chicken
curry; ice cream. **Details:** midnight; D only; no Amex.*

The Lime Tree £ 32 Ⓐ★★
8 Lapwing Ln M20 2WS   (0161) 445 1217
*"Book well in advance" if you want to enjoy the "congenial
sophistication" of this "reliably excellent" modern British brasserie
in West Didsbury – one of the most impressively "consistent"
restaurants of its type in the UK. / **Sample dishes:** grilled asparagus
with red peppers & goat's cheese; sea bass with sautéed potatoes & capers;
chocolate truffle cake. **Value tip:** set 2-crs L & early eve £9.95, set 3-crs Sun
L £12.95. **Details:** nr Withington Hospital; 10.30 pm; closed Mon L & Sat L;
no smoking area.*

The Lincoln £ 40
1 Lincoln Sq M2 5LN   (0161) 834 9000
*With its "distinctive", "modern" décor, this "cool" and "relaxed"
yearling (just off Albert Square) has many fans who say its
"brilliant, contemporary food" is "expensive, but worth it" –
others though, find standards rather "amateurish", considering.
/ **Sample dishes:** beef satay with glass noodles; warm salad of sea bass
& spinach; sticky toffee pudding. **Value tip:** set 2/3-crs L £14.50/£16.50, set
3-crs D (Mon only) £22. **Details:** opp Manchester Evening News building;
10.30 pm, Fri & Sat 11 pm; closed Sat L & Sun D.*

Little Yang Sing   £ 26   ★
17 George St M1 4HE   (0161) 228 7722
*"As good as its big brother" (well, almost), this "bustling" and
"efficient" China Town spot offers similarly "first-class" fare in
a no-frills setting (which was once the site of YS Senior). / **Sample
dishes:*** spicy meat & nut dumplings; deep-fried prawn balls with straw
mushrooms; toffee apples. ***Value tip:*** set 3-crs L £9.50. ***Details:*** 11.30 pm.

Malmaison Hotel   £ 29
Piccadilly M1 3AQ   (0161) 278 1000
*The once-fashionable brasserie of this city-centre design-hotel has
not lived up to its initial promise – the reporter who complained
of "dull and overpriced food, bad service and a dingy setting"
summarised the complaints of many. / **Sample dishes:*** smoked
salmon with lemon; roast spring lamb with Dijon crust; bitter chocolate tart.
Value tip: set 2/3-crs L £9.50/£12.50. ***Details:*** nr Piccadilly Station;
10.30 pm. ***Accommodation:*** 112 rooms, from £75.

Mark Addy   £ 9   ★
Stanley St M3 5EJ   (0161) 832 4080
*A "great river view" is one feature of these convivial cellars;
the special attraction, though, is "the best ploughman's lunches",
featuring a "fabulous range of cheeses". / **Sample dishes:*** chive
& onion cheese; pâté & salad; no puddings. ***Details:*** 8 pm; no credit cards.

The Market   £ 27   𝔸★
104 High St M4 1HQ   (0161) 834 3743
*"Now in its 20th year, the Market has stood the test of time";
it's an "intimate" and "delightful" place with "warm" service
where "gorgeous" eclectic cooking is served on "beautiful antique
crockery", and complemented by a "superb selection of beers,
wines and aperitifs". / **Sample dishes:*** chicken patties with Korean sauce;
Cajun blackened turkey with mango salsa; pavlova with passion fruit.
Details: on corner of Edge St & High St ; 9.30 pm; open only Wed-Sat,
D only.

Metropolitan   £ 24
2 Lapwing Ln M20 2WS   (0161) 374 9559
*It has a "huge and airy" setting (and "an open fire in the
winter"), and this popular Withington gastropub is praised by
supporters for its "cosmopolitan and trendy atmosphere";
its "good pub food" also commands general support. / **Sample
dishes:*** asparagus & smoked salmon; lamb in rosemary & redcurrant jus;
strawberry mousse shortbread. ***Value tip:*** set 2-crs Sun L £9.95. ***Details:*** nr
Withington Hospital; 9.30 pm; no smoking area.

Metz   £ 25
2 Canal St M1 3PJ   (0161) 237 9852
*It's "for an entertaining night out" that this 'gay space' by the
canal – with a pontoon for summer drinking – wins most praise;
the eastern European cooking is somewhere between "decent"
and "disappointing". / **Sample dishes:*** chicken liver terrine with apricot
chutney; lamb & herb casserole with new potatoes; chocolate fudge cake.
Details: nr coach station; 10 pm; children: not at D.

Mr Thomas Chop House   £ 23   𝔸
52 Cross St M2 7AR   (0161) 832 2275
*This "busy Victorian bar and lunchtime restaurant" is an
"unspoiled" city-centre institution that's "popular with the
legal and surveying communities"; its sandwiches and other
"wholesome" pub fare get a consistent thumbs-up, but views
on the kitchen's more ambitious efforts are mixed. / **Sample
dishes:*** black pudding; bacon & kidney pudding with mash; baked Alaska.
Details: L only; closed Sun.

Nico Central £ 36

Crowne Plaza, Mount St M60 2DS (0161) 236 6488
*Some do praise "superb" food and "wonderful" service in the
Gallic brasserie of this landmark hotel, and the "fixed-price
lunches and pre-theatre dinners are a bargain"; it's far too
unreliable, though, and there are numerous reports of
"shamefully poor" experiences; note, such connection as
Nico Ladenis ever had with this venture has now ceased.* / **Sample
dishes:** smoked salmon roulade with saffron dressing; potato scone with puy
lentils & tomato herb sauce; raspberry crème brûlée. **Value tip:** early evening
menu £14.95 available until 6.30pm. **Details:** opp St Peter's Square;
10.30 pm, Fri & Sat 11 pm; closed Sat L & Sun L.

On The Eighth Day £ 8 ★

111 Oxford Rd M1 7DU (0161) 273 4878
*"A large choice" of "excellent home-made vegetarian dishes" that
are "cheap and filling" – generates numerous recommendations
for this café on the campus of the Metropolitan University; BYO.*
/ **Sample dishes:** Armenian lentil soup; Mexican filo parcel with organic brown
rice; chocolate & orange pudding. **Details:** 7 pm; closed Sat D & Sun;
no smoking.

Pacific £ 25 ★

58-60 George St M1 HF (0161) 228 6668
*Culinary schizophrenia – "first floor Chinese, second floor Thai" –
has done little to diminish the enormous instant appeal of this
large newcomer, which wins consistent praise for the "exquisite"
flavours of its "attractively served" cuisine, and whose
"contemporary style is of a kind much needed in Chinatown".*
/ **Sample dishes:** dim sum; kung po spicy chicken; toffee bananas.
Details: in Chinatown; 11 pm; no smoking area.

Palmiro £ 27 ★★

197 Upper Chorlton Rd M16 OBH (0161) 860 7330
*This "simply wonderful" Whalley Range newcomer is one of
the most culinary exciting openings to hit Manchester in years;
"worlds apart from a standard Italian", it earns a hymn of praise
for its "terrific" and "original" cooking, its "great" service and its
"very friendly and relaxed" atmosphere.* / **Sample dishes:** avocado,
Mozzarella, tomato & basil salad; grey mullet saltimbocca with spaghetti
& lentils; chocolate torte with vanilla sauce. **Details:** 10.30 pm; D only, closed
Mon; no Amex.

Pearl City £ 21 ★

33 George St M1 4PH (0161) 228 7683
*This "very large Chinatown Cantonese" delivers "ample portions"
of "excellent and authentic" dishes – "even at 2 o'clock in the
morning" – from a "tantalising" menu of enormous proportions;
"the décor has seen better days".* / **Sample dishes:** dim sum;
Szechuan beef with yellow peppers; ice cream. **Details:** in Chinatown; 2 am,
Fri & Sat 3 am, Sun 11 pm.

Punjab Tandoori £ 17 ★

177 Wilmslow Rd M14 5AP (0161) 225 2960
*"Fabulous vegetarian dishes, hot and heavily spiced but always
fresh and clean" win unanimous local approval for this "top"
Rusholme subcontinental.* / **Sample dishes:** lamb tandoor; chicken
& mango curry; kulfi. **Details:** midnight.

Rhodes & Co   £ 31

Waters Reach M17 1WS   (0161) 868 1900

*Gary R's English brasserie suffers from a "strange location"
(by Old Trafford) and "functional" décor that's "rather lacking in
atmosphere" – in the face of such disadvantages, you might
hope for cooking which was more than "consistent". / **Sample
dishes:** potted chicken liver pâté; roast beef with bitter onions; dark chocolate
brownie. **Value tip:** set 2-crs L £11.50. **Details:** next to Quality Hotel at
Old Trafford; 9.45 pm; closed Sat L & Sun L.*

Royal Orchid   £ 22

36 Charlotte St M1 4FD   (0161) 236 5183

*This "consistent" and "friendly" city-centre Thai offers a "great"
choice of "tasty, freshly cooked" dishes. / **Sample dishes:** fishcakes;
Thai roast duck with tamarind sauce; ice cream. **Details:** nr Piccadilly Gardens;
11.30 pm; closed Sun.*

Sanam   £ 15   ★

145-151 Wilmslow Rd M14 5AW   (0161) 224 1008

*Yet another contender for the "best curry restaurant in
Rusholme" award – this well-known, "cheap and cheerful"
venue offers "consistently good" cooking with Pakistani influences;
no alcohol. / **Sample dishes:** chicken tikka; chicken curry; rasmalai (cream
cheese dessert). **Details:** 3m from centre of Rusholme; 11.30 pm.*

Sangam   £ 17   ★

13-15 Wilmslow Rd M14   (0161) 257 3922

*It's grown to be "extensive" over its ten years in business,
but "the quality is always great" at this "busy" Curry Mile
establishment, whose "delicious" cooking attracts impressively
consistent praise. / **Sample dishes:** onion bhaji; lamb balti; chocolate
gâteau. **Details:** 2m from city centre; 12.30 am; no smoking area.*

Shere Khan   £ 17

52 Wilmslow Rd M14 5TQ   (0161) 256 2624

*This large establishment, with its "modern" and "hygienic"
décor, is certainly "one of the busiest curry houses in Rusholme";
some would claim it's also "the best", but it inspires rather too
many complaints of "identikit gloop". / **Sample dishes:** lamb tikka
chops & kebabs; chicken tikka masala; kulfi. **Details:** midnight.*

Shezan   £ 18

119 Wilmslow Rd M14 5AN   (0161) 224 3116

*As a "cheap and cheerful, tasty fast food, take your own booze,
good after-pub curry sort of place", this "matey" Rusholme
institution has many supporters; it may be an "acquired taste",
but incidents such as "a fight between two customers" and
"being locked in after we refused to pay" only seem to add to
reporters' enthusiasm. / **Sample dishes:** garlic mushrooms; chicken tikka
masala; rasmalai (cream cheese dessert). **Details:** midnight; no smoking area.*

Shimla Pinks   £ 28

Dolefield, Crown Sq M3 3EN   (0161) 831 7099

*This "elegant" city-centre Indian newcomer, with its "imaginative"
and "different" menu, has made quite an impression on
a restaurant scene which hardly wants for subcontinental
competition; it's a "bit pricey", though, and some have it marked
down as "a poseurs' paradise". / **Sample dishes:** tandoori prawns;
Southern Indian garlic chilli chicken; kulfi. **Value tip:** set 2-crs L £8.95.
Details: by Crown courts; 10.45 pm, Sat & Sun 11.30 pm; closed Sat L & Sun
L.*

Siam Orchid £ 22
54 Portland St M1 4QU   (0161) 236 1388
"Friendly service and a wide choice of exotic tastes" (including *"good veggie options"*) help make this small, city-centre Thai, behind Piccadilly station, a *"consistently good"* choice; BYO. / **Sample dishes:** chicken satay; beef curry; banana fritters. **Details:** on edge of Chinatown; 11.30 pm; -open Sunday at 5pm.

Simply Heathcote's £ 36
Jackson Row, Deansgate M2 5WD   (0161) 835 3536
Some find this well-known central brasserie – branded with the name of the North West's most eminent chef – "a trendy and relaxing experience"; far too many reporters, though, leave disappointed by "mediocre" and "overpriced" cooking, by a setting "devoid of atmosphere" or by staff who "need to lighten up". / **Sample dishes:** spiced chicken liver risotto; lamb cutlets with roast tomatoes; orange & walnut tart. **Value tip:** set 2/3-crs L & pre-theatre £10.50/£12.50. **Details:** nr Opera House; 11 pm, Sun 9 pm.

Stock £ 40
4 Norfolk St M2 1DW   (0161) 839 6644
The city's old stock exchange building provides a "sophisticated setting" for this "upmarket" Italian newcomer; bearing in mind that the place is rather "expensive", though, the consensus is that the food is only "OK". / **Sample dishes:** linguine with crayfish tails; calves liver in balsamic vinegar sauce; caramelised peach tartlet. **Details:** off Upper King St; 10.30 pm; closed Sun.

Tai Pan £ 29 ★
81-97 Upper Brook St M13 9TX   (0161) 273 2798
Such is the competition that this "vast" Chinese is not quite, as some claim, "the best in Manchester", but many admirers approve its "consistently good" all-round standards and, in particular, its "fantastic" dim sum. / **Sample dishes:** Peking aromatic crispy duck; shredded beef with chilli & garlic; Chinese desserts. **Details:** 2m from city centre; 11 pm; closed Sat D & Sun D.

Tampopo £ 20 ★
16 Albert Sq M2 5PF   (0161) 819 1966
"A copy of Wagamama, but cheaper"; the enthusiasm evident in reports on this modern basement Thai, off Albert Square – with its "imaginative use of the freshest ingredients" and "vibrant tastes exploding on the palate" – recalls the glory days of London's once path-breaking canteen-oriental. / **Sample dishes:** coconut deep-fried prawns; pad Thai; passion fruit syllabub. **Value tip:** set 2-crs L £5.50. **Details:** in front of town hall; 11 pm; no Amex; no smoking; children: 7+.

Tandoori Kitchen £ 19 ★
131-133 Wilmslow Rd M14 5AW   (0161) 224 2329
"Delicately aromatised Indian regional cooking" wins a very wide following for this "long-standing favourite"; reputedly the oldest curry house in Rusholme, it's "not gaudy and touristified, like the others", and it reminds some "of how the area used to be"; BYO. / **Sample dishes:** onion bhaji with selection of chutneys; minted lamb; home-made kulfi. **Details:** midnight; no smoking area.

constantly updated at www.hardens.com

La Tasca £ 22 🄰

76 Deansgate M3 2FW (0161) 834 8234
It's the "buzzy" atmosphere that wins most praise for this large, well-known, central tapas bar, but the "wide variety" of "tasty" and "reasonably-priced" dishes generally come as a "nice surprise" in what is – in essence – a theme place. / **Sample dishes:** crispy pork in red wine sauce; Valencian paella with chicken & seafood; dark chocolate truffle & ice cream. **Details:** 100 yds from Kendals; 10.30 pm; need 8+ to book.

This & That £ 6 ★

3 Soap St M4 1EW (0161) 832 4971
A "huge cross-section" of fans from central Manchester and beyond are drawn to this "transport café-style" spot near Victoria Station for its "Kashmiri food with a home-cooked taste" at "ridiculously cheap" prices (particularly if you go for the "famous three-for-one deal – a meal for £3"). / **Sample dishes:** shish kebabs; chicken with vegetables; no puddings. **Value tip:** buffet all day, every day £3-£4 . **Details:** 5 pm; closed Sat; no credit cards.

Velvet £ 28 🄰★

2 Canal St M1 3HE (0161) 236 9003
With its "stunning decoration" ("goldfish in the floor!") and "interesting selection of tasty meals" (from a "frequently-changing menu") – not to mention the occasional "transvestite waitress" – this "relaxed" and "easy-going" bar is reporters' top Gay Village recommendation by a very long way. / **Sample dishes:** soup of the day; steak with pepper sauce & chips; chocolate fudge cake. **Details:** 10 pm, Fri & Sat midnight.

Wong Chu £ 19 ★

Faulkner St M1 (0161) 236 2346
"This is where Chinatown's residents eat", say aficionados of this "transport café-style" joint, which offers "fantastic portions at very good prices". / **Sample dishes:** roast chicken with egg noodles; roast pork with stir-fried vegetables; ice cream. **Value tip:** set menus available all day: 3crs £10.50/ 4crs £11- £14- £16- £18- 3crs for two £21.50.. **Details:** 11.30 pm; no Amex.

Woodstock Tavern £ 19

139 Barlow Moor Rd M20 2DY (0161) 448 7952
"You may have a long wait" at this "cool" Chorlton-cum-Hardy pub, which is "always very busy"; realisation of the "out-of-the-ordinary food" – an "unusually varied choice" from veggie fare to kangaroo – can be "hit and miss", but even when "quality is only passable, quantity is king!" / **Sample dishes:** spicy chicken wings; kangaroo steak with roast vegetables; chocolate tart. **Details:** 0.5m from junction for Princes Gateway on M56; 7.30 pm; no Amex; no smoking area; no booking.

Yang Sing £ 35 ★★

34 Princess St M1 4JY (0161) 236 2200
"Back with a vengeance, and better than ever" – some 300 reports (a record for anywhere outside London) justify the "immense reputation" of "the best Chinese restaurant in England", now re-installed in its old premises after a fire; Harry Yeung's cooking is "very sophisticated", and reports of the "odd lapse" in the "gracious" service is about the closest anyone comes to a complaint. / **Sample dishes:** spicy meat & nut dumplings; fried prawn balls with straw mushrooms; toffee apples. **Details:** close to city art gallery; 11 pm.

MANNINGTREE, ESSEX

Stour Bay Café £ 25 ★

39-43 High St CO11 1AH (01206) 396687

"An ever-changing menu, and a homely style with laid-back, but professional service" are the hallmarks of this "lovely", "friendly" bistro, which serves an interesting "fusion" menu. / **Sample dishes:** salmon with honey & chilli; Angus beef with yam & potato confit; raspberry panna cotta. **Value tip:** set 2/3-crs L £8.50/£10. **Details:** 9.30 pm; closed Mon, Sat L & Sun.

MAPPERLEY, CITY OF NOTTINGHAM 5–3D

Travellers Rest £ 24

Mapperley Plains, Plains Rd NG3 5RT (0115) 926 4412

An "extensive blackboard menu" realised to dependable standards make this popular, "relaxed" pub near Nottingham a place that lives up to its name. / **Sample dishes:** tiger prawns with wild rice; pappardelle with Mediterranean vegetables; apple pie & custard. **Value tip:** 1-crs Sunday Lunch £6.65. **Details:** take B684 from Nottingham towards Woodborough; 10 pm; no smoking area; no booking.

MARKET HARBOROUGH, LEICESTERSHIRE 5–4D

Han's £ 22 ★

29 St Mary's Rd LE16 7DS (01858) 462288

"Well-prepared and interesting food" and "good service" make this popular town-centre Chinese a unanimously popular choice. / **Sample dishes:** meze; mixed kebab; rhum baba. **Details:** nr town centre; 11 pm; closed Sat L & Sun.

MARLOW, BUCKINGHAMSHIRE 3–3A

Compleat Angler £ 55

Marlow Bridge SL7 1RG (01628) 484444

The "spectacular river view" is the only dependable attraction of this famous – but now "corporate hotel-style" – Thames-side fixture; its "snotty" service and "overpriced" cooking earned it one of the survey's most egregious overall assessments. / **Sample dishes:** deep-fried courgette flowers with aubergine purée; pork with slow-roasted tomatoes; rhubarb parfait with strawberries. **Value tip:** set 2/3-crs weekday L £21.50/£25.50. **Details:** 10 pm; no jeans; no smoking area. **Accommodation:** 64 rooms, from £225.

MARSTON TRUSSELL, LEICESTERSHIRE 5–4D

The Sun Inn £ 28

Main Street LE16 9TY (01858) 465531

This "excellent country inn", not far from Market Harborough, can get "very busy", thanks to its reputation for "no-nonsense" Gallic cooking at "reasonable prices"; let's hope the new man at the stoves will keep up the good work. / **Sample dishes:** Thai fishcakes; fillet steak in red wine sauce; apple tarte Tatin. **Value tip:** set 3-crs Sun L £12.95. **Details:** 3.5m from Market Harborough; 9.30 pm. **Accommodation:** 20 rooms, from £69.

MELBOURNE, DERBYSHIRE 5–3C

Bay Tree £ 39

4 Potter St DE73 1DW (01332) 863358

"Good food and service" win a consistent press for this "moderately priced modern bistro", housed in a former 17th-century, town-centre coaching inn. / **Sample dishes:** beef carpaccio; calves livers with tomato sauce; pancakes with syrup. **Value tip:** set 4-crs Sun L £17.50. **Details:** nr East Midlands Airport; 9.45 pm; closed Mon, Sun D, all bank holidays; no smoking area.

Pink Geranium   **£ 48**

25 Station Rd SG8 6DX   (01763) 260215

TV chef Steven Saunders sold this charmingly-located thatched restaurant in late-Spring 2000, leaving too little time for significant survey feedback (and, consequently, there is no grading); the new chef is Mark Jordan. / Sample dishes: scallops with pea pureé & pancetta; baked lamb with Stilton soufflé; autumn pudding. Value tip: set 2-crs D £18.50. Details: off A10 from Royston to Cambridge, 2nd exit (opp church); 10 pm; closed Mon & Sun; jacket; no smoking; children: discouraged.

Sheene Mill   **£ 36**

Station Rd SG8 6DX   (01763) 261393

Steven Saunders is now mainly focussed on this "attractive", "bistro-style" operation, next to the Pink Geranium; perhaps full time attention from the boss will cure the fact that the place has recently seemed "understaffed" at times, and that results have been "a bit hit-and-miss". / Sample dishes: poached egg muffin with spinach & cheese; calves liver with garlic mash & deep-fried onions; banana blinis with maple syrup. Details: off A10, 10m S of Cambridge; 10 pm; no smoking at L; booking advisable. Accommodation: 9 rooms, from £65.

Oddfellows Arms   **£ 25**   A★

73 Moor End Rd SK6 5PT   (0161) 449 7826

A "varied" menu – "not just fish specialities, but good curries too" – is "extremely well cooked" at this 18th-century pub, whose "relaxing atmosphere" is also praised. / Sample dishes: cured dill salmon; roast sea bass with green beans; bread & butter pudding. Details: 9.30 pm; closed Mon; no smoking in dining room.

Shepherd's Inn   **£ 20**   ★

CA10 1HF   (01768) 881217

"An excellent pub in a lovely area"; Martin Bauchtt's inn is consistently praised for its "unusual and varied" traditional menu, which includes "exceptional cheeses and chutneys" and "puddings to die for". / Sample dishes: oriental chicken wings; venison & cheese crumble; tangy lemon cheesecake. Details: on village green; 9.45 pm; no smoking area; no booking.

Village Bakery   **£ 23**   ★

CA10 1HE   (01768) 881515

"Ample" and "excellent" fare makes it "worth the detour" (11 miles from J40 of the M6) to this long-established bakery, which now uses only organic ingredients. / Sample dishes: soup of the day; penne with cream, sun-dried tomato & pesto sauce; lemon tart with raspberry sauce. Details: 10m NE of Penrith on A686; L only; no Amex; no smoking.

Nant Ddu Lodge   **£ 29**   ★

Brecon Rd CF48 2HY   (01685) 379111

The "unexpected location" – a riverside Georgian hunting lodge, where you can eat in either the bar or the restaurant – is just part of the attraction of this "nice all-rounder"; it offers "a wide selection of delicious food at reasonable prices". / Sample dishes: duck & pork rilettes with pickled damsons; char-grilled marlin with lentil salsa; vanilla parfait with Victoria plums. Details: 6m N of Merthyr on A470; 9.30 pm; closed Sun D; no smoking; booking: max 8. Accommodation: 22 rooms, from £69.50.

King William IV　　　　　**£ 23**　　　★

Byttom Hl RH5 6EL   (01372) 372590

The food at this "small, traditional pub" is "always good, no matter what you choose" from an "extensive", "old-fashioned" menu. / Sample dishes: garlic bread with Mozzarella; steak & kidney pie; treacle tart. Details: off A24; 9.30 pm; no Amex; bookings taken for Fri-Sun D only; children: 12+.

Purple Onion　　　　　**£ 33**　　　🄰

80 Corporation Rd TS1 2RF   (01642) 222250

Even detractors say that this "comfortable", "French-style bistro" has a "nice atmosphere"; fans say that the cooking is "really good" too, but quite a few grumble about "overpricing" or "small portions". / Sample dishes: skewer of king prawns; fillet steak with mustard & peppercorn sauce; chocolate brownie. Details: by law courts & Odeon cinema; 10.30 pm; closed Sun D; no Amex.

Jaipur　　　　　**£ 25**

502 Eldergate MK9 1LR   (01908) 669796

"An oasis"; this "comfortable, airy, modern" Indian "never fails to deliver", so far as its large local fan-club is concerned, with "unobtrusive" service contributing to the "pleasant" overall experience. / Sample dishes: minted lamb kebab; pistachio & chicken korma; melon & lemon ice cream. Value tip: set 3-crs Sun L £9.95. Details: next to railway station; 11.30 pm; no smoking area.

Marsh Goose　　　　　**£ 35**

High St GL56 0AX   (01608) 653500

An "intriguing" and "imaginative" menu served in an "attractive rustic dining room" near the centre of the village makes this small ten-year old a "perfect all-round" destination for many reporters; however, when it misfires – as it occasionally does – the whole approach can just seem "pretentious". / Sample dishes: foie gras & chicken liver parfait; salmon with leeks & flageolet beans; sticky toffee pudding. Details: 9.30 pm; closed Mon, Tue L & Sun D; no smoking area.

Morston Hall　　　　　**£ 43**　　　★

Main Coast Rd NR27 7AA   (01263) 741041

"Course after course of pure gastronomic heaven" – the "fabulous", rather traditional cooking and "good wines" are roundly praised at this "superb hotel", occupying a 17th-century house, set in "lovely" gardens on the North Norfolk coast. / Sample dishes: squab with puy lentils; roast beef with bubble & squeak; warm chocolate fondant. Details: between Blakeney & Wells on the A149 coastal road; 8 pm; D only, ex Sun open L & D; no smoking during D. Accommodation: 6 rooms, from £190, incl D.

Moss Nook £ 46

Ringway Rd M22 5WD (0161) 437 4778

"Old-fashioned plush" décor and "rich" Gallic cooking contribute to the "feeling of well-being" which some experience at this long-established restaurant near Manchester Airport; other, however, decry all aspects of an operation whose décor is likened to "a Victorian bedroom". / **Sample dishes:** asparagus with sautéed scallops; fillet steak with sweet & sour sauce; crème brûlée. **Value tip:** set 3-crs L £18.50. **Details:** on B5166, 1m from Manchester airport; 9.30 pm; closed Mon, Sat L & Sun; no jeans; children: 11+.

Beetle & Wedge £ 44   A★

Ferry Ln OX10 9JF (01491) 651381

A "superb riverside setting" and an "intimate" ambience help make this "relaxed" Thames-side fixture a deservedly popular destination – both the less formal 'boathouse' (where charcoal grills are a mainstay) and the conservatory restaurant proper (which offers "generous portions of English fare"). / **Sample dishes:** Cornish crab & avocado salad; Gressingham duck with oyster mushrooms; hot Cointreau soufflé. **Details:** on A329 between Streatley & Wallingford, take Ferry Lane at crossroads; 9.45 pm; closed Mon & Sun D; no smoking area. **Accommodation:** 10 rooms, from £135.

Black Bull £ 36   A★

DL10 6QJ (01325) 377289

A "wonderful" dining room in a former Pullman railway carriage is the special attraction of this long-established pub/restaurant; "fantastic fish" is the highlight of a "quality" British menu that "never disappoints". / **Sample dishes:** seafood pancakes; Dover sole with lemon sauce; hot liqueur pancakes. **Value tip:** set 3-crs L £15.50. **Details:** 1m S of Scotch Corner; 10.15 pm; closed Sun; children: 7+.

Cornish Range £ 31

Chapel St TR19 6SB (01736) 731488

This "happy and cosy restaurant", set a little way back from the harbour, serves dependable fish and seafood "at reasonable prices"; it's a good idea to book. / **Sample dishes:** roast pear & Gorgonzola salad; salmon, John Dory & prawns in lobster sauce; lime parfait with passion fruit coulis. **Details:** on coast road between Penzance & Lands End; 9.30 pm (9 pm in winter); D only (closed Mon-Wed in winter); no Amex; mostly non-smoking.

Pandora Inn £ 30   A

Restronguet Creek TR11 5ST (01326) 372678

A "wonderful location" on a picturesque inlet (the pub has showers for visiting yachties) helps ensure that this slightly remote but "very popular" thatched waterside pub is often "very busy"; "good traditional pub food" is served in the bar, on the pontoon, and in the (more expensive) upstairs restaurant. / **Sample dishes:** spinach & Roquefort salad; scallops & tiger prawns with Thai spices; fresh fruit brûlée. **Details:** signposted off A390, between Truro & Falmouth; 9.30 pm (9 pm in winter); no Amex; no smoking.

NAYLAND, SUFFOLK 3–2C

White Hart £ 33

11 High St C06 4JF (01206) 263 382
The make-over last year of this country coaching inn seems to
have gone down like a lead balloon – many reporters finding that
a previously "charming" formula has been replaced with one
that's "stuffy", "boring" and "expensive". / **Sample dishes:** smoked
chicken Thai salad; roast wood pigeon; pistachio crème brûlée. **Details:** off
A12, between Colchester & Sudbury; 9.30 pm. **Accommodation:** 6 rooms,
from £69.50.

NETHER ALDERLEY, CHESHIRE 5–2B

Wizard £ 34 A

Macclesfield Rd SK10 4UB (01625) 584000
This rurally-located old coaching inn is "full of atmosphere",
and is consistently praised for its "elegant" cooking – worth
knowing about in an area without too many competing
attractions. / **Sample dishes:** king scallops with spinach & nut salad;
char-grilled swordfish niçoise with spinach; raspberry crème brûlée & walnut
cookies. **Details:** from A34, take B5087; 9.30 pm; closed Mon & Sun D;
no smoking area.

NEW MILTON, HAMPSHIRE 2–4C

Chewton Glen £ 57 A

Christchurch Rd BH25 6QS (01425) 275341
"Everything is first-class", say the many fans of this famous
country house hotel on the fringe of the New Forest, where
the "impeccable", "pampering" service wins particular praise;
a vocal minority, however, suspects the place is "only interested in
the super-rich", and slams "very poor" standards at "exorbitant"
prices. / **Sample dishes:** cheese soufflé; stuffed pork cheeks & lobster;
chocolate fondant. **Details:** between New Milton & Highcliffe on A337;
9.30 pm; closed Mon L; jacket at D; no smoking; children: 7+.
Accommodation: 59 rooms, from £275.

NEWCASTLE UPON TYNE, TYNE & WEAR 8–2B

The going-out heart of Newcastle is to be found in the old
docks, the Quayside – an area utterly transformed over the
past few years. It is sad that the year has seen the demise of
its star resident, 21 Queen Street, but one must hope that
the new format Café 21 will find a greater market following.
There are also a couple of notable Indians (Leela's, Vujon).

The hill leading up from the Quayside to the town centre is
the location for a number of good, slightly quirky places and
also the leading trendy brasserie, the Metropolitan. In the
centre of town, Barn Again Bistro is a great favourite as an
informal venue. A short taxi-ride from town, and leafily-
located in Jesmond Dene, the city's grandest restaurant,
Fisherman's Lodge, enjoys a particularly picturesque situation.

Barn Again Bistro £ 34 A★

21a Leazes Park Rd NE1 4PF (0191) 230 3338
The culinary combinations can seem "scatty", but the "food is
always interesting" and "flavoursome" at this "fun", and "quirky"
barn-conversion; it delivers "consistently high standards", and is
very popular. / **Sample dishes:** king prawn tempura with noodle salad; pan-
fried sea bass with shrimp & basil mash; hot fallen chocolate soufflé.
Details: nr St James's Park football ground; 10 pm; closed Mon & Sun.

constantly updated at www.hardens.com

Café 21 £ 27 ★

21 Queen St, Princes Whf NE1 3UG (0191) 222 0755

Terry Laybourne has given up the struggle to persuade Newcastle folk to pay good money for French cooking of the highest quality, and has relaunched his Quayside spot (formerly called 21 Queen Street) in a cheaper and more informal style; we've awarded the rating shown on the basis of his brasserie operations elsewhere. / **Sample dishes:** grilled black pudding with crispy onions; turbot with pasta & green beans; iced banana parfait. **Details:** 10 pm; closed Sun.

Café Paradiso £ 24 Ⓐ

3 Market Ln NE1 6QQ (0191) 221 1240

This "cool" and "trendy", "younger generation" Italian café offers "quality" snacks at "great-value" prices, and it's very popular. / **Sample dishes:** ricotta, spinach & rosemary tartlet; lamb shank with rosemary & mustard mash; egg custard tart with redcurrants. **Value tip:** set 2-crs L £5.95. **Details:** opp fire station; 10.45 pm; closed Sun; no smoking area.

Dragon House £ 23

30-32 Stowell St NE1 4XQ (0191) 232 0868

"A decent city-centre restaurant"; this "predictable but reliable" Chinese is a "friendly" place, serving "tasty" dishes in an "unhurried" atmosphere. / **Sample dishes:** chicken & sweetcorn soup; chicken in black bean sauce; orange sorbet. **Value tip:** set 2/3-crs L £5.50/£7.25. **Details:** 11 pm; no Amex.

Fisherman's Lodge £ 46 Ⓐ

Jesmond Dene NE7 7BQ (0191) 281 3281

"A pleasant woodland setting" helps make this old house, "tucked away" in the Jesmond Dene valley "a special place" for many; they claim it's "the best restaurant in Newcastle" – it's certainly the most expensive, but then "substantial" portions of "delicious" seafood rarely come cheap. / **Sample dishes:** sun-dried tomato risotto; roast cod & borlotti beans; raspberry & chocolate ganache tart. **Value tip:** set 3-crs L £19.50. **Details:** 2m from city centre on A1058, follow signposts to Jesmond Dene; 10.45 pm; closed Sat L & Sun; no smoking; children: 8+.

Fox Talbot £ 23

46 Dean St NE1 1PG (0191) 230 2229

"It appears to have gone downmarket, price-wise and in standards" – there are too many reports of "delusions of culinary grandeur" and "rude" or "slow" service to make this formerly admirable café-style venture, above the Quayside, a reliable recommendation. / **Sample dishes:** goat's cheese & walnut salad; Cajun chicken with lemon rice; chocolate fondue with marshmallows. **Value tip:** set 2-crs L £4.87. **Details:** nr Theatre Royal; 11 pm; no Amex.

Francesca's £ 19 ★

Manor House Rd NE2 2NE (0191) 281 6586

"Even on a rainy Tuesday in January, there's always a queue" at this "hugely popular" family-run Italian; "very fine pasta" and "the best garlic prawns" are highlights from its range of "cheap but reliably good" fare. / **Sample dishes:** king prawns in garlic; chicken in arrabiata sauce with penne; tiramisu. **Details:** right off Osborne Rd in Jesmond; 9 pm; closed Sun; no Amex; no booking.

King Neptune £ 26

34-36 Stowell St NE1 4XQ (0191) 261 6657

The "extensive" selection of "delicious" dishes helps ensure that this "relaxed", "friendly" and "reliable" Chinese is "always full". / **Sample dishes:** hot & sour soup; Szechuan beef; ice cream. **Value tip:** set 3-crs L & Sun L £6.50. **Details:** in Chinatown; 10.45 pm.

Komal Balti House £ 14

277 Stanhope St NE4 5JU (0191) 226 1726

The setting here may be "down-to-earth", to say the least, but the "cheap and plentiful" Indian grub offers "delicious varieties on taste and texture"; BYO. / **Sample dishes:** samosas; lamb balti; ice cream. **Details:** nr General Hospital; 11.15 pm.

Leela's £ 30 ★

20 Dean St NE1 1PG (0191) 230 1261

"Lovely, warm" service (from Leela Paul herself) and "delicious and healthy" vegetarian dishes make this south Indian near the Quayside the "best curry house in town" for many reporters. / **Sample dishes:** spiced prawn & cashew nut salad; pork marinated in herbs; roast vermicelli in coconut milk. **Value tip:** set 3-crs L £9.95. **Details:** 11.30 pm; closed Sun; no Switch; no smoking area.

Magpie Room £ 36

St James's Park Football Ground NE1 4ST
(0191) 201 8511

Whether a "superb view of Newcastle United's ground" is a positive attraction is a matter on which every reader will have his or her own view; what's surprising, though, is that the food at the stand's top-floor dining room "does not disappoint" – a trend which will hopefully continue under new chef Ian Lowrey. / **Sample dishes:** cheddar & spinach souffle; sirloin steak with béarnaise sauce & chips; custard tart with nutmeg ice cream. **Value tip:** set 2/3-crs L £10.50/£13. **Details:** 10.30 pm; closed Mon, Sat L & Sun D; tie required.

Metropolitan £ 27 A★

35 Grey St NE1 6EE (0191) 230 2306

The "trendy" but "relaxed" style of this "Art Deco-inspired" café-restaurant wins it a high degree of local popularity, with "earlybird" menus (5.30pm-7pm), in particular, hailed for their "tremendous value"; a vociferous minority finds the place "over-rated". / **Sample dishes:** fish soup with pesto croutons; crispy cod with bacon & pea fritters; chocolate & Newcastle Brown Ale cake. **Value tip:** set 2-crs L £8.95. **Details:** nr Theatre Royal; 10.45 pm; closed Sun; no smoking area.

Pani's £ 14 A★

61 High Bridge NE1 6BX (0191) 232 4366

"It feels more like Rome than Newcastle" at this "great traditional Italian" café in the city centre, which fans say is "the only one in town worth considering", thanks to its "delicious", "authentic" and "very cheap" cooking and its "warm" and "lively" ambience. / **Sample dishes:** Mozzarella & tomato salad; chicken with mushrooms & bacon; tiramisu. **Details:** 10 pm; closed Sun; no Amex; no booking at L.

Sachins £ 25 ★

Forth Banks NE1 3SG (0191) 261 9035

"Consistently good Punjabi cooking" – "full of flavour, with each dish distinct" – helps make this large and "friendly" curry house one of the most popular in town. / **Sample dishes:** mixed tandoori platter; chicken in tomato & onion sauce; kulfi. **Details:** behind Central Station; 11.15 pm; closed Sun.

Tasca £ 23

106 Quayside NE4 3DX (0191) 230 4006

"Good fun, cheap and enjoyable", this "busy" tapas bar is a "very popular" place, and it's "great for a group outing". / **Sample dishes:** crispy pork in red wine sauce; Valencian paella with chicken & seafood; dark chocolate truffle & ice cream. **Details:** 10.30 pm; booking: need 8 to book.

Valley Junction £ 26 Ⓐ

Old Jesmond Station, Archbold Ter NE2 1DB
(0191) 281 6397
"A converted signal box and railway carriage" provide the
"unusual surroundings" for this notably "pleasant", "friendly"
and "efficient" Indian restaurant. / **Sample dishes:** onion bhaji; lamb
with tomato, pepper & coriander; gulab jaman (Indian sweets). **Details:** nr
Civic Centre, off Sandyford Rd; 11.30 pm; closed Mon; no smoking area.

Vujon £ 29 ★

29 Queen St NE1 3UG (0191) 221 0601
"Stylish and delicately spiced" cuisine puts this "tranquil" Indian –
on the "increasingly popular" Quayside – into "a different class"
for many reporters. / **Details:** 11 pm; closed Sun L.

NEWLAND, GLOUCESTERSHIRE 2–2B

Ostrich Inn £ 25 Ⓐ★★

GL16 8NP (01594) 833260
Richard Dewe's "remarkable historic inn" is a highly "popular"
destination, thanks to his "large and eclectic" menu (realised
"using the highest-quality ingredients"), the "good real ales" and
"extensive wine list". / **Sample dishes:** Greek salad; monkfish thermidor;
summer pudding. **Details:** 2m SW of Coleford; 9.30 pm; no booking; children:
14+.

NEWPORT, NEWPORT 2–2A

Junction 28 £ 28 Ⓐ★

Station Approach NP1 8LD (01633) 891891
This converted railway station offers a much more "wonderful"
experience than its name might suggest; attractions include
sometimes "exceptional" cooking from a wide-ranging menu,
an "easy-going" atmosphere and some "well-priced" wines.
/ **Sample dishes:** king scallops with bacon & balsamic vinegar; roast duck tart
with caramelised onions; deep-fried profiteroles with fudge. **Details:** off M4, J8
towards Caerphilly; 9.30 pm; closed Sun D; no Amex.

NEWTON-ON-THE-MOOR, NORTHUMBERLAND 8–2B

Cook & Barker £ 27 ★

LA65 9JY (01665) 575234
"This has to be the best pub food in Northumberland, especially
the Sunday lunch" is typical of feedback on this "consistently
good" destination; options include bar meals as well as the more
substantial restaurant fare. / **Sample dishes:** seafood tapas; supreme of
chicken with lobster sauce; crème brûlée. **Details:** 12m N of Morpeth, just off
A1; 9 pm; no smoking area. **Accommodation:** 4 rooms, from £70.

NEWTON, CAMBRIDGESHIRE 3–1B

Queens Head £ 12 Ⓐ★

Fowlmere Rd CB2 5PG (01223) 870436
The "traditional" menu may "very simple" and quite "restricted",
but this hidden-way inn ("40 years under the same landlords and
reliable") is worth seeking out for its "great atmosphere", and for
the "good quality" of its provisions. / **Sample dishes:** brown soup; cold
meat platter with pickles; no puddings. **Details:** off A10; 9.30 pm;
no credit cards; no booking.

Kristian Fish Restaurant £ 7 ★

5 Union Quay NE30 1HJ (0191) 258 5155

"Juicy and cheap" fish and "real" chips, with a pot of tea and a slice of bread – all at rock-bottom prices – is a winning combination for the small but devoted fan club of this "no-frills" chippy. / **Sample dishes:** *no starters; cod & chips; no puddings.* **Details:** *8.50 pm; closed Sun D; no credit cards.*

Seven Stars £ 31

High St DH1 2NN (0191) 384 8454

A "lovely setting" and "very reasonable prices" are among the attractions of this "cosy village pub", whose "tasty" cooking rarely disappoints. / **Sample dishes:** *chicken tortillas with salsa & guacamole; roast lamb with crushed garlic potatoes; passion fruit & lemon tart.* **Details:** *off A177; 9.30 pm; no Amex; no smoking.* **Accommodation:** *8 rooms, from £50.*

Hundred House £ 34 🅐★

Bridgnorth Rd TF11 9EE (01952) 730353

It's not just the "wonderful gardens" which make this characterful old inn "no ordinary pub" – its "good, varied" menu offers some "excellent" results. / **Sample dishes:** *grilled scallops with sesame rice cakes; venison with red cabbage & blue cheese polenta; raspberry & meringue ice cream terrine.* **Details:** *on A442 between Bridgnorth & Telford; 9.30 pm.* **Accommodation:** *10 rooms, from £95.*

Adlards £ 49

79 Upper Giles St NR2 1AB (01603) 633522

"The best in the region (though the region is not great)"; it's a shame that some reporters find David Adlard's charmingly-located city-fringe establishment a mite "pompous" and "pricey", as his "idiosyncratic" Anglo-French cooking can be "most enjoyable" and he maintains a "very good" cellar. / **Sample dishes:** *scallops with apple & ginger purée; duck in Parma ham; orange soufflé & orange sorbet.* **Details:** *nr the Roman Catholic Cathedral; 10.30 pm; closed Mon L & Sun; no smoking during D.*

Garden House £ 26

Southouse Rd NR13 6AA (01603) 720007

"Fresh, well-cooked pub food" makes this "frantic" boozer worth knowing about in this under-provided city. / **Sample dishes:** *mushroom rarebit; rack of lamb with redcurrant sauce; caramelised oranges with butterscotch ice cream.* **Details:** *8.45 pm; closed Mon & Sun D; no smoking.* **Accommodation:** *6 rooms, from £50.*

Siam Bangkok £ 26 ★

8 Orford Hill NR1 3QD (01603) 617817

"Very fresh" cooking and "lovely" service are among the features which differentiate this "warm" and "cosy" city-centre Thai. / **Sample dishes:** *chicken satay; sizzling mixed seafood; ice cream.* **Value tip:** *set 3-crs L £8.95.* **Details:** *nr Timber Hill; 10.30 pm; closed Mon L & Sun L; children: 5+.*

Tatlers £ 29 ★

21 Tombland NR3 1RF (01603) 766670

"Innovative cuisine from a consistently good young chef" and
an *"understated"* setting make Samuel Clifford's *"splendidly-
situated"* restaurant, just a few yards from the Cathedral,
a *"real find"*. / **Sample dishes:** caramelised onion tart; cod in Parma ham
with leek confit; white chocolate & vanilla mousse. **Value tip:** set 3-crs
L £12.50. **Details:** nr Cathedral; 10 pm.

The Tree House £ 19 ★

14-16 Dove St NR21 1DE (01603) 763258

A *"veggie with character"* (run as a workers' co-operative), whose
"imaginative and very tasty food" (and at *"good prices"*) makes it
a popular local choice; improving ratings support those who say
"the service has definitely improved". / **Sample dishes:** soup with
garlic croutons; potatoes & mushrooms in blue cheese sauce; chocolate banana
cake. **Details:** 9 pm; closed Mon D, Tue D, Wed D & Sun; no credit cards;
no smoking; no booking at L.

NOTTINGHAM, CITY OF NOTTINGHAM 5–3D

Though it's fair to say that it does not have a particular name
for gastronomy, Nottingham is one of the better English
cities for dining. It is unusual in that it boasts two modern
brasseries – *Hart's* and *Sonny's* – that have been consistently
successful for a number of years.

Some of the better places in town are actually outside the
city centre, in Beeston, just the other side of the University
campus.

Bees Make Honey £ 29

12 Alfreton Rd NG7 3NG (0115) 978 0109

*Though this "very small" BYO restaurant strikes some as
"quite ordinary" – and with a "simple" setting that verges on the
"Spartan" – it's "a continuing favourite" for a good number of
locals who praise its "tasty" international cooking and its
"relaxed" approach. / **Sample dishes:** asparagus with scallops & ginger;
monkfish & king prawns with Thai basil; white chocolate cheesecake.
Details: 5 mins from Playhouse & Theatre Royal; 10.15 pm; D only, closed
Mon & Sun; no credit cards; booking: max 14.*

Beeston Tandoori £ 16 ★

150-152 High Rd NG9 2LN (0115) 922 3330

"Great food, quite cheap" makes this *"cramped"* but *"friendly"*
Indian *"well known, especially to the locals"*. / **Sample
dishes:** butterfly king prawns; chicken tikka masala; sorbet.
Details: 11.45 pm; no Amex; no smoking area.

La Boheme £ 35 Ⓐ

Barker Gt, Lace Mkt NG1 1JU (0115) 912 7771

"Live jazz" (some nights) and *"delightful"* service (usually) are
among the attractions of this *"elegant"* but *"unpretentious"*
city-centre venture; though opinions differ on the Eastern
European-influenced menu, most find it *"interesting and
different"*. / **Sample dishes:** chicken liver parfait with walnut bread; roast
duck with peppercorn sauce; tiramisu with coffee bean syrup. **Value tip:** set 3-
crs L £13.50. **Details:** 11 pm; closed Sun; no smoking.

French Living £ 20

27 King St NG1 2AY (0115) 958 5885

"Consistent, authentic, friendly and cheap" – local supporters find that this *"intimate"* and *"authentic"* Gallic bistro lives up to its name. / **Sample dishes:** *moules marinière; beef with roasted shallots; tarte Tatin.* **Details:** *nr Market Square; 10 pm; closed Mon & Sun; no smoking in café; booking: max 10, Sat pm.*

Grenouille £ 25

32 Lenton Boulevard NG7 2ES (0115) 941 1088

It attracts few reports, but local fans speak well of the cooking at this "unpretentious" Gallic fixture of over a quarter of a century's standing, where an "impressive" wine list is a feature. / **Sample dishes:** *grilled goat's cheese salad; roast pork with Dijon mustard sauce; pear tart with custard.* **Value tip:** *set dinner menu available on weds only.* **Details:** *close to A52 & Queens Medical Centre; 9.30 pm; D only, closed Mon & Sun; no Amex.*

Hart's £ 34   Ⓐ★

Standard Ct, Park Rw NG1 6GN (0115) 911 0666

Tim Hart's "first-class provincial restaurant" is often compared – for good and ill – with those in the capital; it's "just ever so slightly impersonal", and some gripe of prices on the "high" side and a "yuppie clientele", but it's a "stylish" place which dependably offers "very good" modern brasserie food. / **Sample dishes:** *potted crab & tomato salad; turbot with samphire & wild mushrooms; chocolate pudding & pistachio ice cream.* **Value tip:** *set 2-crs L £9.90.* **Details:** *nr castle; 10.30 pm, Sun 9 pm.*

Laguna Tandoori £ 22   ★

43 Mount Street NG1 6AG (0115) 941 1632

"Consistently very good, and with reasonable prices", this "proper" Indian is, say locals, a "first-class act". / **Sample dishes:** *chicken tikka; lamb bhuna; kulfi.* **Details:** *nr Nottingham Castle; 11 pm; closed Sat L & Sun L; booking advisable.*

Mem Saab £ 26

12-14 Maid Marian Way NG1 6HS (0115) 957 0009

"A proper restaurant, rather than a curry house", this "modern, light and airy" Indian yearling gets nothing but praise from locals for its "fresh" and "authentic" cooking. / **Sample dishes:** *tandoori salmon salad; lamb in yoghurt, chilli & ginger sauce; kulfi.* **Details:** *nr Nottingham Castle; 11 pm, Fri & Sat 11.30 pm; D only, closed Sun; no smoking area.*

Merchants £ 34

Lace Market Hotel, 29-31 High Pavement NG1 1HS (0115) 852 3232

This city-centre venture may, in two years of its existence, have attracted the attention of the Michelin men, but for far too many reporters it's now a "second-division" affair – "dreadful", "inexperienced" service is at the root of many unhappy experiences, but disasters on the culinary front are also reported. / **Sample dishes:** *goat's cheese fondue; brill with baby spinach salad; sticky toffee pudding.* **Value tip:** *set 2/3-crs L £9.50/£12.50.* **Details:** *10.30 pm; closed Sat L & Sun D.* **Accommodation:** *29 rooms, from £89.*

Pretty Orchid £ 26

12 Pepper Street NG1 2GH (0115) 958 8344

"Tasty" and extremely consistent Thai cooking, "beautifully presented", has made this city-centre ten-year-old one of the most popular restaurants in town; service is "sympathetic". / **Sample dishes:** *tom yum soup; Thai green chicken curry; sticky rice & mango.* **Details:** *behind Marks & Spencer; 11 pm; closed Sun; no Amex.*

Royal Thai £ 21 ★

189 Mansfield Rd NG1 3FS (0115) 948 3001

*"Consistently good" cooking and "genuine hospitality" make this "reasonably priced" oriental a local favourite, where "the traditional Thai setting, with waitresses in native dress, adds to the ambience". / **Sample dishes:** tom yum soup; Thai green curry with chicken; pancake rolls with coconut. **Value tip:** 6crs 14.00/ 7crs 17.00/ 8crs 19.00/ vegetarian-14.00 (6crs)/ 17.00 (7crs). **Details:** 11 pm; closed Sun L; no Amex.*

Saagar £ 26 ★

473 Mansfield Rd NG5 2DR (0115) 962 2014

*"Fresh ingredients" and "authentic" Indian flavours make the cooking here a "consistent" success, and – even though it's some way from the city centre, it's many reporters' top choice in town; the décor is "less than tasteful", however, and service can be "grumpy". / **Sample dishes:** king prawn pakora; chicken masala; Indian sweets. **Details:** 1.5m from city centre; midnight; closed Sun L; no smoking area; children: 5+.*

Shimla Pinks £ 26

38-46 Goosegate NG1 1FF (0115) 958 9899

*"Trendy, busy and young", this "sleek" two-year-old Indian offers the "different" approach to the cuisine which is the group's hallmark; as in other cities, it pleases most – but not all – reporters, and here a minority finds it "very disappointing". / **Sample dishes:** chicken tikka; crispy chicken with vegetables; pistachio kulfi. **Details:** off Mansfield Road; 11 pm; no smoking area.*

Siam Thani £ 23

16-20a, Carlton St NG1 1NN (0115) 958 2222

*This large and "busy" Thai restaurant is consistently praised by locals for its "beautifully presented" cooking and its "elegant" decor. / **Sample dishes:** chicken satay; Thai green chicken curry; banana fritters. **Details:** 10.30 pm; closed Sun L; no Amex; no smoking area.*

Sonny's £ 34 ★

3 Carlton St NG1 1NL (0115) 947 3041

*Notwithstanding the odd gripe that it's "getting tired", this "bright and modern" brasserie is still – for its fans – "the most relaxed smart eat in Nottingham", thanks to its "easy-going" approach and to cooking that's "consistently interesting without being OTT". / **Sample dishes:** beetroot-cured salmon with pickles; roast lamb with rosemary marmalade; sticky toffee pudding. **Value tip:** set 2/3-crs weekday L £10/£13.95. **Details:** nr Victoria Centre; 10.30 pm, Fri & Sat 11 pm.*

La Toque £ 37 ★

61 Vollaton Rd NG9 2NJ (0115) 922 2268

*"Still needing to be more widely discovered" say local fans of Swede Mattias Karlsson's two-year-old venture near Beeston "on a site that has been through many incarnations"; his "original", "beautifully presented" Gallic cooking provides the "best meal out in a long time" for many who comment and he maintains a "good-value" wine list. / **Sample dishes:** duck terrine with bacon salad; lamb with caramelised shallots; baked prune soufflé. **Details:** off A52 towards Beeston; 10.30 pm; closed Sun; no Amex; no smoking area; children: 6+.*

Victoria Hotel £ 21

Dovecote Ln NG9 1JG (0115) 925 4049

This "great" railway-side pub is a very popular destination, thanks to its "live music", "real ales" and, of course, its "reasonably priced" and ever-changing menu of "reliable" "staples". / *Sample dishes:* red onion tart; Lincoln sausages & mash; Mars bar cheesecake. **Details:** by Beeston railway station; 9.15 pm; no Amex; no smoking; children: before 8 pm only.

OCKLEY, SURREY 3–4A

Bryce's At The Old School House £ 30 ★

RH5 5TH (01306) 627430

"It's difficult enough to get a booking here, so please don't put it in", says one regular customer for the "wonderful" fish and seafood – presented in "good-sized servings" – at this popular pub/restaurant. / *Sample dishes:* Dijon mustard scallops with spinach; Cornish monkfish in Parma ham with celeriac rosti; butterscotch & honeycomb cheesecake. **Details:** 9 pm; closed Sun D until November; no smoking in restaurant.

ODIHAM, HAMPSHIRE 2–3D

The Grapevine £ 33 A ★

121 High St RG29 1LA (01256) 701122

"They care" at this "very nice" village bistro; it offers "excellent value for money". / *Sample dishes:* smoked haddock tartlet; roast ostrich with saffron mash; mango & sage crème brûlée. **Value tip:** set 2-crs L £8.95, set 3-crs early eve £14.95. **Details:** follow signs from M3, J5; 10 pm; closed Sat L & Sun.

OLD BURGHCLERE, BERKSHIRE 2–2D

Dew Pond £ 37 ★

RG20 9LH (01635) 278408

The Marshalls' "delightful, family-run restaurant" offers "good-value" French cooking and "low-key but effective" service in a "cottagey" setting. / *Sample dishes:* chicken & Parma ham salad; roe deer with wild mushrooms, apple & port; chocolate cake. **Details:** 6m S of Newbury, off A34; 10 pm; D only, closed Mon & Sun; no smoking area; children: 5+.

OLDHAM, GREATER MANCHESTER 5–2B

Ho Ho's £ 28 ★

57-59 High St OL4 3BN (0161) 620 9500

A "sophisticated Chinese restaurant with Italian-style décor" may sound a bit odd, but "reliable, top-quality" cooking and "nice surroundings" make quite a hit of this "striking", "modern" oriental, which Oldham folk rate "the best Manchester restaurant away from the city centre". / *Sample dishes:* seafood spring rolls; hot & spicy chicken casserole; deep-fried coconut balls. **Value tip:** set 3-crs L £7.95. **Details:** follow signs from M62, J20; 11 pm; closed Mon L-Wed L.

ONGAR, ESSEX 3–2B

Smiths Brasserie £ 34 ★

Fyfield Rd CM5 0AL (01277) 365578

"Excellent for fish" – the theme of reports on this busy town-centre bistro is consistent. / *Sample dishes:* stuffed mussels; scallops marinière; crème brûlée. **Value tip:** set 3-crs L £13.50. **Details:** left off A414 towards Fyfield; 10.30 pm; closed Mon; no Amex; children: 12+.

ORFORD, SUFFOLK
Butley Oysters   £ 24   3–1D

Market Hill IP12 2LH   (01394) 450277
This "unique" establishment "may resemble a '50s café" –
that's pretty much what it is – but it wins high praise for its
"superb" fish, which "tastes as if it was caught 10 minutes ago";
even admirers admit that the ambience is of the "bring your
own" variety, and critics slam sometimes "grudging" service.
/ **Sample dishes:** smoked salmon pâté; sea bass in lemon & butter; rum cake.
Details: 10m E of Woodbridge; 8:30 pm; closed D Mon-Thu (Oct-Mar , also
closed Sun D); no Amex; no smoking.

ORKNEY ISLANDS
The Creel   £ 36   𝔸★

Front Rd, St Margaret's Hope, S Ronaldsay KW17 2SL
(01856) 831311
Allan Craigie's "superb fish" and "more-ish puddings" win
a unanimous thumbs-up from those who have made the
pilgrimage to this unpretentious restaurant-with-rooms.
/ **Sample dishes:** moules marinière; roast monkfish & leeks with ginger;
baked lemon tart. **Details:** off A961 S of town, 13m across Churchill barriers;
9 pm; D only; closed Jan-Mar; no Amex & no Switch; no smoking.
Accommodation: 3 rooms, from £65.

ORPINGTON, KENT
Xian   £ 22   ★   3–3B

324 High St BR6 0NG   (01689) 871881
"Delicate, carefully prepared" cooking and "very good service"
ensure that this "well above-average" Chinese is usually "very
busy". / **Sample dishes:** crispy aromatic duck; crispy fried beef with noodles;
toffee bananas. **Details:** 11.15 pm; closed Sun L.

OSWESTRY, SHROPSHIRE
Sebastians   £ 36   ★   5–3A

45 Willow St SY11 1AQ   (01691) 655444
The appearance – a "small shop front and a cramped interior" –
"belies the quality cooking" on offer at the Fishers' "hide-away",
where "meticulous attention to detail" is the hallmark of all
aspects of the operation. / **Sample dishes:** cheese & walnut soufflé;
lamb with tomato, aubergine & sweet pepper sauce; steamed sponge with
strawberry sauce. **Details:** nr town centre, follow directions to Selattyn;
9.45 pm; closed Mon & Sun; no smoking. **Accommodation:** 4 rooms,
from £50.

OTFORD, KENT
Bull   £ 24   𝔸★   3–3B

High St TN14 5PG   (01959) 523198
"Fine fish" is highlighted amongst the "interesting" dishes which
make this "congenial" and "atmospheric" pub of more than
average note. / **Sample dishes:** fried meadow mushrooms; lemon sole;
passion fruit parfait. **Details:** 10 pm; children: before 5 pm only.

OVER PEOVER, CHESHIRE
Dog Inn   £ 26   5–2B

Well Bank Ln WA16 8UP   (01625) 861421
"Traditional British food as it should be" ("great game pies" and
so on) are served at this "consistent" and "friendly" boozer.
/ **Sample dishes:** black pudding with English mustard sauce; braised lamb
shank with parsley sauce; sticky toffee pudding. **Details:** off A50; 9.30 pm;
no Amex; no smoking. **Accommodation:** 6 rooms, from £75.

Bush   £ 27   Ⓐ

SO24 0RE   (01962) 732764

A "perfect rural riverside" setting adds lustre to this popular pub,
which offers "big portions of high-quality, simple grub". / **Sample
dishes:** pan-fried wild mushrooms; roast venison with root vegetables; sticky
toffee pudding. **Details:** just off A31 between Winchester & Alresford;
9.30 pm; closed Sun D.

OXFORD, OXFORDSHIRE   2–2D

The non-ethnic restaurants in this rich and beautiful city
tend to be comfortable and charming places, but – almost
without exception – their cooking is second-rate. Sadly, this
includes Raymond Blanc's *Petit Blanc*, even though it attracts
a huge amount of commentary. (What many would claim as
England's greatest restaurant, Blanc's *Manoir aux Quat'
Saisons*, is but a few miles away at Great Milton.) For above-
average cooking, you generally need to seek out one of the
good number of quality ethnics. Sadly, most of these either
lack any particular charm or are not especially convenient
for the city centre. Two Thais, however, *Chaing Mai* and
Bangkok House – which offer superior cooking in pleasant
central premises – provide the best of both worlds.

Al Shami   £ 26   ★

25 Walton Cr OX1 2JG   (01865) 310066

A "good variety" of "tasty, freshly cooked" Lebanese food makes
this "Spartan" Jericho spot a very popular destination; some
visitors found "the meze so good we didn't get as far as the main
course!" / **Sample dishes:** tabbouleh & houmous; grilled lamb skewers with
garlic sauce; Lebanese sweets. **Details:** 10 mins from A40; 11.45 pm;
no Amex; no smoking area.

Aziz   £ 27   ★

228-230 Cowley Rd OX4 1UH   (01865) 794945

"The best Indian in Oxford" – "a luxury curry house at
non-luxury prices" – is a "stylish" venture south east of the city;
it's extremely popular, with "clean" cooking "prepared with an
unusual lightness of touch", and there's "not a sign of velour or
red wallpaper". / **Sample dishes:** lentil cakes with yogurt & tamarind;
lamb tikka with ginger & onion; gulab jaman (Indian sweets). **Value tip:** 3-crs
Sunday buffet £8.50. **Details:** 10.45 pm; closed Fri L; no smoking area.

Baguicha   £ 22

15 North Parade Ave OX2 6LX   (01865) 513773

It's a relatively recent opening, but this north Oxford
subcontinental already has a strong local following for its "broad
menu" of "fresh" and "tasty" dishes. / **Sample dishes:** samosas;
chicken tikka masala; kulfi. **Details:** 11.30 pm; no smoking area.

Bangkok House   £ 24   Ⓐ★

42a High Bridge St OX1 2EP   (01865) 200705

An "excellent range of authentic Thai food", "beautifully
presented", together with "wonderful" décor make this central
oriental an "always reliable" choice. / **Sample dishes:** prawn soup;
red Thai curry; mango & sticky rice. **Details:** between BR & bus stations;
10.45 pm; closed Mon & Sun L.

Browns £ 27

5-11 Woodstock Rd OX2 6HA (01865) 319655
*Trading on its status as "a legend", the over-popular original
of what is now a nationwide chain of English brasseries has
"gone severely downhill since Bass took it over"; "routine"
cooking and "disinterested" service are now the norm. / **Sample
dishes:** Mozzarella & plum tomato salad; steak, Guinness & mushroom pie;
hot fudge brownie.* **Details:** 11.30 pm; no smoking area; no booking at D.

Chaing Mai £ 30   A★★

130a High St OX1 4DH (01865) 202233
*"Lovely old buildings" may seem ten-a-penny in central Oxford,
but not those which also serve "incredible" Thai cooking –
no wonder this place, with its "combination of old-world Tudor
beams and fragrant, spicy specialities", has such a huge following.
/ **Sample dishes:** chicken satay; fish dish with rice; ice cream.* **Details:** nr
Carfax; 10.30 pm, Fri & Sat 10.45 pm; no smoking area.

Cherwell Boat House £ 27   A

Bardwell Rd OX2 6ST (01865) 552746
*"A chauffeured punt is highly recommended" if you want to
arrive in style at this "cramped" but "nicely-located" riverside
spot; "very friendly" service and an "excellent" wine list are
among its attractions – the food is "satisfying, but not at all out
of the ordinary". / **Sample dishes:** gravadlax with roast onion mayonnaise;
thyme-roasted trout; baked raspberry tart.* **Details:** 1m N of St Giles, by
Dragon School playing fields; 10 pm; 1 wk over Xmas and New Years;
no smoking.

Chutney's £ 21   ★

36 St Michael St OX1 2EB (01865) 724241
*"Non-standard cooking served in a light and airy setting" and
a "good, central location" have helped make this "enjoyable"
Indian a very "popular" destination; "vegetarian dishes are
particularly good". / **Sample dishes:** chicken tikka; chicken bhuna; kulfi.*
Details: off George St; 11 pm.

Edamame £ 16   ★

15 Holywell St OX1 3SA (01865) 246916
*"Cheap and not nasty at all!"; this "simple" restaurant, offering
"Japanese home cooking", is "fast", "welcoming" and "authentic"
– no surprise, then, that it's also "very popular". / **Sample
dishes:** Japanese soft seaweed salad; deep-fried chicken in soy & ginger;
oolong tea.* **Details:** opp New College; 8.30 pm; L only, ex Fri & Sat when L &
D, closed Mon; no Amex; no smoking; no booking.

Elizabeth's £ 38

82 St Aldates OX1 1RA (01865) 242230
*For its devotees, this Gallic classic (est 1966) offers "simply
amazing" cooking, "charming" service and a "great location"
(by Christ Church); to its critics, though, it just seems "to have got
stuck in the 1970s". / **Sample dishes:** snails with garlic butter; beef
stroganoff; chocolate mousse.* **Value tip:** set 3-crs L & Sun L £16.
Details: 11 pm; closed Mon.

Fishers £ 33

36-37 St Clements OX4 1AB (01865) 243003

Even some advocates of this busy fish bistro admit that "not every dish shines" or that it's rather "expensive for what it is"; some would go further in these criticisms ("overhyped and dreadful"), but, even so, you "need to book". / **Sample dishes:** pan-fried scallops with a ginger & tomato sauce; sea bass with thyme & chilli dressing; iced mango parfait with coconut coulis. **Value tip:** set 2-crs L £10.50. **Details:** by Magdalen Bridge; 10.30 pm; closed Mon L; no Amex; no smoking area.

Gees £ 33 Ⓐ

61 Banbury Rd OX2 6PE (01865) 553540

A Victorian conservatory provides a "delightful" setting for this well-known restaurant just north of the city centre; although the menu is "expensive", results are "mixed" and service can be "inattentive". / **Sample dishes:** king scallops with samphire; char-grilled veal with red wine mustard; summer berries. **Details:** 11 pm; no smoking.

The Lemon Tree £ 35 Ⓐ

268 Woodstock Rd OX2 7NW (01865) 311936

Though the "beautiful" and "stylish" setting and "brilliant" atmosphere makes it as popular as ever, this "hugely overpriced" north Oxford villa "promises more than it delivers" – especially as regards the "unexciting" realisation of its modish menu. / **Sample dishes:** crab with coconut leeks & chilli salsa; Aberdeen Angus steak; pressed chocolate cake. **Value tip:** set 2/3-crs L £11.50/£13.50. **Details:** 1.5m N of city centre; 11 pm; Mon-Thu D only, Fri-Sun open L & D.

The Old Parsonage £ 40 Ⓐ

1 Banbury Rd OX2 6NN (01865) 310210

This "most attractive" medieval townhouse is a "smart" but "relaxed" place, that provides a "quiet retreat" only a few minutes from the city centre; the modern British cooking may not be the prime attraction, but some find it "surprisingly interesting". / **Sample dishes:** twice-baked spinach & Parmesan soufflé; guinea fowl & potato pancakes with wild mushroom sauce; pear tarte Tatin. **Details:** 0.5m N of city centre; 11 pm. **Accommodation:** 30 rooms, from £125.

Le Petit Blanc £ 35

71-72 Walton St OX2 6AG (01865) 510999

For its many fans, Raymond Blanc's "cramped", "very busy" modern Gallic brasserie in Jericho is just "excellent all round"; the cooking is "seriously patchy", though, and there is a strong undercurrent of feeling that the place "doesn't have to try too hard... so it doesn't". / **Sample dishes:** foie gras & chicken liver pâté; confit of guinea fowl with wild mushrooms; floating island marrons blanc. **Value tip:** set 2-crs L & pre-theatre £12.50. **Details:** 11 pm; smoking only allowed at D, Fri & Sat.

Quod £ 29

Old Bank Hotel, 92-94 High St OX1 4BN (01865) 202505

Given its pedigree – this is the latest brainchild of Jeremy Mogford, founder of Brown's – the 'success' of this would-be "groovy" newcomer is 'mixed' to a perplexing extent; some do report "very interesting" Italian cooking, but the predominant theme is that it's "bland" or "overpriced". / **Sample dishes:** fresh crab salad; lamb shank with aubergine caponata; panna cotta with raspberries. **Details:** opp All Souls College; 11 pm; no smoking area; no bookings for L Fri-Sun. **Accommodation:** 44 rooms, from £155.

Radcliffe Arms £ 11
67 Cranham St OX2 6ED (01865) 514762
"The prices have to be seen to be believed", say supporters of this "bargain" student boozer near the Phoenix cinema; it's the "remarkable value" – rather than the quality – of the menu which dominates feedback. / **Sample dishes:** garlic mushrooms; lasagne & salad; chocolate fudge cake & ice cream. **Details:** 9 pm; no Amex.

Shimla Pinks £ 26
16 Turl St OX1 3DH (01865) 244944
Fans praise the "wonderful combination of modern surroundings and excellent food" at this Indian two-year-old; for doubters, though, "reluctant" service contributes to a "boorish" overall impression. / **Sample dishes:** vegetable samosas; chicken tikka masala; ice cream. **Details:** nr Exeter & Lincoln colleges; 10.30 pm; no Amex; no smoking area.

White House £ 32
2 Botley Rd OX2 0AB (01865) 242823
"Good food for a pub" makes this inn near the railway station a very useful rendezvous; "babies are welcome". / **Sample dishes:** French mussels with orange & leeks; crispy of lamb with stir-fried noodles; baked cheesecake with strawberries. **Details:** W of Oxford, past railway station; 9.30 pm; no Amex.

Xian £ 20
197 Banbury Rd OX2 7AR (01865) 554239
With its "pretty conservatory", this good all-rounder is unanimously complimented for its "flavourful" Chinese cooking and "friendly" service. / **Sample dishes:** sweet & sour soup; chicken chow mein; ice cream. **Details:** in Summertown, next to bank; 11 pm; closed Sun L.

PADSTOW, CORNWALL   1–3B

Margot's £ 33 ★
11 Duke St PL28 8AB (01841) 533441
Adrian and Julie Oliver's "thoroughly charming bistro" is a "small and intimate" spot, universally praised for its "very good" food and "delightful" service. / **Sample dishes:** scallop, bacon & pistachio salad; confit of duck with mustard cream sauce; cappuccino ice cream. **Details:** 9 pm; closed Mon & Tue; no smoking; booking advisable.

Seafood Restaurant £ 52 ★
Riverside PL28 8BY (01841) 532700
Thanks to Rick Stein's TV celebrity, it's "almost impossible to book" for his "unpretentious" harbourside restaurant; those who succeed for the most part report that "flawless fish" cooking contributes to a "memorable" experience; "prices which are the same as the West End", jar with some, however, as does service that can be "abrupt" and "condescending". / **Sample dishes:** scallops in lentil & Chardonnay sauce; wild salmon with sorrel sauce; panna cotta with baked plums. **Value tip:** set 3-crs L £31.50. **Details:** 10 pm; no Amex; no smoking in dining room; children: 3+. **Accommodation:** 13 rooms, from £90.

constantly updated at www.hardens.com   228

St Petrocs House Bistro   £ 35

4 New St PL28 8BY   (01841) 532700

"As good as the Seafood Restaurant but without the hassle"
is how fans view the simpler formula at Rick Stein's No. 2
establishment; rather too many reporters, though, complain
of "uninspired" cuisine and "crammed in" tables. / **Sample**
dishes: *moules marinière; grilled lemon sole; sticky toffee pudding.*
Details: *9.30 pm; closed Mon; no Amex; no smoking.* **Accommodation:** *13*
rooms, from £90.

PARK GATE, HAMPSHIRE   2–4D

Kam's Palace   £ 31

1 Bridge Rd SO31 7GD   (01489) 583328

This "large, pagoda-style restaurant" is worth knowing about in
a part of the world not overprovided with culinary destinations –
even the occasional reporter disappointed by the service thought
the cooking of "a good standard". / **Sample dishes:** *Chinese hors*
d'oeuvres; crispy duck & pancakes; toffee bananas. **Value tip:** *£24.50 3crs/*
£28.50 4crs with lobster/ £16.50 vegetarian menu. £36.00 3crs for two
people/ two people, 3crs £21.50 a head. **Details:** *head towards Park Gate*
from A27, J9; 10.30 pm, Fri & Sat 11 pm.

PAULERSPURY, NORTHANTS   2–1D

Vine House   £ 37   ★

100 High St NN12 7NA   (01327) 811267

"Effective but unfussy service" wins particular praise at Julie
and Marcus Springett's "consistent" and "friendly" country house,
whose "cosy" dining room offers a "beautifully balanced" menu.
*/ **Sample dishes:** potato crust tart with fresh mackerel; duck with white bean*
purée; hot apricot bread pudding. **Details:** *2m S of Towcester just off A5;*
9.15 pm; closed Mon-Wed L, Sat L & Sun; no Amex & no Switch; no smoking
in restaurant. **Accommodation:** *6 rooms, from £69.*

PAXFORD, GLOUCESTERSHIRE   2–1C

Churchill Arms   £ 28   ★

GL55 6XH   (01386) 594000

With its "refreshingly modern approach to pub food", this
"nice" inn in a "lovely" village – under the same ownership as the
Marsh Goose at Moreton-in-Marsh – is tipped by some for "the
best pub food in the Cotswolds"; unsurprisingly, it's "too popular",
and "the non-booking rule can be problematic". / **Sample**
dishes: *warm pigeon salad; braised lamb shank with herb mash; sticky toffee*
pudding. **Details:** *on Fosse Way; 9 pm; no Amex; no booking.*
Accommodation: *4 rooms, from £60.*

PENARTH, VALE OF GLAMORGAN   2–2A

Tomlins   £ 24   𝔸★

46 Plassey St CF64 1EL   (029) 2070 6644

"Wales's best-kept secret"; David and Lorraine Tomlinson's
"incredible" veggie is hailed by fans as "one of the best eateries
round Cardiff". / **Sample dishes:** *deep-fried wontons with black bean*
sauce; black olive polenta with grilled vegetables; steamed syrup pudding.
Details: *10.30 pm; closed Mon, Tue L, Wed L, Thu L & Sun D& alt Sun L;*
no smoking.

PENMAENPOOL, GWYNEDD

4–2D

George III　　　　£ 35　　A★

LL40 IYD　(01341) 422525

A "charming location" adds special magic to a visit to this restaurant of this 17th-century inn, where a traditional menu using "excellent Welsh produce" is "beautifully cooked and prepared". / **Sample dishes:** seared scallop & crispy bacon salad; roast rack of Welsh lamb; poached pears. **Details:** take A493 towards toll bridge from A470 bypass; 9 pm; no Amex; no smoking. **Accommodation:** 11 rooms, from £70.

PENSHURST, KENT

3–3B

Spotted Dog　　　　£ 24　　A

Smarts Hill　TN11 8EP　(01892) 870253

"A quaint pub, in an excellent location, with beautiful views from the beer garden in summer"; the blackboard menu offers "good" and "varied" fodder. / **Sample dishes:** chicken liver pâté; halibut in lemon & butter sauce; bread & butter pudding. **Details:** nr Penshurst Place; 9.15 pm; no Amex.

PERTH, PERTH & KINROSS

9–3C

Let's Eat　　　　£ 31　　A★

77-79 Kinnoull St　PH1 5EZ　(01738) 643377

Cooking that's "always reliable and interesting" and the "nice people and atmosphere" make it worth seeking out this "relaxing", bric à brac-filled bistro; they also now have a branch (Let's Eat Again) at 33 George St, tel 633771. / **Sample dishes:** smoked haddock, bacon & sweetcorn chowder; chicken & banana in bacon with sweetcorn pancakes; warm raspberry tart. **Details:** opp North Inch Park; 9.45 pm; closed Mon & Sun; no smoking area.

PETERSFIELD, HAMPSHIRE

2–3D

River Kwai　　　　£ 24　　★

16-18 Dragon Hs　GU13 4JJ　(01730) 267077

"Really individual-tasting" and "well-presented" cooking makes this "top-notch" Thai an acclaimed local destination. / **Sample dishes:** Thai fishcakes; chicken chow mein; green tea ice cream. **Details:** 10.30 pm; closed Sun; no smoking area.

PETWORTH, WEST SUSSEX

3–4A

Well Diggers Arms　　　　£ 28　　★

Pulborough Rd　GH28 0HG　(01798) 342287

"No frills, just exceptionally good meat and fish" are the strengths of this traditionally-minded Georgian inn, which offers "fresh produce prepared to haute cuisine standards". / **Sample dishes:** home-made fish soup; steak with buttered vegetables; apple pie & cream. **Details:** 1m out of town on Pulborough Road; 9.30 pm; closed Sun.

PHILLEIGH, CORNWALL

1–4B

Roseland Inn　　　　£ 23　　A

TR2 5NB　(01872) 580254

It's the "wonderful, peaceful setting" which is the special attraction of this cottagey 16th-century inn, but its "simple" and "well-priced" cooking has many admirers too. / **Sample dishes:** goat's cheese; braised lamb with rosemary & thyme; chocolate bread & butter pudding. **Details:** nr King Harry ferry; 9 pm; no Amex.

White Swan £ 32 🅰 ★

Market Pl YO18 7AA (01751) 472288

"Pub meals are excellent, the restaurant meals exceptional, the St Emilion collection unbelievable" – no surprise, then, that "reservations are essential" at this old coaching inn in the centre of the town, which offers "inventive" cooking in "ample" portions. / **Sample dishes:** Yorkshire blue cheese tart; steamed monkfish with spinach hash; chocolate cake with coffee cream. **Details:** 9 pm; no smoking; booking advisable; children: 5+ after 8 pm. **Accommodation:** 12 rooms, from £90.

La Giralda £ 24

66-68 Pinner Green HA5 2AB (020) 8868 3429

WIth its "Mediterranean atmosphere", this Spanish old trooper can still offers "a great night out", though authenticity is not exactly the linchpin. / **Sample dishes:** smoked salmon with prawns; lamb steak with redcurrant sauce; poached pears with syrup. **Details:** A404 to Cuckoo Hill Junction; 10 pm; closed Mon & Sun D.

Perkins £ 30

Old Railway Station NG12 5NA (0115) 937 3695

"Good value bistro-style food" and "a view of the old railway lines" makes Tony & Wendy Perkins' converted station "worth a visit". / **Sample dishes:** monkfish & aubergine fritters; roast Gressingham duck with corn muffins; lime torte with dark chocolate pastry. **Details:** off A606 between Nottingham & Melton Mowbray; 9.30 pm; closed Mon & Sun D; no smoking area.

Chez Nous £ 45 ★

13 Frankfort Gate PL1 1QA (01752) 266793

The "confirmed excellence" of the "fine" Gallic cooking and the "good service" at Suzanne & Jacques Marchal's Gallic fixture is doubly unexpected, give its tiny, unassuming premises and their location in what can only be described as a concrete jungle. / **Sample dishes:** crab & orange salad; fillet steak with morels; tarte Tatin. **Details:** nr Theatre Royal; 10.30 pm; closed Mon, Sat L & Sun.

The China Garden £ 29 ★

17/19 Perrys Cross PL1 2SW (01752) 664472

"The best Chinese in the South West" – or a contender, at least – whose "authentic" cooking is consistently of "good quality". / **Sample dishes:** deep-fried seaweed; chicken with mushrooms & cashew nuts; ice cream. **Details:** in city centre; 11.15 pm; closed Sun.

Thai Palace £ 26 ★

3 Elliot St, The Hoe PL1 2PP (01752) 255770

"Genuine and relaxed", this "very good all round" oriental is all the more worth knowing about in this under-provided town. / **Sample dishes:** spicy Thai soup; chicken with parsley & egg fried rice; sticky rice with mango. **Value tip:** 2-crs menus available 6 days a week £17/ £20. **Details:** 11 pm; D only, closed Sun.

Veggie Perrins £ 17

97 Mayflower St PL1 1SD (01752) 252888

Quite "out of the ordinary, for Plymouth" – this "non-smoking, vegetarian Indian" offers "an imaginative menu, very cheaply"; BYO. / **Sample dishes:** onion bhaji; bell pepper jalfrezi; no puddings. **Value tip:** set 2-crs L £3.50. **Details:** nr Copthorne; 9.30 pm; closed Sun; no Amex; no smoking.

The Wet Wok   **£ 25**

West Hoe Rd PL1 3   (01752) 664456
The "wave-lapped, seaside location", with its "lovely views" over
the Sound, is the special strength of this "decent" Chinese whose
cooking is "good, for this town". / **Sample dishes:** deep-fried crispy
squid; roast duck Cantonese style; fruit fritters. **Details:** 11.30 pm.

PONTELAND, NORTHUMBERLAND   8–2B

Café 21   **£ 27**

35 The Broadway, Darras Hall NA20 9PW
(01661) 820357
It may have a "strange location" (in a housing estate, near
Newcastle Airport), but "good modern British cooking" and
a "buzzing" atmosphere make this shop-conversion bistro
"very popular". / **Sample dishes:** grilled black pudding with crispy onions;
turbot with tomato pasta & fine beans; iced banana parfait. **Value tip:** set 2-
crs D £11.50. **Details:** 1m past Newcastle Airport, off A1; 10 pm; D only,
closed Sun.

POOL-IN-WHARFEDALE, WEST YORKSHIRE   5–1C

Monkmans   **£ 27**

Pool Bank, New Rd LS21 1EH   (0113) 284 1105
This "genuine" bistro gets rather a mixed press – for some it's
a "lovely place, with lovely food and lovely atmosphere" whereas
others say it's "crowded" and "expensive, for what's on offer".
/ **Sample dishes:** French ham & pork terrine; roast duck in fruit & port sauce;
lemon tart with passion fruit coulis. **Value tip:** set 3-crs Sun L £14.50.
Details: 5m from Leeds, on road to Otley; 10 pm; closed Sun D; no Amex;
no smoking area. **Accommodation:** 6 rooms, from £80.

POOLE, DORSET   2–4C

Mansion House   **£ 29**   ★

Thames St BH15 1JN   (01202) 685666
"Reliably superior 'home' cooking" makes this "fine period house"
the "best place in the area" for most reporters; those who are
not club members pay a small surcharge. / **Sample dishes:** twice-
baked cheese soufflé; duck with honey, ginger & lavender sauce; bread
& butter pudding. **Details:** follow signs for Poole Ferry, turn off to quay; 9 pm;
closed Sat L & Sun D; no smoking in dining room; children: 5+.
Accommodation: 32 rooms, from £100.

PORT APPIN, ARGYLL & BUTE   9–3B

Airds Hotel   **£ 56**   Ⓐ★

PA38 4DF   (01631) 730236
It's "a real find", say fans of the Allen Family's "friendly" luxury
hotel on the shoreside of Loch Linnhe; the dining room offers
"beautifully-cooked local produce", complemented by "an
outstanding list of Burgundies". / **Sample dishes:** roast quail with bacon
& croutons; roast venison & potato cakes with juniper sauce; raspberry
& almond tart. **Details:** 25m N of Oban; 8.30 pm; closed much of Dec & Jan;
no Amex; no smoking; children: 8+. **Accommodation:** 12 rooms, from £141.

Pier House Hotel   **£ 29**   Ⓐ★

PA38 4DE   (01631) 730302
"Excellent fresh seafood" and "great views of the loch" make this
"incredible" place – "beautifully located" by the Lismore Island
ferry – a very popular gastronomic recommendation. / **Sample
dishes:** crab cakes; scallop, langoustine, mussel, smoked salmon & oyster
platter; sticky toffee pudding. **Details:** just off A828 by pier; 9.30 pm;
no Amex; no smoking area. **Accommodation:** 12 rooms, from £70.

Portaferry Hotel £ 34 𝔸★
10 The Strand BT22 1PE (028) 4272 8231
"Stunning oysters, brilliant scallops, a very good cellar" and
"soda bread to dream about" – such are the traditional Irish
treats at this ferry-side hotel, which overlooks Strangford Lough.
/ **Sample dishes:** prawn tail salad; smoked monkfish; crème brûlée.
Details: 9 pm. **Accommodation:** 14 rooms, from £90.

Harbour Lights £ 35 ★
SA62 5BL (01348) 831549
Anne Marie Davies's "small and intimate quayside restaurant"
delivers "excellent seafood" and "the best laver bread in the
world". / **Sample dishes:** laverbread with smoked bacon & garlic; grilled
Dover sole with rocket & parsley oil; seasonal fruit compote. **Details:** 7.5m NE
of St Davids; 8.30 pm; open only Thu-Sat D, open for lunch in July and August;
no Amex; no smoking area.

Portmeirion Hotel £ 39 𝔸★
LL48 6ER (01766) 770000
"The food is equal to any of the capital's eateries, and the
setting exceeds them all", says one of the many reporters smitten
by the charms of this dining room at the heart of Sir Clough
Williams-Ellis's fantasy-Mediterranean village; it offers "superb",
"freshly-prepared" food, from "a different menu every day".
/ **Sample dishes:** onion soup with Cheddar croutons; seared tuna with rice,
leeks & poached egg; chocolate gâteau with basil parfait. **Value tip:** set 3-crs
L £14 (Sun L £15). **Details:** off A487 at Minffordd; 9 pm; closed Mon L;
no smoking. **Accommodation:** 40 rooms, from £110.

Crown Hotel £ 26
North Cr DG9 8SX (01776) 810261
"Good local seafood", a "cheerful atmosphere" and "fine sea
views" commend this busy harbourside pub and restaurant.
/ **Sample dishes:** herring & prawn platter; venison in pepper & brandy sauce;
strawberry shortcake. **Value tip:** set 3-crs D £14.95. **Details:** 10 pm;
no smoking area. **Accommodation:** 12 rooms, from £72.

Ramore Wine Bar £ 32 ★
The Harbour BT56 8D3 (028) 9082 4313
"Still excellent" is one early report on this stylish establishment,
where the chef has changed and where there has also been
a major revamp – wine bar and restaurant have swapped places,
so the former now benefits from the view. / **Sample dishes:** scallop
& avocado ceviche; roast monkfish with butter beans & basil pesto; baked
peaches & cream. **Details:** 10 pm; D only, closed Mon & Sun; no Amex;
children: 12+.

White House　　　　　　　　　　　　**£ 40**

New Rd SK10 4DG   (01625) 829376

Given its location at the heart of this legendarily bijou Cheshire village, the "fair prices" for the "consistently-good" modern British cooking at this popular restaurant are all the more remarkable. / **Sample dishes:** *twice-cooked Cornish crab soufflé; crispy roast duckling with berry fruits; chocolate galaxy cake.* **Value tip:** *set 3-crs L £13.95.* **Details:** *2m N of Macclesfield on A538; 10 pm; closed Mon L & Sun D.* **Accommodation:** *11 rooms, from £70.*

The Crabmill　　　　　　　　　　**£ 30**　　　★

B95 5DR   (01926) 843342

New owners (from the Boot at Lapworth) "have made all the difference" to this "unusual" Mediterranean restaurant; its "high standard of food and presentation" are consistently praised. / **Sample dishes:** *smoked haddock with fondant potatoes; duck confit with Toulouse sausage, lentils & olive mash; Greek panna cotta with honeycomb biscuits.* **Details:** *9.30 pm; closed Sun D; booking advisable at D, max 11.*

Simply Heathcote's　　　　　　　　　**£ 30**

23 Winckley Sq PR1 3JJ   (01772) 252732

"London prices, but fab franglais food" is one fan's view on this smart, "light and modern" town-centre brasserie (which wins particular praise as a "perfect lunchtime venue"); as with Paul Heathcote's other ventures, however, a lot of reporters find it "over-rated", and some rail at what they see as a "customer-is-always-wrong" attitude. / **Sample dishes:** *caramelised shallot & goat's cheese tart; lamb with peppered leeks & potatoes; bread & butter pudding.* **Details:** *nr railway station; 10.30 pm; closed Sun.*

Polecat　　　　　　　　　　　　　**£ 24**

170 Wycombe Rd HB16 0HJ   (01494) 862253

"Interesting daily specials" and other "varied" traditional pub grub make this "roadside pub" – where a couple of rooms are dedicated to dining – a popular local destination. / **Sample dishes:** *kipper pâté; red snapper in coconut milk with Thai spices; bitter chocolate tart.* **Details:** *on A4128 between Great Missenden & High Wycombe; 9 pm; closed Sun D; no credit cards; no smoking; children: not in dining room.*

Woodhouse at Princethorpe　　　　　**£ 30**　　★

Leamington Rd CV23 9PZ   (01926) 632303

A "splendid choice" of "simple" but "substantial" dishes is praised at this "busy" restaurant, which numbers "fine views" among its attractions. / **Sample dishes:** *avocado prawns & marie rose sauce; roast duck with cranberry sauce; crème caramel.* **Details:** *nr Princethorpe College on the B4453; 9.30 pm.* **Accommodation:** *18 rooms, from £60.*

Butchers Arms   £ 35   ★

Church End CV47 7SN   (01327) 260504

*Reflecting the nationality of the owners, the menu at this "delightful old inn" in a "pretty village" shows the occasional Portuguese influence – dishes may be "simple", but they can be "excellent". / **Sample dishes:** fresh grilled sardines; steak with mustard & chips; parfait roll. **Details:** 9 pm; closed Sat L & Sun D.*

PWLLHELI, GWYNEDD   4–2C

Plas Bodegroes   £ 39   Ⓐ★★

Nefyn Rd LL53 5TH   (01758) 612363

*The "local-produce-based haute cuisine" earns some of the highest food ratings in Wales for the "small" dining room at the Chowns' "restaurant with rooms" – a manor house with an "idyllic location" in "beautiful" grounds. / **Sample dishes:** sea trout wrapped in Parma ham; roast tenderloin with bacon & black pudding; bread & butter pudding. **Details:** on A499 1m W of Pwllheli; 9.30 pm; D only, ex Sun open L & D; no Amex; no smoking. **Accommodation:** 11 rooms, from £35.*

RAMSGILL-IN-NIDDERDALE, NORTH YORKSHIRE   8–4B

Yorke Arms   £ 34   Ⓐ★

HG3 5RL   (01423) 755243

*"All round excellence" characterises all reports on this "small country hotel" in the middle of nowhere, where Frances Atkins' cooking is "consistently very good". / **Sample dishes:** Cornish crab with foie gras & avocado; grouse with celeriac purée & blackberry jus; nougatine parfait with peaches. **Details:** 4m W of Pately Bridge; 9.45 pm; closed Sun D; no smoking; booking: max 6. **Accommodation:** 13 rooms, from £80.*

RAWTENSTALL, LANCASHIRE   5–1A

Samrat   £ 17

13 Bacup Rd BB4 7NG   (01706) 216183

*Reports on the service at this "welcoming local restaurant" confirm that the gong given to its "award-winning manager" was well justified; the "good, basic Indian food" is also praised. / **Sample dishes:** mixed kebabs; Karahi lamb balti; chocolate bombe. **Value tip:** £22.00 set meal for two people. **Details:** nr Asda; 11.30 pm, Sat & Sun 12.30 am; D only; no Amex; children: 6+.*

READING, BERKSHIRE   2–2D

Bens Thai   £ 21

Royal Ct, Kings Rd RG1 4AE   (0118) 959 6169

*"Fresh and zingy cooking" and "good value for money" ensure that this "wine bar-style" riverside Thai is "always packed", even if it does have "no atmosphere". / **Sample dishes:** spring rolls; chicken & pork stir-fry; egg custard. **Details:** 10 pm; closed Sun.*

Old Siam   £ 27   ★

Kings Wk, Kings St RG1 2HG   (0118) 951 2600

*The copious volume of survey feedback suggests that – despite its "strange location" in a shopping centre – this "unexpected" Thai restaurant is no longer "Reading's best-kept secret"; it's a "warm and hospitable" place, and fans say the cooking is "excellent". / **Sample dishes:** king prawn rice paper rolls; stir-fried chicken with fresh chilli; mango & sticky rice. **Details:** in centre of shopping complex; 9 pm; closed Sun; no smoking.*

The Peacock Inn £ 27 A★

Church Corner NG13 0GA (01949) 842554

With its "great" setting, this "characterful" inn near Belvoir Castle offers "fantastic", "cheap and cheerful" French cooking. / **Sample dishes:** spiced crab & papaya salad; lamb with cucumber fricassée; chocolate & brandy mousse. **Details:** Grantham exit from A52, then follow signs; 9.30 pm; no smoking. **Accommodation:** 10 rooms, from £80.

REIGATE, SURREY 3–3B

La Barbe £ 38

71 Bell St RH2 7AN (01737) 241966

This "good local bistro" is "always full, so it has a lively atmosphere"; some question whether the "rich" Gallic cooking is holding its own in the face of increasing local competition. / **Sample dishes:** puff pastry with mussels & ginger; roast rabbit in mustard sauce; smooth chocolate & cherry cake. **Details:** nr Safeways; 9.45 pm; closed Sat L & Sun; no smoking area.

Dining Room £ 41 ★

59a High St RH2 9AE (01737) 226650

The "hidden-away", first-floor town-centre dining room of TV chef Tony Tobin may be quite closely packed, but his Mediterranean-influenced approach generally offers "excellent ingredients, cooked with flair and simplicity". / **Sample dishes:** crispy squid with fried green tomatoes; crispy duck with melted onions; banana tart with vanilla ice cream. **Value tip:** set 2/3-crs weekday L £10/£13.50. **Details:** 10 pm; closed Sat L & Sun D; no smoking.

REYNOLDSTON, SWANSEA 1–1C

Fairyhill £ 49 A★★

SA3 1BS (01792) 390139

It may be "a top-class hotel", but there's a "very homely and relaxing" atmosphere at this "lovely" spot "in the middle of nowhere" (on the Gower Peninsula); "fine local ingredients are cooked and presented with flair", and the results are "quite superb, even when the place is busy". / **Sample dishes:** scrambled egg with cockles & peppers; seared sea bass with laver butter sauce; iced mango parfait. **Value tip:** set 2-crs L £14.50. **Details:** 20 mins from M4, J47 off B4295; 9 pm; no smoking; children: 8+. **Accommodation:** 8 rooms, from £110.

RICHMOND, SURREY 3–3B

Burnt Chair £ 37 A

5 Duke St TW9 1HP (020) 8940 9488

"A congenial owner" and "a terrific wine list" are the key strengths of this above-average (for Richmond) local; the modern British cooking has its moments. / **Sample dishes:** seared scallops with pickled vegetables; roast pineapple & coconut. **Value tip:** set 2-crs D £15. **Details:** nr Richmond Theatre; 11 pm; D only, closed Sun & Mon; no Amex; no smoking before 11 pm; children: "love them".

Canyon £ 37 A

Riverside TW10 6UJ (020) 8948 2944

A "great location on the river" helps make this Richmond yearling a "beautiful" spot; it's also "grossly overpriced and pretentious", and offers "terrible" south west American cooking, so its appeal is pretty much limited to sunny day brunching. / **Sample dishes:** spicy tomato soup; char-grilled tuna with spinach & butternut squash; crème caramel. **Details:** 11 pm; no smoking area.

Old Vicarage £ 60 ★

Ridgeway Moor S12 3XW (0114) 247 5814

For fans, "superb, imaginative cooking" and a "Jane Austen-fantasy setting" set the scene for some "wonderful" meals at Tessa Bramley's restored Victorian vicarage; the place can seem a trifle "stiff", however, and some do feel it "rests on its laurels". / **Sample dishes:** sea bass & vanilla risotto with crab bisque; roast duck with mustard-coated figs; baked chocolate pudding with custard. **Value tip:** set 3-crs L & Sun L £32. **Details:** 10 mins SE of city centre; 10 pm; closed Mon & Sun D; no smoking in dining room.

The Boar's Head £ 26 🄰★

Ripley Castle Estate HG3 3AY (01423) 771888

"Beautiful surroundings" are an undoubted attraction of Sir Thomas and Lady Ingilby's "comfortable", "upmarket" hotel (set in a village mostly owned by the family); the contemporary cooking generally wins praise too, particularly in the more informal bistro, and there are "excellent wines". / **Sample dishes:** rabbit with caramelised apples; pan-fried duck with summer vegetable risotto; hot strawberry soufflé. **Details:** off A61 between Ripon & Harrogate; 9 pm. **Accommodation:** 25 rooms, from £115.

Michels £ 46

High St GU23 6AQ (01483) 224777

A rather "individual" style proves rather a mixed blessing at this grandly-housed restaurant "on a cobbled high street"; "when Erik Michel is on form, the cooking's great", but even some fans say that results "can be a bit twee", and others rail against the "disastrous staff attitude" and the "dull" and "pompous" atmosphere. / **Sample dishes:** grilled prawn & scallop kebabs; hare stuffed with spinach & foie gras; rhubarb crème brûlée. **Value tip:** set 2-crs L £14, set 3-crs D £23. **Details:** 9 pm; closed Mon, Sat L & Sun D; no smoking.

Owd Betts £ 22 🄰★

Edenfield Rd OL12 7TY (01706) 649904

A "snug" pub that's an especially welcome find in its moorland setting; it offers a "great choice" of "home-cooked" fare, and "good beer" too. / **Sample dishes:** duck & orange paté; salmon with new potatoes; sticky toffee pudding. **Details:** 9.30 pm; closed Sun; no credit cards; booking: some restrictions.

Jack in the Green Inn £ 28 ★

London Rd EX5 2EE (01404) 822240

"A good selection of meals in bar and restaurant" – "well presented and of consistently high quality" – makes a trip to this "nice" pub a welcome break from the A30. / **Sample dishes:** plate of Parma ham; duck with potatoes & peppercorn sauce; warm rice pudding with pralines. **Details:** off new A30; 9 pm; no Amex; children: Sun L only.

ROMALDKIRK, COUNTY DURHAM 8–3B

The Rose & Crown £ 33 Ⓐ★

DL12 9EB (01833) 650213

This "excellent country restaurant and hotel", set amidst
"beautiful surroundings" – near the High Force waterfall –
serves "splendid game and home-made accompaniments"
and other "good" traditional fare; lunch is served in the bar.
/ **Sample dishes:** hot chive & potato pancake; roast lamb with black pudding
& mushroom broth; honey & whisky ice cream. **Value tip:** set 3-crs Sun
L £13.50. **Details:** 6m NW of Barnard Castle on B6277; 9 pm; closed Mon-
Sat L & Sun D; no Amex; no smoking; children: 6+. **Accommodation:** 12
rooms, from £86.

ROMSEY, HAMPSHIRE 2–3D

Old Manor House £ 39 ★

21 Palmerston St SO51 8GF (01794) 517353

"Not cheap, but a real experience in every way", the Bregolis'
tiny Italian restaurant of over 20 years' standing specialises "in
local game and wild mushrooms" and offers "classy" food with
a "very good wine list"; service, though, can be "snooty".
/ **Sample dishes:** hot salami & lentil salad; venison escalope with spiced fruit;
home-made ice cream. **Details:** 9.30 pm; closed Mon & Sun D.

ROTHWELL, NORTHANTS 5–4D

The Thai Garden £ 26

3 Market Hl NN14 6EP (01536) 712345

This may be a "plainly decorated ethnic diner", but, thanks to
the quality of its cooking, it's "often booked up". / **Sample
dishes:** Thai fishcakes; coriander chicken with egg fried rice; Thai pancakes.
Details: off A14 nr Kettering; 10.45 pm; no smoking area.

ROWDE, WILTSHIRE 2–2C

George & Dragon £ 35 ★

High St SN10 2PN (01380) 723053

"Surprisingly, given the location, the fish is superb" at Tim and
Helen Withers's excellent "restaurant-quality pub"; it's "difficult to
find" in the back roads of the West Country, but "well worth the
effort" – "you generally need to book". / **Sample dishes:** warm salad
of scallops & bacon; cod in beer batter with chilli sauce; raspberry posset.
Value tip: set 2/3-crs L £10/£12.50. **Details:** on A342 between Devizes
& Chippenham; 10 pm; closed Mon & Sun; no Amex; no smoking.

ROYAL LEAMINGTON SPA, WARWICKSHIRE 5–4C

Emperors £ 29 Ⓐ★

Bath Pl CV31 3BP (01926) 313666

"Interesting décor" and "wonderfully-flavoured" cooking make
this a "top-class" Chinese, say enthusiastic locals; it's "often fully
booked". / **Sample dishes:** spring rolls; Cantonese style beef; toffee apples.
Details: at the bottom of the Parade, behind Iceland; 10.45 pm, Fri & Sat
11.15 pm; closed Sun.

Thai Elephant £ 28

20 Regent St CV32 5HQ (01926) 886882

"Hurrah, a decent restaurant in Leamington!"; this "quality"
oriental newcomer is proving "a very welcome addition to the
area". / **Sample dishes:** duck pancakes; Thai chicken curry; ice cream.
Details: 10.30 pm; closed Sat L.

RYE, EAST SUSSEX 3–4C

Landgate Bistro £ 28 ★

5-6 Landgate TN31 7LH (01797) 222829

"Warm, friendly, and full of happy regulars", this bistro of over 20 years standing offers "delicate cooking of a high standard". / **Sample dishes:** salmon & salt cod fishcakes; pigeon in red wine sauce; compote of quinces. **Value tip:** tues/weds/thurs set menu £16.90. **Details:** 50 yrds below Landgate Arch; 9.30 pm, Sat 10 pm; D only, closed Mon & Sun.

SALISBURY, WILTSHIRE 2–3C

Jade £ 26 ★

109a Exeter St SP1 2SF (01722) 333355

"Unusual fish dishes" and "amazing seafood" – together with "attentive" and "discreet" service – are roundly praised by the local fan club of this well-established Cantonese, near the Cathedral. / **Sample dishes:** prawn toast; octopus with water chestnuts; ice cream. **Details:** opp Cathedral; 11.30 pm; closed Sun; no Amex.

LXIX £ 33 ★

69 New St SP1 2PH (01722) 340000

"An oasis in a gastronomic wilderness"; at last this historic town has a non-ethnic restaurant worth talking about in this "chic" yearling; it offers "delicious" modern British cooking and a "friendly" welcome. / **Sample dishes:** char-grilled veal kidneys & heart; roast sea bass in lapsang oil; almond & Amaretto meringue. **Details:** adjacent to Cathedral Close, 50yds from main entrance; 10 pm; closed Sat L & Sun; no smoking; children: 12+.

SALTAIRE, WEST YORKSHIRE 5–1C

Salts Diner £ 20 Ⓐ

Salts Mill BD18 3LB (01274) 530533

The "good, fresh, inviting food" (including "marvellous salads") helps make this "American-style diner in an old mill" a popular lunch spot; it may be on the "Spartan" side, but it's "always buzzing". / **Sample dishes:** goat's cheese; sea bass with roasted vegetables; sticky toffee pudding. **Details:** 2m from Bradford on A650; 5 pm; L only; no Amex; no smoking area.

SANDGATE, KENT 3–4D

La Terrasse £ 44 ★★

Sandgate Hotel CT20 3DY (01303) 220444

"Superb French food", "gracious service" and a "stunning sea view" ("ask for a window table") make the "small" dining room of the Gicqueau family's seaside hotel an almost universal hit – to the extent, indeed, that "it's difficult to get a table". / **Sample dishes:** goose & duck foie gras terrine; sole with roasted tomatoes; chocolate cake with almond cream. **Value tip:** set 3-crs L & D £22. **Details:** on A259 (main coastal road); 9.30 pm; closed Mon, Tue L & Sun D; no shorts; no smoking in dining room; booking: max 8. **Accommodation:** 14 rooms, from £51.

SANDIWAY, CHESHIRE 5–2B

Nunsmere Hall £ 54

Tarporley Rd CW8 2ES (01606) 889100

"Cheshire's most peaceful and luxurious hotel" – on the fringe of Delamere forest – offers "first-class" cooking; limited feedback suggests that it's "worth the money… just". / **Sample dishes:** grilled smoked salmon; rib-eye steak in red wine; dark chocolate fondant. **Value tip:** set 3-crs Sun L £22.50. **Details:** off A49, 4m SW of Northwich; 10 pm; no jeans; no smoking; children: 12+ at D. **Accommodation:** 36 rooms, from £160.

SAWBRIDGEWORTH, HERTFORDSHIRE

3–2B

Star of India   £ 21

51 London Rd CM21 9JH   (01279) 726512

This "very nice curry house" of long standing receives only praise – "they put more care into achieving delicate flavours than many Indian restaurants". / *Sample dishes:* chicken samosas; king prawn garlic chilli; coconut supreme. *Details:* 11.30 pm; no smoking area.

SAWLEY, LANCASHIRE

5–1B

Spread Eagle   £ 26   ★★

BB7 4NH   (01200) 441202

A "great setting", with charming views of the River Ribble, sets the tone at this "superior" hostelry (under the same ownership as Crosthwaite's Punch Bowl) – its "innovative" and "reasonably-priced" cooking is "difficult to beat", and there's a "great wine list" too. / *Sample dishes:* fish hors-d'oeuvres; braised lamb with root vegetable sauce; tarte Tatin. **Value tip:** set 2/3-crs L £7.95/£9.95 (Sun £10.95/£12.95). *Details:* NE of Clitheroe off A59; 9 pm; no smoking. *Accommodation:* 5 rooms, from £55.

SAWSTON, CAMBRIDGESHIRE

3–1B

Jade Fountain   £ 22

42-46 High St CB2 4BG   (01223) 836100

An "interesting" and "inventive" menu (with "tasty vegetarian options") helps make this "classic Chinese" the top oriental for miles around. / *Sample dishes:* spare ribs; crispy chilli beef; toffee apples. *Details:* 1m from M11, J10; 9.30 pm.

SAXTON, NORTH YORKSHIRE

5–1D

Plough Inn   £ 16

Headwell Ln LS24 9BP   (01937) 557242

There's "always a warm welcome" at this "unpretentious" pub (with bar and "polished" dining room), which numbers "excellent fish" amongst its specialities; some reckon the midweek meals "more interesting" than the popular Sunday lunches. / *Sample dishes:* prawn cocktail; steak & kidney pie; chocolate fudge cake. *Details:* off A162 between Tadcaster & Sherburn in Elmet; 9.15 pm; closed Mon & Sun D; no Amex; smoking in bar only.

SCAWTON, NORTH YORKSHIRE

8–4C

Hare Inn   £ 26   𝔸★

YO7 2HG   (01845) 597289

With its "wonderful location" in a "tiny village", Graham Raina's "small pub/restaurant" wins heartfelt endorsements for its "good atmosphere", "great food" and "charming service". / *Sample dishes:* smoked haddock fishcakes; roast suckling pig with cider gravy; chocolate brownie. *Details:* off A170; 9.30 pm; closed Mon L; no smoking area.

SEAVIEW, ISLE OF WIGHT

2–4D

Seaview Hotel   £ 30   𝔸★

High St PO34 5EX   (01983) 612711

"Simple fresh food" served in a "traditional but relaxed" environment makes a winning combination for the dining room of this "lively" seaside hotel. / *Sample dishes:* smoked herring on toast; coconut & coriander chicken with curry leaves; brandy snaps with coconut ice cream. **Value tip:** set 3-crs Sun L £13.95. *Details:* 9.30 pm; closed Sun D except on Bank Holidays; no smoking area; children: 5+. *Accommodation:* 16 rooms, from £90.

constantly updated at www.hardens.com

SEDGEFIELD, CLEVELAND 8–3B

Dun Cow £ 27 ★

43 Front St TS21 3AT (01740) 620894

This "comfy pub" offers a "good" and "imaginative" blackboard menu, which may include the likes of "very good fish" and "excellent sausages". / **Sample dishes:** freshwater king prawns with lime dressing; medallions of pork with apple sauce; fresh cream cheesecake. **Details:** 9.30 pm. **Accommodation:** 6 rooms, from £65.

SHANAGARRY, COUNTY CORK, *EIRE* 10–4B

Ballymaloe Hotel IR £ 42 Ⓐ★★

(021) 465 2531

"A meal you'll remember for ever" – Rory O'Connell's "incredibly fresh" cooking (especially of fish and shellfish), "lovely" staff and a "smart but comfortable setting" makes the Allen family's "beautiful" and "secluded" hotel a "magical" place. / **Sample dishes:** crab & grapefruit salad; fish mousse with shrimp butter sauce; Worcesterberry tart. **Details:** exit M25 before Cloyne; 9.30 pm; no Switch; no smoking; children: 4+. **Accommodation:** 33 rooms, from IR £55.

SHARDLOW, DERBYSHIRE 5–3C

Thai Kitchen £ 21

3 Wilne Ln DE72 2HA (01332) 793311

"Authentic food in a pleasant setting" wins consistent praise from the locals for this "simple" oriental. / **Sample dishes:** crispy spring rolls; stir-fried beef with ginger; banana fritters. **Details:** 11 pm; closed Mon L; no smoking area.

SHEFFIELD, SOUTH YORKSHIRE 5–2C

Bahn Nah £ 25 ★

19-21 Nile St S10 2PN (0114) 268 4900

"Authentic" Thai food "at its best" makes Mrs Low's "very small", "simple" and "welcoming" ten-year old one of the top places in town. / **Details:** off A57; 11 pm; D only, closed Sun; no smoking.

Candy Town Chinese £ 18

27 London Rd S2 4LA (0114) 272 5315

"Cheap and cheery décor", "circular spinning tables for large groups" and "accommodating staff" contribute to the "party atmosphere" at this popular Chinese, near the city centre. / **Sample dishes:** crispy spring rolls; sweet & sour pork; toffee apples. **Details:** nr town centre; 11.15 pm; no smoking area.

Everest £ 19

59-61 Chesterfield Rd S8 0RL (0114) 258 2975

This "very enjoyable and reasonably-priced" curry house is praised for its "freshly cooked and spicy fare", and décor that's "better than most Indians". / **Sample dishes:** garlic prawns; chicken masala with naan bread; gulab jaman (Indian sweets). **Value tip:** tues evening 2crs buffet £8.95 including coffee. **Details:** close to Newbridge; 12.45 am, Thu 1.45 am, Fri & Sat 2.45 am; D only.

Kashmir Curry Centre £ 12 ★

123 Spital Hill S4 7LD (0114) 272 6253

The setting may be a bit "like a school cafeteria", but the food at this self-explanatory spot is "very cheap and flavoursome", and "you can bring in a pint from the pub across the road". / **Sample dishes:** onion bhajis with raita; tomato & coriander bhuna; kulfi. **Details:** midnight; no credit cards; no smoking area.

Marco @ Milano   £ 39
Archer Rd S8 0LA   (0114) 235 3080
*Is this year-old Italian a "cool", "stylish" and "very easy-going"
place that serves "absolutely top-class food"? – most reporters
think so, though there is a minority view that it's "a triumph of
style over content".* / **Sample dishes:** *avocado, Mozzarella & tomato
salad; chicken in white wine sauce with asparagus; tiramisu.* **Value tip:** *set 2/3-
crs pre-theatre £10.95/£12.95.* **Details:** *11.30 pm; closed Sat L & Sun;
no Amex.*

Nirmals   £ 22   ★
189-193 Glossop Rd S10 2GW   (0114) 272 4054
*Mrs Nirmal Gupta is a "gregarious proprietress" and her
presence dominates this "Sheffield standard-bearer", where
the "original and tasty" Indian cooking is "consistently good".*
/ **Sample dishes:** *swordfish salad; lamb masala with spinach; almond
& pistachio kulfi.* **Details:** *nr West St; midnight, Fri & Sat 1 am; closed Sun L;
no smoking area.*

Nonnas   £ 33   ★
539-541 Eccleshall Rd S11 8PR   (0114) 268 6166
*"I've never been to Italy, but this must be what it's like" –
"wonderful", "freshly-cooked" fare is served "con gusto" at this
"cosy" and "slightly cramped" outfit (which incorporates a deli
and espresso bar).* / **Sample dishes:** *Mozzarella with roasted vine
tomatoes; rosemary-skewered chicken with garlic oil; grappa panna cotta.*
Details: *M1, J33 towards Bakewell; 9.45 pm; no Amex.*

Smiths of Sheffield   £ 30
34 Sandygate Rd S10 5RY   (0114) 266 6096
*On a good day, "delicious simple food" can be had at Richard
Smith's "relaxed" bar/restaurant; it can "lack atmosphere",
though, and some feel it "doesn't live up" to its great local
reputation.* / **Sample dishes:** *Tuscan vegetable gâteau; roast lamb with wild
mushroom & shallot purée; white chocolate & Malibu mousse.* **Details:** *off
A57; 9.30 pm; D only, closed Mon & Sun; no smoking area.*

Zing Vaa   £ 22
55 The Moor S1 4PF   (0114) 275 6633
*Chinese cooking "as good as you can get in Sheffield" helps
makes this "good value" destination "popular with the local
oriental community".* / **Sample dishes:** *tomato & sweetcorn soup;
Chinese chicken & straw mushrooms; ice cream.* **Value tip:** *set 3-crs L £5.50
(Sun £9.50).* **Details:** *11.30 pm; no smoking area.*

SHELLEY, WEST YORKSHIRE   5–2C

Three Acres   £ 34   Ⓐ★
Roydhouse HD8 8LR   (01484) 602606
*"A complete pleasure on an unfriendly winter's night"; this "cosy"
and "homely" old coaching inn may be "difficult to find, but it's
worth it", thanks to its "beautiful setting" and "varied" menu;
"excellent fish and seafood" are the specialities.* / **Sample
dishes:** *potted shrimps; pan-fried calves liver & bacon with mushrooms;
passion fruit jelly.* **Value tip:** *set 3-crs L & Sun L £16.95.* **Details:** *nr Emley
Moor TV transmitter; 9.45 pm; closed Sat L.* **Accommodation:** *20 rooms,
from £60.*

SHEPPERTON, SURREY 3–3A

Edwinns £ 34

Church Rd TW17 9JT (01932) 223543

This "small" and "cosy" restaurant in a Thames-side village is "usually full", thanks to its "reliable" cooking and its "very polite" service. / **Sample dishes:** warm duck salad; beef Wellington; sticky toffee pudding. **Details:** opp church & Anchor Hotel; 10.15 pm, Fri & Sat 10.45 pm; closed Sat L & Sun D; no smoking area.

SHEPTON MALLET, SOMERSET 2–3B

Charlton House £ 53 A ★

Charlton Rd BA4 4PR (01749) 342008

Mulberry-lovers – the fancy goods company, not the fruit – will be in heaven at this "charming little hotel" owned by its founders; it's not just the bijou décor which makes this a "very comfortable" destination, though – the cooking is "absolutely mouthwatering" too. / **Sample dishes:** rainbow trout, rocket & exotic fruit salad; roast duck with juniper & cardamoms; chocolate & candied raspberry mousse. **Details:** on A361 towards Frome; 9 pm; no smoking. **Accommodation:** 16 rooms, from £140.

SHERE, SURREY 3–3A

Kinghams £ 32 A ★

Gomshall Ln GU5 9HB (01483) 202168

"The food is always imaginative and well presented" and "staff put you at your ease", say devotees of Paul Baker's "lovely", "cosy" thatched cottage-restaurant, set in a pretty, old village. / **Sample dishes:** shellfish fricasée; pork stuffed with prunes & pistachio nuts; butterscotch tart with brandy ice cream. **Details:** off A25 between Dorking & Guildford; 9.30 pm; closed Mon & Sun D; no smoking.

SHIPLEY, WEST YORKSHIRE 5–1C

Aagrah £ 23 ★

27 Westgate BD18 3QX (01274) 530880

It's "hard to choose" from the "huge" menu of "tasty" dishes – which includes "a good range of veggie options" – at this branch of the well-established Indian chain notable for its "consistent quality". / **Sample dishes:** chicken tikka; chicken achar; kulfi. **Details:** off Saltaire Rd; midnight, Fri & Sat 1 am; D only; no smoking area.

SHREWSBURY, SHROPSHIRE 5–3A

Cromwells Hotel £ 29 ★

11 Dogpole SY1 1EN (01743) 361440

An "excellent-value", "varied" menu helps make this wine bar/restaurant, part of a small hotel, a "consistently good" choice in a thinly-served area. / **Sample dishes:** linguine with fresh baby clams; millefeuille of wild chestnuts & mushrooms; dark chocolate & pistachio marquise. **Details:** opp the Guildhall; 10 pm; no smoking. **Accommodation:** 7 rooms, from £45.

Floating Thai Restaurant £ 23 A

Welsh Bridge, Frankwell SY3 8JQ (01743) 243123

"Good unless its flooded!"; at least two features make this rather an "unusual" spot for Shrewsbury – it offers "excellent Thai food" and does so on an "in an interesting location, floating on the River Severn". / **Sample dishes:** Thai fishcakes; tiger prawn stir-fry; ice cream. **Value tip:** 4-crs set D £15. **Details:** 10.30 pm; D only.

constantly updated at www.hardens.com 243

SIBSON, WARWICKSHIRE
5–4C

Cock Inn £ 25 Ⓐ

Main Rd CV13 6LB (01827) 880357

It's the "exceptional atmosphere" which really distinguishes this ancient inn (where Dick Turpin was once a regular); some claim the cooking is "superb", but its ratings suggest that "generally fine" is closer to the mark. / **Sample dishes:** Chinese chicken salad; duck with strawberry & blackcurrant sauce; bread & butter pudding. **Details:** off A444 between Nuneaton & Burton; 9.45 pm; closed Sun D; booking advisable at weekends.

SNAPE, SUFFOLK
3–1D

The Crown Inn £ 30 Ⓐ

Main St IP17 1SL (01728) 688324

A "pleasant olde worlde pub atmosphere", a "fresh" and "varied" menu and "good beer" are among the attractions of this "friendly" hostelry-cum-restaurant, near The Maltings. / **Sample dishes:** tiger prawn & noodle salad; rack of lamb; lemon tart. **Details:** off A12 towards Aldeburgh, follow signs to Snape Maltings; 9 pm; no Amex; no smoking in restaurant; children: 14+. **Accommodation:** 3 rooms, from £50.

SOLIHULL, WEST MIDLANDS
2–2D

Shimla Pinks £ 26 ★

44 Station Rd B91 3RX (0121) 704 0344

"Defining the new curry attitude" for some reporters, this branch of the trendy national chain is unanimously praised for its "nouvelle Indian cuisine" – it's "beautifully presented" and includes "good veggie options". / **Sample dishes:** chicken tikka; lamb in tomato sauce; kulfi. **Details:** 11 pm; closed Sat L.

SONNING, WOKINGHAM
2–2D

Bull Inn £ 29

High St RG4 6UP (0118) 969 3901

This "olde worlde pub" is a "Sunday lunchtime favourite" sort of place; it offers "a superb choice of good traditional pub grub", but "high prices" undercut support. / **Sample dishes:** tricolore salad; Peking pork; cheese cake. **Details:** off A4, J10 between Oxford & Windsor; 9 pm; no smoking area; no booking. **Accommodation:** 7 rooms, from £60.

The French Horn £ 60

RG4 6TN (0118) 969 2204

"A marvellous setting by the river" is the undoubted attraction of this "wonderfully old-fashioned" restaurant on the Thames; the "classically-presented" cooking is commended by most reporters (as are the "spit-roasted ducks in the bar"), but a disgruntled minority wonder if the place has not "seen better days". / **Sample dishes:** fresh crab salad; spit-roasted duck with carrot purée; bread & butter pudding. **Value tip:** set 3-crs L £22.50. **Details:** M4, J8 or J9, then A4; 9.30 pm. **Accommodation:** 20 rooms, from £110.

SOUTHALL, GREATER LONDON
3–3A

Madhu's Brilliant £ 24 ★

39 South Rd UB1 1SW (020) 8574 1897

For Indian grub, Southall – it is said – is the place to be; this well-known fixture (five minutes from the station) offers some "very tasty", "authentic" dishes, even if, in our experience, they are not quite the stuff of urban legend. / **Sample dishes:** butter chicken; spring lamb chops in spicy sauce; almond kulfi. **Details:** nr railway station; midnight; closed Tue, Sat L & Sun L.

Kuti's £ 22

37-39 Oxford St SO14 3DP (023) 8022 1585

Fans say "this is the best Indian restaurant in Hampshire" –
there may not be much competition, but this is also the most
celebrated restaurant in town of any type, and, thanks to the
popular buffets, it "gets lively at the weekends". / **Sample
dishes:** chicken tikka; chicken korma; vanilla ice cream. **Details:** nr Ocean
Village; midnight; closed Sat L.

Pipe of Port £ 21 A★

84 High St SS1 1JN (01702) 614606

"Always good home-cooked English fare" and "excellent" service
make it worth seeking out this unpretentious spot of nearly
twenty years standing; fans say it has a "brilliant" atmosphere
too. / **Sample dishes:** orange & avocado salad with chutney mayo; roast
halibut with spinach & lobster sauce; lemon meringue pie. **Details:** at junction
with Tylers Ave; 10.30 pm; closed Sun; children: 16.

L'Auberge Bistro £ 24

1b Sea Bank Rd PR9 0EW (01704) 530671

A "cosy" and "intimate" Gallic bistro whose dishes come at
"reasonable prices". / **Sample dishes:** goat's cheese soufflé; lamb with
carrot & courgette tagliatelle; baked Alaska. **Details:** 10.30 pm.

Hesketh Arms £ 19

Botanic Rd PR9 7NA (01704) 509548

"Steak and kidney pie to die for" and "superb roasts" (with
"home-cooked fresh vegetables") are the sort of fare which is
done well at this popular local. / **Sample dishes:** soup of the day; steak
& kidney pie; apricot flan. **Details:** nr Botanical gardens; 8.30 pm; closed Mon
D & Sun D; no smoking area.

Warehouse Brasserie £ 30 ★

30 West St PR8 0DP (01704) 544662

"It's quite funky and modern, for a retirement town", says
a London visitor to this "buzzy, light and airy" spot, which is
unanimously praised for its "interesting" cooking and
"reasonable" prices. / **Sample dishes:** Thai chicken noodle salad;
peppered lamb with lemon & thyme relish; trio of mini desserts.
Value tip: set 2/3-crs early eve £8.95/£10.95. **Details:** 10.15 pm; closed
Sun.

The Crown £ 32 A★

High St IP18 6DP (01502) 722275

"Arrive at opening time to be sure of a slot" in the "bustling"
bar of this "real favourite" Adnams tavern "in the main street of
a delightful coastal town" – the solid fare is cooked with "flair
and finesse" and there is a "splendid" and "notably reasonably
priced" wine list; the pricier dining room is fine, but less of
a draw. / **Sample dishes:** salmon mousse with ginger & chilli; king prawn
& watermelon curry; chocolate cake with orange sauce. **Value tip:** set 2-crs
L £14.50. **Details:** off A12; in the town centre; 9.30 pm; no smoking.
Accommodation: 14 rooms, from £75.

The Swan £ 36 𝔸★

The Market Pl IP18 6EG (01502) 722186

*Though it's "stuffier" than the nearby Crown, this genteel fixture overlooking the market square is still relatively "relaxing and unfussy"; the solid British cooking is "enjoyable" – though the prix-fixe menu offers better value than the carte – and access to Adnams' cellar provides "very good" wines at notably reasonable prices. / **Sample dishes:** smoked & roast duck terrine; Adnam's pork with mustard gravy; passion fruit soufflé. **Details:** 9 pm; closed L, Oct-Dec; no jeans or shorts; no smoking; children: 7+ at D. **Accommodation:** 43 rooms, from £100.*

SOWERBY BRIDGE, WEST YORKSHIRE 5–1C

Gimbals £ 25 ★

Wharf St HX6 2AF (01422) 839329

*This small and "cosy" bistro is "a real find, off the beaten track", and its "wide range of dishes" (which includes "a good choice for vegetarians") finds unanimous approval. / **Sample dishes:** shredded duck & cashew pancake; smoked haddock & potato pie; blueberry crème brûlée. **Details:** off M62, J22, then A672/A58 for 4m; 9.15 pm; D only, closed Tue; no Amex; no smoking during D; booking advisable.*

Java £ 22 ★

Wharf St HX6 2AF (01422) 831654

*"Lots of small and delightful dishes" make this "authentic" Indonesian a consistent recommendation. / **Sample dishes:** deep-fried chicken with sweet & sour sauce; roast chicken with plum sauce & mixed vegetables; home-made ice cream. **Value tip:** 3crs set menu for two £36.00. **Details:** 11 pm; D only; no Amex; no smoking.*

SPARSHOLT, HAMPSHIRE 2–3D

Plough Inn £ 31

SO21 2NW (01962) 776353

*This "rambling rural inn with many rooms" is really "more a restaurant than a pub"; though the staff are usually "helpful" and "attentive", the cooking "varies from exceptional to dull". / **Sample dishes:** smoked chicken & Parma ham with walnuts; roast rack of lamb; poached pears with cream. **Details:** left off Stockbridge Rd from Winchester after 1.5m; 8.30 pm, Fri & Sat 9.30 pm; no Amex; no smoking area.*

SPEEN, BUCKINGHAMSHIRE 3–2A

Old Plow £ 39

HP27 OP2 (01494) 488300

*There's "good cooking", but it's "not cheap", at this converted Chilterns pub, which incorporates an informal bistro and quite a smart restaurant. / **Sample dishes:** bang-bang chicken with peanut sauce; veal with wild mushroom & cream sauce; peach ice cream with shortbread. **Details:** 20 mins from M40, J4 towards Princes Risborough; 8.45 pm; closed Mon & Sun D and last 3 weeks in August; smoking in bar only.*

ST ALBANS, HERTFORDSHIRE 3–2A

Thai Rack £ 24

13 George St AL3 4ER (01727) 850055

*"Very passable in central St Albans", this "very popular" restaurant offers "good-quality" Thai cooking, if in a "slightly uninspiring" setting. / **Sample dishes:** spring rolls; Thai green chicken curry; pancakes with ice cream. **Value tip:** 4-crs £19.00/ 6-crs £23.00. **Details:** 10.30 pm; no Amex.*

Vine Leaf Garden   £ 31   ★
131 South St KY16 9UN   (01334) 477497
"The owner is on occasion both chef and waiter" at Ian and
Morag Hamilton's small establishment, but the daily-changing
menu of *"varied"* and *"interesting"* fare can sometimes achieve
"perfect" results. / **Sample dishes:** scallops & tiger prawns with noodles;
pigeon, venison & wild boar with wild mushrooms; lemon pavlova.
Details: 9.30 pm; D only, closed Mon & Sun; no smoking.

Al Fresco   £ 32   Ⓐ★
Harbourside Wharf Rd TR26 ILF   (01736) 793737
It's "situated by the picturesque quay", but a *"beautiful location"*
is not the only strength of this *"unpretentious"* harboursider;
it also offers *"superbly prepared and presented"* modern British
cooking, with *"excellent fish"* the speciality. / **Sample dishes:** crab
cakes; monkfish & smoked bacon cassoulet; chocolate tart with cherries.
Details: on harbour front; 9.30 pm; no Amex.

Porthminster Beach Café   £ 24   Ⓐ★
Porthminster TR26 2EB   (01736) 795352
This "scenic beachside restaurant" has *"a beautiful location
overlooking the Bay"*, and offers *"fantastic fresh fish"* (*"with
a Mediterranean/Asian slant"*), *"presented by a charming
hostess"*. / **Sample dishes:** smoked salmon sushi; John Dory with sun-dried
tomato risotto; vanilla bean ice cream with figs. **Details:** 10 pm; closed end of
Oct- Easter.

Rosers   £ 45   ★
64 Eversfield Place TN37 6DB   (01424) 712218
"Just splendid and nice people" say fans of Gerald & Jenny
Roser's fixture, near the seafront, which despite its *"dated"*
appearance is known for its *"first-class"* Gallic cuisine using
"the finest ingredients". / **Sample dishes:** pike soufflé; roast guinea fowl;
caramelised lime cream. **Value tip:** set 3-crs set L £19.95. **Details:** opp
Hastings Pier on A259; 10 pm; closed Mon, Sat L & Sun, closed 1st two weeks
in January, 2nd two weeks in June; smoking discouraged.

Walletts Court   £ 51
Westcliffe CT15 6EW   (01304) 852424
*Some claim that the Oakley family's country house hotel,
scenically located at the top of a cliff, has a dining room
"to rival any city restaurant"*; *"poor"* and *"arrogant"* service,
however, has contributed to a number of *"disappointing"* recent
reports. / **Sample dishes:** grilled baby squid & blackened green peppers;
roast partridge stuffed with game parfait; crème brûlée with raspberries. **Value
tip:** set 3-crs L £27.50. **Details:** on B2058 towards Deal, 3m NE of Dover;
9 pm; no smoking. **Accommodation:** 16 rooms, from £75.

ST MAWES, CORNWALL
1–4B

Hotel Tresanton　　　　　　£ 42

Lower Castle Rd TR2 5DR　(01326) 270055

"Fantastic sea views" are an undoubted strength of Forte scion Olga Polizzi's rural designer-hotel; some say *"you can't get better simple food"* than is served in its dining room, but for others the place is *"OK, but not up to the hype"*. / **Sample dishes:** deep–fried squid & oysters; monkfish saltimbocca with salsa verde; panna cotta with grappa. **Details:** nr St Mawes Castle; 9.30 pm; D only; no smoking at D. **Accommodation:** 28 rooms, from £180.

STADDLEBRIDGE, NORTH YORKSHIRE
8–4C

McCoys at the Tontine　　　£ 39　　A★★

DL6 3JB　(01609) 882671

Though the *"first-class"* cooking – with a *"wide range of fish dishes"* the speciality – is *"comparable"* throughout, the basement bistro is generally tipped in preference to the more sedate restaurant at the McCoy brothers' *"friendly"* hotel, on the fringe of the North Yorks Moors. / **Sample dishes:** crab & tuna with avocado gazpacho; roast lamb & aubergines in cherry vinegar sauce; crème brûlée with oranges. **Value tip:** set 2/3-crs early eve £17/£21. **Details:** junction of A19 & A172; 10 pm; bistro open all week, restaurant open Sat D only. **Accommodation:** 6 rooms, from £90.

STAITHES, NORTH YORKSHIRE
8–3C

Endeavour　　　　　　　　£ 30　　★

1 High St TS13 5BH　(01947) 840825

As you might expect, *"imaginative"* fish dishes are the highlight of an *"extensive"* choice of dishes at Lisa Chapman's well-established small restaurant near the quay; its daily-changing blackboard menu also includes *"a good range of meat and vegetarian options"*. / **Sample dishes:** mint & honey marinated scallops; hot lobster with garlic butter; crème brûlée with raspberries. **Details:** 10m N of Whitby, off A174; 9 pm; closed Nov, Xmas, mid Jan to mid March, Sun & Mon excluding bank holidays; no credit cards; no smoking area; booking essential. **Accommodation:** 3 rooms, from £42.

STAMFORD, LINCOLNSHIRE
6–4A

The George Hotel　　　　　£ 46　　A

71 St Martins PE9 2LB　(01780) 750750

This huge and *"wonderful"* traditional coaching inn at the centre of a fine Georgian town inspires widespread affection; despite the expense, people generally prefer the *"atmospheric dining room"* to the cheaper, slightly tacky Garden Room brasserie – even in the former, however, the *"old-fashioned"* fare is too *"variable"* for a wholehearted recommendation. / **Sample dishes:** chestnut lasagne with ceps; turbot in red wine sauce with savoy cabbage; chocolate cream & coffee sponge. **Value tip:** set 2-crs L £14.50. **Details:** off A1, 14m N of Peterborough, onto B1081; 10.30 pm; jacket & tie. **Accommodation:** 47 rooms, from £130.

STANTON, SUFFOLK
3–1C

Leaping Hare Café　　　　　£ 29　　A★

Wyken Vineyards IP31 2DW　(01359) 250287

"Great tastes" and *"great ingredients"* win high praise at this Anglo-American restaurant in a converted barn, where the menu ranges from *"nibbles to bigger meals"*; *"fruity English wine"* (from the estate) is not the least of the attractions. / **Sample dishes:** tuna carpaccio with truffle oil; roast lamb with basil mash; buttermilk pudding with roast peaches. **Value tip:** set 2-crs L £12.50. **Details:** 9m NE of Bury St Edmunds; follow tourist signs off A143; 9 pm; closed Mon, Tue, Wed D, Thu D & Sun D; no Amex; no smoking.

Stapleford Park £ 59   Ⓐ

LE14 2EF (01572) 787522

Peter de Savary's country house hotel offers a rather "haphazard" culinary experience – "when it's good it's good, when it's off it's miles out" – and produces reports such as "truly awful food in a marvellous setting". / **Sample dishes:** *tomato tarte Tatin; fillet steak with foie gras sauce; soufflé.* **Value tip:** *set 3-crs Sun L £25.* **Details:** *4m from Melton Mowbray on B676; 9.30 pm, Fri & Sat 10.30 pm; jacket and/or tie; no smoking; children: 5+.* **Accommodation:** *51 rooms, from £165.*

Fox & Hounds £ 19   Ⓐ★

BD23 5HY (01756) 760269

"Great food" ("including a huge veggie selection") helps make this "congenial country pub" – which is something of a walkers' haven – an "ever-popular" destination. / **Sample dishes:** *blue cheese soufflé; Whitby scampi & chips; sticky toffee pudding.* **Details:** *on B6160 N of Kettlewell; 9 pm; closed Mon; no Amex; no smoking area; no booking.* **Accommodation:** *2 rooms, from £25.*

Bell Inn £ 31

Great North Rd PE7 3RA (01733) 241066

"Good food in antique surroundings" commends this "fine old coaching inn" to most reporters, though some do find its style a touch "pretentious". / **Sample dishes:** *white bean & truffle soup; roast Gressingham duck with fondant potatoes; vanilla panna cotta with raspberry sauce.* **Details:** *follow signs from A1(M), J16; 9.30 pm; no smoking area; children: 12+.* **Accommodation:** *19 rooms, from £89.50.*

Mayfly £ 18   Ⓐ★

Testcombe SO20 6AZ (01264) 860283

An "idyllic location" by the River Test is the venue for "quality simple food" – "home-made soups" and "good cheeses" from the buffet, for example – at this commendable pub. / **Sample dishes:** *soup of the day; beef steak & vegetable casserole; sticky toffee pudding with custard.* **Details:** *9 pm; no Amex; bookings taken for weekday L only.*

Vineyard at Stockcross £ 61   ★

RG20 8JU (01635) 528770

"Only Raymond Blanc can beat this", say fans of Sir Peter Michael's "sumptuous", "Napa Valley-style" two-year-old; it certainly has the "good American wine list" you might expect, and the cooking can be "exquisite", but we would side with those who find the whole experience "slightly over the top". / **Sample dishes:** *lobster salad; roast lamb with wild mushrooms; poached peaches with tarragon.* **Details:** *from M4 J13, take A34 towards Newbury; 9 pm; no smoking.* **Accommodation:** *33 rooms, from £185.*

STOKE BRUERNE, NORTHANTS
2–1D

Bruerne's Lock £ 34 A★

5 The Canalside NN12 7SB (01604) 863654

Thanks to its "classy canal-side setting" and "excellent" modern British cooking, this "posh" but "friendly" establishment is unanimously acclaimed by the locals as an all-round "enjoyable experience". / **Sample dishes:** smoked chicken, mushroom & apricot terrine; steamed halibut with saffron & squid ink noodles; sticky toffee pudding. **Details:** 0.5m off A508 between Northampton & Milton Keynes; 9.45 pm; closed Mon, Sat L & Sun D; no smoking in dining room.

STOKE BY NAYLAND, ESSEX
3–2C

Angel Inn £ 28 ★

Polstead St CO6 4SA (01206) 263 245

"Sophisticated pub fare" of "consistently good" quality means that "getting a table can be difficult" at this well known, "cosy" inn – a "reliable and popular favourite". / **Sample dishes:** marinated herrings; medallions of beef in red wine sauce; steamed syrup pudding. **Details:** 5m W of A12, on B1068; 9 pm; no smoking area; children: 14+. **Accommodation:** 6 rooms, from £43.

STOKE HOLY CROSS, NORFOLK
6–4C

Wildebeest £ 31

Norwich Rd NR14 8QJ (01508) 492497

It may be "idiosyncratic" – the tables are made of tree-trunks, for instance – but most reporters find this pub-conversion a "pleasing" place, "if you can find it". / **Sample dishes:** twice-baked cheese soufflé with walnuts; pan-fried chicken with Parmesan & green beans; coconut parfait with rum sauce. **Details:** turn left at Dunston Hall, left at T-junction; 10 pm; no smoking area.

STOKE ROW, OXFORDSHIRE
2–2D

The Crooked Billet £ 39 A★

Newlands Ln RG9 5PU (01491) 681048

"Difficult to find, but well worth the effort", this apparently "rustic" Chilterns hostelry is "really more of a country restaurant", and offers superior cooking with "great emphasis on fresh local ingredients"; musical evenings are a feature. / **Sample dishes:** grilled goat's cheese with artichoke hearts; hake escalope & pan-fried scallops; strawberry cheesecake. **Value tip:** set 2-crs L £11.95, set 3-crs Sun L £15.95. **Details:** on A4130; 10 pm; no Amex & no Switch.

STOKESLEY, NORTH YORKSHIRE
8–3C

Y-Thai £ 27

4 High St TS9 5DQ (01642) 710165

"Unusual to find such a good Thai in a small market town" – this "friendly" two-year old is unanimously hailed for its "tasty" cooking and "reasonable" prices. / **Sample dishes:** wrapped king prawns with sweet chilli sauce; spicy fried chicken with basil leaves; sticky rice pudding with sweetcorn & coconut. **Details:** 10 pm; no smoking; booking advisable.

STONEHAVEN, ABERDEEN
9–3D

Lairhillock Inn £ 34 A★

Netherley AB39 3QS (01569) 730001

"Well worth a drive into the country" say Aberdeen city dwellers, who rate this an "excellent" place on account of its "very relaxed" style and its "exceptional pub food, using the finest local produce". / **Sample dishes:** chunky seafood chowder; lamb shank with roast parsnips; sticky toffee pudding. **Value tip:** set 3-crs L & Sun L £12.95. **Details:** 7m S of Aberdeen; 9.30 pm; no smoking area.

STONY STRATFORD, MILTON KEYNES

Moghul Palace £ 22 A★
7 St Pauls Ct MK11 1LJ (01908) 566577

Fear not if you see stars at this "lovely" subcontinental – it will be the "fantastic painted ceiling" of this converted church which is to blame, not the cooking, which is of high quality. / **Sample dishes:** shish kebab; chicken masala; chocolate truffle. **Details:** 11 pm, Sun 9 pm; no bookings after 10 pm.

Peking £ 21
117 High St MK11 1AT (01908) 563120

"Crispy duck" wins a particular thumbs up at this popular Chinese, which has a large local following thanks to its "quality food and good service". / **Sample dishes:** crispy aromatic duck; chicken with cashew nuts & egg noodles; ice cream. **Details:** 11.30 pm; no smoking area.

STORRINGTON, WEST SUSSEX 3–4A

Fleur de Sel £ 40 A★
Manley's Hill RH20 4BT (01903) 742331

The site once known as Manley's is now decked out in a "more modern and understated style"; "thank goodness it changed and became this", say fans, who laud its "superb" Gallic cooking and "very helpful" service. / **Sample dishes:** rosemary scallops & king prawns; roast duck with honey & elderberry; poached pears & almond ice-cream. **Value tip:** set 2/3-crs L £12.50/£16.50 (Sun £16.50/£20.50). **Details:** 9.30 pm; closed Mon, Sat L & Sun D.

STOURBRIDGE, WORCESTERSHIRE 5–4B

French Connection £ 33 A★
3 Coventry St DY8 1EP (01384) 390940

"Wonderful French home-cooking" helps ensure that this "consistent" and "well priced" restaurant is "very popular locally", and "always buzzing". / **Sample dishes:** Mediterranean king prawns; boeuf bourguignonne; citron brûlée. **Value tip:** set 3-crs L £9.95, (pre-theatre £11.95). **Details:** 9.30 pm; closed Mon, Tue D, Thu D & Sun; no smoking area.

STRATFORD UPON AVON, WARWICKSHIRE 2–1C

Desports £ 38 ★
13-14 Meer St CV37 6QB (01789) 269304

It's "a cut above the usual Stratford dining experience", and this "friendly", brightly-decorated town-centre yearling is beginning to make quite a name for its "good" and "interesting" modern cooking. / **Sample dishes:** chicken salad with chorizo; roast cod; peach fritters. **Value tip:** set 2/3-crs L £10.50/£14. **Details:** nr marketplace; 10.30 pm; closed all January; no smoking area.

Hussains £ 23 ★
6a Chapel St CV37 6EP (01789) 205804

"Very fresh, well cooked and tasty food" and "good, quick" service commend this Indian to locals and non-locals alike. / **Sample dishes:** chicken kebab; chicken tikka masala; coconut supreme. **Value tip:** set D £32.95 for 2 people. **Details:** 11.30 pm.

Lambs £ 26
12 Sheep St CV37 6EF (01789) 292554

"The food is really quite good" at this "consistently reliable" restaurant; it's "handy for the theatre" and "gets really busy" – "book early". / **Sample dishes:** crispy duck & watercress salad; roast chicken with mango in lime butter; banoffi pie. **Value tip:** set L & early eve £9. **Details:** nr Royal Shakespeare Theatre; 11 pm; no Amex.

Opposition £ 29

13 Sheep St CV37 6EF (01789) 269980

A "broad range of dependable British food" is one of the attractions making this "consistent and good-value" wine bar "a nice place to go"; pre-theatre meals are reliably timed. / **Sample dishes:** Caesar salad; roast chicken & banana in lime butter; hazelnut & caramel iced parfait. **Details:** nr Royal Shakespeare Theatre; no Amex; booking: max 12.

STUCKTON, HAMPSHIRE   2–3C

Three Lions £ 42 ★★

Stuckton Rd SP6 2HF (01425) 652489

"Outstanding and reliable food" from a blackboard menu – served with "great charm in attractive surroundings" – makes Michael and Jayne Womersley's "restaurant-style" pub, on the fringe of the New Forest, a most "engaging" destination. / **Sample dishes:** wild mushroom salad; crispy roast lamb with garlic mash; hot chocolate sponge dessert. **Value tip:** set 2-crs L £14.50. **Details:** 1m E of Fordingbridge off B3078; 9.30 pm; closed Mon & Sun D; no Amex; no smoking. **Accommodation:** 3 rooms, from £65.

STURMINSTER NEWTON, DORSET   2–3B

Plumber Manor £ 28 Ⓐ

DT10 2AF (01258) 472507

This "delightful" manor house is now a "friendly, family-run hotel" (of over 25 years standing); "impeccable service and presentation" is a particular strength. / **Sample dishes:** crab mousseline with sherry & tomato sauce; guinea fowl with black cherries & cinnamon; lemon meringue pie. **Details:** off A357 at Sturminster Newton towards Hazelbury Bryan; 9.30 pm; D only, except Sun when L only; closed Feb; booking essential. **Accommodation:** 16 rooms, from £95.

SUDBURY, SUFFOLK   3–1C

Red Onion Bistro £ 22 ★

57 Ballingdon St CO10 6DA (01787) 376777

This small and unpretentious bistro wins support with its "interesting" cooking, its "helpful staff" and its "relaxed atmosphere". / **Sample dishes:** potted crab & prawns; roast lamb with olive & thyme jus; Bailey's crème brûlée. **Value tip:** set 2/3-crs L £7.50/£9. **Details:** on A131; 9.30 pm; closed Sun; no Amex.

SUNDERLAND, TYNE & WEAR   8–2C

Café 21 £ 27

Wylam Whf, Low St SR1 2AD (0191) 567 6594

Recently renamed (from Brasserie 21), this "restored warehouse", overlooking the river and quay, is generally thought to offer the "creative modern cooking" associated with the offshoots of Newcastle's 21 Queen Street (as it was formerly called); some, though, feel it "fails to live up to the rest of the group". / **Sample dishes:** Cheddar & spinach soufflé; confit of duck with warm potato & shallot salad; treacle tart with Chantilly cream. **Details:** 10.30 pm; closed Mon & Sun.

---

constantly updated at www.hardens.com 252

throwingstones £ 21 ★
National Glass Ctr, Liberty Wy SR6 0GL (0191) 565 3939
A "glass roof, with people walking on it" is just one of the
features which wins unanimous approval for the "light" and
"airy" restaurant of the National Glass Centre – the "remarkable
value" of its "imaginative" modern British cooking also receives
a big thumbs-up. / **Sample dishes:** roasted tomato & Mozzarella salad;
lamb with roasted plum tomatoes & red pesto; sticky toffee pudding.
Details: A19 to Sunderland, follow sign to National Glass Centre; 9.30 pm;
L only, ex Fri & Sat when L & D.

SUNNINGHILL, BERKSHIRE 3–3A

Jade Fountain £ 30 ★
38 High St SL5 9NE (01344) 627070
"Excellent" food, "unobtrusive service" and "nice surroundings"
make this "pricey" Chinese a consistently popular destination.
/ **Sample dishes:** crispy duck; beef chow mein; ice cream. **Details:** 2m from
Ascot town centre, follow A329; 10.30 pm; no smoking area.

SUTTON COLDFIELD, WEST MIDLANDS 5–4C

New Hall £ 53 Ⓐ
Walmley Rd B76 1QX (0121) 378 2442
The menu may seem a touch "pedestrian" (especially in contrast
to "the beautiful china"), but it's the "delightful" setting – in the
oldest manor house in England, only eight miles from Brum city
centre – which is the special attraction here. / **Sample dishes:** baked
goat's cheese with roasted peppers; roast pigeon with cabbage, foie gras
& redcurrant jus; banana pancake with caramel sauce. **Value tip:** set 3-crs
L £12.50. **Details:** from A452, right onto B4148, past Walmley; 10 pm;
closed Sat L; tie required; no smoking; booking essential; children: 8+.
Accommodation: 60 rooms, from £160.

SWANSEA, SWANSEA 1–1D

L'Amuse £ 27 ★
93 Newton Rd SA3 4BN (01792) 366006
"Delicious French cuisine" and "very friendly service" make
chef/patronne Kate Cole's "classic" bistro one of the most
consistently popular destinations in town; an "excellent
cheeseboard" is a highlight. / **Sample dishes:** aubergine, tomato & basil
tart; sea bass with wild mushrooms & thyme; roasted nectarines in Marsala.
Value tip: set 2/3-crs L £10.95/£13.95. **Details:** 9.30 pm; closed Mon D &
Sun D.

La Braseria £ 32 Ⓐ
28 Wind St SA1 1DZ (01792) 469683
Most reporters "always enjoy" this large and "lively"
"Spanish-style brasserie", which serves "no-frills meat and fish" –
you choose your own – "simply and well cooked"; the formula is
very similar to La Brasserie in Cardiff, to which it was once
connected. / **Sample dishes:** calamari; char-grilled fillet steak; crème
caramel. **Details:** 11.30 pm; closed Sun; need 6+ to book; children: 6+.

Moghul Brasserie £ 21
81 St Helen's Rd SA1 4BQ (01792) 475131
"Very good vegan dishes" are among the "extensive" range of
"well presented" and "reasonably priced" choices at this popular
subcontinental. / **Sample dishes:** chicken tikka; chicken tikka masala
& mushroom bhaji; mango kulfi. **Details:** follow the King's Way; 11.30 pm;
no Switch.

Opium Den £ 18 Ⓐ

20 Castle St SA1 1JF (01792) 456160

You'd hope for a "good atmosphere", given the name, and this "reliable" central spot does not disappoint; neither does its "varied" and "tasty" cooking. / Sample dishes: crispy spring rolls; Cantonese style chicken; ice cream. Details: 11.30 pm.

Patricks £ 28 ★

638 Mumbles Rd SA3 4EA (01792) 360199

Thanks to its "great, reasonably-priced" modern British cooking, this "friendly", family-run bistro — which looks over Swansea bay from the Mumbles — is usually "bustling". / Sample dishes: bacon salad with Stilton dressing; Barbary duck with strawberry sauce; peanut butter & chocolate sandwich. Details: in Mumbles, 1m before pier; 9.50 pm; closed Sun D; no Amex.

SWINTON, SCOTTISH BORDERS 8–1A

Wheatsheaf Inn £ 32 ★

Main St TD11 3JJ (01890) 860257

"Interesting and well-presented country food" — from "a new menu every day" — is served at this "secret Borders jewel". / Sample dishes: pigeon, black pudding & lentil salad; roe deer with juniper & redcurrant sauce; iced Drambuie parfait. Details: opp Village Green midway between Kelso and Berwick-upon-Tweed; 9.15 pm; closed Mon & Sun D (to non-residents); no Amex; no smoking. Accommodation: 7 rooms, from £80.

TADCASTER, NORTH YORKSHIRE 5–1D

Aagrah £ 23 ★

York Rd LS24 8EG (01937) 530888

"An excellent range of veggie options" is just one of the attractions which makes for the consistent popularity of this "exemplary" subcontinental, which occupies "a well-converted former pub". / Sample dishes: chicken tikka; chicken achar; kulfi. Details: 7m from York on A64; 11.30 pm; D only; no smoking area.

TALSARNAU, GWYNEDD 4–2C

Maes y Neuadd £ 31 ★

LL47 6YA (01766) 780200

"Attention is paid to every detail" — not least the "well-balanced" modern British cooking and the fine wine list — at this "perfect", family-run country hotel, now entering its twentieth year. / Sample dishes: sea bass with tomato fondue; Welsh lamb with mustard mash; gingered apple & bramble tarte Tatin. Value tip: set 3-crs Sun L £14.95. Details: 3m N of Harlech off B4573; 9 pm; no smoking. Accommodation: 16 rooms, from £127, incl D.

TAPLOW, BERKSHIRE 3–3A

Waldo's at Cliveden £ 77

Berry HI SL6 0JF (01628) 668561

"Oh dear, Mr Winner was right"; the basement dining room of the Astors' grandiose palazzo may provide a "gorgeous" setting, but the experience of eating there is widely dismissed as "pretentious, very boring and overpriced". / Sample dishes: vanilla-roasted monkfish & lobster risotto; clove & honey-glazed duck with mushrooms; vanilla & cherry soufflé. Details: M4, J7 then follow National Trust signs; 9.30 pm; D only, closed Mon & Sun; jacket & tie; no smoking; booking: max 6; children: discouraged. Accommodation: 38 rooms, from £290.

Brazz £ 27

Castle Bow TA1 3NF (01823) 252000
"A real buzz" and an "imaginative" menu helps make this
"smart" brasserie – an adjunct to the famous Castle Hotel –
an unusual find in a town of this size; "service suffers at busy
times". / **Sample dishes:** deep–fried goat's cheese salad; lamb shank with
rosemary jus; knickerbocker trifle. **Details:** 10.30 pm.

The Castle Hotel £ 48

Castle Green TA1 1NF (01823) 272671
This landmark hotel dining room has always seemed a trifle
"dull", but the culinary distinction which enveloped it when
Phil Vickery was at the stoves has now wholly evaporated; many
now just find it thoroughly "over-rated". / **Sample dishes:** tomato
consommé; slow-cooked mutton with rosemary mash; strawberry & rhubarb
vacheron. **Details:** follow brown tourist information signs; 9 pm; no smoking.
Accommodation: 44 rooms, from £145 for 2.

Tayvallich Inn £ 25 ★

PA31 8PL (01546) 870282
"Fresh seafood, prepared simply in an idyllic setting" helps
make this small bar near the water's edge of Loch Sween a very
popular tourist-season destination. / **Sample dishes:** pan-fried scallops
with parsley; Tayvallich seafood platter; lemon posset with shortcake.
Details: signposted off Crinan canal at Bellanoch, 9 miles from Lochgilphead;
9 pm; closed Fri L & Sat L (& Mon Nov-Easter); no Amex; no smoking area.

Fox On The River £ 22

Queens Rd KT7 0QY (020) 8339 1111
A "beautiful" riverside setting "facing the back of Hampton Court
Palace" makes this old inn an ideal refreshment point for those
on a day out; the traditional cooking – "wonderful roasts" and so
on – is surprisingly "professional". / **Sample dishes:** home-made soup;
chicken with cheddar mash; caramelised apple cobbler. **Details:** across the
river from Hampton Court Palace grounds; 10 pm, Sun 9.30 pm; no Amex;
no smoking area; no booking.

Old Trout £ 37

29-30 Lower High St OX9 2AA (01844) 212146
This thatched cottage-conversion produced rather up-and-down
feedback this year; for some, a visit is "always a real pleasure",
whereas, for a minority, "poor" service contributed to general
disappointment. / **Sample dishes:** spicy fishcake with lemongrass sauce;
pan-fried halibut with asparagus & olives; roasted peaches. **Details:** 10 pm;
closed Sun; no Amex. **Accommodation:** 7 rooms, from £75.

Thornbury Castle £ 53

Castle St BS35 1HH (01454) 281182
Sadly, "the food lags behind the location" at this sumptuous
Tudor landmark – some "flawless" meals are reported, but also
some "almost inedible" ones. / **Sample dishes:** goat's cheese in pastry
with asparagus; pan-fried cod with parsley mash & Sevruga caviar; orange
crème brûlée with chocolate sorbet. **Value tip:** set 2/3-crs L £16.50/£17.50.
Details: nr intersection of M4 & M5; 9.30 pm, Sat 10 pm; jacket & tie;
no smoking in dining room. **Accommodation:** 20 rooms, from £120.

Lifeboat Inn £ 26

PE36 6LT (01485) 512236

This 16th-century smugglers' inn is "far too popular" – "it's packed, even out of season" – but it "copes well", considering, and maintains "high standards of food and service"; "very fine mussels" are a highlight. / **Sample dishes:** duck confit with grape & apple chutney; medallions of beef with roast shallots; iced nougat parfait with raspberries. **Details:** 20m from Kings Lynn on A149; 9.30 pm; no Amex. **Accommodation:** 12 rooms, from £74.

Bakers Arms £ 28 Ⓐ

Main St LE16 7TS (01858) 545201

A "wonderful thatched pub in deepest rural Leicestershire", which is almost "more a restaurant than a pub", with a "warm" and "intimate" atmosphere; "great fish" is the highlight on a "reliable quality" menu. / **Sample dishes:** fresh mussels; roast sea bass with sweet potato mash; chocolate tart with caramelised bananas. **Details:** nr Market Harborough off the A6; 9.30 pm; closed Mon, L (Tue-Fri) & Sun D; no smoking area; children: 12+.

Rupali £ 27 ★

337 Tile Hill Ln CV4 9DU (024) 7642 2500

"A taste bud sensation" is reported at this "consistently good" Indian; even those who "aren't sure about the authenticity" concede it's "a nice place to eat". / **Sample dishes:** tikka platter; chicken jalfrezi; rasmalai (cream cheese dessert). **Details:** off A45, follow signs; 10.30 pm; no smoking area.

Stagg Inn £ 27 ★

HR5 3RL (01544) 230 221

Steven Reynolds' "imaginative and wide-ranging" cooking – using "fresh local ingredients" – wins this "lively" pub a vocal local fan club; some reporters find "poor" service, though. / **Sample dishes:** scallops with spinach & black pepper oil; stuffed pork with aubergine sauce & mash; baked figs with honey ice cream. **Details:** on B4355, NE of Kington; 9.30 pm; closed Mon, close first week in November; no Amex; no smoking area. **Accommodation:** 2 rooms, from £50.

Berghoff Brandstatter £ 27 Ⓐ★

Cross Stone Rd OL14 8RQ (01706) 812966

"No need to travel to Austria, Germany or Switzerland" – for "fine continental food", you need go no further than Peter Brandstatter's "cosy" and "welcoming" fixture; all "rather unexpected on a hillside overlooking a small Yorkshire town!" / **Sample dishes:** wild boar dumplings; pan-fried rib-eye steak with garlic; apple strudel. **Details:** on Calder Way; 9.30 pm; Mon-Thu D only, Fri-Sun open L & D; mostly non-smoking; booking essential.

The Old Hall Restaurant £ 27 A ★
Hall St OL14 7AD (01706) 815998
*Complete with "wonderful 16th-century hall", this Elizabethan
house – "in the middle of nowhere" – provides a "marvellous"
setting; the modern British cooking isn't of huge ambition, but
it is "delicious" and notably "competitively priced", and staff are
"charming".* / **Sample dishes:** black pudding with chorizo & poached eggs;
pork on parsnip mash with crab apple & kumquat sauce; hot chocolate
steamed pudding. **Details:** 15 mins from M62; 9 pm, Sat 9.45 pm; closed
Mon & Sun D; no Amex; no smoking in dining rooms.

TONBRIDGE, KENT 3–3B

Bottle House £ 26
Coldharbour Rd TN11 8ET (01892) 870306
*"Huge portions from a large and interesting menu" commend
this "typically picturesque Kent pub"; "booking is essential for
Sunday lunch".* / **Sample dishes:** smoked salmon; calves liver with garlic
mash; banoffi pie. **Details:** SW of Penshurst on B2188; 10 pm; no Amex;
no smoking area.

TREBURLEY, CORNWALL 1–3C

Springer Spaniel £ 22 ★
PL15 9NS (01579) 370424
*Home-cooking that's "reliably of a high standard" makes this
"relaxed" and welcoming pub a perennially popular destination.*
/ **Sample dishes:** seafood bouillabaisse; beef with Stilton sauce; chocolate
brandy cake. **Details:** 4m S of Launceston on A388; 9 pm; no Amex;
no smoking before 10 pm.

TREEN, CORNWALL 1–4A

Gurnards Head £ 24 ★
TR26 3DE (01736) 795313
*"A coastal road inn that serves simple fresh seafood"; the cooking
makes "imaginative" use of local produce, and fans say the place
offers "excellent value for money".* / **Sample dishes:** trio of smoked
Cornish fish; confit of duck with fresh vegetables; marmalade tart. **Details:** off
coastal road between Land's End and St Ives, near Zennor; 9.15 pm;
no smoking. **Accommodation:** 6 rooms, from £50.

TROON, SOUTH AYRSHIRE 9–4B

The Oyster Bar £ 31 ★
The Harbour, Harbour Rd KA10 6DH (01292) 319339
*"Quality" fish and seafood cooking using "fresh locally caught
produce" wins praise for this "down-to-earth" mill-conversion,
overlooking the harbour.* / **Sample dishes:** oysters in half shell; grilled
lobster in garlic butter; raspberry crème brûlée. **Details:** follow signs for Sea
Cat Ferry Terminal, past shipyard; 9.45 pm; closed Mon & Sun D; no Amex.

TROUTBECK, CUMBRIA 7–3D

Queen's Head £ 27 A ★
Townhead LA23 1PW (01539) 432174
*"Rambling" and "atmospheric", this "unspoilt" 17th-century
coaching-inn set amidst "stunning" Lakeland scenery offers
"well-prepared meals – both traditional and contemporary" –
plus "a great range of beer"; "get there early" if you want to eat
in the bar.* / **Sample dishes:** smoked duck breast; medallions of beef; bread
& butter pudding. **Details:** A592, on Kirkstone Pass; 9 pm; D only; no Amex;
no smoking area. **Accommodation:** 9 rooms, from £70.

---

constantly updated at www.hardens.com

Hotel du Vin et Bistro   £ 35
Crescent Rd TN1 2LY (01892) 526455
*Though satisfied customers speak of "good-quality food"
and "a wine list to die for" at this "boutique hotel" (part of
a growing chain), it inspires too many reports of "fancily
described, but only passable" cooking and markedly "indifferent"
service. / **Sample dishes:** baked aubergine & goat's cheese; chicken with
herb ratatouille; watermelon & port soup. **Value tip:** set 3-crs Sun L £22.50.
Details: 9.30 pm; booking: max 10. **Accommodation:** 25 rooms, from £75.*

Signor Franco   £ 36
5a, High St TN1 1UL (01892) 549199
*In this under-served town, it's worth knowing about this
"good-standard Italian", with its "polite and attentive" staff;
"ask for a window seat". / **Sample dishes:** baked Roman artichokes;
beef stuffed with Parmesan & garlic; pancakes with vanilla ice cream.
Details: opp railway station; 11 pm; closed Sun; no Amex.*

Thackeray's House   £ 44
85 London Rd TN1 1EA (01892) 511921
*This wine bar/restaurant, elegantly housed where the writer
once lived, incites mixed reviews; for the majority, it's a
"very comfortable" place with "ever-changing" and "imaginative"
cooking – there are still doubters, though, who say it's "expensive
if you stray from the set menu", and complain that "erratic"
service can take the edge off the atmosphere. / **Sample dishes:** red
mullet, crab & rocket salad; roast guinea fowl; apricot & walnut toffee pudding.
Value tip: set 2-crs L £13.50. **Details:** 9.30 pm, Fri & Sat 10 pm; closed
Mon & Sun D; no Amex; no smoking area.*

Turnberry Hotel   £ 66   𝔸
KA26 9LT (01655) 331000
*This famous golfing hotel – boasting two world-class courses
and a great sea view – has a "beautiful" setting; it's "expensive",
but most form the view that the Mediterranean-influenced
cooking is "worth it". / **Sample dishes:** oak-smoked Scottish salmon;
seared monkfish with basil polenta; fresh raspberries & mango. **Details:** A77,
2m after Kirkswald turn right, then right again after 0.5m; 9.30 pm.
Accommodation: 132 rooms, from £270.*

Bull & Butcher   £ 30
RG9 6QU (01491) 638283
*On a good day, you can find some "excellent" cooking at this
"wonderful" pub, which has a "great location" in a very "pretty"
Chilterns village; it can get "chaotic" at the weekends, though,
and standards suffer accordingly. / **Sample dishes:** chicken liver & pork
pâté with chutney; roast lamb with Middle Eastern spices; redcurrant pie.
Details: off M40, J5 to Ibstone, right at T-junction in village; 9.45 pm; closed
Tue D & Sun D; no Amex; no smoking area; children: 14+.*

Olde Dog & Partridge £ 25

High St DE13 9LS (01283) 813030

*Even those who "don't do carveries" acclaim the quality and "excellent value for money" of the one at this half-timbered coaching inn dating back to Tudor times; some – even fans – think it can be "variable", though; there's also a brasserie. / **Sample dishes:** cheese soufflé; chicken stuffed with herbs & lemon; pear tarte Tatin. **Value tip:** set 2/3-crs pre-theatre £6.95/£7.95. **Details:** N of Burton on Trent on A444; 9.45 pm; closed Sun L; no smoking area. **Accommodation:** 20 rooms, from £60.*

Sidney's £ 22 A ★

3-5 Percy Park Rd NE30 4LZ (0191) 257 8500

*"An oasis of taste on the coast"; this "excellent", year-old modern bistro is carving out a big name for itself locally, thanks to its "simple food, skillfully prepared", its "super young staff" and its "relaxed" style. / **Sample dishes:** orange & coconut tempura king prawns; roast duck with sweet potato rosti; crème brûlée. **Details:** 10 pm; closed Sun D; no smoking before 9 pm.*

Altnaharrie Inn £ 88 A ★★

IV26 2SS (01854) 633230

*Can a place really be "perfect in every way"?; that's certainly reporters' view on Gunn Eriksen and Fred Brown's "relaxing", "gourmet paradise" – an isolated former drovers' inn, "accessible only by boat" – where "the food is never less than stunning, and usually better!" / **Sample dishes:** crab & lobster soup with ginger; chicken liver & mushroom cake with truffle mash; roast pineapple with cloudberry ice cream. **Details:** 8 pm; D only, closed Nov-Easter; no smoking; children: 8+. **Accommodation:** 8 rooms, from £165, incl D.*

Ceilidh Place £ 36

14 West Argyle St IV26 2TY (01854) 612103

*This café appended to a folk music venue is "quite a find in such a remote location", especially – with its "fresh seafood" and selection of veggie dishes – for those in search of non-carnivorous fare. / **Sample dishes:** three fish paté with citrus dressing; grilled prawns with tarragon & dill sauce; chocolate terrine. **Details:** 55m NW of Inverness on A835; 9 pm; no smoking. **Accommodation:** 13 rooms, from £45.*

Sharrow Bay £ 54 A ★★

CA10 2LZ (01768) 486301

*"Superlatives abound" for the original and, for many, still the leading country house hotel, whose location enjoys "the best view in England"; "traditional dishes are done exceptionally well" (but with "sufficient choice and options to avoid too much richness"), and almost everyone is charmed by the "highly professional" but "unstuffy" service. / **Sample dishes:** roast quail & smoked bacon salad; lamb with marinated vegetables & thyme jus; white chocolate & raspberry bombe. **Value tip:** set 3-crs L £30 (incl service). **Details:** on Pooley Bridge Rd towards Howtown; 8 pm; no Amex; jacket & tie; no smoking; children: 13+. **Accommodation:** 28 rooms, from £290, incl D.*

Bay Horse £ 38 ★

Canal Foot LA12 9EL (01229) 583972

It's "a real treat" to visit this well known pub, whose "edge-of-the-world" location offers great views over Morecambe Bay; "excellent results" from an "imaginative" menu are praised by many reporters, but the occasional "disaster" is not unknown. / **Sample dishes:** crab & avocado salad; steak with honey & raspberry vinegar sauce; raspberry & Mascarpone cheesecake. **Value tip:** set 3-crs L £16.75. **Details:** after Canal Foot sign, turn left & pass Glaxo factory; 7.30 pm; closed Mon L & Sun L; no Amex; no smoking; children: 12+. **Accommodation:** 9 rooms, from £75, incl D.

Lords of the Manor £ 53 A★

GL54 2JD (01451) 820243

"The food is equal to the surroundings" at this "lovely", "small luxury hotel" in the Cotswolds, where "impeccable" service contributes to an "exceptional" overall experience. / **Sample dishes:** smoked haddock; John Dory with pickled lamb's tongue; warm chocolate fondant with passion fruit. **Value tip:** set 2/3-crs L £11.95/£15.95 (Sun £21). **Details:** 2m W of Stow on the Wold; 9.30 pm; no jeans; no smoking; children: 7+. **Accommodation:** 27 rooms, from £145.

Lake Isle £ 32

16 High St East LE15 9PZ (01572) 822951

"A good destination, for the area", this well-established, quite informal hotel dining room in a charming small town offers fairly traditional cooking that's "pleasant, without hitting the heights"; a "fantastic choice of wines by the half-bottle" is a feature of the quality list. / **Sample dishes:** smoked haddock & prawn fishcakes; chicken stuffed with ham & apricots; chocolate & nut pudding. **Details:** 9.30 pm; closed Mon L; no smoking. **Accommodation:** 12 rooms, from £65.

Five Arrows £ 32

High St HP18 0JE (01296) 651727

This "Rothschild-owned pub" is liked by many for its "French-style" food and "excellent" service; some do find the menu "rather limited" and the wines – from the family's estates – "too pricey". / **Sample dishes:** carpaccio of beef; roast salmon; honeycomb ice cream. **Details:** off A41; 9.30 pm; no Amex; no jeans; mostly non-smoking; booking advisable at weekends. **Accommodation:** 11 rooms, from £80.

Aagrah £ 23 ★

Barnsley Rd WF1 5NX (01924) 242222

As at the other branches, this member of the prominent Yorkshire chain of "slightly upmarket curry houses" offers "quality across the board". / **Sample dishes:** chicken tikka; chicken achar; kulfi. **Details:** from M1, J39 follow Denby Dale Rd to A61; 11.30 pm; no smoking area. **Accommodation:** 19 rooms, from £39.95.

Bell Inn £ 24 A★

Ferry Rd IP18 6TN (01502) 723109

This "very established" boozer – well, you'd hope so after half a millennium – offers "superb ambience and food"; "good fish" is the highlight. / **Sample dishes:** Suffolk smokies; slow-roasted lamb with mint sauce; strawberry cheesecake. **Details:** off A12 on B1387 (no access from Southwold); 9 pm; no Amex; no smoking area; booking advisable at weekends; children: 14+. **Accommodation:** 6 rooms, from £70.

Priory £ 45 A★

Church Green BH20 4ND (01929) 551666

An "exquisite" setting helps make it quite an experience to visit this long-established restaurant on the banks of the River Frome, whether you dine in the "superb" grounds or in the "stylish" cellar; "great" cooking completes a winning package. / **Sample dishes:** salmon, lobster & citrus fruit terrine; fillet steak with Stilton mash; amaretto bread & butter pudding. **Details:** 10 pm; no smoking area; children: 8+. **Accommodation:** 19 rooms, from £110.

Three Horseshoes £ 20 A★

Bridge St NR23 1NL (01328) 710547

"A great log fire and a huge shared table" (not to mention the "vintage one-armed bandit") set the tone at this "super country pub", which offers "huge" portions of "home-cooked food" that takes "pride in local produce and recipes"; popularity is such that some find a visit "best out of season". / **Sample dishes:** shellfish bake; steak & kidney pie; spotted dick. **Details:** 1m off A148; 8.30 pm; no credit cards; no smoking area; no booking. **Accommodation:** 6 rooms, from £24.

Aggra £ 17

32 East St BA12 9BN (01985) 846941

"Good food" ("at reasonable cost") and a "friendly" welcome have made this "intimate" Indian a "reliable" local choice; let's hope this continues under its new owners. / **Sample dishes:** mixed kebabs; chicken passanda; ice cream. **Details:** 11 pm.

Bishopstrow House £ 48 A★

BA12 9HH (01985) 212312

This "splendid hotel" in a Georgian house has a "charmingly decorated conservatory dining room"; the modern-ish British cooking is "very expensive, but very good too". / **Sample dishes:** char-grilled scallops on goat's cheese crostini; salmon with crayfish risotto; sticky toffee pudding. **Details:** on Boreham Rd; 9 pm; no smoking. **Accommodation:** 31 rooms, from £170.

WATERHOUSES, STAFFORDSHIRE
5–3C

Old Beams £ 50   A★

Leek Rd ST10 3HW (01538) 308254

Nigel Wallis's "posh restaurant in an area with few such establishments" has – for over twenty years now – offered "consistently good" cooking and a "warm" reception; "the ambience is nicer in the summer, when full use can be made of the conservatory". / **Sample dishes:** confit of duck leg with cardamom sauce; venison with wild mushroom ravioli; apricot & almond crumble. **Value tip:** set 2/3-crs L £16.95/£22. **Details:** on A523 between Leek & Ashbourne; 9.30 pm; closed Mon, Tue L, Sat L & Sun D; no smoking. **Accommodation:** 5 rooms, from £75.

WATH-IN-NIDDERDALE, NORTH YORKSHIRE
8–4B

Sportsman's Arms £ 33

HG3 5PP (01423) 711306

Some find it "a bit stuffy at times", but "lovely beer and food" continue to win a strong local following for this "thriving" inn, on the fringe of the North York Moors. / **Sample dishes:** warm goat's cheese & pepper salad; roast lamb on olive mash with roasted garlic; summer pudding. **Value tip:** set 3-crs Sun L £17. **Details:** take Wath Road from Pateley Bridge; 9 pm; D only, closed Sun; no Amex; no smoking. **Accommodation:** 13 rooms, from £60.

WATTON AT STONE, HERTFORDSHIRE
3–2B

George & Dragon £ 27   ★

High St SG14 3TA (01920) 830285

"Long-standing excellence in pub food" of a traditional bent helps make this "lovely old inn" a consistently popular recommendation. / **Sample dishes:** smoked haddock & tomato gratin; pot-roasted lamb with tomato; bread & butter pudding. **Details:** A602 from Stevenage; 10 pm; closed Sun D.

WEST BRIDGFORD, NOTTINGHAMSHIRE
5–3D

New Oriental Pearl £ 22

42-44 Bridgford Rd NG2 6AP (0115) 945 5048

"Good service and good value" make this "friendly" Chinese a "pleasant" local destination. / **Sample dishes:** crispy aromatic duck; lemon chicken; apple & banana fritters. **Details:** close to cricket ground; 11 pm; no smoking area.

WEST BYFLEET, SURREY
3–3A

Chu Chin Chow £ 27

63 Old Woking Rd KT14 6LF (01932) 349581

It may be a touch on the "pricey" side, but most find "good value" at this "fancy Chinese". / **Sample dishes:** sesame chicken; chicken in black bean sauce; toffee bananas & apples. **Value tip:** 34 .50 for two set menu or £75.00 for four. **Details:** opp Waitrose; 11 pm.

WESTERHAM, KENT
3–3B

Tulsi £ 26

20 London Rd TN16 1BD (01959) 563397

"Well cooked dishes" from a "wide-ranging menu" make this "tasteful" Indian a popular local destination. / **Sample dishes:** chicken tandoor; murgh makhani; melon sorbet. **Details:** 11.30 pm.

Colony   **£ 29**

3 Balfour Rd KT13 8HE   (01932) 842766

"Solid, undemanding, authentic Peking cuisine" makes this well-established oriental a consistently *"great"* local recommendation. / **Sample dishes:** spare ribs, spring rolls & crispy seaweed; sizzling beef; toffee apples. **Value tip:** set menus available every day. **Details:** on A317 nr M25; 10.30 pm.

WHASHTON, NORTH YORKSHIRE   8–3B

Hack & Spade   **£ 24**   ★

DL11 7JL   (01748) 823721

"Friendly, comfortable and personal", Adrian & Gill Barrett's restaurant-like pub offers a *"lovely"* atmosphere, and results from the weekly-changing menu are often *"excellent"*. / **Sample dishes:** grilled goat's cheese with black pudding & chutney; grilled turbot with minted pea risotto; glazed Grand Marnier tart. **Details:** 4m N of Richmond; 9 pm; closed Mon D & Sun D; closed 3 weeks in Jan; no Amex; no smoking area.

WHITBY, NORTH YORKSHIRE   8–3D

Magpie Café   **£ 23**   ★★

14 Pier Rd YO21 3PU   (01947) 602058

"The best fish and chips in the universe" are widely reported to emanate from this *"tearoom"*-style café, and it offers *"a real by-the-sea experience"* too; *"the only problem is that you often have to face a huge queue"*, but *"it moves fast, and it's worth it"*. / **Sample dishes:** seafood in wine & garlic broth; deep-fried cod with tartare sauce & chips; banana cheesecake. **Details:** opp Fish Market; 9 pm; no Amex; no smoking.

The White Horse & Griffin   **£ 28**   𝔸★

Church St YO22 4AE   (01947) 604857

"Gourmet cooking" (fish in particular) and *"attentive service"* makes this *"civilised"* town-centre tavern a *"real find"*. / **Sample dishes:** Whitby scallops with mango salsa; roast cod with black olive crust & tomato risotto; plum & almond pizza. **Details:** centre of old town, on Abbey side of river; 9.30 pm; no Amex. **Accommodation:** 11 rooms, from £50.

WHITCHURCH, HAMPSHIRE   2–3D

Red House   **£ 26**   ★

21 London St RG28 7LH   (01256-) 895558

This *"cheerful and friendly"* 16th-century coaching inn owes a good deal of its popularity to its *"exciting selection"* of *"contemporary cuisine"* that's unanimously hailed as *"unpretentious"* and *"good value"*. / **Sample dishes:** scallops with minted pea purée; roast duck with truffle oil mash; double chocolate mousse. **Details:** nr Whitchurch silk mill; 9.30 pm; no Amex; no smoking; booking essential; children: 12+.

WHITEBROOK, MONMOUTHSHIRE   2–2B

The Crown at Whitebrook   **£ 38**

NP5 4TX   (01600) 860254

It's *"not too easy to find"* this Wye Valley restaurant with rooms, but it's worth it for its *"friendly"* service, its locally-sourced menu and its *"good wine list"*. / **Sample dishes:** leek & wild mushroom risotto; quail stuffed with bacon & chicken; rosemary & pear crème brûlée. **Value tip:** set 3-crs L & Sun L £15.95. **Details:** 2m W of A466, 5m S of Monmouth; 9 pm; closed 2 weeks in Jan and Aug; no smoking; children: 12+. **Accommodation:** 10 rooms, from £56.

Whitstable Oyster Fishery Co.   **£ 34**
Horsebridge Beach CT5 1BU   (01227) 276 856
A *"fabulous seaside location"*, atmospheric premises and *"great"*
seafood have won a big reputation for this *"basic"* spot – 90
minutes from The Smoke – as a great *"day-out destination"*;
sadly, it's just got *"too big for its boots"* nowadays – the food
often seems *"indifferent"*, service *"surly"* and prices *"high"*.
/ **Sample dishes:** Whitstable oysters with lemon & chilli; Dover sole with salsa;
crème brûlée. **Details:** off A299; 9 pm; closed Mon & Sun D in winter.
Accommodation: 30 rooms, from £40.

Stile   **£ 30**   ★
97 High St DL15 0PE   (01388) 746615
The cottage setting may be *"plain"*, but the *"interesting range
of mainly French dishes"* at this *"lovely, quiet"* dining room
of over fifteen years standing is very positively received,
and some say the results are *"amazing"*. / **Sample dishes:** flat
mushrooms stuffed with bacon & cheese; confit duck with lentils & Toulouse
sausage; chocolate & brandy marquise. **Details:** 9.30 pm; closed L , Wed-Sun;
no Amex; no smoking.

Bank Square   **£ 38**
4 Bank Sq SK9 1AN   (01625) 539754
The *"modern bistro food"* at this town centre brasserie
is *"better than most in north Cheshire"*, and it's a shame
that support is undercut by incidents of *"sloppy"* or *"dismissive"*
service; some feel the *"loud bar"* on the ground floor *"destroys
the atmosphere"*. / **Sample dishes:** shredded duck parcels; peppered
lamb rump; trio of chocolate desserts. **Details:** 10 pm; closed Sun.

Chili Banana   **£ 22**
Kings Arms Hotel, Alderley Rd SK9 1PZ   (01625) 539100
"Authentic" and *"interestingly presented"* Thai cooking makes
it a *"real pleasure"* to visit this restaurant attached to the King's
Arms public house. / **Sample dishes:** chicken satay; Penang dry chicken
curry; banana fritters. **Value tip:** 4crs menu for two £39.50/ 5crs menu for
two £44.50/ sunday lunch buffet £11.95. **Details:** hotel on crossroad with
Knutsford Road; 11 pm; D only, closed Mon.

Wesley House   **£ 36**   ★
High St GL54 5LJ   (01242) 602366
This *"friendly and well-run establishment"* resides in
a half-timbered house, *"tucked away in the high street"*; it wins
enthusiastic endorsements for its *"exceptional food and service"*
and its *"excellent wine list"*. / **Sample dishes:** terrine of salmon & leeks;
lamb with salad potatoes & rosemary sauce; apple tart & lemon curd ice
cream. **Details:** next to Sudley Castle; 9.30 pm; no smoking; booking: max 6.
Accommodation: 5 rooms, from £65.

Hotel du Vin et Bistro   £ 35   A
14 Southgate St SO23 9EF   (01962) 841414
*There's no doubt that the original of this "stylish" hotel chain is "much slicker than its Tunbridge Wells branch", and many affirm its "simple, high-class cooking in a relaxed, soothing atmosphere" and appropriately "impressive" wine list; there are continuing complaints, however, that the place is "complacent" and "expensive". / **Sample dishes:** skate roulade with lemongrass dressing; rack of lamb with celeriac & thyme mash; chocolate cake & orange sauce. **Value tip:** set 3-crs Sun L £22.50. **Details:** 9.45 pm. **Accommodation:** 23 rooms, from £89.*

Old Chesil Rectory   £ 50   ★
1 Chesil St S023 OHU   (01962) 851555
*Chef/patron Philip Storey offers some "brilliant" cooking – with "every dish distinctive and original" – and service at this "beautiful" and "historic" Tudor building is "friendly" too; yet in spite of all these advantages, some find the atmosphere here a trifle "dull". / **Sample dishes:** twice-baked Roquefort soufflé; pork & black pudding with mustard mash; apple strudel. **Value tip:** set 2/3-crs L £16/£20. **Details:** 9.15 pm, Sat 9.45 pm; closed Mon & Sun; no Amex; no smoking area.*

Wykeham Arms   £ 30   A
75 Kingsgate St SO23 9PE   (01962) 853834
*"Unsullied by modern tat", this "fabulous" pub boasts a "convivial", "'old school" atmosphere" – appropriately, as it's next to the College – and comes "highly recommended" for its "traditional", "wholesome" cooking and "reasonably priced" wines. / **Sample dishes:** curried parsnip soup; lamb & redcurrant casserole; passion fruit crème brûlée. **Details:** between Cathedral and college; 8.45 pm; closed Sun; no smoking area; booking: max 8; children: 14+. **Accommodation:** 13 rooms, from £79.50.*

Beech Hill Hotel   £ 28   A★
Newby Bridge Rd LA23 3LR   (01539) 442137
*"Consistently imaginative" cooking (with a twist that seems "very Californian" for the Lake District) wins very positive support for this "excellent" hotel dining room, which has a "beautiful" location overlooking Windermere. / **Sample dishes:** red snapper; monkfish with curried sauce; soufflé. **Details:** 9.15 pm; D only, ex Sun open L & D; no smoking. **Accommodation:** 58 rooms, from £99.*

Gilpin Lodge   £ 40   A★
Crook Road LA23 3NE   (01539) 488818
*"A sense of in-depth competence and reliability" envelopes visitors to this "welcoming" and "comfortable" country house hotel, where "attentive but not OTT" service complements the "exceptional" cooking and "well priced" wine list. / **Sample dishes:** Scottish scallops with red onion salsa; roast lamb with minted pea risotto; tiramisu & tuille biscuits. **Details:** 9 pm; no smoking; children: 7+. **Accommodation:** 14 rooms, from £70.*

constantly updated at www.hardens.com

Holbeck Ghyll £ 55   A

Holbeck Ln LA23 ILU (01539) 432375

This country house hotel has been an "excellent" destination in all respects, not least for its "imaginative" and "artistically presented" cuisine and its "superb" setting, which offers fine Lakeland views; new chef David McLaughlin arrived in late-summer 2000 (too late to rate) — let's hope he's maintaining the star-worthy standards of his predecessor. / Sample dishes: Scottish oysters & clams; roast lamb with shallot purée; shortbread biscuit & strawberries. Details: 3m N of Windermere, towards Troutbeck; 9.30 pm; no smoking. Accommodation: 20 rooms, from £170.

Jerichos £ 34   ★

Birch St LA23 IEG (01539) 442522

This "friendly local restaurant" in the town-centre wins high praise for its "professional" service and "fresh and well prepared" modern British grub, albeit from a slightly "limited" menu. / Sample dishes: black pudding & white wine risotto; seared sea bass with balsamic asparagus; chocolate & mint marquise. Details: 9.30 pm; D only, closed Mon; no Amex; no smoking; children: 12+.

WINDSOR, WINDSOR & MAIDENHEAD   3–3A

Al Fassia £ 27

27 St Leonards Rd SL4 3BP (01753) 855370

"There's only one problem" with this "mouth-watering Moroccan", say most of its fans, and that's "managing to book a table"; others do find it a bit "dingy". / Sample dishes: filo parcels with chicken & almond; lamb stew with sweet prunes; Moroccan dessert 'Bastilla à la glacé'. Details: 10.30 pm, Fri-Sat 11 pm; closed Sun.

WINKLEIGH, DEVON   1–2D

Pophams £ 33   A★

Castle St EX19 8HQ (01837) 83767

Given that it's "tiny" (10 seats) and only open for lunch (and then only on certain days), it's no surprise that it's "often difficult to get in" to this rather eccentric spot; those who make it, however, speak of cooking of "fabulous" quality, and of "lovely, friendly" service. / Sample dishes: roast cod with tomato & ginger; lamb in puff pastry with mushroom pâté; rum & hazelnut ice cream. Details: off A377 between Exeter & Barnstaple; L only; open Wed-Fri only; closed Feb; no Amex & no Switch; no smoking; children: 14+.

WINTERINGHAM, NORTH LINCOLNSHIRE   5–1D

Winteringham Fields £ 65   A★★

DN15 9PF (01724) 733096

"Out-of-this-world" Swiss-French cooking — on reporters' ratings, the best in the country — helps earn a hymn of praise for Annie and Germain Schwab's "stunning" 16th-century manor house; it's a "relaxed" place, which is just "exceptional in every way". / Sample dishes: langoustine with samphire & gazpacho; roast grouse with Muscat-soaked raisins; apricot tiramisu. Value tip: set 2-crs L £21. Details: 4m SW of Humber Bridge; 9.30 pm; closed Mon & Sun; no smoking. Accommodation: 10 rooms, from £90.

WITHAM, ESSEX   3–2C

Lian £ 29   ★

5 Newland St CM8 2AF (01376) 570684

Chef/patron Kim Man "makes all customers feel special" at this "pleasant" oriental — "the best Chinese for miles". / Sample dishes: tea smoked chicken; chicken with chilli & pepper; toffee apples. Value tip: 5crs menus £24/ £34. Details: 10 pm; closed Sun.

WITHERSLACK, CUMBRIA 7–4D
Old Vicarage £ 36 A ★
Church Rd LA11 6RS (01539) 552381
"The tenderest venison and the tastiest baby vegetables ever" are the kind of dishes which make this delightful country house hotel a *"sublime"* experience for the few reporters who comment on it. / **Sample dishes:** Dolcelatte torte & herb roulade; char-grilled lamb with minted saffron polenta; date & ginger slice. **Details:** from M6, J36 follow signs to Barrow on A590; 9 pm; no smoking. **Accommodation:** 14 rooms, from £65.

WOBURN, BEDFORDSHIRE 3–2A
Paris House £ 59
Woburn Pk MK17 9QP (01525) 290692
Though fans find a visit to sample the French cooking at this half-timbered house in the grounds of Woburn Abbey *"superb from start to finish"*, there are a good number for whom *"food and décor are stuck in the '80s"*, and bills are *"way too high"*. / **Sample dishes:** smoked salmon & crayfish salad; fillet steak with red wine sauce; hot raspberry soufflé. **Value tip:** set 2-crs L £18 (Sun L £22). **Details:** on A4012; 9.30 pm; closed Mon & Sun D.

WOLLATON, NOTTINGHAMSHIRE 5–3D
Mr Man's £ 26 ★
Wollaton Park NG8 2AD (0115) 928 7788
"A wide variety of dishes" and *"good service, for such a huge place"* has made this *"comfortable"* and *"reassuringly expensive"* Chinese one of the more popular dining destinations in town. / **Sample dishes:** spare ribs; sizzling steak Cantonese style; apple fritters. **Details:** 11 pm.

WOLTERTON, NORFOLK 6–4C
Saracen's Head £ 22
NR11 7LX (01263) 768909
For a *"country adventure"*, chef/patron Robert Dawson's *"isolated gastropub"* is *"well worth finding"*; a traditional menu is offered, with *"game a speciality"*. / **Sample dishes:** crispy fried aubergine with garlic mayonnaise; medallions of venison with red fruit; treacle tart. **Details:** difficult to find, call for directions; 9 pm; no smoking area. **Accommodation:** 4 rooms, from £60.

WOLVERHAMPTON, WEST MIDLANDS 5–4B
Bilash £ 28 ★
2 Cheapside WV1 1TU (01902) 427762
"I told the waiter what I liked, and the chef cooked an exceptional meal" – high praise is bestowed by fans of Sitab Khan's *"one-off"* curry house. / **Sample dishes:** kebabs & pancake rolls; tiger prawn masala; Indian ice cream. **Value tip:** banquet meal offer £20.00. **Details:** opp Civic Centre; 11 pm; no smoking area.

WOODSTOCK, OXFORDSHIRE 2–1D
The Feathers Hotel £ 52
Market St OX20 1SX (01993) 812291
"Nice-enough food, shame about the prices" is probably the fairest overview of this well-known luxury hotel, in the *"lovely village"* by Blenheim Palace – the modern British cooking may be *"adventurous"*, but the final bill is *"unjustified"*. / **Sample dishes:** caramelised foie gras; pot-roasted duck with olive oil mash; dark chocolate parfait. **Details:** 8m N of Oxford on A44; 9.15 pm; no smoking. **Accommodation:** 22 rooms, from £115.

constantly updated at www.hardens.com

Brown's   £ 42   A ★
24 Quay St WR1 2JJ   (01905) 26263
A "lovely setting" in "a spacious former warehouse" contributes
to the charms of this riverside spot (which has nothing to do with
the national brasserie chain); "it's expensive, but it's the best in
the city", with modern British cooking that's "consistently"
realised. / *Sample dishes:* warm salad of black pudding; sautéed cow's liver
with onion gravy & mash; crème brûlée. **Value tip:** set 3-crs L £19.50.
Details: nr the Cathedral; 9.45 pm; closed Mon, Sat L & Sun D;
no smoking area; children: 8+.

Lemon Tree   £ 32   ★
12 Friar St WR1 2LZ   (01905) 27770
"Imaginative" Mediterranean cooking, "great" staff and
an "intimate" atmosphere are highly praised at this "tiny"
venture; its "relaxed" ambience is "ideal for a between-the-shops
moment". / *Sample dishes:* ciabatta with houmous & olives; Old Spot pork
with roasted pears & bacon; banana pavlova. **Details:** 2 mins walk from
Guildhall; 9.30 pm; closed Mon, Tue D, Wed D & Sun; no Amex; no smoking.

Pant Yr Ochan   £ 27   ★
Old Wrexham Rd LL12 8TY   (01978) 853525
"Rustic" food served in a "beautiful" old house (with "many
nooks") makes this "relaxed" and "unpretentious" establishment
very popular locally – "it can get very busy, even during the
week". / *Sample dishes:* Thai beef vegetable salad; chicken with leeks
& shiitake mushrooms; nectarines in butterscotch sauce. **Details:** 1m N of
Wrexham; 9.30 pm; no smoking area; children: before 6 pm only.

Wife of Bath   £ 33
4 Upper Bridge St TN25 5AF   (01233) 812540
"Great food in a remote part of Kent" makes this "friendly, small
restaurant" worth knowing about; even some fans say the
"French oriented" cooking is "perhaps not what is was", though,
and the consensus is that it is "satisfying, but not special".
/ *Sample dishes:* smoked duck breast salad; pan-fried venison with red
cabbage; sticky toffee pudding. **Details:** off A28 between Ashford
& Canterbury; 10 pm; closed Mon & Sun. **Accommodation:** 6 rooms,
from £60.

George Hotel   £ 47   A ★
Quay St PO41 0PE   (01983) 760331
There's both a brasserie and a restaurant at this impressive hotel;
the former has the better of the harbour view (and "makes
a lovely setting for lunch") while the latter "aims to be clubby
and grand" – "outstanding ingredients" and "faultless service"
are praised throughout. / *Sample dishes:* trio of duck starters; millefeuille
of red mullet & artichokes; trio of chocolate desserts. **Details:** nr harbour;
10 pm; D only, closed Mon & Sun; children: 8+. **Accommodation:** 17 rooms,
from £130.

YARM, STOCKTON ON TEES

D P Chadwicks £ 35 ★

104B, High St TS15 9AU (01642) 788558

"The food is always up to scratch", say the supporters of this "busy, modern bistro", where "impressive" results are achieved from a decidedly "eclectic" menu. / **Sample dishes:** twice-baked Swiss cheese soufflé; calves liver & bacon with bubble & squeak; baked cherry cheesecake. **Details:** just after Yarm Bridge; 9.30 pm; closed Mon & Sun (open one Sunday a month); no Amex; no smoking area; no booking.

YATTENDON, BERKSHIRE 2–2D

Royal Oak Hotel £ 39

The Square RG18 0UG (01635) 201325

Reports on this famously "perfect country pub" have been "variable" this year, and though many still proclaim "top notch" French fare, the approach strikes others as bordering on "pretentious"; enthusiasm remains high amongst those sticking to the "good-value bar meals". / **Sample dishes:** warm crab salad; Jamaican jerk chicken; banana parcels. **Value tip:** set 2/3-crs set L £12.50/£15. **Details:** 5m W of Pangbourne, off B4009; 9.45 pm; closed Sun D; no smoking. **Accommodation:** 5 rooms, from £115.

YORK, CITY OF YORK 5–1D

Bettys £ 25 A

6-8 St Helen's Sq YO1 8QP (01904) 659142

"The Bettys experience is an essential part of a day out in York", say devotees of the "best tearooms ever" (well, apart from the Harrogate original, of course); all agree that a visit is "sheer indulgence", and the only real drawback is "the queues". / **Sample dishes:** Betty's Yorkshire rarebit; Swiss rosti with bacon & raclette cheese; fresh cream strawberry heart. **Details:** down Blake St from York Minster; 9 pm; no Amex; no smoking area; no booking.

Blue Bicycle £ 35 A★

34 Fossgate YO1 9TA (01904) 673990

For many reporters, this "lovely", "relaxed" central bistro is "by far and away York's leader" ("especially for its fresh fish"); this year, however, did give rise to the odd grumble about "ordinary" standards. / **Sample dishes:** fishcakes; tuna, monkfish & salmon chowder; lemon tart. **Details:** nr Marks & Spencer; 10 pm; no smoking; booking: max 6.

Café Concerto £ 26

21 High Petergate YO1 2EN (01904) 610478

This "busy and friendly café/restaurant", by the Minster, "appeals to young and old" alike, and its many fans insist that – with its "inexpensive" and "imaginative" menu – it's "the perfect casual eating place". / **Sample dishes:** goat's cheese crostini with roasted vegetables; filo parcel of salmon, asparagus & pesto; pecan nut crème brûlée. **Details:** by the W entrance of York Minster; 9.30 pm, Fri & Sat 10 pm; no Amex; no smoking area; no booking at L.

Melton's £ 29 ★

7 Scarcroft Rd YO23 1ND (01904) 634341

"Inspired" results endear this "enthusiastic" restaurant, housed in Victorian shop premises, to many, and the "fixed margin on wines" creates some notable bargains at the top end of the list; a few reporters wonder if the place is beginning to "rest on its laurels". / **Sample dishes:** home-smoked chicken & herb salad; roast venison with damsons; hot raspberry soufflé. **Value tip:** set 2/3-crs L £13.25/£16. **Details:** 10 mins walk from Castle Museum; 10 pm; closed Mon L & Sun D; no Amex; no smoking area.

Middlethorpe Hall £ 42 A★

Bishopthorpe Rd YO23 2GB (01904) 641241

Set in "lovely tranquil gardens", this country house hotel and spa just outside the city offers a "heavenly" experience to all who comment on it; "excellent food and wine" and "very attentive service" play no small part. / **Sample dishes:** hot home-smoked salmon; lamb fricassée; hot chocolate fondant. **Value tip:** set 2/3-crs L £14.50/£17.50 (Sun £18.50). **Details:** next to racecourse; 9.45 pm; no Amex; jacket & tie; no smoking area; children: 8+. **Accommodation:** 30 rooms, from £155.

UK & EIRE MAPS

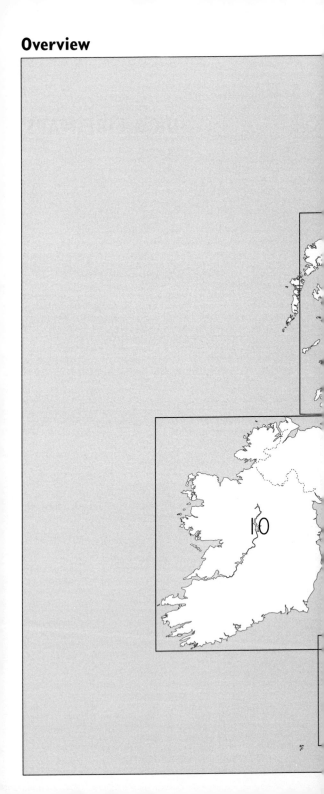

10

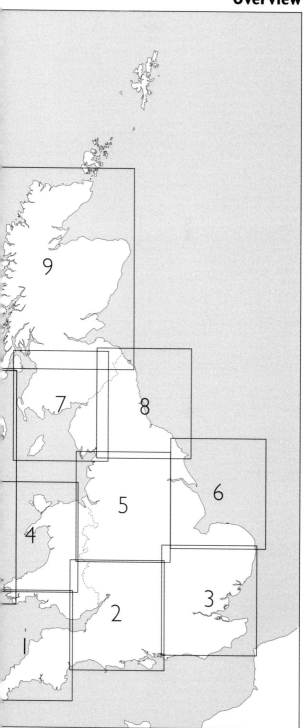

Map 1

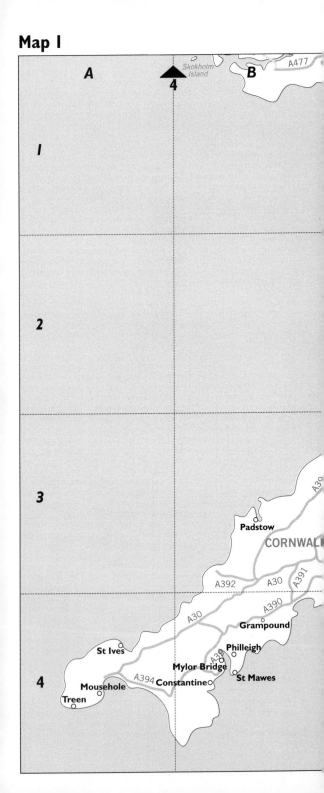

Map I

Map 2

Map 2

C WARWICKSHIRE   D

A425

Stratford upon Avon **5**   Priors Hardwick

A46   A423   Stoke Bruerne

A44   A46   A422   A43   A5

Chipping Campden   Banbury   Paulerspury

Broadway   Paxford   Blockley   Stony Stratford

Winchcombe   Moreton-in-Marsh   Great Tew

Upper Slaughter   Chipping Norton   BUCKINGHAM-SHIRE

Cheltenham   Lower Oddington   M40

Lower Slaughter   A361   Woodstock   A34   A41

Birdlip   Burford   Church Hanborough   Lower Wolvercote   Gibraltar

Coln St Aldwyns   **OXFORD**   Long Crendon   Thame

A417   A40   Cumnor   A40   Chinnor

A419   OXFORDSHIRE   Gt Milton   M40

Ewen   Buckland   Fyfield   Britwell Salome

Brinkworth   A420   A338   Maidensgrove

M4   Stoke Row   A4130   Fawley

A361   A346   Moulsford   Goring

BERKSHIRE   Yattendon   Sonning   Reading

Lacock   A4   Stockcross   M4

Rowde   **3**

WILTSHIRE   A338   A34   A33

A342   Old Burghclere   A339

Salisbury Plain   Basingstoke   M3   Odiham

A303   Whitchurch   A303

Longstock   HAMPSHIRE

A338   A30   M34   M3

Stockbridge

Salisbury   Sparsholt   Ovington   A31   A3

A30   Winchester   A272

A354   A338   A36   Romsey   A31   Petersfield

Stuckton   Cadnam   A32

A31   Southampton   A3(M)

New Forest   Lyndhurst   M27   Emsworth

A35   Brockenhurst   Park Gate

Poole   Lymington

A348   New Milton

Bournemouth   Yarmouth   Seaview

Wareham   Isle of Wight

A3055

Map 3

A427 · A6116 · A1 · A605 · **A** · A141 · **B** · A10

○ Stilton

▲ **6**

○ Ely

CAMBRIDGESHIRE

A43 · A45 · A14 · A14 · A10 · A14

NORTHAMPTONSHIRE

1 A45 · A6

○ **Huntingdon**

Histon ○

A428 · A428 · A1198

Madingley ○

○ **Cambridge**
Little Shelfor

Horton

M1 · A428 · A505 · A421

Newton ○ M11 **Sawston**
Fowlmere ○ **Duxford**
Melbourn ○ A13

Milton
Keynes

A421

BEDFORDSHIRE

A1

○ **Heydon**

A505

Houghton-Conquest

A505

Woburn ○

A421

A6 M1

Luton ○ ✈ HERTFORDSHIRE

A507 **Clavering** ○

A1(M)

A120

BUCKINGHAM-
SHIRE

Ivinghoe

A5

Lemsford ○ **Watton At Stone**

A602

Sawbridgewor

2 **Aylesbury**
Waddesdon ○

Harpenden ○

M11

Prestwood

A613 · A41

Frithsden

○ **St Albans**

Amersham

M10 · A10

Ongar ○

M40 · Speen

2 **Beaconsfield**

Bushey M1

○ **E Barnet** ○ **Loughton**

A12 · M25

Turville ○ **Marlow**
Taplow ○ **Cookham**

Pinner ○ **Hatch End**

A406

Gants H

A4 · **Windsor**
A329(M) · ○ **Bray**
Eton ○

Southall ○

A41

LONDON ✈

A13

Ascot ○

Hersham A40

○ **Richmond**

A2 · **Orpington** ○

3

Shepperton ○
Chobham ○
Brookwood ○ **West**
Byfleet
Ripley ○ **Mickleham**

Esher ○ **Kingston**
○ **Thames Ditton**

A205

Locksbottom ○

Weybridge
Claygate
○ **Cobham**

Croydon A232

Otford

A23 · A22

M25 · M26

M25

Dogmersfield ○

Guildford ○
Compton ○

SURREY

Dorking ○
Shere ○ **Reigate**

A25 · A24

Westerham ○

A21

A31

M23

Penshurst ○

Tonbridg

Ockley ○

East
Grinstead

Tunbridge Wells ○

Langton Gree

A264 · A22 · A267

A3 · **Lickfold** ○

Haywards
Heath

○ **Fletching**

A272

Petworth ○

A272 · A29 · A104 · A23

A272 · E. SUSSE

4 WEST SUSSEX
○ **Chilgrove**

○ **Storrington**
○ **Amberley**

○ **East Chiltington**

A26 · A272

A27

○ **Chichester**

South Downs

A27

BRIGHTON ●

Alciston ○

Chidham ○

Jevington ○

Map 3

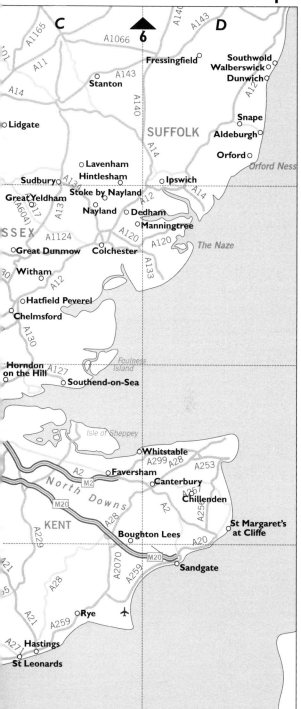

C

D

6

A1066

A1165

A11

A143

A14

A143

A140

A14

Fressingfield○

Stanton
○

Southwold○
Walberswick○
Dunwich○

A12

Lidgate○

SUFFOLK

Snape

Aldeburgh○

Orford○

Orford Ness

Lavenham○
Hintlesham
○

Ipswich
○

A14

A14

Sudbury○

A134

Stoke by Nayland

A12

Great Yeldham

A1017

A13

Nayland
○

Dedham
○

A14

Manningtree
○

ESSEX

A1124

A120

A120

The Naze

Great Dunmow○

Colchester

A133

Witham
○

A12

Hatfield Peverel○

Chelmsford●

A130

A130

Horndon
on the Hill●

A1127

Foulness
Island

Southend-on-Sea●

Isle of Sheppey

Whitstable○

A299

A28

A253

A2

M2

Faversham○

Canterbury
○

A257

Chillenden

North Downs

A2

A256

M20

KENT

A28

A258

A229

Boughton Lees●

A20

St Margaret's
at Cliffe

A2070

A259

M20

Sandgate●

A21

A28

A259

Rye○

A21

A27

Hastings●

St Leonards●

Map 4

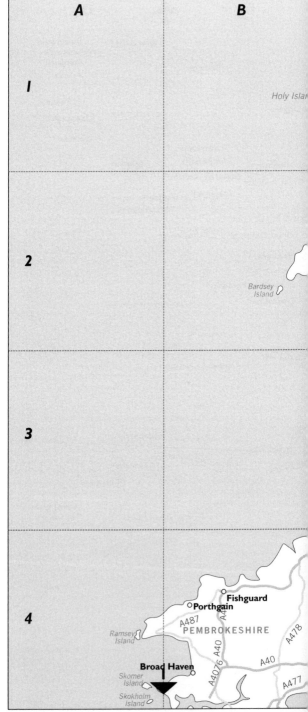

	A	**B**
1		Holy Islan
2		Bardsey Island
3		
4	Ramsey Island · Porthgain · **Fishguard** A487 PEMBROKESHIRE A478 **Broad Haven** A4076 A40 A40 A477 Skomer Island Skokholm Island	

Map 4

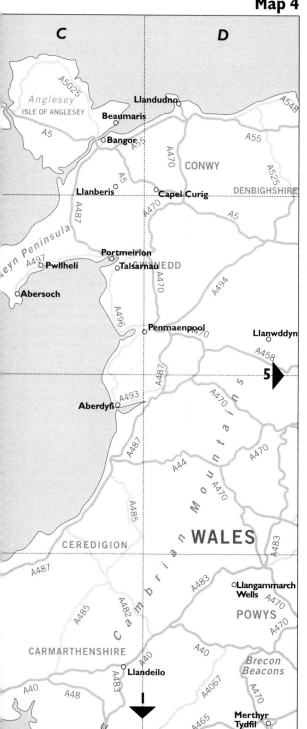

C   D

A5025

Anglesey
ISLE OF ANGLESEY

A5

Llandudno

A548

Beaumaris

Bangor
A55

A55

A470

CONWY

A525

DENBIGHSHIRE

A5

Llanberis   **Capel Curig**

A487

A470

A5

Lleyn Peninsula

Portmeirion

GWYNEDD

A497   **Pwllheli**

Talsarnau

A470

A494

Abersoch

A496

Penmaenpool

A470

Llanwddyn

A458

5

A487

A470

Cambrian Mountains

Aberdyfi   A493

A487

A470

A470

A44

A470

A485

WALES

A483

CEREDIGION

A487

A483

Llangammarch Wells

A470

A485

A482

POWYS

A470

CARMARTHENSHIRE

A40

Llandeilo

A40

A40

Brecon Beacons

A40

A48

A483

A4067

A465

A470

Merthyr Tydfil

Map 5

Map 5

Map 6

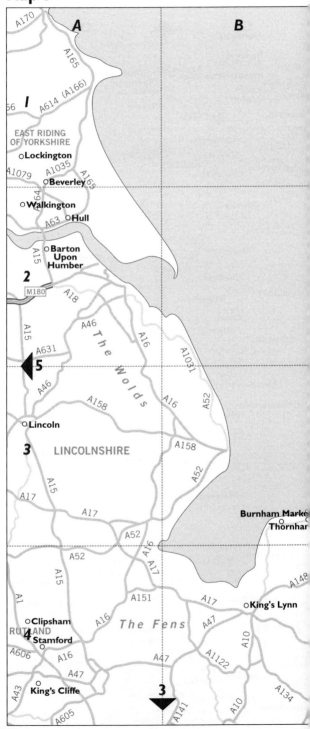

A

B

A170

A165

A614 (A166)

66

I

EAST RIDING
OF YORKSHIRE

○Lockington

A1079 A1035 A165

○**Beverley**

A63

○**Walkington**

A63 ○Hull

2

○**Barton
Upon
Humber**

A15

M180 A18

A46 A16

A15

A631

◀**5**

A46

T h e   W o l d s

A1031

A52

A158

A16

○**Lincoln**

3 LINCOLNSHIRE

A158

A52

A17

A15

A17

A52

A16

A52

A15

A16

A17

A52 A16 A17

Burnham Marke
Thornhar

A148

A151

A17

A47

○**King's Lynn**

A1

A16

T h e   F e n s

A10

○**Clipsham**

RUTLAND

4 Stamford

A606 A16

A47 A1122

A43 **King's Cliffe**

A47

A605

3

▼

A141

A134

A10

Map 6

C

D

Morston

A149

Warham
All Saints

A148

Holt

Wolterton

A140

A149

A1067

A47

The

Norwich

A47 Broads

NORFOLK

A146

A143

A11

Stoke Holy Cross

3

A140

A143

Map 7

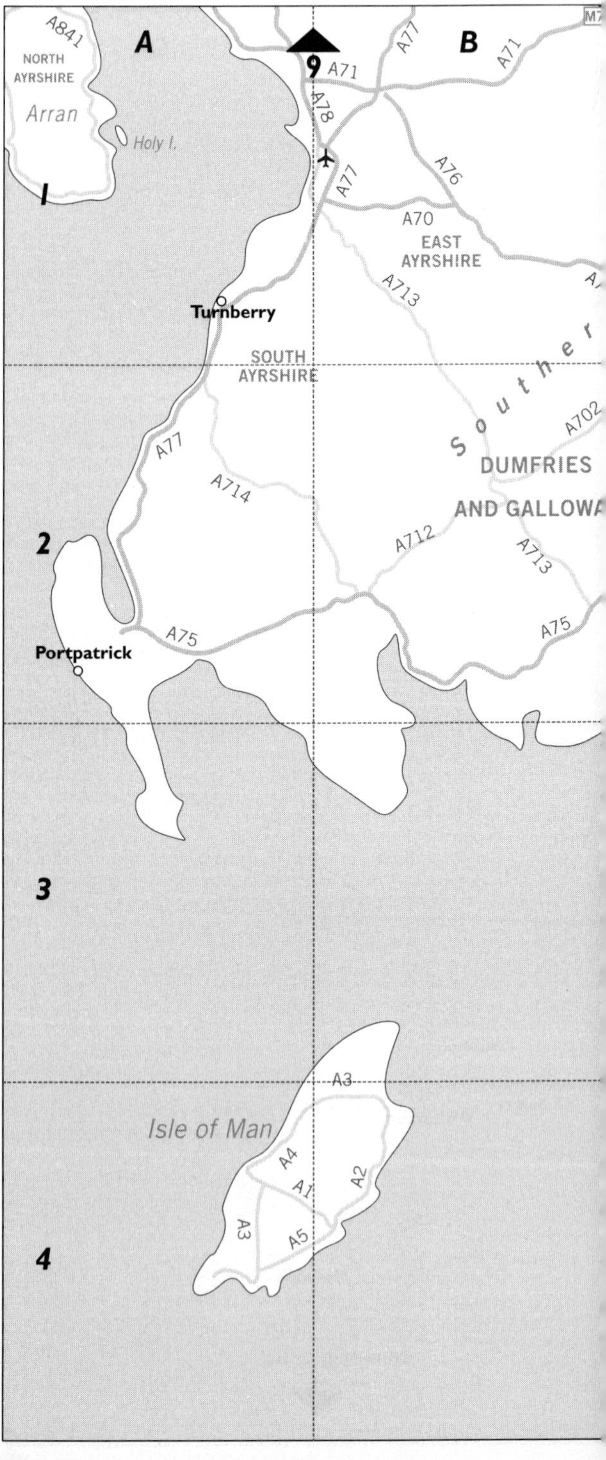

A841

A

NORTH
AYRSHIRE

Arran

Holy I.

1

M7

9

A71

A77

B

A71

A78

A77

A76

A70

EAST
AYRSHIRE

A713

Turnberry

SOUTH
AYRSHIRE

S o u t h e r

A702

DUMFRIES

AND GALLOWA

A77

A714

2

A712

A713

A75

Portpatrick

A75

3

A3

Isle of Man

A4

A2

A1

A3

A5

4

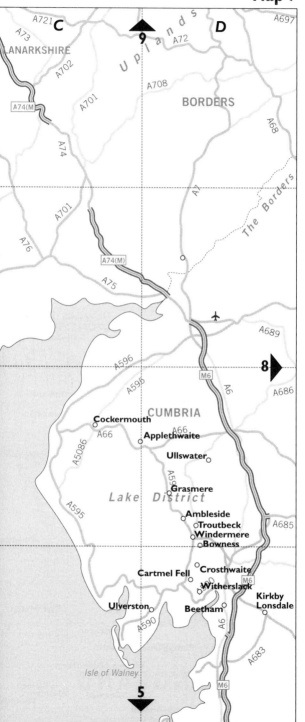

Map 7

A721

C

A73

A697

A72

LANARKSHIRE

A702

U p l a n d s

D

A701

A708

BORDERS

A74(M)

A68

A74

9

A701

A7

T h e   B o r d e r s

A76

A74(M)

A75

✈

A689

A596

A596

M6

8

A6

A686

CUMBRIA

Cockermouth ○

A66

A66

A5086

Applethwaite ○

A5086

Ullswater ○

A592 ○

Lake   District

Grasmere ●

A595

Ambleside ●
○**Troutbeck**
●**Windermere**
○**Bowness**

A685

○ **Crosthwaite**

Cartmel Fell ●

M6

●**Witherslack**

**Kirkby
Lonsdale** ○

Ulverston ○

A590

Beetham ○

A6

Isle of Walney

5

A683

M6

Map 8

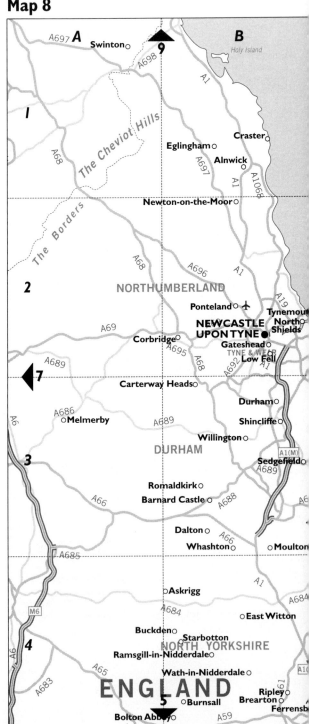

A697 **A** Swinton○

B Holy Island

I

A698

9

The Cheviot Hills

A1

A68

The Borders

○Craster

Eglingham○

A697

Alnwick○

A1

A1068

Newton-on-the-Moor○

2

A68

A696

A1

NORTHUMBERLAND

A19

Ponteland○ ✈

NEWCASTLE UPON TYNE ●

Tynemouth

North○ Shields

A69

Corbridge○

A695

A68

Gateshead○

TYNE & WEAR

Low Fell

A692

A1

7

A689

Carterway Heads○

A686

○Melmerby

A689

Durham○

Shincliffe○

Willington○

A1(M)

DURHAM

Sedgefield○

A689

A6

A66

A686

3

Romaldkirk○

Barnard Castle ○

A688

A6

Dalton○ A66

Whashton○

○Moulton

A685

A1

○Askrigg

A684

A684

○East Witton

M6

Buckden○

Starbotton

NORTH YORKSHIRE

Ramsgill-in-Nidderdale○

A10

4

A65

Wath-in-Nidderdale ○

A683

ENGLAND

Ripley○

Brearton○

5

○Burnsall

Ferrensb

Bolton Abbey○

A59

A6

Map 8

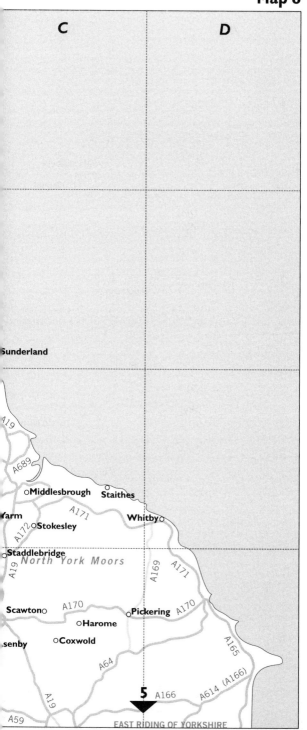

C

D

Sunderland

A19

A689

oMiddlesbrough   Staithes

A171

Whitbyo

Yarm

A172 oStokesley

Staddlebridge

A19   *North York Moors*

A169   *A171*

Scawtono   *A170*

Pickering   *A170*

oHarome

senby   oCoxwold

A165

A64

A614 (A166)

5   A166

A19

EAST RIDING OF YORKSHIRE

A59

Map 9

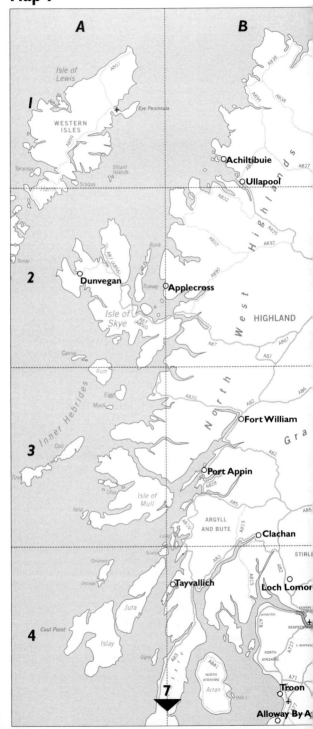

A

B

I

Isle of Lewis

A857

+ *Eye Peninsula*

WESTERN
ISLES

A855

Taransay

Shiant Islands

Scalpay

Harris

○●Achiltibuie

○Ullapool

A837

A838

A841

A838

A837

2

Rona

○Dunvegan

A850 (A856)

Raasay

○Applecross

Isle of Skye

A87
A851

A87

A863

A832

A835

A832

A890

North West HIGHLAND

A87

A87

A87

Rona

Canna

Rum

Eigg

Muck

3

Inner Hebrides

Coll

Tiree

A830

○●Fort William

A82

A86

North

Isle of Mull

Diva

Iona

○●Port Appin

A828

A85

A619

A85

○Clachan

Luing

ARGYLL
AND BUTE

Gra

4

Coul Point

Oronsay

Colonsay

Jura

Islay

Gigha

A816

○Tayvallich

A83

A815

○
Loch Lomor

A82

STIRLI

DUNBAR
TON

RENFREW

E. RENFREW

A727

A78

Arran

NORTH
AYRSHIRE

NORTH
AYRSHIRE

Holy I.

A737

A71

○Troon
+

○Alloway By A

▼
7

Map 9

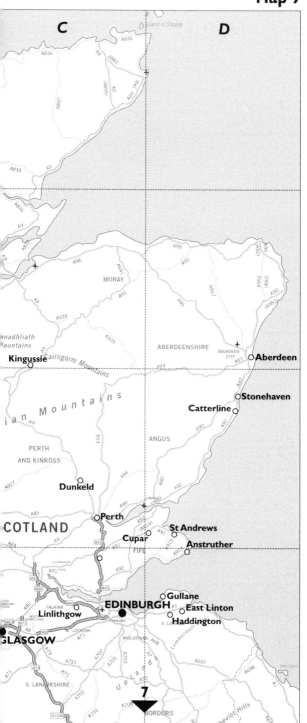

Map 10

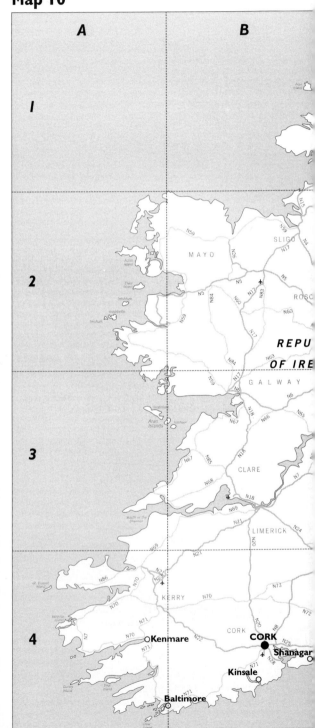

Map 10

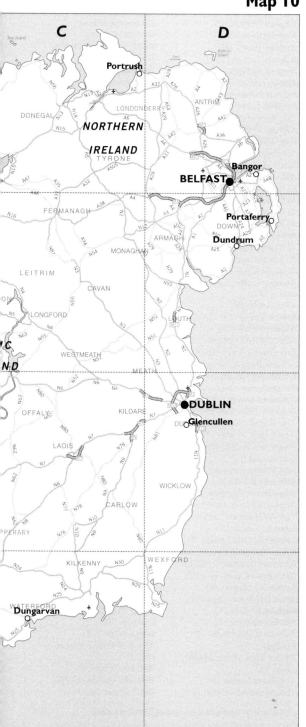

ALPHABETICAL INDEX

ALPHABETICAL INDEX

constantly updated at www.hardens.com

ALPHABETICAL INDEX

constantly updated at www.hardens.com

ALPHABETICAL INDEX

ALPHABETICAL INDEX